ALEXANDRIA

EDITED BY DAVID FIDELER

4

PHANES PRESS
1997

ALEXANDRIA

David Fideler
EDITOR

Walter Bakes
PROOFREADING

Port City Fulfillment
Lisa Grillo
SUBSCRIPTIONS

The Alexandria Society
FUNDING

Associated Publishers Group (USA)
Airlift Books (UK and Europe)
DISTRIBUTION

PUBLISHED BY

Phanes Press
PO Box 6114
Grand Rapids, Michigan 49516
USA

E-mail: *phanes@cris.com*
Web site: *www.cosmopolis.com*

ISBN 0-933999-39-9

Contents

Acknowledgments

"The Cosmic Religious Feeling" and "Science and Religion" first appeared in Albert Einstein, *Ideas and Opinions* (New York: Crown Publishing, 1954) • "Science and the Beautiful" first appeared as "The Meaning of Beauty in the Exact Sciences" in Werner Heisenberg, *Across the Frontiers* (Woodbridge, CT: Ox Bow Press, 1990) • James Robertson's review of *When Corporations Rule the World* first appeared in *Network*, the journal of the Scientific and Medical Network, Gibliston Mill, Colinsburgh, Leven, Fife KY9 1JS, Scotland.

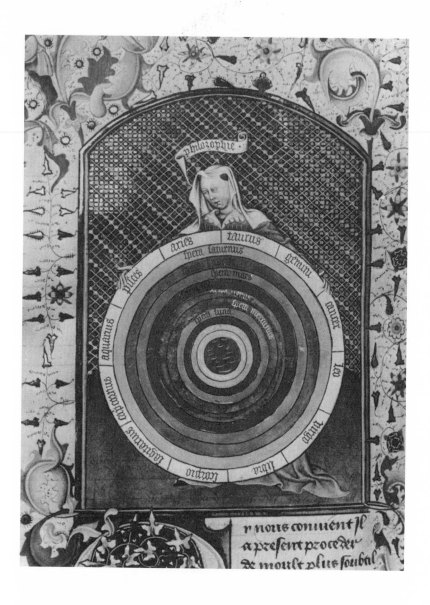

r nous convient il
a present procede
de moult plus soubtil

Introduction:
Philosophy Embracing the World

WHAT would it be like to embody a living philosophy? And what is the role of philosophy in the world? Like all deep questions, perhaps no single, definitive answer is possible. Nonetheless, many valuable hints, suggestions, and signposts can be discovered in the following pages.

Kathleen Damiani reminds us that living philosophy involves a direct, existential encounter with the unknown. Such an encounter poses risks, not only individually in a psychological sense, but also to our received assumptions and belief systems on a personal and collective level. The greatest philosophers have been willing to accept this challenge, even if it involved endangering their lives, sanity, or personal reputations. The classical example of Socrates is well known. But another good example is the philosopher Spinoza, who, for suggesting that the universe is "God in extension," was officially shunned and excommunicated by his religious community. He lived in isolation as a lens grinder, an occupation that led to his early death from the inhalation of glass particles. Contemporary individuals do not need to emulate these examples in a literalistic way, but an analogous type of risk always seems to be involved in making the transition between a state of comfortable complacency and a life that is really worth living.

A similar, courageous response is indicated by Christos Evangeliou in "The Lost Spirit of Hellenic Philosophy." The willingness to ask the big and threatening questions involves a risk—but it also results in a spirit of dignity, integrity, and self-autonomy that we humans would otherwise lack. This spirit of intellectual freedom, so characteristic of the Greek philosophers, is something that has been absent in those who, over the centuries, have transformed "philosophy" into a servant for theological, political, or academic agendas.

A central issue in all of this is the ability to live with risk, and the challenge to see deeper and farther than we are invited to look by the status quo—commercial, political, or ecclesiastical—which is always concerned with maintaining its own interests. The defensive habit of maintaining the certainty of the status quo is not just a social dynamic, it is a psychological one. The ego loves nothing more than to believe it is in control and the center of reality. Unwanted intrusions that challenge its comfort are dealt with by repression, avoidance, denial, or in other ways. Yet ultimately, too, the ego must give up its illusory fantasies of control, as Robert Romanyshyn points out, so that we can recognize our true place in a larger field of consciousness and be greened and transformed by the encounter. This encounter can occur through personal shipwreck, or, as Betty and Theodore Roszak describe, through a living encounter with Deep Form in art and nature—and the corresponding realization that we ourselves are embodiments of nature's living intelligence and creative process.

One theme that has been touched upon by the greatest philosophers is the limitation of the discursive intellect—the ego—and the need to a direct, existential encounter with the deepest levels of reality. As Henri Bergson wrote, "The intellect is characterized by a natural inability to comprehend life." This is not a form of irrationalism, but an honest recognition of the limitations of the analytical intellect, which holds life and reality at an arm's length.

One valid criticism of the Western philosophical tradition is its excessive intellectualism or logocentrism. As individuals or civilizations, we start life out enraptured, intoxicated by wonder, beauty, and the luminosity of being. This, according to Socrates, is the beginning of all philosophy. But then the intellect's tendency to organize, systematize, and dogmatize begins to take over. As we grow older and mature, the ego begins to harden; we become estranged from our emotional and life energies. The living sense of wonder and the desire for exploration becomes eclipsed, weeded out, or crucified in the interests of regularity and predictability. In the words of the *Tao Te*

Ching,

> When they lose their sense of awe,
> people turn to religion.
> When they no longer trust themselves,
> they begin to depend on authority.

Or to paraphrase, when people lose their sense of awe they turn to religion, and when they lose their sense of religion, they turn to philosophy or theology. Sadly, *philosophy has now become a dead way of looking at the world.* It is no wonder why most normal people recoil from what has become a gray, lifeless, and moribund pursuit. Their natural impression—that philosophy has been transformed into a minefield of false dichotomies, disembodied abstraction, and intellectual hairsplitting—is in many ways correct. That is because, since antiquity, there has been a tendency for philosophers and intellectuals to divide reality up into artificial categories of their own creation; the second part of the game involves sorting out and systematizing the relationship between the artificial categories while a verdant and beautiful world recedes in the background. As ecophilosopher Henryk Skolimowski points out, "Academic philosophy of our time is written by pure brains. It has become unreadable to ordinary persons and even well educated ones. It stands out as a curious marred monument abounding in intellectual labor and yet leaving us totally dry and uninspired. This *philo-sophia* has renounced all claims to *sophia.*"

We are living in a time when the Western philosophical tradition has deconstructed itself and is no more. But if philosophy is really dead, paradoxically, there is nothing that the world needs more than true philosophy. Thus, in the death of philosophy—as in the unseating of the monotheistic ego—vital possibilities for growth and rebirth are opened up. But what would a living philosophy look and *feel* like?

One clue is that a living philosophy would embrace the world and its beauty in deep, life enhancing ways. It would move beyond the ego, logocentrism, and mere cleverness, to embrace wisdom—that rare, elusive quality that can only be won through the risky, alchemical encounter with life's existential uncertainties. It would challenge the ego's puritanical reaction against life, vitality, and exuberance. If modern philosophy has been characterized by intellectual detachment and a devaluation of relatedness, the personal, and the feminine, a living philosophy might reflect the qualities of intimacy, attachment, and creative unfolding.

If philosophy is to have any meaningful future, it must once again embrace the world, the nonhuman, and the larger-than-human. This in itself calls for an enlarged epistemology that embraces the various ways of knowing in such a way that art, music, and the other modalities of human experience are recognized as valid, non-verbal pathways to authentic knowledge. Philosophy can no longer afford to play the self-defeating game which assumes that the rational intellect is the only valid pathway to true knowledge. As Bruce Nelson notes, the "ego loves the hermetic, the complex and the distant—it is always stepping back, avoiding directness." Because the ego is always looking from the outside and lacks a deep connection with the inner nature of things, the spirit of modernity has assumed that the world is dead and Other. But the world itself remains alive. As Nelson writes, "It is not a problem of a dead world, for the world has always possessed soul, but of a dead vision, one which numbs and deadens us until we extricate ourselves from it."

In our contemporary, post-modern and post-mortem time, we are standing at an important turning point in which our planetary situation is calling forth the seeds of a new, more adequate worldview or cosmovision. If philosophy has the wisdom, the knowledge, and the courage to embrace the psyche, nature, the feminine, beauty, and *all* the ways of knowing—in a living spirit of intimacy, attachment, and feeling—then not only will philosophy be reborn, it will have an important contribution to make to the world.

—DAVID FIDELER

The Cosmic Religious Feeling

ALBERT EINSTEIN

EVERYTHING that the human race has done and thought is concerned with the satisfaction of deeply felt needs and the assuagement of pain. One has to keep this constantly in mind if one wishes to understand spiritual movements and their development. Feeling and longing are the motive force behind all human endeavor and human creation, in however exalted a guise the latter may present themselves to us. Now what are the feelings and needs that have led men to religious thought and belief in the widest sense of the words? A little consideration will suffice to show us that the most varying emotions preside over the birth of religious thought and experience. With primitive man it is, above all, fear that evokes religious notions—fear of hunger, wild beasts, sickness, death. Since at this stage of existence understanding of causal connections is usually poorly developed, the human mind creates illusory beings more or less analogous to itself on whose wills and actions these fearful happenings depend. Thus one tries to secure the favor of these beings by carrying out actions and offering sacrifices which, according to the tradition handed down from generation to generation, propitiate them or make them well disposed toward a mortal. In this sense, I am speaking of a religion of fear. This, though not created, is in an important degree stabilized by the formation of a special priestly caste which sets itself up as a mediator between the people and the beings they fear, and erects a hegemony on this basis. In many cases, a leader or ruler or a privileged class whose position rests on other factors combines priestly functions with its secular authority in order to make the latter more secure; or the political rulers and the priestly caste make common cause in their own interests.

The social impulses are another source of the crystallization of religion. Fathers and mothers and the leaders of larger human communities are mortal and fallible. The desire for guidance, love, and support prompts men to form the social or moral conception of God. This is the God of Providence, who protects, disposes, rewards, and punishes; the God who, according to the limits of the believer's outlook, loves and cherishes the life of the tribe or of the human race, or even life itself; the comforter in sorrow and unsatisfied longing; he who preserves the souls of the dead. This is the social or moral conception of God.

The Jewish scriptures admirably illustrate the development from the religion of fear to moral religion, a development continued in the New Testament. The religions of all civilized peoples, especially the peoples of the Orient, are primarily moral religions. The development from a religion of fear to moral religion is a great step in peoples' lives. And yet, that primitive religions are based entirely on fear and the religions of civilized peoples purely on morality is a prejudice against which we must be on our guard. The truth is that all religions are a varying blend of both types, with this differentiation: that on the higher levels of social life the religion of morality predominates.

Common to all these types is the anthropomorphic character of their conception of God. In general, only individuals of exceptional endowments, and exceptionally high-minded communities, rise to any considerable extent above this level. *But there is a third stage of religious experience* which belongs to all of them, even though it is rarely found in a pure form: I shall call it cosmic religious feeling. It is very difficult to elucidate this feeling to anyone who is entirely without it, especially as there is no anthropomorphic conception of God corresponding to it.

The individual feels the futility of human desires and aims and the sublimity and marvelous order which reveal themselves both in nature and in the world of thought. Individual existence impresses him as a sort of prison and he wants to experience the universe as a single significant whole. The beginnings of cosmic religious feeling already appear at an early stage of development, e.g. in many of the Psalms of

David and in some of the prophets. Buddhism, as we have learned especially from the wonderful writings of Schopenhauer, contains a much stronger element of this.

The religious geniuses of all ages have been distinguished by this kind of religious feeling, which knows no dogma and no God conceived in man's image; so that there can be no church whose central teachings are based on it. Hence it is precisely among the heretics of every age that we find men who were filled with this highest kind of religious feeling and were, in many cases, regarded by their contemporaries as atheists, sometimes also as saints. Looked at in this light, men like Democritus, Francis of Assisi, and Spinoza are closely akin to one another.

How can cosmic religious feeling be communicated from one person to another if it can give rise to no definite notion of a God and no theology? In my view, it is the most important function of art and science to awaken this feeling and keep it alive in those who are receptive to it.

We thus arrive at a conception of the relation of science to religion very different from the usual one. When one views the matter historically, one is inclined to look upon science and religion as irreconcilable antagonists, and for a very obvious reason. The man who is thoroughly convinced of the universal operation of the law of causation cannot for a moment entertain the idea of a being who interferes in the course of events—provided, of course, that he takes the hypothesis of causality really seriously. He has no use for the religion of fear and equally little for social or moral religion. A God who rewards and punishes is inconceivable to him for the simple reason that a man's actions are determined by necessity, external and internal, so that in God's eyes he cannot be responsible, any more than an inanimate object is responsible for the motions it undergoes. Science has, therefore, been charged with undermining morality, but the charge is unjust. A man's ethical behavior should be based effectually on sympathy, education, and social ties and needs; no religious basis is necessary. Man would indeed be in a poor way if he had to be restrained by fear of punishment and hope of reward after death.

It is, therefore, easy to see why the churches have always fought science and persecuted its devotees. On the other hand, I maintain that the cosmic religious feeling is the strongest and noblest motive for scientific research. Only those who realize the immense efforts and, above all, the devotion without which pioneer work in theoretical science cannot be achieved are able to grasp the strength of the emotion out of which alone such work, remote as it is from the immediate realities of life, can issue. What a deep conviction of the rationality of the universe and what a yearning to understand, were it but a feeble reflection of the mind revealed in this world, Kepler and Newton must have had to enable them to spend years of solitary labor in disentangling the principles of celestial mechanics! Those whose acquaintance with scientific research is derived chiefly from its prac-tical results easily develop a completely false notion of the mentality of the men who, surrounded by a skeptical world, have shown the way to kindred spirits scattered wide through the world and the centuries. Only one who has devoted his life to similar ends can have a vivid realization of what has inspired these men and given them the strength to remain true to their purpose in spite of countless failures. It is cosmic religious feeling that gives a man such strength. A contempo-rary has said, not unjustly, that in this materialistic age of ours the serious workers are the only profoundly religious people.

Science and Religion

ALBERT EINSTEIN

DURING THE LAST CENTURY, and part of the one before, it was widely held that there was an unreconcilable conflict between knowledge and belief. The opinion prevailed among advanced minds that it was time that belief should be replaced increasingly by knowledge; belief that did not itself rest on knowledge was superstition and, as such, had to be opposed. According to this conception, the sole function of education was to open the way to thinking and knowing, and the school, as the outstanding organ for the people's education, must serve that end exclusively.

One will probably find but rarely, if at all, the rationalistic standpoint expressed in such crass form; for any sensible man would see at once how one-sided is such a statement of the position. But it is just as well to state a thesis starkly and nakedly, if one wants to clear up one's mind as to its nature.

It is true that convictions can best be supported with experience and clear thinking. On this point, one must agree unreservedly with the extreme rationalist. The weak point of his conception is, however, this, that those convictions which are necessary and determinant for our conduct and judgments cannot be found solely along this solid scientific way.

For the scientific method can teach us nothing else beyond how facts are related to, and conditioned by, each other. The aspiration toward such objective knowledge belongs to the highest of which man is capable, and you will certainly not suspect me of wising to belittle the achievements and the heroic efforts of man in this sphere. Yet it is equally clear that knowledge of what *is* does not open the door directly to what *should be*. One can have the clearest and most complete knowledge of what *is*, and yet not be able to deduct from that what should be the *goal* of our human aspirations. Objective knowledge provides us with powerful instruments for the achievements of certain ends, but the ultimate goal itself and the longing to reach it must come from another source. And it is hardly necessary to argue for the view that our existence and our activity acquire meaning only by the setting up of such a goal and of corresponding values. The knowledge of truth as such is wonderful, but it is so little capable of acting as a guide that it cannot prove even the justification and the value of the aspiration toward that very knowledge of truth. Here we face, therefore, the limits of the purely rational conception of our existence.

But it must not be assumed that intelligent thinking can play no part in the formation of the goal and of ethical judgments. When someone realizes that for the achievement of an end certain means would be useful, the means itself becomes thereby an end. Intelligence makes clear to us the interrelation of means and ends. But mere thinking cannot give us a sense of the ultimate and fundamental ends. To make clear these fundamental ends and valuations, and to set them fast in the emotional life of the individual, seems to me precisely the most important function which religion has to perform in the social life of man. And if one asks whence derives the authority of such fundamental ends, since they cannot be stated and justified merely by reason, one can only answer: they exist in a healthy society as powerful traditions, which act upon the conduct and aspirations and judgments of the individuals; they are there, that is, as something living, without it being necessary to find justification for their existence. They come into being not through demonstration but through revelation, through the medium of powerful personalities. One must not attempt to justify them, but, rather, to sense their nature simply and clearly.

The highest principles for our aspirations and judgments are given to us in the Jewish-Christian religious tradition. It is a very high goal which, with our weak powers, we can reach only very inadequately, but which gives a sure foundation to our aspirations and valuations. If one were to take that goal out of its religious form and look merely at its purely human side, one might state it perhaps thus: free and responsible development of the individual, so that he may place his powers freely and gladly in the service of all mankind. There is no room in this for the divinization of a nation, of a class, let alone of an individual. Are we not all children of one father, as it is said in religious language? Indeed, even the divinization of humanity, as an abstract totality, would not be in the spirit of that ideal. It is only to the individual that a soul is given. And the high destiny of the individual is to serve rather than to rule, or to impose himself in any other way.

If one looks at the substance rather than at the form, then one can take these words as expressing also the fundamental democratic position. The true democrat can worship his nation as little as can the man who is religious, in our sense of the term.

If one holds these high principles clearly before one's eyes, and compares them with the life and spirit of our times, then it appears glaringly that civilized mankind finds itself at present in grave danger. In the totalitarian states, it is the rulers themselves who strive actually to destroy that spirit of humanity. In less threatened parts, it is nationalism and intolerance, as well as the oppression of the individuals by economic means, which threaten to choke these most precious traditions.

A realization of how great is the danger is spreading, however, among thinking people, and there is much search for means with which to meet the danger—means in the field of national and international politics, of legislation, or organization in general. Such efforts are, no doubt, greatly needed. Yet the ancients knew something which we seem to have forgotten. All means prove but a blunt instrument if they have not behind them a living spirit. But if the longing for the achievement of the goal is powerfully alive within us, then shall we not lack the strength to find the means for reaching the goal and for translating it into deeds.

* * *

It would not be difficult to come to an agreement as to what we understand by science. Science is the century-old endeavor to bring together by means of systematic thought the perceptible phenomena of this world into as thorough-going an association as possible. To put it boldly, it is the attempt at the posterior reconstruction of existence by the process of conceptualization. But when asking myself what religion is, I cannot think of the answer so easily. And even after finding an answer which may satisfy me at this particular moment, I still remain convinced that I can never, under any circumstances, bring together, event to a slight extent, the thoughts of all those who have given this question serious consideration.

At first, then, instead of asking what religion is, I should prefer to ask what characterizes the aspirations of a person who gives me the impression of being religious: a person who is religiously enlightened appears to me to be one who has, to the best of his ability, liberated himself from the fetters of his selfish desires and is preoccupied with thoughts, feelings, and aspirations to which he clings because of their superpersonal value. It seems to me that what is important is the force of this superpersonal content and the depth of the conviction concerning its overpowering meaningfulness, regardless of whether any attempt is made to unite this content with a divine Being, for, otherwise, it would not be possible to count Buddha and Spinoza as religious personalities. Accordingly, *a religious person is devout in the sense that he has no doubt of the significance and loftiness of those superpersonal objects and goals which neither require nor are capable of rational foundation.* They exist with the same necessity and matter-of-factness as he himself. In this sense, religion is the age-old endeavor of mankind to become clearly and completely conscious of these values and goals and constantly to strengthen and extend their effect. If one conceives of religion and science according to these definitions then a conflict between them appears impossible. For science can only ascertain what *is*, but not what *should be*, and outside of its domain value judgments of all kinds remain necessary. Religion, on the other hand, deals only with evaluations of human thought and action: it cannot justifiably speak of facts and relationships between facts. According to this interpretation, the well-known conflicts between religion and science in the past must all be ascribed to a misapprehension of the situation which has been described.

For example, a conflict arises when a religious community insists on the absolute truthfulness of all statements recorded in the Bible. This means an intervention on the part of religion into the sphere of science; this is where the struggle of the Church against the doctrines of Galileo and Darwin belongs. On the other hand, representatives of science have often made an attempt to arrive at fundamental judgments with respect to values and ends on the basis of scientific method, and in this way have set themselves in opposition to religion. These conflicts have all sprung from fatal errors.

Now, even though the realms of religion and science in themselves are clearly marked off from each other, nevertheless there exist between the two strong reciprocal relationships and dependencies. Though religion may be that which determines the goal, it has, nevertheless, learned from science, in the broadest sense, what means will contribute to the attainment of the goals it has set up. But science can only be created by those who are thoroughly imbued with the aspiration toward truth and understanding. This source of feeling, however, springs from the sphere of religion. To this there also belongs the faith in the possibility that the regulations valid for the world of existence are rational, that is, comprehensible to reason. I cannot conceive of a genuine scientist without that profound faith. The situation may be expressed by an image: science without religion is lame, religion without science is blind.

Though I have asserted above that, in truth, a legitimate conflict between religion and science cannot exist, I must nevertheless qualify this assertion once again on an essential point, with reference to the actual content of historical religions. This qualification has to do with the concept of God. During the youthful period of mankind's spiritual evolution, human fantasy created gods in man's own image, who, by the operations of their will were supposed to determine or, at any rate, to influence the phenomenal world. Man sought to alter the disposition of these gods in his own favor by means of magic and prayer. The idea of God in the religions taught at present is a sublimation of that old concept of the gods. Its anthropomorphic character is shown, for instance, by the fact that men appeal to the Divine Being in prayers and plead for the fulfillment of their wishes.

Nobody, certainly, will deny that the idea of the existence of an omnipotent, just, and omnibeneficent personal God is able to accord man solace, help, and guidance; also, by virtue of its simplicity, it is accessible to the most undeveloped mind. But, on the other hand, there are decisive weaknesses attached to this idea in itself, which have been painfully felt since the beginning of history. That is, if this being is omnipotent, then every occurrence—including every human action, every human thought, and every human feeling and aspiration—is also His work; how is it possible to think of holding men responsible for their deeds and thoughts before such an almighty Being? In giving out punishment and rewards, He would, to a certain extent, be passing judgment on Himself. How can this be combined with the goodness and righteousness ascribed to Him?

The main source of the present day conflicts between the spheres of religion and of science lies in this concept of a personal God. It is the aim of science to establish general rules which determine the reciprocal connection of objects and events in time and space. For these rules, or laws of nature, absolutely general validity is required—not proven. It is mainly a program, and faith in the possibility of its accomplishment in principle is only founded on partial successes. But hardly anyone could be found who would deny these partial successes and ascribe them to human self-deception. The fact that, on the basis of such laws, we are able to predict the temporal behavior of phenomena in certain domains with great precision and certainty is deeply embedded in the consciousness of the modern man, even though he may have grasped very little of the contents of those laws. He need only consider that planetary courses within the solar system may be calculated in advance with great exactitude on the basis of a limited number of simple laws. In a similar way, though not with the same precision, it is possible to calculate in advance the mode of operation of an electric motor, a transmission system, or of a wireless apparatus, even when dealing with a novel development.

To be sure, when the number of factors coming into play in a phenomenological complex is too large, scientific method in most cases fails us. One need only think of the weather, in which case prediction even for a few days ahead is impossible. Nevertheless, no one doubts that we are confronted with a causal connection whose causal components are in the main known to us. Occurrences in this domain are beyond the reach of exact prediction because of the variety of factors in operation, not because of any lack of order in nature.

We have penetrated far less deeply into the regularities obtaining within the realm of living things, but deeply enough, nevertheless, to sense at least the rule of fixed necessity. One need only think of the systematic order in heredity, and in the effect of poisons, as, for instance, alcohol, on the behavior of organic beings. What is still lacking here is a grasp of connections of profound generality, but not a knowledge of order in itself.

The more a man is imbued with the ordered regularity of all events, the firmer becomes his conviction that there is no room left by the side of this ordered regularity for causes of a different nature. For him, neither the rule of human nor the rule of divine will exists as an independent cause of natural events. To be sure, the doctrine of a personal God interfering with natural events could never be *refuted*, in the real sense, by science, for this doctrine can always take refuge in those domains in which scientific knowledge has not yet been able to set foot.

But I am persuaded that such behavior on the part of the representatives of religion would not only be unworthy but also fatal. For a doctrine which is able to maintain itself not in clear light but only in the dark, will, of necessity, lose its effect on mankind, with incalculable harm to human progress. In their struggle for the ethical good, teachers of religion must have the stature to give up the doctrine of a personal God, that is, give up that source of fear and hope which in the past placed such vast power in the hands of priests. In their labors, they will have to avail themselves of those forces which are capable of cultivating the Good, the True, and the Beautiful in humanity itself. This is, to be sure, a more difficult but an incomparably more worthy task. After religious teachers accomplish the refining process indicated, they will surely recognize with joy that true religion has been ennobled and made more profound by scientific knowledge.

If it is one of the goals of religion to liberate mankind as far as possible from the bondage of egocentric cravings, desires, and fears, scientific reasoning can aid religion in yet another sense. Although it is true that it is the goal of science to discover rules which permit the association and foretelling of facts, this is not its only aim. It also seeks to reduce the connections discovered to the smallest possible number of mutually independent conceptual elements. It is in this striving after the rational unification of the manifold that it encounters its greatest successes, even though it is precisely this attempt which causes it to run the greatest risk of falling a prey to illusions. But whoever has undergone the intense experience of successful advances made in this domain is moved by profound reverence for the rationality made manifest in existence. By way of the understanding he achieves a far-reaching emancipation from the shackles of personal hopes and desires, and thereby attains that humble attitude of mind toward the grandeur of reason incarnate in existence, and which, in its profoundest depths, is inaccessible to man. This attitude, however, appears to me to be religious in the highest sense of the word. And so it seems to me that science not only purifies the religious impulse of the dross of its anthropomorphism, but also contributes to a religious spiritualization of our understanding of life.

The interpretation of religion, as here advanced, implies a dependence of science on the religious attitude, a relation which, in our predominantly materialistic age, is only too easily overlooked. While it is true that scientific results are entirely independent from religious or moral considerations, those individuals to whom we owe the great creative achievements of science were all of them imbued with the truly religious conviction that this universe of ours is something perfect and susceptible to the rational striving for knowledge. If this conviction had not been a strongly emotional one and if those searching for knowledge had not been inspired by Spinoza's *Amor Dei Intellectualis*, they would hardly have been capable of that untiring devotion which alone enables man to attain his greatest achievements.

"Beauty is the proper conformity of the parts
to one another and to the whole."

Science and the Beautiful

WERNER HEISENBERG

PERHAPS IT WILL BE BEST if, without any initial attempt at a philosophical analysis of the concept of "beauty," we simply ask where we can meet the beautiful in the sphere of exact science. Here I may perhaps be allowed to begin with a personal experience. When, as a small boy, I was attending the lowest classes of the Max-Gymnasium here in Munich, I became interested in numbers. It gave me pleasure to get to know their properties, to find out, for example, whether they were prime numbers or not, and to test whether they could perhaps be represented as sums of squares, or eventually to prove that there must be infinitely many primes. Now since my father thought my knowledge of Latin to be much more important than my numerical interests, he brought home to me one day from the National Library a treatise written in Latin by the mathematician Leopold Kronecker, in which the properties of whole numbers were set in relation to the geometrical problem of dividing a circle into a number of equal parts. How my father happened to light on this particular investigation from the middle of the last century I do not know. But the study of Kronecker's work made a deep impression on me. I sensed a quite immediate beauty in the fact that, from the problem of partitioning a circle, whose simplest cases were, of course, familiar to us in school, it was possible to learn something about the totally different sort of questions involved in elementary number theory. Far in the distance, no doubt, there already floated the question whether whole numbers and geometrical forms exist, i.e., whether they are there outside the human mind or whether they have merely been created by this mind as instruments for understanding the world. But at that time I was not yet able to think about such problems. The impression of something very

25

beautiful was, however, perfectly direct; it required no justification or explanation.

But what was beautiful here? Even in antiquity there were two definitions of beauty which stood in a certain opposition to one another. The controversy between them played a great part, especially during the Renaissance. The one describes beauty as the proper conformity of the parts to one another, and to the whole. The other, stemming from Plotinus, describes it, without any reference to parts, as the translucence of the eternal splendor of the "one" through the material phenomenon. In our mathematical example, we shall have to stop short, initially, at the first definition. The parts here are the properties of whole numbers and laws of geometrical constructions, while the whole is obviously the underlying system of mathematical axioms to which arithmetic and Euclidean geometry belong—the great structure of interconnection guaranteed by the consistency of the axiom system. We perceive that the individual parts fit together, that, as parts, they do indeed belong to this whole, and, without any reflection, we feel the completeness and simplicity of this axiom system to be beautiful. Beauty is therefore involved with the age-old problem of the "one" and the "many" which occupied—in close connection with the problem of "being" and "becoming"—a central position in early Greek philosophy.

Since the roots of exact science are also to be found at this very point, it will be as well to retrace in broad outline the currents of thought in that early age. At the starting point of the Greek philosophy of nature there stands the question of a basic principle, from which the colorful variety of phenomena can be explained. However strangely it may strike us, the well-known answer of Thales—"Water is the material first principle of all things"—contains, according to Nietzsche, three basic philosophical demands which were to become important in the developments that followed: first, that one should seek for such a unitary basic principle; second, that the answer should be given only rationally, that is, not by reference to a myth; and third and finally, that in this context the material aspect of the world must play a deciding role. Behind these demands there stands, of course, the unspoken recognition that understanding can never mean anything more than the perception of connections, i.e., unitary features or marks of affinity in the manifold.

But if such a unitary principle of all things exists, then—and this was the next step along this line of thought—one is straightway brought up against the question how it can serve to account for the fact of change. The difficulty is particularly apparent in the celebrated paradox of Parmenides. Only being is; non-being is not. But if only being is, there cannot be anything outside this being that articulates it or could bring about changes. Hence being will have to be conceived as eternal, uniform, and unlimited in space and time. The changes we experience can thus be only an illusion.

Greek thought could not stay with this paradox for long. The eternal flux of appearances was immediately given, and the problem was to explain it. In attempting to overcome the difficulty, various philosophers struck out in different directions. One road led to the atomic theory of Democritus. In addition to being, non-being can still exist as a possibility, namely as the possibility for movement and form, or, in other words, as empty space. Being is repeatable, and thus we arrive at the picture of atoms in the void—the picture that has since become infinitely fruitful as a foundation for natural science. But of this road we shall say no more just now. Our purpose, rather, is to present in more detail the other road, which led to Plato's Ideas, and which carried us directly into the problem of beauty.

This road begins in the school of Pythagoras. It is there that the notion is said to have originated that mathematics, the mathematical order, was the basic principle whereby the multiplicity of phenomena could be accounted for. Of Pythagoras himself we know little. His disciples seem, in fact, to have been a religious sect, and only the doctrine of transmigration and the laying down of certain moral and religious rules and prohibitions can be traced with any certainty to Pythagoras. But among these disciples—and this was what mattered subsequently—a preoccupation with music and mathematics played an important role. Here it was that Pythagoras is said to have made the famous discovery that vibrating strings under equal tension sound together in harmony if their lengths are in a simple numerical ratio. The mathematical structure, namely the numerical ratio as a source of harmony, was certainly one of the most momentous discoveries in the history of mankind. The harmonious concord of two strings yields a beautiful sound. Owing to the discomfort caused by beat-effects, the human ear finds dissonance disturbing, but consonance, the peace of harmony, it finds beautiful. Thus the mathematical relation was also the source of beauty.

Beauty, so the first of our ancient definitions ran, is the proper conformity of the parts to one another and to the whole. The parts here are the individual notes, while the whole is the harmonious sound. The mathematical relation can, therefore, assemble two initially independent parts into a whole, and so produce beauty. This discovery effected a breakthrough, in Pythagorean doctrine, to entirely new forms of thought, and so brought it about that the ultimate basis of all being was no longer envisaged as a sensory material—such as water, in Thales—but as an ideal principle of form. This was to state a basic idea which later provided the foundation for all exact science. Aristotle, in his *Metaphysics*, reports that the Pythagoreans, ". . . who were the first to take up mathematics, not only advanced this study, but also having been brought up in it they thought its principles were the principles of all things. . . . Since, again, they saw that the modifications and the ratios of the musical scales were expressible in numbers; since, then, all other things seemed in their whole nature to be modeled on numbers; and numbers seemed to be the first things in the whole of nature, they supposed the elements of numbers to be the elements of all things, and the whole heaven to be a musical scale and a number."

Understanding of the colorful multiplicity of the phenomena was thus to come about by recognizing in them unitary principles of form, which can be expressed in the language of mathematics. By this, too, a close connection was established between the intelligible and the beautiful. For if the beautiful is conceived as a conformity of the parts to one another and to the whole, and if, on the other hand, all understanding is first made possible by means of this formal connection, the experience of the beautiful becomes virtually identical with the experience of connections either understood or, at least, guessed at.

The next step along this road was taken by Plato with the formulation of his theory of Ideas. Plato contrasts the imperfect shapes of the corporeal world of the senses with the perfect forms of mathematics; the imperfectly circular orbits of the stars, say, with the perfection of the mathematically defined circle. Material things are the copies, the shadow images, of ideal shapes in reality; moreover, as we should be tempted to continue nowadays, these ideal shapes are actual because and insofar as they become "act"-ive in material events. Plato thus distinguishes here with complete clarity a corporeal being accessible to the senses and a purely ideal being apprehensible not by the senses but only through acts of mind. Nor is this ideal being in any way in need of man's thought in order to be brought forth by him. On the contrary, it is the true being, of which the corporeal world and human thinking are mere reproductions. As their name already indicates, the apprehension of Ideas by the human mind is more an artistic intuiting, a half-conscious intimation, than a knowledge conveyed by the understanding. It is a reminiscence of forms that were already implanted in this soul before its existence on earth. The central Idea is that of the Beautiful and the Good, in which the divine becomes visible and at sight of which the wings of the soul begin to grow. A passage in the *Phaedrus* expresses the following thought: the soul is awe-stricken and shudders at the sight of the beautiful, for it feels that something is evoked in it that was not imparted to it from without by the senses but has always been already laid down there in a deeply unconscious region.

But let us come back once more to understanding and thus, to natural science. The colorful multiplicity of the phenomena can be understood, according to Pythagoras and Plato, because and insofar as it is underlain by unitary principles of form susceptible of mathematical representation. This postulate already constitutes an anticipation of the entire program of contemporary exact science. It could not, however, be carried through in antiquity, since an empirical knowledge of the details of natural processes was largely lacking.

The first attempt to penetrate into these details was undertaken, as we know, in the philosophy of Aristotle. But in view of the infinite wealth initially presented here to the observing student of nature and the total lack of any sort of viewpoint from which an order might have been discernible, the unitary principles of form sought by Pythagoras and Plato were obliged to give place to the description of details. Thus there arose the conflict that has continued to this day in the debates, for example, between experimental and theoretical physics; the conflict between the empiricist, who by careful and scrupulous detailed investigation first furnishes the presuppositions for an understanding of nature, and the theoretician, who creates mathematical pictures whereby he seeks to order and so to understand nature—mathematical pictures that prove themselves, not only by their correct depiction of experience, but also and more especially by their simplicity and beauty, to be the true Ideas underlying the course of nature.

Aristotle, as an empiricist, was critical of the Pythagoreans, who, he said, "are not seeking for theories and causes to account for observed facts, but rather forcing their observations and trying to accommodate them to certain theories and opinions of their own" and were thus setting up, one might say, as joint organizers of the universe. If we look back on the history of the exact sciences, it can perhaps be asserted that the correct representation of natural phenomena has evolved from this very tension between the two opposing views. Pure mathematical speculation becomes unfruitful because from playing with the wealth of possible forms it no longer finds its way back to the small number of forms according to which nature is actually constructed. And pure empiricism becomes unfruitful because it eventually bogs down in endless tabulation without inner connection. Only from the tension, the interplay between the wealth of facts and the mathematical forms that may possibly be appropriate to them, can decisive advances spring.

But in antiquity this tension was no longer acceptable and thus, the road to knowledge diverged for a long time from the road to the beautiful. The significance of the beautiful for the understanding of nature became clearly visible again only at the beginning of the modern period, once the way back had been found from Aristotle to Plato. And only through this change of course did the full fruitfulness become apparent of the mode of thought inaugurated by Pythagoras and Plato.

This is most clearly shown in the celebrated experiments on falling bodies that Galileo probably did not, in fact, conduct from the leaning tower of Pisa. Galileo begins with careful observations, paying no attention to the authority of Aristotle, but, following the teaching of Pythagoras and Plato, he does try to find mathematical forms corresponding to the facts obtained by experiment and thus, arrives at his laws of falling bodies. However, and this is a crucial point, he is obliged, in order to recognize the beauty of mathematical forms in the phenomena, to idealize the facts, or, as Aristotle disparagingly puts it, to force them. Aristotle had taught that all moving bodies not acted upon by external forces eventually come to rest, and this was the general experience. Galileo maintains, on the contrary, that, in the absence of external forces, bodies continue in a state of uniform motion. Galileo could venture to force the facts in this way because he could point out that moving bodies are, of course, always exposed to a frictional resistance and that motion, in fact, continues the longer, the more effectively the frictional forces can be cut off. In exchange for this forcing of the facts, this idealization, he obtained a simple mathematical law, and this was the beginning of modern exact science.

Some years later, Kepler succeeded in discovering new mathematical forms in the data of his very careful observations of the planetary orbits and in formulating the three famous laws that bear his name. How close Kepler felt himself in these discoveries to the ancient arguments of Pythagoras, and how much the beauty of the connections guided him in formulating them, can be seen from the fact that he compared the revolutions of the planets about the sun with the vibrations of a string and spoke of a harmonious concord of the different planetary orbits, of a harmony of the spheres. At the end of his work on the harmony of the universe, he broke out into this cry of joy: "I thank thee, Lord God our Creator, that thou allowest me to see the beauty in thy work of creation." Kepler was profoundly struck by the fact that here he had chanced upon a central connection which had not been conceived by man, which it had been reserved to him to recognize for the first time—a connection of the highest beauty. A few decades later, Isaac Newton in England set forth this connection in all its completeness and described it in detail in his great work *Principia Mathematica*. The road of exact science was thus pointed out in advance for almost two centuries.

But are we dealing here with knowledge merely, or also with the beautiful? And if the beautiful is also involved, what role did it play in the discovery of these connections? Let us again recall the first definition given in antiquity: "Beauty is the proper conformity of the parts to one another and to the whole." That this criterion applies in the highest degree to a structure like Newtonian mechanics is something that scarcely needs explaining. The parts are the individual mechanical processes—those which we carefully isolate by means of apparatus no less than those which occur inextricably before our eyes in the colorful play of phenomena. And the whole is the unitary principle of form which all these processes comply with and which was mathematically established by Newton in a simple system of axioms. Unity and simplicity are not, indeed, precisely the same. But the fact that in such a theory the many are confronted with the one, that in it the many are unified, itself has the undoubted consequence that we also feel it at the same time to be simple and beautiful. The significance of the beautiful for the discovery of the true has at all times been recognized and emphasized. The Latin motto *"Simplex sigillum veri"*— "The simple is the seal of the true"—is inscribed in large letters in the physics auditorium of the University of Göttingen as an admonition to those who would discover what is new; another Latin motto,

SCIENCE AND THE BEAUTIFUL   33

"Pulchritudo splendor veritatis"—"Beauty is the splendor of truth"—
can also be interpreted to mean that the researcher first recognizes
truth by this splendor, by the way it shines forth.
Twice more in the history of exact science, this shining forth of the
great connection has been the crucial signal for a significant advance.
I am thinking here of two events in the physics of our own century: the
emergence of relativity theory and the quantum theory. In both cases,
after years of vain effort at understanding, a bewildering plethora of
details has been almost suddenly reduced to order by the appearance
of a connection, largely unintuitable but still ultimately simple in its
substance, that was immediately found convincing by virtue of its
completeness and abstract beauty—convincing, that is, to all who
could understand and speak such an abstract language.
   But now, instead of pursuing the historical course of events any
further, let us rather put the question quite directly: What is it that
shines forth here? How comes it that with this shining forth of the
beautiful into exact science the great connection becomes recogniz-
able, even before it is understood in detail and before it can be
rationally demonstrated? In what does the power of illumination
consist, and what effect does it have on the onward progress of science?
   Perhaps we should begin here by recalling a phenomenon that may
be described as the unfolding of abstract structures. It can be illustrated by the example of number theory, which we referred to at the
outset, but one may also point to comparable processes in the evolution of art. For the mathematical foundation of arithmetic, or the
theory of numbers, a few simple axioms are sufficient, which, in fact,
merely define exactly what counting is. But with these few axioms we
have already posited that whole abundance of forms which has entered
the minds of mathematicians only in the course of the long history of
the subject—the theory of prime numbers, of quadratic residues, of
numerical congruences, etc. One might say that the abstract structures
posited in and with numbers have unfolded visibly only in the course
of mathematical history, that they have generated the wealth of
propositions and relationships that makes up the content of the

complicated science of number theory. A similar position is also occupied—at the outset of an artistic style in architecture, say—by certain simple basic forms, such as the semicircle and rectangle in Romanesque architecture. From these basic forms there arise in the course of history new, more complicated, and also altered forms, which yet can still, in some way, be regarded as variations on the same theme; thus, from the basic structures there emerges a new manner, a new style of building. We have the feeling, nonetheless, that the possibilities of development were already perceivable in these original forms, even at the outset; otherwise, it would be scarcely comprehensible that many gifted artists should have so quickly resolved to pursue these new possibilities.

Such an unfolding of abstract basic structures has assuredly also occurred in the instances I have enumerated from the history of the exact sciences. This growth, this constant development of new branches, went on in Newtonian mechanics up to the middle of the last century. In relativity theory and the quantum theory we have experienced a similar development in the present century, and the growth has not yet come to an end.

Moreover, in science, as in art, this process also has an important social and ethical aspect; for many men can take an active part in it. When a great cathedral was to be built in the Middle Ages, many master masons and craftsmen were employed. They were imbued with the idea of beauty posited by the original forms and were compelled by their task to carry out exact and meticulous work in accordance with these forms. In similar fashion, during the two centuries following Newton's discovery, many mathematicians, physicists, and technicians were called upon to deal with specific mechanical problems according to the Newtonian methods, to carry out experiments, or to effect technical applications; here, too, extreme care was always required in order to attain what was possible within the framework of Newtonian mechanics. Perhaps it may be said in general that by means of the underlying structures, in this case Newtonian mechanics, guidelines were drawn or even standards of value set up whereby it could be objectively decided whether a given task had been well or ill discharged. It is the very fact that specific requirements have been laid down, that the individual can assist by small contributions in the attainment of large goals, and that the value of his contribution can be objectively determined, which gives rise to the satisfaction proceeding from such a development for the large number of people involved. Hence even the ethical significances of technology for our present age should not be underestimated.

The development of science and technology has also produced, for example, the Idea of the airplane. The individual technician who assembles some component for such a plane, the artisan who makes it, knows that his work calls for the utmost care and exactitude and that the lives of many may well depend upon its reliability. Hence he can take pride in a well-executed piece of work, and delights, as we do, in the beauty of the aircraft, when he feels that in it the technical goal has been realized by properly adequate means. Beauty, so runs the ancient definition we have already often cited, is the proper conformity of the parts to one another and to the whole, and this requirement must also be satisfied in a good aircraft.

But in pointing thus to the evolution of beauty's ground structure, to the ethical values and demands that subsequently emerge in the historical course of development, we have not yet answered the question we asked earlier, namely, what it is that shines forth in these structures, how the great connection is recognized even before it is rationally understood in detail. Here we ought to reckon in advance with the possibility that even such recognition may be founded upon illusions. But it cannot be doubted that there actually is this perfectly immediate recognition, this shuddering before the beautiful, of which Plato speaks in the *Phaedrus*.

Among all those who have pondered on this question, it seems to have been universally agreed that this immediate recognition is not a consequence of discursive (i.e., rational) thinking. I should like here to cite two statements, one from Johannes Kepler, who has already been referred to, and the other, in our own time, from the Zurich atomic physicist Wolfgang Pauli, who was a friend of the psychologist, Carl Jung. The first passage is to be found in Kepler's *Harmony of the World*:

> That faculty which perceives and recognizes the noble proportions in what is given to the senses and in other things situated outside itself must be ascribed to the soul. It lies very close to the faculty which supplies formal schemata to the senses, or deeper still, and thus adjacent to the purely vital power of the soul which does not think discursively, i.e., in conclusions, as the philosophers do, and employs no considered method, and is thus not peculiar only to man, but also dwells in wild animals and the dear beasts of the field. . . . Now it might be asked how this faculty of the soul, which does not engage in conceptual thinking, and can therefore have no proper knowledge of harmonic relations, should be capable of recognizing what is given in the outside world. For to recognize is to compare the sense perception outside with the original pictures inside, and to judge that it conforms to them. Proclus has expressed the matter very finely in his simile of awakening, as from a dream. For just as the sensorily presented things in the outer world recall to us those which we formerly perceived in the dream, so also the mathematical relations given in sensibility call forth those intelligible archetypes which were already given inwardly beforehand so that they now shine forth truly and vividly in the soul, where before they were only obscurely present there. But how have they come to be within? To this I answer that all pure Ideas or archetypal patterns of harmony such as we were speaking of are inherently present in those who are capable of apprehending them. But they are not first received into the mind by a conceptual process, being the product rather of a sort of instinctive intuition of pure quantity, and are innate in these individuals, just as the number of petals in a plant, say, is innate in its form principle, or the number of its seed chambers is innate in the apple.

So far Kepler. He is, therefore, referring us here to possibilities already to be found in the animal and plant kingdoms, to innate archetypes that bring about the recognition of forms. In our own day,

Adolf Portmann, in particular, has described such possibilities, pointing, for example, to specific color patterns seen in the plumage of birds, which can possess a biological meaning only if they are also perceived by other members of the same species. The perceptual capacity will therefore have to be just as innate as the pattern itself. We may also consider bird song at this point. At first, the biological requirement here may well have been simply for a specific acoustic signal, serving to seek out the partner and understood by the latter. But to the extent that this immediate biological function declines in importance, a playful enlargement of the stock of forms may ensue, an unfolding of the underlying melodic structure, which is then found enchanting as song by even so alien a species as man. The capacity to recognize this play of forms must, at all events, be innate to the species of bird in question for certainly it has no need of discursive, rational thought. In man, to cite another example, there is probably an inborn capacity for understanding certain basic forms of the language of gesture and thus, for deciding, say, whether the other has friendly or hostile intentions—a capacity of the utmost importance for man's communal life.

Ideas similar to those of Kepler have been put forward in an essay by Pauli. He writes:

> The process of understanding in nature, together with the joy that man feels in understanding, i.e., becoming acquainted with new knowledge, seems therefore to rest upon a correspondence, a coming into congruence of preexistent internal images of the human psyche with external objects and their behavior. This view of natural knowledge goes back, of course, to Plato and was ... also very plainly adopted by Kepler. The latter speaks, in fact, of Ideas, preexistent in the mind of God and imprinted accordingly upon the soul, as the image of God. These primal images, which the soul can perceive by means of an innate instinct, Kepler calls archetypes. There is very wide-ranging agreement here with the primordial images or archetypes introduced into modern psychology by C. G. Jung, which function as instinctive patterns of ideation. At this stage, the place of clear

concepts is taken by images of strongly emotional content, which are not thought but are seen pictorially, as it were, before the mind's eye. Insofar as these images are the expression of a suspected but still unknown state of affairs, they can also be called symbolic, according to the definition of a symbol proposed by Jung. As ordering operators and formatives in this world of symbolic images, the archetypes function, indeed, as the desired bridge between sense perceptions and Ideas, and are therefore also a necessary precondition for the emergence of a scientific theory. Yet one must beware of displacing this *a priori* knowledge into consciousness and relating it to specific, rationally formulable Ideas.

In the further course of his inquiries, Pauli then goes on to show that Kepler did not derive his conviction of the correctness of the Copernican system primarily from any particular data of astronomical observation, but rather from the agreement of the Copernican picture with an archetype which Jung calls a mandala and which was also used by Kepler as a symbol for the Trinity. God, as prime mover, is seen at the center of a sphere; the world, in which the Son works, is compared with the sphere's surface; the Holy Ghost corresponds to the beams that radiate from center to surface of the sphere. It is naturally characteristic of these primal images that they cannot really be rationally or even intuitively described.

Although Kepler may have acquired his conviction of the correctness of Copernicanism from primal images of this kind, it remains a crucial precondition for any usable scientific theory that it should subsequently stand up to empirical testing and rational analysis. In this respect, the sciences are in a happier position than the arts, since for science there is an inexorable and irrevocable criterion of value that no piece of work can evade. The Copernican system, the Keplerian laws, and the Newtonian mechanics have subsequently proved themselves—in the interpreting of phenomena, in observational findings, and in technology—over such a range and with such extreme accuracy that after Newton's *Principia* it was no longer possible to doubt that they were correct. Yet even here there was still an idealization involved, such as Plato had held necessary and Aristotle had disapproved.

This only came out in full clarity some fifty years ago when it was realized from the findings in atomic physics that the Newtonian scheme of concepts was no longer adequate to cope with the mechanical phenomena in the interior of the atom. Since Planck's discovery of the quantum of action, in 1900, a state of confusion had arisen in physics. The old rules, whereby nature had been successfully described for more than two centuries, would no longer fit the new findings. But even these findings were themselves inherently contradictory. A hypothesis that proved itself in one experiment failed in another. The beauty and completeness of the old physics seemed destroyed, without anyone having been able, from the often disparate experiments, to gain a real insight into new and different sorts of connection. I don't know if it is fitting to compare the state of physics in those twenty-five years after Planck's discovery (which I, too, encountered as a young student) to the circumstances of contemporary modern art. But I have to confess that this comparison repeatedly comes to my mind. The helplessness when faced with the question of what to do about the bewildering phenomena, the lamenting over lost connection, which still continue to look so very convincing—all these discontents have shaped the face of both disciplines and both periods, different as they are, in a similar manner. We are obviously concerned here with a necessary intervening stage, which cannot be bypassed and which is preparing for developments to come. For, as Pauli told us, all understanding is a protracted affair, inaugurated by processes in the unconscious long before the content of consciousness can be rationally formulated.

At that moment, however, when the true Ideas rise up, there occurs in the soul of him who sees them an altogether indescribable process of the highest intensity. It is the amazed awe that Plato speaks of in the *Phaedrus*, with which the soul remembers, as it were, something it had unconsciously possessed all along. Kepler says: *"Geometria est archetypus pulchritudinis mundi"*; or, if we may translate in more general terms: "Mathematics is the archetype of the beauty of the world." In atomic physics this process took place not quite fifty years ago and has again restored exact science, under entirely new presuppositions, to that state of harmonious completeness which for a quarter of a century it had lost. I see no reason why the same thing should not also happen one day in art. But it must be added, by way of warning, that such a thing cannot be made to happen—it has to occur on its own.

I have set this aspect of exact science before you because in it the affinity with the fine arts becomes most plainly visible and because here one may counter the misapprehension that natural science and technology are concerned solely with precise observation and rational, discursive thought. To be sure, this rational thinking and careful measurement belong to the scientist's work, just as the hammer and chisel belong to the work of the sculptor. But in both cases they are merely the tools and not the content of the work.

Perhaps at the very end I may remind you once more of the second definition of the concept of beauty, which stems from Plotinus and in which no more is heard of the parts and the whole: "Beauty is the translucence, through the material phenomenon of the eternal splendor of the 'one.'" There are important periods of art in which this definition is more appropriate than the first, and to such periods we often look longingly back. But in our own time it is hard to speak of beauty from this aspect, and perhaps it is a good rule to adhere to the custom of the age one has to live in, and to keep silent about that which it is difficult to say. In actual fact, the two definitions are not so very widely removed from one another. So let us be content with the first and more sober definition of beauty, which certainly is also realized in natural science, and let us declare that in exact science, no less than in the arts, it is the most important source of illumination and clarity.

Soul and the World:
A Conversation with Thomas Moore

SUZI GABLIK AND THOMAS MOORE

THOMAS MOORE is a psychotherapist best known for his work in the field of archetypal and Jungian psychology. He also holds advanced degrees in theology, music, art, and philosophy. As a young man Moore lived for twelve years as a monk in a Catholic religious order; he now describes himself as a "self-employed, poetic-minded, independent scholar who was also a former cleric." When his book *Care of the Soul* appeared in 1992, it unexpectedly brought the house down. I say "unexpectedly," because although he had published several other books, only a few people had read them, and Moore mistakenly assumed that few would read this one as well. When *Care of the Soul* began its slow-motion ascent on the bestseller charts, no one was more stunned by the intensity of the response than the author himself. "I'm used to writing books that no one reads," he says.

Our estrangement from the world, according to Moore, is a result of our depersonalizing philosophies and the culture we have made. If we truly wish to care for the soul, we cannot continue to live the life we are living. Care of the soul involves a fundamental reorientation to what's going on. What we need is to become more artful about our lives instead of mechanical. The soul is not amenable to mechanical and structural thinking, it works alchemically. When a radio interviewer, who was commenting on Moore's extensive travels, said to him, "Your battery must be running down," Moore replied: "I have no battery." In the modern world, we tend to see everything as if it were a machine, and our use of language reflects this. A better metaphor, according to Moore, would be to imagine ourselves as huge, deep, mysterious, and awe-inspiring as the night sky. Seeing oneself as a universe, and not as a machine that needs fixing, takes us closer to the mystery of soul.

The soul loves the labyrinth rather than the ladder (which symbolizes "getting somewhere"), and it prefers relatedness to distancing. Paradox, mystery, being sick, failures, foolishness, blank spaces, not knowing where one is going, are all good for the soul, which is ripened by making mistakes. Magic, not reason and will, accomplishes what the soul needs, allowing its eccentricity to emerge. The soul does not have an urgent need for understanding or achievement; rather, it loves intimacy. According to Moore, conversation is one of the "technologies of intimacy," an inherently soulful activity that gives us an appreciation for unresolved complexity. Care of the soul is more a process of listening and following than of hanging on fiercely to our own interpretations and programs. Soul has little to do with our intentions, expectations or moral requirements, and slight shifts in imagination, Moore claims, have more impact on living than major efforts at change. With his friend and mentor James Hillman, Moore argues for a new soul ecology: a responsibility to the things of the world based on appreciation, affection, and relatedness rather than on obligation or abstract principle. Ultimately this is where the fields of psychology, ecology, and art overlap.

For Moore, the arts are central to finding ways to nourish the soul. Art gets us away from problem-solving and into the mystery. But we forfeit opportunities for soul when we leave art only to the accomplished painter and the museum. Moore feels that professionalism can be lofty and remote, while soul is ordinary, daily, communal, felt, intimate, attached, engaged, involved, and poetic. In a world where soul is neglected, beauty is placed last on its list of priorities. The implication is that the arts are dispensable: we can't live without technology, but we can live without beauty. To begin building a culture that is sensitive to matters of the heart, says Moore, and to care for the soul, we will have to expose ourselves to beauty, risking "the interference it can place in the way of our march toward technological progress. We may have to give up many projects that seem important to modern life, in the name of sacred nature and the need for beautiful things." All this is part of our effort to replace modernist psychology with care of the soul.—*Suzi Gablik*

SUZI GABLIK: Tom, you've said that the great malady of the twentieth century, implicated in all our troubles, and affecting us individually and socially, is loss of soul. It seems as if you've taken on as your primary work to think about how we can bring soul back into life, back into the world. It's a subject that is very close to my own heart, and I was particularly struck with your comment in this regard that "care of the soul is a step outside the paradigm of modernism and into something entirely different." What is it that's so entirely different?

THOMAS MOORE: The first thing I might say—a very simple thing—is that care of the soul as I am presenting it is not something that you do within the present cultural system, or paradigm, or habits that we have now. It seems like a lot of people would like to be able to find some way to keep what we have, the life that we live, and make some adjustments so we'll all be happy. That's not what I'm trying to suggest at all. What I'm suggesting is something deeper: we have to get rid of certain things. To bring soul in means other things go out.

SUZI GABLIK: What things have got to go?

THOMAS MOORE: I guess when you think about modernism and about the modern world, there are obvious dimensions of it that make it difficult to live a soulful life. One of the primary things is trying to get along in this world relying on reason, on mind. Even today, I read the brightest, most interesting people, full of imagination, talking about the mind-body paradigm, and to me, that just doesn't do it. That's the old world; it's still a dualistic way of looking at the world. It still relies on mind—in fact, there's a lot of brain talk in all of it—and I think there's no room in that for soul.

SUZI GABLIK: So you're saying that even the people who are trying to change the old Cartesian body-mind split are still trapped in it in some way?

THOMAS MOORE: Yes.

SUZI GABLIK: Because the new body-mind paradigm that they're talking about still doesn't address issues of soul?

THOMAS MOORE: Exactly. I wish I could have said it that way myself. It's an interesting problem, because if you look at certain religious traditions—the most obvious one would be Zen—it seems to me that in certain schools of Zen, there's an insight that the only way you can really find a solution to the questions that you have is to reach a point where your questions dissolve. There's a personality dimension there that has to break apart, and that I think is being bolstered, actually, in that other response.

SUZI GABLIK: When you talk about needing to let certain things go, surely part of that must include the way we frame issues to ourselves, and the way that we talk and think about things.

THOMAS MOORE: Yes: the language that we use, the style of our talking, the way in which we do things. To be a little more specific, I think with this mind-body talk in medicine, what happens is that we try to get out of the split by making mind more attractive—like, OK, let's have a higher form of consciousness. Let's be more imaginative in our mental life. In other words, we're digging the hole deeper by making it more attractive.

SUZI GABLIK: So what is the mysterious element, or component, called "soul" that is somehow absent from this picture? And how could we better put it there?

THOMAS MOORE: I have actually learned a lot of things since this book has come out. I didn't know what it was about when it first appeared, really. Just now, after a year and a half, I'm beginning to get a better picture of what it is.

SUZI GABLIK: Is this through the feedback you've had, and the many interpretations others have laid on your work?

THOMAS MOORE: Yes, and also having to speak about it so much. Over and over again I've had to simplify, and I've had to realize, very concretely, especially when speaking on an AM radio station, that you can't be too subtle about things. You have to try to convey, in a few minutes before they announce the sports scores, what soul is all about and what care of the soul is. So I've had to really hone this down, and one of the things I've learned that pertains to the question is, we have to find ways of talking that are not in that split place of mind and body, or in that rationalism. And so, I'm very interested in talking to people who don't have any education around these philosophies of modernism and postmodernism. For example, I do not see my book *Care of the Soul* as a popularization of these questions, even though it has sold a lot of copies. Some people might look at it and say, "You're trying to be accessible." I often hear that. I'm really not trying to be accessible, that's not one of my purposes. What I am interested in is finding a language that in itself is not stuck in this dualism, and avoiding situations where the language itself becomes so removed from even my own daily experience that I have to figure out how to pull it down and apply it to my life.

SUZI GABLIK: One of the qualities of the book that I experienced most strongly when I read it did have to do with language, and the use of language in it. What I experienced was almost like a physical alteration in my body, a kind of cellular realignment, or direct transmission, which might be comparable, say, to the effect of listening to certain types of music. I felt as if the words were making me know something through my body while I was reading them. Is that anything you consciously worked for?

THOMAS MOORE: Well, not too consciously. Maybe artfully. You know, I try to see myself as a writer, and as I said at the beginning of the book, "this is fiction," at a certain level.

SUZI GABLIK: It certainly has an alchemical quality. Maybe it's because you're so steeped in those traditions from the Renaissance that you're able to bring an alchemical force into the way you write.

THOMAS MOORE: I'm actually surprised how much the studies of alchemy and astrology, world religions and music, have affected my work—it's not terribly conscious, though. I do notice, looking back on it and hearing people respond to me, that yes, I guess there is a lot of that in there.

SUZI GABLIK: We never really got to the heart of what it is in the modern paradigm that needs to be left behind if we're going to have a more soulful existence.

THOMAS MOORE: One of the things that needs to be left behind, as I suggested, is too much reliance on reason and mind, especially on what my Renaissance sources would call a schizoid, or split-off, mind—not having soul. When our reasoning and our education and teaching have soul, they have more imagination; they're more poetic in style. They're not going toward solutions to problems. They're not objectified, or quantified. And also, technology is not divorced from other dimensions. You see, the one thing about soul that's very interesting—it's in this new book of mine, *Soul Mates*—is that soul is *convivial.* That's the word I'm using for it: it's convivial in itself. So, let's say with technology: as long as technology is convivial with the arts, and with other dimensions of our experience, then I see no difficulty with technology. But to make technology convivial in the sense I'm thinking about would mean to leave modernism, because modernism has been built around a monotheism of technology. It's a little like James Hillman's idea of "psychological polytheism," only I'm emphasizing the erotic aspect of multiplicity. I don't want to speak at all against technology—it's crazy to do that.

SUZI GABLIK: What would make for a convivial technology that was somehow linked with the arts?

THOMAS MOORE: I think we can learn from our ancestors that it's possible to be a technologist while at the same time being a poet. Emerson writes about this when he says that only the poet knows astronomy.

SUZI GABLIK: It sounds as if you're suggesting a model like that of the Renaissance person.

THOMAS MOORE: I think that idea of the Renaissance individual as being someone who can do a little bit of everything has been misunderstood to some extent. What it really means, I think, is that this Renaissance person is living in a world where all the arts, and all the activities we do, are convivial with each other. They're distinct, but they have a relationship where one acknowledges and supports the other, and they do not allow any of them to become so dominant that the others go into eclipse.

SUZI GABLIK: It seems that we're moving, culturally speaking, into a more interdisciplinary, interdependent, multicultural kind of environment right now.

THOMAS MOORE: Well, that's a good move, but I think that this idea has got to be deeper, even, than that.

SUZI GABLIK: I think what makes all this relevant to the struggles art is going through at this point is how modernism made art into a highly specialized pursuit, practiced only by trained professionals. As I understand your sense of the soulful life, it would mean bringing art back into a more vernacular, everyday world, and taking it out of the more rarefied sphere of professionalism. You mentioned in the letter you wrote to me that you are very interested in the role of the arts in the world today. Do you see art as being an important vehicle for the return of soul?

THOMAS MOORE: Probably its most important vehicle.

SUZI GABLIK: Do you want to elaborate on this?

THOMAS MOORE: Yes, there's so much to say here. First, though, I'd like to pick up on this point of yours about everyday life. There are a number of ways in which we could bring the artist back into everyday life, so that we don't just have this fringe art world that doesn't really touch on the values of the way we live, essentially. One way would be for the artist truly to feel a sense of—here's that word again— conviviality in the society, in being part of that community, so that there's a responsibility, and a pleasure, in going into the world and being part of, say, actually designing the city. I agree with someone like Ficino from the Renaissance that architecture is probably, from a certain point of view, our most important art, because it creates the space we live in and work in every day. And it is part of ordinary life. We have allowed people who see life as primarily functional to create our buildings, so our buildings are very much like our psychology. Everyone now talks about dysfunctional families, and it's so much like the way we build our buildings: they're either functional or dysfunctional. It's a terrible way to talk about family, I think, and it's an awful way to build buildings. Now, as long as we live in a world where we're building buildings as functions—with a little trim around them— we're going to be talking about dysfunctional families, because there's a direct relationship between our lives and the world we live in, whether it has imagination, whether it's artful, or not. We can't suddenly begin living a more artful life, which is the avenue to soul, if in the public life around us, and in everything we see and inhabit, like this building we're in now, art is invisible.

SUZI GABLIK: And so, in your thinking, that could be a whole new paradigm for a socially relevant kind of art—not precisely in the sense that's being talked about in the art world now of "political correctness" and social critique, but rather a kind of art that celebrates and participates robustly in the life-world.

THOMAS MOORE: Exactly. And does so with pleasure. Here's another point about soul. A whole tradition about soul is Epicurean, in the West. The philosophers and poets who write about soul, like the Renaissance Neoplatonists, and like John Keats and Oscar Wilde and Emily Dickinson, people like this recognize that soul enters life through pleasure. It's an erotic activity: psyche and eros going together, rather than principle and responsibility. Responsibility suggests a kind of outward superego coming in and saying, "You know, this is what you should be doing." Again, that is not a new paradigm; we're not moving out of the modernistic world then. We're just feeling we should do something different and more responsible.

SUZI GABLIK: "If we are going to care for the soul," you say in the book, "and if we know that the soul is nurtured by beauty, then we will have to understand beauty more deeply and give it a more relevant place in life." It's not only pleasure and conviviality, but also beauty that is necessary for the return of soul. This is something Hillman talks about, too. It's interesting, don't you think, that archetypal psychologists are the ones who seem to be taking the lead for a renaissance of beauty in our lives, even more than artists or aestheticians?

THOMAS MOORE: Isn't it true that many artists are not terribly interested in talking about philosophy and psychology?

SUZI GABLIK: Do you think they're interested in talking about beauty?

THOMAS MOORE: No.

SUZI GABLIK: Why do you suppose that's true?

THOMAS MOORE: It's possible that some artists, at least, have bought into the modernist philosophy of the time very unconsciously, and in buying into that world, they think that doing their art is a matter of self-expression. I hear that a lot from many artists, though they're not necessarily the most accomplished ones.

SUZI GABLIK: The notion of self-expression has certainly been a prominent feature of the worldview of individualism, and is a theme I take up a lot in my own work. One of the things that's happening in our culture right now, I believe, is this moving beyond the worldview of individualism in many spheres. Art in modern society has had almost no communal dimension. Do your ideas about care of the soul have any relationship with the more interdependent and communal worldview that seems to be overtaking our radically individualistic society?

THOMAS MOORE: I think my ideas relate to a different kind of individualism, a deeper kind of individualism. There's a paradox at work here. The traditions say that soul is in the community and in nature; but, it's also in the individual and in culture. Soul overlaps in all these areas. You can't really care for the soul totally as an individual. What happens, I think, is that as you care for the soul communally and also in relation to nature, then people are able to touch places in themselves that are less controlled, and have less ego. Whatever we are made of at a deep level is full of mystery that we can never really know, but it comes out then, and a certain individuality is increased in our expression of ourselves. But it's not something that's done consciously, it's not a self-conscious individuality, where I am expressing my philosophy and my ideas—

SUZI GABLIK: Imposing myself upon the world.

THOMAS MOORE: It's not that at all. I think there's an even deeper and sharper individualism that comes through when you get away from that. The insistence on being an individual is a sign—this is Freudian talk—that we don't have it. You don't insist psychologically and emotionally on something if you've really got it in its fullness. You insist when you feel the lack. We insist on individualism and self-expression because we haven't touched deep enough roots of what it is to be an individual. And I suspect that as we get closer to it, we'll discover that it is not as remote from community as we now believe.

SUZI GABLIK: Another paradox about all this is how the loss of the communal dimension in our particular culture has actually truncated our sense of individuality, because we have such a distorted experience of the world that comes to us exclusively through the limited ego-self. We know only about separateness; we know so little about interdependence. But returning soul to the world and leaving behind the modern paradigm seem to be linked, wouldn't you say, with a dismantling of patriarchal consciousness and lifting the repression of the feminine? Is this kind of terminology acceptable to you?

THOMAS MOORE: It's not a question of whether it's acceptable— I don't use it. I'm not interested in it; I'm very suspicious of it and I don't like it.

SUZI GABLIK: You don't feel, then, that the modern worldview has been an overweeningly masculine framework?

THOMAS MOORE: No, and I don't think we have yet discovered at all what wonderful things patriarchy can be. To blame patriarchy for all these things that are wrong I think is an awful simplification. I could go on and on about this.

SUZI GABLIK: Please do.

THOMAS MOORE: Well, starting at the bottom line, one of the problems is that there's no way all of that talk about patriarchy won't bleed into talk of men versus women and therefore increase the divisions, and I think that's a sad situation. That's not this new world we're talking about, to have men and women divided, almost to the point where I get the feeling sometimes that we could have another civil war here. It's that bad. The divisiveness of the genders is so difficult at the present moment.

SUZI GABLIK: Has the men's movement not been helpful, then, from that point of view?

THOMAS MOORE: I can't say that. No, I think that both the men's movement and the women's movement have been important in raising critical questions, but they have not been taken with nearly enough subtlety yet, as far as I can see. I don't think we need those metaphors of masculine and feminine; first of all, they're dualistic, like mind-body. Dichotomies don't work: right brain-left brain doesn't work.

SUZI GABLIK: Have you found some other terminology that you like better?

THOMAS MOORE: Well, you told me that you thought the language in *Care of the Soul* had more body to it. I'm trying to find language where the words are individual words. I'm not trying to create any system. For instance, I don't use the words conscious and unconscious; I use my own vocabulary.

SUZI GABLIK: When I made that comment earlier about your writing, it didn't refer so much to the choice of words, although maybe that's part of it. I was thinking more about the pace, and how the slowness and deliberation and subtlety of the writing cause one's whole being to pause and take a breath, to decelerate. I once heard someone on NPR—it was on the "New Dimensions" program—say that the most important thing any of us can do for the planet right now is to slow our individual lives down. Of course, it's the very opposite of what's really happening. Just look at any of us. Even the people who most understand the need to slow things down, who are the most dedicated to this idea, don't seem able to achieve it. We're all in orbit. Do you feel hopeful that our present culture will succeed at any of this in an intentional kind of way, or are we going to be slammed before anything changes significantly?

THOMAS MOORE: Oh, I think we're going to be slammed, we probably need that. There's no indication that we're listening to what's going on. We have an atrocious situation in our cities; our cities are unbelievable. One thing I've learned from traveling a lot is the terrible shape so many American cities are in, because of crime, businesses closing down, people not able to live in neighborhoods anymore.

SUZI GABLIK: One of the triggers for these conversations was Michael Ventura's comment, in *We've Had a Hundred Years of Psychotherapy—And the World's Getting Worse*, that Western civilization is over and there's no way to stop the avalanche of its collapse. In that book, the question is posed as to what therapy should be doing in such a time, and I've presumed to pirate the question by asking the same thing about art. Do you share the perception that Western civilization is collapsing?

THOMAS MOORE: Well, the question I think you're really asking is what is my fiction? What is my myth of this? You can see this through an apocalyptic myth, but I don't. I agree with people that things are pretty bad, and I do think that there's no place for hope. One of my favorite authors is Samuel Beckett. He was asked by someone once if there wasn't some glimmer of hope in one of his plays, and he said, "No, not the slightest."

SUZI GABLIK: What does it mean for you that there's no place for hope?

THOMAS MOORE: It means that we have to empty our thoughts about hope so that we can feel the hopelessness, really feel it. We have to allow ourselves, and have the courage, to feel our hopelessness, right to the bottom of it. And I don't think we're doing that: we're trying to find all these defenses against it. I think a lot of what we're doing in our optimism is trying to defend ourselves against the hopelessness.

SUZI GABLIK: And to fall back on a belief in all those technological wonders and panaceas that will solve everything eventually. But if we were *not* on the path of denial—if we were truly on the path of experiencing our hopelessness and our despair—do you think this would change the course of things? What might be happening then?

THOMAS MOORE: I want to say that my own style is not to speak from a hopeless place. I find myself trying to get out there and inspire people, getting up and saying, "Get out there and do something."

SUZI GABLIK: It's the same for me. But is your personal sense of things that there's no hope for us?

THOMAS MOORE: I think it works this way, that the deeper you get into the hopelessness, the more genuine your optimism is. These are paradoxes again, and we need to get beyond the opposites here—of hope and despair. And the only way to do that is to really deepen both sides. I have been going everywhere and quoting a line that someone in one of my audiences gave me from Yogi Berra. He said, "When you come to the fork in the road, take it." And that's what I've been trying to do. [Laughter] It's a tough thing to do. And so, when you ask me about hopelessness, I have to realize that, yes, I want to get down that road of hopelessness as far as I can, but I'm not going to give up the path of optimism.

SUZI GABLIK: That's incredibly well put, the fork in the road signifying that you can go down two paths at once, simultaneously; and if you do that, at some point, perhaps even parallel lines may actually meet, right?

THOMAS MOORE: Yes. You get to a point where, suddenly, you don't even see two paths anymore. You're in something else entirely. The something else is what soul is. This gets back to your first question, how do you bring soul into this culture? It's something else. It's beyond any divisions that we are perceiving at the moment. We don't know what it's like to have a soulful culture, because we're still trying to learn to stand out of the way so that what can be will manifest itself—and it will not be what we think now it could be, because we're thinking still in modernist terms, all of us. That's my huge complaint about this talk of patriarchy.

SUZI GABLIK: Do you feel that other cultures, or civilizations, besides our modernist one, were soulful cultures, or not?

THOMAS MOORE: No, I don't. I think this is an archetypal struggle that all cultures have to deal with. I also think it's a mistake to ask: how did we get into this mess, and who's responsible? No one's responsible: it's an ultimate issue. We're always trying to make soul; soulmaking is a process that is always going on. And I don't think there's any culture that has ever been "soulful" with big capital letters.

SUZI GABLIK: Ellen Dissanayake, who is a Darwinist, suggests that we have somehow managed to create a society to which the human species is not adapted. I wonder a lot, myself, about whether the human race is a dysfunctional species and is on a track of destroying itself, not to mention the thousands of other species that we are destroying as well.

THOMAS MOORE: See, I don't feel that. I was trained as a theologian, and I think theologically. More and more so every day—it shocks me.

SUZI GABLIK: Does your spiritual sense of life keep you from feeling hopeless about the human race?

THOMAS MOORE: Not exactly. What I meant was, I'm very conscious of the story of Adam and Eve, and of the Christian doctrine of original sin—meaning that there's something in the very nature of things, not just in human beings, but in the nature of *things*, that makes them not perfect. Life is full of holes and failure and incapacity, and is self-destructive and self-creative.

SUZI GABLIK: Living with soul would be to fully acknowledge and embody that understanding.

THOMAS MOORE: Yes, and the less literal that is, the more you see that this all makes some kind of sense. If we could own up to our destructiveness, and allow life to be destroyed more than we do, and not be so aimed toward "goodness" and "success" and living life without blemish, I think if we really could look and see these two sides more stereophonically, or whatever, then I think that we would not have a backlash from all this shadow material.

SUZI GABLIK: What is your next book, *Soul Mates*, about?

THOMAS MOORE: It applies the ideas in *Care of the Soul* to relationships: to marriage, family, friendship, community.

SUZI GABLIK: Does it suggest that we need to conduct ourselves in those realms rather differently than we have been?

THOMAS MOORE: Yes. This book is primarily about allowing ourselves to imagine relationship to be what it is, rather than trying to have some fantasy that relationships are only valuable if they're good, and work out and don't have pain. I'm trying to give a place to all those things that happen and suggest that relationship is very much like art, like an artist's canvas or an empty staff of notes. It's the field on which we can do our soul work. It's an alchemical vessel, you might say. I think relationship can be imagined as being terribly important and essential to a soulful life. Just the fact of having a family is a tradition that connects you to the past. A family provides some of the eternity the soul needs. Soul can't just live on this personal life, it needs a much bigger context.

SUZI GABLIK: Talking about a bigger context, what do you see as the path for artists today who are seeking soul?

THOMAS MOORE: One thing I get from Ficino in the Renaissance is that the soul needs a vacation, regularly. Now that can be taken lightly, but it means something much deeper than we mean by vacation. It means that the soul, in order to thrive, needs to get out of this life, regularly, every day.

SUZI GABLIK: You mean, out of humdrum chores and tasks?

THOMAS MOORE: Out of the world.

SUZI GABLIK: Where does it need to go?

THOMAS MOORE: It needs to go somewhere—as long as it's not here. [Laughter] It needs to vacate, that's the first thing. I want to emphasize that, because we immediately want to think about what does it do, when the important thing is that it needs to be vacant. It needs to empty itself out, and go somewhere that's empty. One of the things that art does is to provide that: art arrests our attention. It stops us, so that the world is not going on for a few minutes. But you can see that this would be a problem with propagandistic art, or political art.

SUZI GABLIK: What's an example of art that arrests our attention successfully?

THOMAS MOORE: A Bach partita.

SUZI GABLIK: Does any contemporary art do this?

THOMAS MOORE: Oh, yes. Any art that arrests us, and does not lead us back into life with an opinion about it, is inviting us out and is performing a very important service. What it is giving us is an occasion for contemplation. We've lost the capacity, as a culture, for real contemplation. We do not contemplate easily—it feels like we're not accomplishing anything when we contemplate. Now if we don't have contemplation in our lives, we're probably going to be going after it symptomatically—a lot of our spectating is like this.

SUZI GABLIK: Like couch-potato TV-watching.

THOMAS MOORE: Couch-potato TV-watching is totally symptomatic, it seems to me. It's a real symptom, not that this person needs to get active and get off that couch. That person needs to get deeper into the couch. There's another point about soul and art that's very important to me: soul also thrives on mystery. The French Catholic philosopher Gabriel Marcel distinguished, many years ago, between a problem and a mystery. Today we seem to deal with every issue in our cultural life as a problem, and never take it as a mystery. A problem is there to be solved; mystery is there to be initiated into, or to be entered into fully. But I don't mean mystery in the sense of a black hole. An example would be, say, the mystery of Annunciation. That's a positive, specific mystery that I think all of us live. All of us can, in our contemplation, be visited by an angel, an inspirer of some kind, a muse —and this is what that mystery is about. Another mystery from my Catholic background would be the Crucifixion of Jesus—a tremendous mystery that we all live. I think all of us get crucified, and that's a very real way to appreciate that mystery.

SUZI GABLIK: Are any contemporary images able to match those?

THOMAS MOORE: We have as much of a wealth of those things as people ever did. I believe that these mysteries are always present and show themselves according to the styles of the times.

SUZI GABLIK: So it's really a matter of tapping into the collective unconscious and its store of images and then finding a way to bring that forward with new meaning for our time.

THOMAS MOORE: I would never use that language, but yes. That's a structural way of looking at what's going on. I would rather say that there's a great profundity of what creates our human life, and what invites us into the various dimensions of our lives—toward pain, or happiness, or love, or death. All these things that we've invited into our lives are beyond us. I don't like to talk about that as the collective unconscious, though; it's too defined.

SUZI GABLIK: Would you say that by being beyond us, these things also lure us toward them?

THOMAS MOORE: They lure us toward our own fulfillment, and, in a way, toward who we are going to be. That's what I had in mind when I quoted Picasso in *Care of the Soul*, when he says that if he were to connect the dots of all the events of his life, then he would draw a minotaur. It's a very nice image to think about. Our lives are fashioned, not by our intentions, but by responding to these invitations that come from fate, and from other people and events, mysteriously. And I think that what art can do that reason can't do is provide us with images that help us contemplate these mysteries.

Stall Moor Stone Circle, 1982
Etching, 16" x 20"

Retrieving an Ancient Ecology

CHRISTOPHER CASTLE

AS WE MOVE from mindless exploitation of the physical world to a more awakened understanding based on unity and interconnection, we do well to have at least one eye on the ancient past. Archaeology has revealed that patterns and symbols of prehistoric peoples enfold in their layers of meaning a perception of the world which, though of another context, has deep significance for our way forward.

Patterns previously reduced and approximated to "decoration" or "primitive," in light of new science and systems theory, now can be seen to offer forms of consciousness that demonstrate precisely the kind of thinking that is required today. Concentric circles on a stone from Neolithic Ireland no longer merely represent an arcane significance beyond our knowledge. Rather, they are specific to their location and express an awareness of the energetic ontology of that place. Neolithic stone circles are receptacles of a vanished cosmology linking people to place and the cycles of time. Such sites gather the influences in the land around them and focus the subtle networks of connections in the region: geographical, mythological, geological, biological, meteorological, astronomical. This awareness, however, presupposes a profound sensitivity on the part of the observer or participant in the location. It is also identical to contemporary ecological understanding of place.

With electricity pulsing in the wiring of our houses, electromagnetic waves of all wavelengths, visible and invisible, permeating the space in which we live our lives, and all the other less subtle forms of interference intruding, it is little wonder our senses no longer respond and interact with the subtle energies our ancestors could feel.

Through my work I actively seek to develop my senses and engage the world in a kind of conversation. I am not an observer. My own part is as a player, yet science forms the base from which I explore intuitively and emotionally.

The interpersonal and environmental become one at the level of sensitivity I am referring to here. Interdependence is not a theoretical idea but a living, dynamic experience. Wonder at nature is not a romantic fantasy but a renewal of the ancient, polytheistic, pagan vision, a healthy involvement of the heart and mind in the processes of life of which we are a part.

My work spans several media. All are utilized as a means to awaken, first in myself, then later in my viewer or audience, this ancient experience of an integral world. Drawing is (unfashionably) at the heart of my visual work. My studies of the physical and metaphysical structure of trees gave rise to a series of large scale charcoal drawings. Utilizing the transient, even entropic forms of tree life, the carbon of charcoal, the series on the redwood tree of California sprang to life. From leaf to the full canopy of the tree, from an architectural study of the cone to an aerial vista of a full forest, the exploration was conceived of as a whole and led eventually to including the cellular structure of the tree's root. Perceptual shifts inspire changes of medium. In this case the voice of the tree became audible when the rhythmic pattern became visible.

My recent musical compositions are living maps of terrain at many scales. Specific land forms, cellular structure, animal tracks, stellar geometries, and human statistics are some of the systems for which I am finding visual and musical equivalents. The merging of visual and musical modes effects an engagement of human perception and emotion in the particulars of place. This represents a renewal of our covenant with the patterns of life encoded in the forms and processes of nature, and especially with the depths and details of our locale.

Campbell Hot Springs (detail), 1985
Etching, 17" x 25"

Boscawen-Un Stone Circle, 1980–81
Oil on canvas, 36" x 48"

Wesiory Stone, Poland, 1980
Watercolor/gouache, 22" x 30"

Newgrange II, 1976
Oil on canvas, 42" x 30"

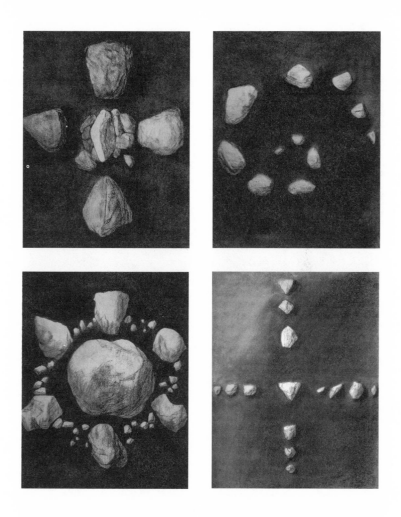

Wayside Shrine I, II, III, IV, 1983
Charcoal, 25" x 19" each

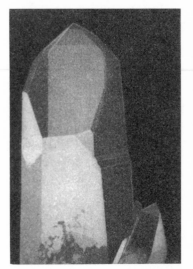 

Quartz Crystals I & II, 1986
Etching, 5" x 3.5" each

Redwood Leaf, 1983
Charcoal, 60" x 48"

Redwood Canopy, 1983
Charcoal, 60" x 48"

Pine Cones, 1985
Etching, 3.5" wide

Cross Species Collaboration, 1993
Rattlesnake tracks, heron track, artist's hand
Charcoal, 60" x 48"

Deep Form in Art and Nature

BETTY AND THEODORE ROSZAK

> The poet makes poetry as the rain and earth
> make trees . . . The poet produces poetic
> objects as electricity produces light.
>
> —Octavio Paz[1]

THE SPIRITUAL CRISIS of the modern world has been described in many ways. From the viewpoint of the arts, Herbert Read's diagnosis is among the most incisive. Read believed a serious loss of aesthetic sensitivity has paralleled our progressive estrangement from nature. We suffer, he said, from an "atrophy of sensibility." Art as well as science and technology harbor the illusion that we live *outside* or *above* the natural world, and so may treat it as we please, turning it into an object of exploitation for the exclusive benefit of our species. Over the past century whole philosophical and aesthetic movements have been predicated upon and even dedicated to our alienation from nature as if it were the inevitable human condition. As the atrophy deepens, the experience grows familiar, even chic. "Nature and I are *two*," quips Woody Allen, turning our environmental disconnection into one-liner angst.

The essence of modernism has been a deepening immersion in extremes of despair, anxiety, or outright cynicism. Few would dispute that it is the role of art to reflect its times. But reflection should include what art itself has to offer to the soul in need; it must look beyond the contemporary wasteland to find life-enhancing possibilities. Otherwise even heroic despair easily cheapens into a cliché. Settling for the

71

fashionably anguished or fashionably cynical, mainstream art stops at the city limits of a culture that has lost or forgotten its ecological roots. In a time when so many artists have learned to confabulate with extremes of horror and alienation, the most daring thing an artist can do is to fill a book, a gallery, or a theater with joy, hope, and beauty. This is more than a matter of calling for a new "movement" or "style." As the degradation of the planetary environment worsens, we are being forced to recognize that a culture divorced from the biological foundations of life is simply not sustainable. Both environmental ignorance and aesthetic atrophy are rapidly approaching terminal status. To refuse despair has become an ecological imperative.

In her provocative survey of the outer limits of modernism, the art critic Suzi Gablik asks: "After the avant garde, what?" Her answer can be found in the title of her book: *The Reenchantment of Art*. There she writes hopefully of a new art "ushered in by twentieth century physics, ecology, and general systems theory, with its call for integrative and holistic modes of thinking." The terminology Gablik uses is drawn from modern science, but the re-enchanted sensibility she calls for takes us back to the shamanic roots of art. On the far side of modernism artists may find they have a great deal to "learn from Lascaux." This is not a matter of scavenging the "primitive." There has been enough of that in the twentieth century. Too often the effort to salvage ancestral images has been animated by a domineering consciousness, one that insensitively ransacks or even plunders the tribal cultures. Lately, spokespeople for traditional societies have taken issue with such invasive practices. Jerome Rothenberg's "ethno-poetics" is a better approach. It seeks to redress this essentially colonialist attitude by preserving and enhancing the human values that connect us with primary people. Our goal should not be to borrow from elsewhere, but to search among our own cultural resources, perhaps even in modern science and industrialism, for ways to restore art to the status it has always held in traditional societies as a form of knowledge.

In the modern Western world, the Romantics were the last major cultural movement to assert the "truth of the imagination," defending art as a way of knowing the world that equalled or surpassed scientific reason. In their resistance to what Blake called "Satan's Mathematik Holiness," their goal was not to reject science but to enlarge it. Newtonian science sought to understand the world by a process of reductionism. The method may be legitimate enough, but it can carry over into reducing in *value*. Phenomena deprived of their dignity and vitality become "nothing but . . . nothing but." They are cheapened by the very act of knowing. In contrast, the Romantics sought to understand by *augmentation*. In Blake's terms, they sought "fourfold vision" rather than "single vision." From the Romantic perspective, a landscape by Constable makes our knowledge of nature bigger; art adds to what we learn from any combination of physics, biology, geology, and chemistry. It tells us the world is (to offer a poor verbal translation) magnificent, perhaps sacred, therefore deserving of reverence. At its highest level, it transforms our consciousness by uniting us with Deep Form in the natural world.

By "Deep Form" we mean the correspondence between formative processes of mind and formative processes in nature. As Coleridge put it, "The rules of the imagination are themselves the very powers of growth and production." For the Romantics, recognizing this congruency between creativity in art and in nature was not a *mere* subjective reflex; it was as much a fact as anything a botanist tells us about photosynthesis or a geologist about continental drift. Deep Form offers us the knowledge that an authentically Deep Ecology requires in order to place us in a respectful, sustainable relationship with nature.

"Great works of art," Goethe believed, "are works of nature just as truly as mountains, streams, and plains." The oneness of art and nature has not been wholly beyond the reach of scientists themselves. Even as tough-minded a Darwinian as Thomas Huxley once admitted to the fact that "in travelling from one end to the other of the scale of life, we are taught one lesson, that living nature is not a mechanism, but a poem."

Georg Groddeck, Freud's most eccentric follower, was among the few psychotherapists who granted art an epistemological status of its own. An admirer of Goethe, Groddeck regarded art as the key criterion of sanity. Healthy art creates a healthy soul; sick art creates neurosis. Groddeck believed that, since the Renaissance, the art of Western society has been corrupted by an excessive humanism. He warned that when we turn away from nature we lose "the chance of cultural development, cease to recognize our dependence upon the universal whole, and direct our love, fear, and reverence only upon the strivings and sufferings of our fellow men." This degenerates into a narrow psychologism especially as our lives come to be bounded by what the neo-Romantic poet Robinson Jeffers called "the incestuous life of the cities."

It is heartening to see how the sense of Deep Form has managed to survive in the arts despite all that urban industrial society has done to shatter the natural continuum. We can find celebrations of Deep Form among some of the masters of modernism, a small, gallant contingent who never lost their nourishing connection with the earth beneath the pavement. While their style is distinctly of our time and place, their sensibility allies them to the dawn of human culture. Paul Klee is a leading example. He once gave this advice to a fellow art teacher:

> Lead your students to Nature, into Nature! Let them learn by experience how a bud is formed, how a tree grows, how a butterfly opens its wings, so that they will become as rich, as variable, as capricious as Nature herself. Perception is revelation.... Follow the ways of natural creation, the becoming, the functioning of forms. That is the best school.[2]

Werner Haftmann writes that in his studio

> Klee collected skeletons of small animals, mosses, bark and lichen, shells and stones, beetles and butterflies. They were ... most carefully selected, for if one can see through them and master the laws governing their

existence and their form, nature itself becomes transparent, the spirit
moves and the artist feels compelled to attempt similar acts of formal
creation.[3]

Similarly, Emil Nolde subscribed to a deeply organic aesthetic. He too
sensed the forces of nature that work within the artist, bringing us the
knowledge of an *animated* universe. "My aim," he said, "was that
colours should be transmitted to the canvas, through myself as the
painter, with the same inevitability as when Nature herself is creating
forms, just as minerals and crystals are formed, just as moss and
seaweed grow."

One can name many others whose work in an expression of Deep
Form. They are not the dominant movement in twentieth-century art,
but they appear here and there like upstart springs that flow from the
distant shamanic sources of their vocation. The voice of the earth
sounds throughout Walt Whitman and his major disciple Pablo
Neruda. Georgia O'Keeffe must be numbered among the company;
and so too Emily Carr, who so vividly recalls in her diaries the unitive
experience that comes with the discovery of Deep Form:

> I woke up this morning with "unity of movement" in a picture strong in
> my mind.... For long I have been trying to get the movement of the parts.
> Now I see there is only *one* movement. It sways and ripples. It may be slow
> or fast but it is only one movement sweeping out into space but always
> keeping going—rocks, sky, one continuous movement.

The artist, like a tree, drinks up nourishment from the depths and
from the heights, from the roots and from the air, to bring forth a
crown of leaves. The organic metaphor is essential here to the concept
of Deep Form. Nature is reborn through artistic vision.

"Think what it would be like," Italo Calvino once wrote, "to create
a work outside the limited perspective of the individual ego, not only
to enter into selves like our own, but to give speech to that which has
no language, to the bird perching on the edge of the gutter, to the tree

in spring."

Yes, and to the stones, clouds, and stars.

Deep Form reveals the web of vital relationships embedded in all things; its vision of the universe is what Read called "a prodigious animism." It reminds us that the great drama of our time is the discovery that all things and creatures on earth share a common destiny. We are linked to one another in what the poet Robert Duncan once called a "symposium of the whole." Duncan's poetry is among the most eloquent appeals for the creation of what the Deep Ecologists have called an "ecocentric community." He writes:

> To compose such a symposium of the whole, such a totality, all the old excluded orders must be included. The female, the proletariat, the foreign; the animal and vegetative; the unconscious and the unknown, the criminal and failure—all that has been outcast and vagabond must return to be admitted in the creation of what we consider we are.[4]

The words echo Klee's profession: "I sink myself beforehand in the universe and then stand in a brotherly relationship to my neighbors, to everything on this earth."

What then is the contemporary artist's task in recognizing that our humanity and our art arise out of these natural processes, share in them and celebrate them? Can our art become an instrument of rediscovery? Can we devise a new education in aesthetic imagination, a knowledge of the diversity of images in the great network of earthly life? It requires a sensitization to all forms of perception: dreams, memories, states of consciousness other than the "normal" cultural trance.

As examples of work that embodies the full ecological significance of Deep Form in the visual arts, we have chosen two artists—both are English, now living in California.

Gordon Onslow Ford began his artistic life as a surrealist. From that school he took his powerful introspective orientation. Now in his eighties, Onslow Ford has gone well beyond the purely personal subconscious that delimited surrealism. In his major work we enter territory where inside and outside, microcosmos and macrocosmos merge and mirror each other. He inhabits "an inner world beyond dreams" where "the world is the subject and the painter eventually becomes one with what is happening in the world." Onslow Ford's is an activated space where, in an instant, matter becomes energy and energy matter. He speaks of his paintings as experiments in "ecomorphology" that offer us the inner, visionary experience of such otherwise speculative scientific concepts as the black hole and the Big Bang. His canvases become visual hymns to the material foundations of life and mind in the cosmos.

Christopher Castle's art is also a vision of the inner energetic spaces, the worlds of inner earth. Both he and Onslow Ford are concerned with an organic concept of space and matter. Castle, who identifies his work as "geomantic," creates layered archaic images that reverberate with those hidden, telluric forces that our ancestors experienced as animate and divine. This requires the closest attention of the viewer: lines of force, growth patterns, seeds, stones, the folds and fissures of land, and the dark, pulsating symbols of ancient sites. In Castle's work we view the landscape, usually a sacred site, simultaneously from above, from below, from the air, from beneath the earth. A widely-travelled artist, Castle often approaches the sites he paints by living, dreaming, and envisioning his way into them in a sort of psychic archaeological dig that seeks to recapture the ancestral experience of the land.

Both artists present us with a world of unbroken inter-relationship, with a space vibrating with energy, with a depth not of perspective but of multiplicities. Oscillations of figure and ground occur in which images appear, disappear, then appear again. In Onslow Ford's work, as in the tracings of subatomic particles in a cloud chamber, form appears and disappears mysteriously in that boundary zone at the moment of creation. Castle draws upon neolithic patterns: spirals and zig-zags imprinted on sky or earth. He reclaims the runic script of nature, the sinuous serpentine movement of dark, telluric powers, rising from great depths to mirror the heavens. As stylistically different as the two painters may seem at first glance, both assert the vital link between the artistic celebration of form and the real existence of form in the world. In their work, aesthetic pleasure becomes knowledge; the mind is thrown open to that primordial form-making power from which the cosmos has arisen, this thing that our ancestors could see in the trees, mountains, rivers, and stars about them and which grows more beautiful with every advance modern science makes into quantum depths and astronomical vastness.

These and other artists of Deep Form teach us that we can no longer afford to reject the sacred, nor fail in the task of re-animating nature. If we are to meet the challenge of our common ecological dilemma, an art that limits itself to expressions of urban angst and heroic despair becomes too small and too ephemeral.

Deep Form offers the artist a new repertory of gestures: instead of grasping, seizing, mastering, struggling, it attempts a tender touching, a non-interfering gaze, a receptive bonding with earth and the other. The dark, submerged feminine reappears as image and informing spirit, a new *anima mundi* with her rich welter of sensuous experience in color, scent, and sound. Wherever Deep Form wells up among the poets, the painters, the architects, the performers, life is made whole again and the universe comes alive. The creative imagination returns us to an aesthetic both old and new, to a mode of knowing the natural world which can be the ally of science. The human again becomes an integral part of nature; life and mind become part of a vital matrix as vast and as old as the universe. This primary ecological insight views human art not as an anomaly or arbitrarily fashionable decoration, but as integral to the natural order, the common root being inherent formative processes at work at every level of reality from the structure of atoms to the formation of galactic clusters.

Notes

1. Octavio Paz, *Children of the Mire: Modern Poetry from Romanticism to the Avant Garde* (Harvard: Harvard University Press, 1974), 140.

2. Werner Haftmann, *The Mind and Work of Paul Klee* (New York: Praeger, 1954), 113.

3. Werner Haftmann, *The Mind and Work of Paul Klee*, 113.

4. Jerome and Diane Rothenberg, *Symposium of the Whole* (Berkeley and Los Angeles: University of California Press, 1983), 238.

Being Space, 1985
Acrylic on canvas, 81" x 140"

Ecomorphology

GORDON ONSLOW FORD

A TRADITIONAL LANDSCAPE PAINTING is seen from where the painter stands and extends towards the distant horizon. The landscape is seen from the individual painter's point of view.

When the leap is made from the perceived reality of the outer-worlds into an inner-world of the unconscious, the painter as an individual disappears into the nature of the world being expressed.

One way for the painter to catch an invisible inner-world is through spontaneous drawing. Spontaneous drawing begins just faster than thought and speeds up through world after world to arrive at The Deeps of the Mind in the ever present Instant.

Spontaneous lines give off auras and, through contemplation of what has appeared, one line leads to another, and with patience and dedication an aspect of an inner-world inevitably comes into being.

Each inner-world has its own kind of nature, its own kind of space-time-matter-energy. The guiding spirit of an inner-world is the interrelationship between the forms of life that appear.

Each inner-world is in relation with a certain level of reality in the outer-worlds and there is a cross-fertilization between the two. The deeper the awareness of the inner-worlds, the deeper one sees.

The depth at which one sees determines the kind of world in which one lives—hence the importance of becoming aware of the inner-worlds and what I call Ecomorphology: the spirit that holds all forms of life together.

Nature Breathing, 1993
Acrylic on paper, 25" x 22.5"

Finding the Child, 1986
Acrylic on canvas, 35" x 54"

All One's Company, 1993
Acrylic on canvas, 78" x 134"

Two Poems by Betty Roszak

You, Spark

In the fire-dazzle
a flower stirs
a star moves
cities of fire
spring from the sun
a star stirs
the sky trembles.

After-glow burns in the blood.
Gravity spirals into the hunger of space.
Starworld rings and sings
low bronze tremors,
blue earth opens
veins, strata, clefts,
swampy fossils.

Of what are we made?
Tunnels of emptiness,
fierce plunging stars
dissolve and mix
dissolve again
return to the dark time
before time.

You, spark
inward tree, world skull,
mask of bone,
leave your house
to stare under

gardens of stars.

Earth extends
to unimagined regions
of light.
You, spark,
tender green heart,
ground tremble,
violent root dance,
are part of it,

fibers, feathers, fur,
scales, skin, hair,
cells streaming in rivers
and waters, mother blood
flooding the stars.

Asleep inside animal earth
flag in the wind
banner of wrinkled rags
hanging threads
feathery gestures.

Deep darkness
reaches the first seed.
Ancestral earth
light desires you.

Shining back
the mirror turns
flashing so bright
it darkens
whirring of wings
increases, deafens

until sound overflows
to silence.

worlds split open
images into fragments
oracle words
touch then shatter

trees think leaves
weave air into prayer
the branch's particular
incantation,
a great stone stairway
to inner eyes
that speak
in dreams.

Oracle Call Down the Stars

Shadow hand. Blood star
reach down to roots.
Bend leap shine
pour down your glittering body
on parched and waiting
hearts. Oracle call down.

The apocalypse never arrived.
Instead this slow dissolution,
this gradual surrender,
a late menacing question.
Crowds gather before the weeping Madonna.
They have persistent dreams,
wounds that never heal.

Oracle call down
your tiger-streaked beasts,
your thousand names,
call down canyons and cliffs
and rushing fields of stars.

Constellations open.
Face to astonished face
the warning smile destroys.
Call down your house,
not even your house,
but your door, not even your door,
but your lock, not even your lock,
but your key. If there is a key.
If the door exists.
Call down a landscape of desires,
lavender, cinnabar, gold,

granules of crystal sand
under a microscope.

Oracle each month
the crescent grows full.
Call down drowned maps of memory.
Ask darkness for permission
to live. Every garden
a rainbow, every flower
an answer in a maze.

Once more awake and knowing
the mirror brightens,
enters eyes. Call down oracle
your webwork of radiating light.
Lean down
your dark length of hair
awake from sleep
blind but seeing
lean down
your dark hair around me,
covering
until nothing is left but shadows
and shells, nothing left
but a singing stone.

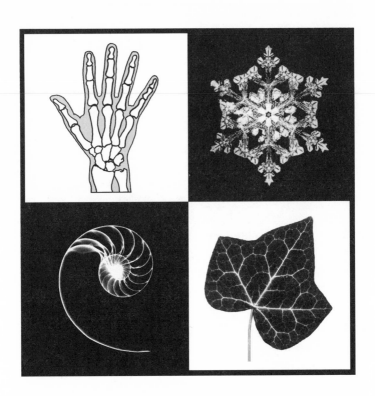

Cosmology, Ethics, and the Practice of Relatedness: A Conversation on Philosophy, the Patterns of Nature, and the Ways of Knowing

DAVID FIDELER

Mark and Christopher, two philosophers, are spending several days relaxing at Sleeping Bear National Lakeshore in Michigan's lower peninsula. Today they are starting a walk along the Empire Bluff trail.

I can't tell you how wonderful it is to be here. And what a fine day.

Yes, everything seems to be just right. I'd say that it's a perfect day. The ground is still moist with dew, and the Earth is being gently warmed by the sun. The sky is deep blue with only an occasional cloud. And the birds are singing everywhere.

We are lucky to be able to take this walk. The trail goes through different types of terrain. First through fields and what used to be an old orchard. Then through deep woods under a canopy of high trees. Finally we come out on the Empire Bluff, a three-hundred foot high dune overlooking Lake Michigan. The view is exquisite and you can see for miles.

Thanks for bringing me here. I know that I'm going to enjoy this.

The two move on past the trail head and hear a soft hum coming from a large, luxuriant patch of goldenrod.

Do you hear that sound?

Yes . . . and look what it is . . .

Amazing. There are dozens of bees attracted to this goldenrod.
Their combined sound is so loud that you can hear them from twenty
feet away.

It's a comforting hum, but also a sound that inspires alertness. I've
seen and heard the bees here many times, but I've never been bothered
by them. They are harmless if you don't provoke them.

Novalis said that "We are bees gathering the pollen of the invisible."
I always liked that very much. Of course, like these other bees, we are
also gathering the pollen of the visible!

Yes. This idea of gathering pollen is a very good description of what
we are doing. Marsilio Ficino also spoke of men as bees. He said that
under the guidance of the Muses they gather pollen, and ripen it into
the honey of knowledge and insight.

That's a wonderful analogy.

They continue up a slight incline.

So what's on the agenda for today?

I'm not sure. Perhaps we should just have a walk and not worry
about things. This might be a good time to leave the world of ideas
behind and enjoy the beauty of this wonderful place. I've been reading
so much stuff lately that my brain is ready to fall out. I recently
attended an academic conference, too. There were a few papers that
I enjoyed, but the rest were so abstract that they seemed impossible to
relate to.

I know what you are saying. Philosophy has become such an
academic pursuit that it seems in danger of losing its social relevance.
Of course, that is true of much of the academic world in general. The
specialization leads to a fragmentation of knowledge and, in my view,
a diminished view of reality and human nature.

This is something that we'll have to talk about some more. I don't
mean to be rude, but when I look at what many academics are doing,
it reminds me of dogs peeing on small patches of territory to mark
their turf. The pieces of territory are so small that they can claim
expertise, but the dominions claimed are so tiny that they also lack any

wider relevance to human life. Rather than creating human beings who embody depth, graduate schools focus on the creation of specialists.

It's a sad situation. And if you really think about it, it can lead to a deep sense of personal alienation. Academic specialization embodies alienation by virtue of its minute focus, and if you are looking for something more—for an understanding of the whole—the ethos of specialization will itself lead to a sense of personal estrangement.

How has this come about, in your opinion?

Well, that is a big topic and one that we could probably not exhaust quickly. But it's interesting to compare the philosophy of education in ancient times with the academic world today. In the Platonic Academy, for example, different branches of learning and research were pursued, but they were pursued toward a certain end. The aim of all learning was ultimately to grasp the nature of the Good in some nonverbal way. This essential experience of the Good would result in a transformation of the self and also provide a starting point for seeing and cultivating the good in particular situations. Today, however, the academic world has adopted a scientific methodology that aims for a neutral type of objectivity that precludes the ideas of value, *telos*, personal experience, and personal transformation as a foundation of knowledge. So, rather than leading to a vision of the whole and the Good, the emphasis is toward specialization and, in my opinion, fragmentation.

Like it or not, there seems to be no way of avoiding the pre-Socratic question of the relationship between the One and the Many!

Yes, not only are Unity and Multiplicity unavoidable conceptual categories, they are realities as well. In the case of living organisms, for example, we cannot understand the part without reference to the entire organism, and we cannot understand the whole without reference to the parts. As the ancient philosophers could clearly see, like living things, the entire universe itself is a one–many, or a harmonically differentiated image of unity.

I like the emphasis that you place on vision and seeing. It suggests that the end of philosophy is not analytical, but in some sense perceptual and intuitive in a way that transcends language.

Well, analysis certainly has its place, but it cannot be the final end. The lesson of modern philosophy is that analysis alone ultimately caves in on itself. Without a sense of the whole as both a starting and finishing point, you will inevitably end up with the type of situation that prevails in the academic world.

Yes. I recently read *The Passion of the Western Mind* by Richard Tarnas and found his comment about modern philosophy to be very telling.

What did he have to say?

It made such an impression, that I can probably quote it from memory . . . Hold on a moment while I try and call it forth. Okay. He said that

> modern philosophy has brought forth some courageous intellectual responses to the post-Copernican situation, but by and large the philosophy that has dominated our century and our universities resembles nothing so much as a severe obsessive-compulsive sitting on his bed repeatedly tying and untying his shoes because he never gets it right— while in the meantime Socrates and Hegel and Aquinas are already high up the mountain on their hike, breathing the bracing alpine air, seeing new and unexpected vistas.[1]

That is a very good way of putting it, and I like the way that he has given us helpful images rather than abstractions.

Yes, and the theme of the hike relates very well to our walk today.

I'd like to go back to what we were saying about the whole–part relationship. It seems to relate to the meaning of philosophy and ethics in today's world, and perhaps even to our survival as a species.

Yes, it's a big topic, and an important one.

What you were suggesting is that the alienation reflected in the academic world is based on a one-sided epistemology that is rooted in the idea of objective, scientific knowledge that claims to be value-free.

Well, yes, that is what I was getting at. Of course there is a place for analysis, specialization, and science as a way of knowing. But if we look at the situation today from a whole–part perspective, there is far too much emphasis on specialization, which leads to the unhappy consequences that we've mentioned. . . . Now that we've taken the world apart, how do we put it back together again?

So what you're saying is that specialization is not inherently harmful, but there needs to be some way to relate the parts back to the whole.

Yes, that's what I think. And if we had a better sense of the whole, much of the specialization that is mere nonsense could be avoided. The point is not that specialization is worthless, but that it becomes meaningless and destructive if it is pursued for its own sake, and not illuminated by a vision of the greater whole.

Ideally, the university itself would function as an organism, in which there was true interdisciplinary dialogue. In the same way that touch, sight, hearing, and thought are necessary for my survival as a living being, in a properly functioning university there would be a similar relationship between the different disciplines and ways of knowing. In the same way that my own senses and faculties contribute to my continued survival and flourishing, the university-as-organism would contribute meaningfully to the larger social organism.

If we were to describe this in symbolic terms, the university would be a mandala that integrates the ways of knowing. But perhaps the image of an organism is better, because it is more dynamic—after all, an organism embodies a living and breathing metabolism.

Yes, and the idea of the organism points toward the vital nature of our undertaking. Because if a harmony between the parts is not maintained, disease and sickness result in any living thing. The words *health* and *wholeness* come from the same Indo-European root, and ultimately mean the same thing.

What we are describing seems quite revolutionary. Perhaps we should sit down and talk about it.

The two philosophers take a comfortable seat on a fallen tree.

This idea of envisioning the world as an organism seems to be an important task of contemporary philosophy. But it is also something that is needed in a larger cultural sense. What role do you see the field of contemporary philosophy playing in this?

As you point out, this may appear to be a revolutionary idea, but it only *seems* to be revolutionary because we moderns have forgotten what philosophy is all about. And again it comes down to the fragmentation of knowledge. For some individuals, philosophy is nothing other than the study of analytical method; for others, a study in the history of ideas. In truth, however, the vision of the world-as-organism is very traditional. If it appears strange, it is only because we have become so lost in mental abstractions.

The very word *abstraction* literally means "to pull away." Rather than showing us how to follow the patterns of nature's own thinking, many philosophers seem to have pulled away from the world to dwell in a world of pure abstraction.

That's why I very much like Stephen Rowe's idea of philosophy as "the practice of relatedness."[2] On the one hand, it incorporates the understanding that the world—and life itself—consists of organic relatedness. On the other hand, it suggests that philosophy is a tangible practice of actualizing our engagement *with* the world, rather than pulling away from it. Along a similar line, I once heard him say that ethics is nothing else than the study of the relationship between the self and the world.

Yes, that is a very lucid idea, and perhaps the most succinct formulation possible. It also delivers a rather devastating blow to those individuals who overly-complexify the study of ethics and make it into a subject that is incomprehensibly abstract or meaningless, like the aptly named noncognitivists.

That's very funny!

After sharing a brief moment of laughter, the two sit in silence listening to the birds. A light wind rustles the leaves of the forest canopy.

This idea of philosophy as the practice of relatedness throws an illuminating light on the relevance of philosophy in today's world, and also helps us to understand the connection between cosmology, ecology, and ethics.

Perhaps we should get up and continue walking? I'm sure that this topic can keep us going for a while.

Okay. I'm ready to resume our peripatetic approach. And soon we'll be at the dune overlook where we sit and look at the lake.

The philosophers return to the trail and resume their journey.

The relationship between cosmology, ecology, and ethics sounds like a daunting topic, and one that could be very complex.

Well, like anything else, it *could* be made into something that is unnecessarily complex. But the basic relationships are quite simple. I've been thinking about it a lot recently, and I know that you have been reading some ancient philosophers who are helpful in this regard. So perhaps we can work out the broad outline together.

I'm certainly willing to give it a try.

What I would like to suggest is that we try not to get too abstract, unless it is absolutely necessary.

And how do you think that we can do that?

First of all, it will be necessary to talk about ideas-in-themselves, so some level of abstraction will be necessary. But what I'd like to do is also investigate the way that ideas are embodied in living things and living relationships. That way, like the bees, we can gather our pollen from the forms of nature and distill it into the nectar of understanding.

It sounds that you are suggesting something like what the medieval and Renaissance philosophers had in mind when they spoke about "reading the Book of Nature."

Yes, that is exactly what I would like to do. Rather than pulling away from reality, I would like to read the Book of Nature. For ideas are not entirely abstract things, but they are embodied in the fabric of the world and living things. If we can learn how to see ideas and relations embodied in living things, then the world itself will become transparent, and we can learn how to see other levels of being shining through the forms of nature.

This sounds like a supremely important undertaking, and one that should interest all curious people—including all philosophers, if philosophy is indeed born from wonder, as Socrates suggested.

They proceed a few paces.

So where do we begin?

First of all, I'd like to begin with a few premises. The first premise is that in some way the universe is a whole, or one thing manifesting itself in a variety of ways.

Obviously, this is true in some sense, and I don't see how anyone could deny it.

Certainly it is a traditional premise in both science and philosophy, and one that can scarcely be avoided. Some postmodernists with their fear of metanarratives might try to deny it for the sake of denying it, but such protests carry little weight for people of good sense. In fact, the only reason that I bring it up in the first place is because much of contemporary life has an atomistic character, and in this type of environment it's easy to forget that the universe, or reality, is one thing.

So you are really raising this premise just as a reminder, of something that we all know but tend to forget?

Yes, and it relates to our talk about specialization, which, when carried to extremes, is itself a forgetting of the essential nature of reality that results in estrangement and alienation.

We are agreed on this point.

Secondly, I would like to suggest that virtue and goodness is not something that only exists in humans.

So, in other words, you are positing a classical Greek conception of *aretê* or excellence?

Exactly. A thing is good when it is able to realize and fulfill its own nature. A pair of scissors possesses virtue when it is sharp and cuts well; a horse possesses virtue when it is strong, healthy, and fast.

This seems eminently reasonable.

Let's also add another related premise that living things possess some type of inherent value regardless of what use they are put to by humans.

Well, industrial civilization has based its existence on a very anthropocentric denial of this fact, but I certainly agree with you. Even if humans had never come into being on this planet, the horse would still possess virtue and goodness because of the fact that it is strong, healthy, and fast. Its virtue and goodness does not depend on the fact that it might make a meal for someone else. On the other hand, the scissors wouldn't possess much in the way of value if there were no humans around to use them.

I agree, and you have delineated the difference between intrinsic and instrumental value. The horse possesses intrinsic value by its very nature as a living being, but scissors possess instrumental value only in terms of their use. If there were no humans to use them, a pair of scissors would possess no more value than the unformed materials from which they are made. . . . But Christopher, do you have any premises that you'd like to add?

Yes. I would like to suggest that Mind or Intelligence is present not only in human beings, but is reflected throughout the fabric of living nature.

This is a point that many people might have difficulty following. Can you explain it further?

Sure. In fact, I've been reading a book by the late biologist and epistemologist Gregory Bateson entitled *Mind and Nature: A Necessary Unity*. Bateson suggests that Mind and Life are essentially the same thing, and he generously defines Mind as "a circular or more complex system in which information flows that makes a difference." Seen in that way, all living systems, like ecosystems and societies, also possess Mind.

Why do you think that this is a useful premise? Many people do not naturally think along these lines and would find it counter-intuitive.

It is a useful premise for that very reason, because it can help expand our perceptions and allow us to see the world in a more accurate way. Ever since the time of Descartes, there has been a deep bias that the natural world is inert, lifeless, and unintelligent. Descartes himself said that living things are automatons or machines, and that all Mind exists within humans. This type of thinking has had terrible consequences, because on the one hand it suggests that humans are fundamentally different from other living things; on the other hand, it radically devalues the world. Rather than being seen as an epiphany of intelligence and living form, the natural world has grown material and opaque.

This idea that Mind is present in nature is also found in the Greek philosophers, isn't it?

Yes, it's a very common idea. The Greek philosophers saw the universe as being alive because all of reality is a ceaseless flow of activity, and motion itself is a sign of life. Secondly, the ever-shifting universe exhibits recurring patterns of order and form—and order and form are expressions of intelligence.[3] Put another way, order and form are strategies for problem solving, and anything that possesses a strategy also possesses some type of intelligence. In Greek philosophy, the intelligence of the universe was called *Nous* or Mind, and it was seen as being reflected in all of nature. The greatest stumbling block to understanding this Greek conception of Mind is the modern prejudice that all Mind or intelligence must be embodied in a self-conscious, human ego. This is clearly absurd, for flowers don't consciously think about how to reach for the sun, but nonetheless embody life (*psyche*), intelligence (*logos* and *nous*), and goal-directed problem solving abilities. Similarly, the growth of a crystal involves the intelligent organization and placement of one trillion molecules an hour, which is its own life process unfolding in time. From this vantage point, the entire universe is clearly an embodiment of living intelligence, or what Plato called the World Soul.

Do you think that evolution is an embodiment of Mind or intelligence?

Yes. All living species possess memory through their genetic structure, and over the course of their evolutionary sequence make innumerable mental decisions in response to environmental contexts. The result of these decisions becomes embodied in the collective life pattern of the species. From this perspective, evolution is akin to a thought process that is slowly working itself out over time. The mental decisions that various species have made are embodied in their form; even plants have had to make quite a few decisions to get to where they are today!

I can see what you're saying. From this perspective, the world clearly is an embodiment of intelligence, and the understanding that Mind exists in nature is a good one. Do you have any other suggestions for premises that we should adopt?

One thing that I'd like to suggest is that abstract logic is useful for some things, but can be very dangerous for the way that it falsifies reality.

Please explain.

Well, as you know, classical logic draws very precise boundaries between things; it's an either/or type of proposition. In the real world, however, these types of precise dividing lines don't exist. For example, there is no firm dividing line between the lungs and the heart because respiration and circulation are aspects of an inclusive system. If living systems incorporate a logic of either/or, they *also* incorporate a logic of both/and, but classical logic ignores the latter and thereby falsifies reality by painting a one-sided picture. It's based on a divide-and-conquer mentality that overlooks the symbiosis, synergy, and cooperation present in living systems—in the living, breathing world.

Any other points?

Yes, I have one other thought that should be included in our list of premises, and it's related to the past two.

And what is that?

If we want to view the world in an accurate way, we need to realize that the world itself is not a collection of static, discrete things, but a process—a web of interrelated events. We falsify the world by making it into a noun when it is really a verb. A flower is not a "thing" but an "event." And, because all these events are parts of larger living systems, they are all implicated in one another.

I have to agree with this point, and it's an understanding that has important ramifications in grasping the deep nature of the world. If we can see the world as a web of interrelated events, this vision will influence our cosmological, ecological, and ethical thinking. Ultimately, it will influence the very way that we relate to the world, living things, and each other.

Do you have anything else to add in the way of good premises or starting points?

No, not at the moment. But we can always add to our collection later, if the need arises.

Mark and Christopher are silent as they reflect on the points of agreement.

Before we go further, would you be willing to summarize our points?

Yes, that's a good idea. In summary, we have agreed on five premises. We first agreed that the universe is a whole, or one thing manifesting in a variety of ways. Second, we agreed that all living things possess some form of intrinsic value. Third, Mind is not something that exists entirely in humans, because the presence of Intelligence is reflected in all living things and most natural systems. Fourth, abstract logic tends to falsify reality by insisting on rigid distinctions that may not exist in the natural world. Fifth, the world is not just a collection of static things, but a process and web of dynamic relationships.

We are in agreement with all of these points. And whether or not we ever refer back to them, they are all very good premises which I hope that everyone would agree with. In fact, they should be in the tool kit of every thinking individual!

They move forward a few paces.

Let's now try to make clear what we mean by cosmology so that we can outline the relationship that exists between cosmology, community, ecology, and ethics.

Where to begin?

Let us start with the observation that, in the beginning, cosmology and philosophy were synonymous. Pythagoras was the first person to call himself a *philosopher* or a lover of wisdom, *and* he was also the first person to call the universe a *kosmos* on account of its beauty. But perhaps this is something that you could expand upon, given your reading.

I would be most happy to, for I have been studying the Pythagoreans and Stoics, as you well know. Basically, the Greek word *kosmos* has a double meaning that cannot be translated by a single English word, and it refers to an equal presence of order and beauty. The Pythagoreans were also students of mathematical proportion, and the mathematical patterns of nature. They saw proportion as an ordering principle in the natural world, and also taught that the universe is a *harmony* or "fitting together" of various elements through proportional relationships. In Pythagorean thought, there is an intrinsic relationship between number, harmony, cosmos, order, and beauty.

And by this you mean to say that harmonious, proportional relationships underlie the fabric of nature?

That seems to be what the Pythagoreans were getting at, and it is certainly true that many natural phenomena are based on archetypal proportions like the Golden Section. These proportions allow for the harmonious integration of Sameness and Difference, and also radiate beauty. But I am getting abstract now, and we promised not to get too abstract, if it can be avoided!

Well, why don't you give me a concrete example, so that we can stay close to the physical world and read the Book of Nature?

That's a splendid idea and I have an example that is close at hand, if you will pardon the expression.

At this point Mark sticks out his hand and slowly makes a fist. He then opens his hand and closes it again.

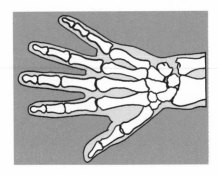

Look at your hand, or, if you like, just at your index finger. As you make a fist, your index finger folds in on itself like a spiral. It does that because there is a proportional relationship between the different joints on the finger. The outermost length is the smallest, the middle length is longer, and the innermost length is the longest yet. The interesting thing is that these three lengths are in perfect geometric proportion with one another, so that the smallest length is related to the middle length as the middle length is related to the longest length. In other words, A is to B as B is to C.

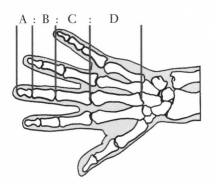

Fascinating.

It's even more interesting when you realize that the proportion of the joints is not some arbitrary ratio, but the Golden Section.

And what's so special about that?

At this point Mark stops in his tracks and draws a line into the sand on the trail. He then draws a notch into the line:

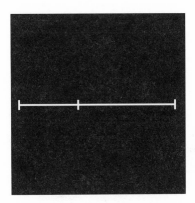

As you can see, I have drawn a line and placed a notch in it. The place of the notch marks the ratio of the Golden Section on the line. It's not perfectly placed, because I'm not using a compass and a straightedge, but it's very close.

Okay, but what's so special about that *one* point on the line?

The thing that is unique about the Golden Section is that it divides the line into two parts, where the smaller part is related to the larger part in exactly the same ratio as the larger part is related to the entire length of the line.

The smaller part is to the larger part as the larger part is to the whole?

Yes. The Golden Section is the only proportion in the entire universe that embodies this relationship. In geometry, it's the ratio of the star pentagon. And in your hand, it's the ratio that determines the spacing of your finger joints. In terms of your height, the navel marks the placement of the Golden Section.

Fascinating.

The Golden Section also appears in plants, flowers, fish, and other animals. When I started to get abstract, I was saying that the proportions of nature harmonize the principles of Sameness and Difference. A good example of that is reflected in a nautilus shell, which perhaps you can envision in your mind.

Yes, I can envision it.

The sea creature needs to grow and change, which is a form of "difference." But by employing continuous geometrical proportion or "sameness," the nautilus can accommodate the change in a regular sort of way. Another way of saying this is that through the use of proportion the nautilus can integrate the polarities of stability and change in an ordered and beautiful way.

Which brings us back to the Pythagorean idea of the cosmos, the world as an embodiment of order and beauty, achieved through proportion.

Yes, and it also goes back to what we were talking about at the beginning of our walk: the balance between the parts and the whole, and how in the academic world we have lost a vision of how the parts fit together.

But Chris, this loss of vision is not limited to the academic world. If we had a clear vision of how things naturally fit together in a scientific and cultural context, it seems unlikely that the ecological crisis would have arisen in the way that it has.

You mean as a symptom of industrial civilization and the idea of unlimited growth?

Yes. The economies of nature are circular, because in an ecosystem waste equals food. Also, in natural economies, growth is limited by proportional relationships which embody the most efficient patterns of organization and sharing . . . .

But wait! Before you go ahead so quickly, I want to point out that we have established—or are very close to establishing—a link between cosmology and ecology. And that is one of the things that we wanted to do.

Okay, let's not rush ahead too quickly. In fact, we have hardly yet touched upon the relationships between cosmos, culture, proportion, and justice in ancient philosophy. Before diving into the relationship between cosmology and ecology, perhaps we should further elaborate the ancient ideas; in that way, the connection might be more firmly established.

I agree—let's retrace our steps and then continue with the ancient philosophers. First of all, we have arrived at a good understanding of what the Pythagoreans meant by cosmos: the order and beauty of the world which arises from proportional relationships or harmony.

This has been explained very clearly with reference to the forms of nature, and I can see how studying nature's harmonies and patterns can be a deeply revealing philosophical pursuit. In fact, it reminds me of the idea of philosophy as the practice of relationship.

Yes, in my book the study of these natural harmonies is certainly an important practice along these lines, though it doesn't exhaust the idea of philosophy as the practice of relationship.

We also suggested that the idea of cosmos arises not from a strictly intellectual form of analysis, but from a way of seeing and perceiving the harmonic patterns of relationship that are present in the natural world. In this sense, the idea of cosmos arises from and reflects a way of knowing or epistemology that is wider, and perhaps deeper, than purely rational analysis.

What about the idea that the universe embodies both order *and* beauty?

Here we have a clear understanding that the worlds of fact and value are conjoined. Pythagoras is saying that we do not inhabit a double-truth universe of objective facts on the one hand and subjective values on the other. The world is not just a collection of meaningless things, but a web of interrelated phenomena that embody beauty.

Are you suggesting that beauty is a form of meaning?

Yes, because beauty is a profound manifestation of value, and value is a form of meaning. When we experience a deep sense of beauty, we also feel a deep sense of belonging, wholeness, and completion. If the fabric of the world emanates beauty, I have to conclude that it is also meaningful. When Pythagoras called the universe a cosmos, he was saying that, from a deep aesthetic perspective, the world is not a senseless configuration of parts, but an embodiment of value and meaning that can never be expressed fully in words.

The modern tendency is to suggest that beauty is subjective, or, as they say, only "in the eye of the beholder."

There seems to be a confusion here between beauty and personal taste! The objective beauty of the world became subjectivized only with the advent of the Scientific Revolution and the rise of logical positivism, which states that only measurable quantities are valid in scientific work. The first clearly articulated example of positivism appears in the work of Galileo. With the quantitative approach, qualities like beauty became irrelevant.

But many of these early scientists were inspired by the intellectual beauty and elegance of the discoveries that they were making. Even contemporary physicists like Einstein and Heisenberg recognized the significance of beauty and were very much in the Pythagorean camp.

Yes, it's impossible to make beauty into a totally subjective phenomenon without falsifying reality. So there is no question that these great men would be inspired and motivated by the beauty of nature. But while beauty is not subjective, it is not quantifiable either. Since the dominant ethos of industrial society has been empirical and quantitative, the intrinsic value and beauty of the world is officially neglected in scientific methodology, the world of business, and so on.

Yes. Positivism is based on the premise that only quantifiable phenomena are worthy of consideration and perhaps even real. From this perspective, it's easy to see how many modern dilemmas have arisen. For as soon as the world is shorn of beauty and intrinsic value, it possesses only utilitarian or instrumental value. Rather than being something valuable in itself, it becomes only a means to some other end—a natural resource to be used up.

The two pause for a moment on the trail.

I think that you are onto something important here, because what you are describing shows how human behavior proceeds in an almost inexorable, deductive fashion from its fundamental premises, whatever they may be. And these premises themselves constitute the basis of a worldview.

I have a sense of what you are getting at, but please explain.

You've practically explained it yourself! The point is this: The Pythagorean idea of cosmos integrates the worlds of order and beauty, of fact and value; inevitably, then, Pythagorean science was both empirical *and* contemplative in orientation. But since modern scientific methodology is strictly empirical in formulation, it can only conceive of the world in strictly quantitative, mechanistic, utilitarian, and instrumental terms, which it then pictures to be the actual state of affairs.

So in the words of biologist Jacques Monod, man now has to face up to the "objective fact" that "he lives on the boundary of an alien world. A world that is deaf to his music, just as indifferent to his hopes as it is to his suffering or his crimes."[4]

You've got it. But as you can see, he is telling us nothing about the way the world really is—he is only telling us what his premises allow him to see. Just because positivism starts with the premise that the "objective world" is value-free, this hardly means that the real world *is* value-free. This is a particularly odious example of what Whitehead referred to as the fallacy of "misplaced concreteness" or confusing maps and concepts with the way the world really is.

For my own sake, I find overwhelming evidence of objective beauty in the world. For example, I can't imagine anyone looking at a snowflake under a microscope and not being impressed by its wholeness, harmony, and radiance, which Aquinas took to be the elements of beauty. In addition, as you know I am a musician, and I have had many wonderful experiences playing music outside, and on many occasions the birds and the crickets would respond and join in with the rhythm and melody. From my own personal experience, the natural world is not deaf to our music!

Perhaps that is your Orphic influence!

The two philosophers pause in laughter.

The point that we have raised about the power of premises is important. Alfred North Whitehead even said that "Philosophy is the search for premises. It is not deduction. Such deductions as occur are for the purposes of testing the starting points by the evidence of the conclusions."[5]

Clearly his point is that philosophy is the search for the *best* premises, the ones that do greatest justice to the nature of things and human experience, which is itself part of the cosmos and not separate from the universe.

I would like to suggest then, by invoking the correspondence theory of truth, that the Pythagorean view that the world embodies beauty and value is *much* closer to the nature of things than is the positivist view that the world is only a quantifiable aggregate of particles, or whatever they think it is.

I absolutely concur and think that we should adopt this with the five other premises that we previously agreed upon. We should also heartily *endorse* this premise for the pragmatic consequences that flow from it!

Good premises are important, because as Edmund Sinnott pointed out, "What man believes about *himself* is of utmost moment, for it will determine the kind of world he will make and even his own fate."[6]

The philosophers arrive at the dune overlook.

Look, here we are at the lake. I knew that this would be a wonderful sight, but I had no idea how truly stunning it would be.

It really is remarkable.

Let's sit down here and continue our conversation.

That sounds wonderful. I'm really enjoying the discussion.

Before going further, let's clear up the point about the word cosmology. We know what the Pythagoreans meant by cosmos, but what do we mean by cosmology?

Well, today cosmology has come to mean in some circles the study of the large-scale structure of the universe, its expansion rate, the red shift of stars, and so on. But for most of Western history, the idea of cosmology has implied the search for a unified worldview or theory of the universe, *including* the nature of humanity and our relationship to the greater cosmos. As we noted earlier, cosmology and philosophy were originally identical. For my own sake, I would describe cosmology as "the study which allows us to come to terms with our place in the world, in the widest possible way."

This idea of cosmology seems to be making a big comeback these days.

I think that you're right. A great need is being felt for a comprehensive worldview that can do better justice to reality and our place in nature. Even contemporary physicists can no longer ignore questions relating to consciousness, epistemology, and teleology in their re-search.

The interest in cosmology seems to reflect a desire for an integrated worldview, a desire to understand and relate to the whole.

We are being haunted by this idea of relatedness!

Well, the universe is all around us. There's nowhere to escape!

The interest in cosmology reflects a desire to overcome the frag-mentation of knowledge and destructive influence of disciplinary specialization that exists in the academic world. I've been reading a book on economics and sustainability by Herman Daly and John Cobb, and they suggest that universities should develop departments for the study of cosmology—not solely in the sense of astrophysics, but in the wider traditional sense.[7]

That could really lead to a rebirth of philosophy and help reinvigo-rate the discipline by reclaiming its lost ground. As you know, natural science was originally a part of philosophy. Galileo and Newton were known as philosophers, not as scientists. The fragmentation of knowl-edge has impoverished both science and philosophy in my opinion.

I have some wonderful illustrations from medieval and Renaissance times relating to the iconography of the liberal arts. I'm planning to do a short book on the mythology of education some day. In any event, one common motif shows *philosophia* as nourishing all the other disciplines with streams of water or perhaps milk. That makes the central role of philosophy quite clear. Other illustrations show phi-losophy holding the celestial sphere or, in short, encompassing the entire universe.

Those are beautiful images, and I can imagine the second one inspiring a song, "Philosophy . . . she's got the whole world in her hands."

You have a *wicked* sense of humor!

Laughter floats above the dunes.

I think that we are approaching an important point about the relationship between philosophy, cosmology, and the ways of knowing that are reflected in the various arts and sciences.

Please tell me what you have in mind.

My thinking is that the world is in a pretty bad state today. There's the problem of the ecological crisis, the exploitation of the Earth and people, the mythology of unlimited economic growth, and so on. Ecologists tell us that every natural system in the world is in decline, and over the next forty years, the planetary population is supposed to double. Advertising and media hype have taken the place of real communication. And for those individuals who do want more out of life than is dished up by popular culture, the available choices seem to be very limited. Many colleges have become vocational schools rather than places of real learning. And to top things off, serious public discussion seems to be at an all time low.

These are things that I have also been thinking about. And we both agree, I think, that these problems are symptoms of a limited, one-sided worldview and epistemology. We've been saying that if people could look at the world and life in deeper, more accurate ways, the situation could be quite different.

I think that there should be some type of serious interdisciplinary discussion of these issues going on. I say interdisciplinary, because we are dealing with a problem that is essentially cosmological in scope. Specialization and narrow self-interest are pulling the world apart. We've lost a vision of the whole and how things fit together. It's like the poem by Yeats where he says "the center cannot hold." But, by the same token, we can't go back to an integrated but dogmatic religious worldview where the priests expect us just to believe and follow their advice.

So what's your proposal?

Well, it makes sense that we should work toward cultivating a larger vision that, at the very least, will assure human survival and flourishing. On the one hand, we want to perpetuate life; on the other hand, we want to perpetuate a life that is truly worth living.

I don't think that any reasonable person would argue with you.

The magnitude of the situation is so great, however—particularly in regard to the issue of sustainability—that no one approach can hope to assure human flourishing and survival. Art, science, religion, ecology, business, political science, economics, and psychology cannot individually lead to a sustainable relationship with the greater web of life, but all have an important part to play in giving birth a larger cosmological vision or worldview.

Once again you are appealing to the idea of wholeness, and perhaps balance.

What I'd like to suggest is that philosophy, above all other disciplines, really needs to lead the way in the academic world, and maybe also in a cultural sense. For if philosophy is envisioned as the practice of relatedness, a metadiscipline of critical thinking, and can return to its roots as a study of whole systems or cosmology, then philosophy itself will have an increasingly important role to play in today's world.

That's an inspiring vision, but how do you think that it can be brought about?

The initiative will have to start with individuals who are interested in doing real philosophy and relating it to contemporary issues in a way that people can understand. Our discussion is a an example of the type of inquiry that needs to be encouraged. But for philosophy to become a real interdisciplinary meeting point, it needs to recover lost ground. I'm also convinced that the idea of epistemology needs to be expanded.

In what way?

As a comparative study of the ways of knowing the world.

I have often thought that the modern trends in epistemology are the most unattractive aspects of philosophy. Kant's idea that we cannot know things-in-themselves has been destructive in the sense that it leads to relativism rather than relatedness. And the vast majority of academic philosophy carries the unstated bias that the discursive intellect is the only valid organ of knowledge—even if accepted in its limited epistemological status as proposed by Kant.

That is why I think that epistemology needs to be revisioned in a much wider sense. Discursive analysis *is* a valid way of knowing in some ways, as far as it goes, but its limitations have been well-documented by philosophers of science. By placing all of its eggs in the intellectual basket, philosophy since Descartes has tended to paint a very one-sided view of human nature and the world.

We could even say that philosophy is part of the problem.

Unfortunately, yes. My own feeling is that the very finest *and* the very worst aspects of human nature have been reflected in the Western philosophical tradition. Rather than contracting human experience to the merely intellectual, genuine philosophy now needs to expand our experience so that we can relate to the whole. This calls for an expanded conception of epistemology.

In this sense, I've always liked Plato very much, with his understanding that intellect can take us only so far. By its very nature, discursive intellect is based on subject–object duality, which entails a form of alienation. For Plato there is a higher, more complete form of knowledge, which is nonverbal.... The other thing that I like is Plato's use of myth, which also points toward a more imaginal, nondiscursive way of knowing. In traditional cultures, art, myth, storytelling, and participation in creative process are all valid ways of knowing. They are ways of knowing through *doing* and *being*, rather than just through thinking.

If I could design the curriculum for a graduate school, I would require that all students practice some art, whether it be music, writing, poetry, dance, gourmet cooking, or whatever. The idea behind this is that the educational system should strive to produce individuals of personal depth, rather than just specialists or intellectuals.

The ideal would be to produce well-rounded individuals who could *talk with one another* in meaningful ways across disciplinary lines. Ultimately, I would like to see each university, in conjunction with the philosophy department, establish a cross-disciplinary Garden of Discourse where the discussion of serious issues can take place from a variety of perspectives. There could be monthly discussions among faculty and students relating to both perennial and contemporary issues.

I think that your proposal could have a very therapeutic effect and lend a great deal of meaning, both to contemporary life and to the university as an institution. In fact, it's astonishing to realize that most colleges and universities don't already have something like this in place. The proposal could reinvigorate philosophy by once again establishing its relevance in the *polis* or the city. In this sense, we could return to the image of Philosophia nourishing the other disciplines, and holding the entire universe in her hands.

Do you have any further thoughts about the relationship between philosophy, cosmology, and culture?

Not for now, at least. Our conversation has pretty well summed it up.

Let's then return to the trail. We've been sitting here a long time and

I'm ready to walk again. And we still have much to discuss.

The two take one last look at the beautiful vista of the dunes towering over Lake Michigan and return to the trail.

We've covered the social relevance of cosmology, and have a good understanding of the Pythagorean idea of cosmos. But how does this idea of cosmos relate to ethics?

There is a very direct relationship between cosmology and ethics because all forms of human behavior are influenced by an underlying worldview or by the absence of one. The industrial worldview, which strips nature of all intrinsic value in its premises, inevitably regards the biosphere as an object of exploitation. The Pythagorean view is quite different, because it emphasizes the kinship and relationship between all things.

How so?

The Pythagorean insight that the cosmos is a harmony carries with it the realization that all things are linked together through proportional relationships. The Pythagoreans identified justice and proportion because it is through proportion that every part receives its proper due. Proportion also links the parts together into a greater whole. From this starting point the Pythagoreans inevitably concluded that there is a relationship and kinship between all living things.

This type of thinking was influential in the thought of Plato, wasn't it?

Absolutely. In fact, the Pythagorean view is clearly stated by Plato in the *Gorgias* when he writes that

> one community embraces heaven and earth and gods and men and friendship and order and temperance and righteousness, and for that reason they call this whole a *kosmos*, my friend, for it is not without order nor yet is there excess. . . . But it has escaped your notice that geometrical equality prevails widely among both gods and men.[8]

And by geometrical equality, he means geometrical proportion?

Right. Just like the proportion that links our finger joints together, which enables the hand to function well as a unit. In this sense, we can see that there is a relationship between good proportion and the virtue or excellence of the hand. It is only through having attained a state of good proportion that the hand itself can work in the best possible way.

Doesn't he also talk about the relationship between proportion, justice, and virtue in the *Republic*?

Yes, in the *Republic* Plato talks about bringing the three parts of the soul into tune with one another like the proportions of the musical scale. When this type of proportional justice exists between the parts or aspects of the soul, then the soul as a unit is able to function in the best possible way and human excellence is achieved.[9]

What about the other dialogues?

Well, the writings of Plato are full of these Pythagorean ideas. Another good source is his cosmological dialogue the *Timaeus*, which is Pythagorean through and through. There he describes the universe as "one Whole of wholes"[10] and as "a single Living Creature which encompasses all of the living creatures that are within it."[11]

What a beautiful image. It is a good description of the whole–part relationship and also suggests that holism and symbiosis are central properties in the structure of the universe.

He concludes the *Timaeus* by describing the cosmos as "a perceptible god, image of the intelligible, greatest and best, most beautiful and most perfect."[12]

That passage really undermines the opinion of some people that Plato was a dualist, who pitted the spiritual realm against the material realm.

It certainly seems to. He is describing the physical universe as a theophany, or a manifestation of divine beauty.

A chickadee lands on a nearby stump as the two move along the path.

Lately I've been reading *The Meditations of Marcus Aurelius* and also brushing up on Stoicism. What I've stumbled across is exciting because it shows that there is a very intimate relationship between cosmology and ethics in Stoicism. In fact, Stoic ethics is based entirely on a cosmological foundation. And as Stephen Toulmin, the philosopher of science, points out, all contemporary ecological theories are essentially Stoic in character.

It sounds like you may have hit upon something important. But to tell you the truth, I'm not all that familiar with the Stoics. Would you be willing to fill me in a bit?

I'd be happy to. In fact, I have a copy of *The Meditations of Marcus Aurelius* here in my pack. We could sit on that log ahead in the clearing and I could read you some passages.

That sounds like a great idea.

The two move toward the log, which is resting in a clearing that is bathed by sunlight.

Okay, here's the book. I looked at all of the available translations and this version, published by Penguin, is by far the best.

I'm just going to sit here and look at the trees, the sun, and the clouds. Why don't you go ahead and tell me whatever you'd like—and let me hear some of those good quotes?

That would be fine. Let me thumb through the book for a moment and find some passages . . .

Clouds drift on by as Christopher pages through the book.

Okay, I'm ready, so here goes . . .

The Stoics divided philosophy into three branches: logic, physics, and ethics. By physics they meant cosmology or the study of the universe. Ultimately, ethics is rooted in cosmology, for humanity is part of the universe, and only by understanding the nature of the universe is it possible to understand human nature. For as Marcus Aurelius writes,

> Without an understanding of the nature of the universe, a man cannot know where he is; without an understanding of its purpose, he cannot

know what he is, nor what the universe itself is. Let either of these discoveries be hid from him, and he will not be able so much as to give a reason for his own existence.[13]

The Stoics were pantheists and held that the entire universe is permeated by an active intelligence that they called by many names: Logos, Mind, Nature, God, Providence, Zeus, Destiny, the World Soul, and so on. In other words, the Stoics were in agreement with our premise that Mind is not something that is entirely in humans.

He fumbles for a piece of paper.

For example, here in my notes I see that Zeno, the founder of Stoicism, argued that

> Nothing which is devoid of life and intelligence can give birth to any living creature which has intelligence. But the universe does give birth to living creatures which partake of intelligence in their degree. The universe is therefore itself a living intelligence.[14]

If you're beginning to think that the Stoics saw the entire universe as being akin to an all-inclusive, intelligent organism, you're absolutely right. For example, Marcus Aurelius reminds himself to

> Always think of the universe as one living organism, with a single substance and a single soul; and observe how all things are submitted to the single perceptivity of this one whole, all are moved by its single impulse, and all play their part in the causation of every event that happens. Remark the intricacy of skein, the complexity of the web.[15]

And here he writes:

> All things are interwoven with one another; a sacred bond unites them; there is scarcely one thing that is isolated from another. Everything is coordinated, everything works together in giving form to the one

universe.[16]

So far, the Stoics are with us in accepting our premises that the universe is one thing manifesting itself in a variety of ways, and that the forms of nature embody intelligence. From these two premises it is only a short step to the conclusion that humanity itself is an embodiment of the order and harmony of the universe. In other words, we are all members of a universal community, one which includes animals, plants, stars, galaxies, and our fellow humans, mirroring Plato's idea that "there is one community which unites heaven and earth."

It is the harmony of the universe that gives birth to human community. For the Stoics, we humans are not strictly members of one particular city, but inhabitants of the entire world. There is a "universal brotherhood of humanity," owing to our common rational nature, which is itself rooted in the deep structure of the cosmos. The Stoics taught that we are all members of the *cosmopolis* or "world-city"; they maintained that we are literally *citizens of the universe*. Human community is not isolated from the underlying harmony of the biosphere and the greater universe, but is a living embodiment of the cosmic order.

The implication is that all beings exist within the context of some community. As Marcus Aurelius writes, "The Mind of the universe is social."[17] Therefore, within the order of the universe and the cosmopolis, it follows that our own individual fulfillment is bound up in a social context, within the greater web of life. Human beings alone have the ability to consciously assist the perfection of Nature by our own efforts. Writing to himself, Marcus Aurelius notes that

> As a unit yourself, you help to complete the social whole; and similarly, therefore, your every action should help to complete the social life.[18]

And elsewhere he writes that "Everything I do, whether by myself or with another, must have as its sole aim the service and harmony of all."[19] In other words, in the same way that the organs of an animal serve the entire organism, so too should a similar relationship hold between individuals and the larger world community. In one of my favorite passages, Marcus makes a play on the Greek words *melos* and *meros*, which mean "limb" and "part" respectively. He writes that

> In a system comprising diverse elements, those which possess reason have the same part to play as the bodily limbs in an organism that is a unity; being similarly constituted for mutual cooperation. This reflection will impress you more forcibly if you constantly tell yourself, "I am a 'limb' (*melos*) of the whole complex of rational things." If you think of yourself as a 'part' (*meros*) only, you have as yet no love from the heart for mankind, and no joy in the performance of acts of kindness for their own sake. You do them as a bare duty, and not yet as good offices to yourself.[20]

Well, that is about all that I have to say at this point. But I hope this summary has thrown some light on the relationship between cosmology and ethics in Stoic thought. As you can see, for the Stoics cosmos and community are synonymous, and we can achieve a state of fulfillment only through engagement with the World Soul, which is simultaneously a cosmological, ecological, and social reality. By realizing our innate connection with the larger web of life, and understanding that we are limbs of the universe rather than mere parts, we will be inspired to act for the common good out of love rather than duty.

The two sit silent basking in the warmth of the sun. A light breeze envelopes the terrain, carrying the cry of a gull over the dunes.

That was an absolutely wonderful summary! You have left no doubt in my mind about the relationship that exists between cosmology, ecology, and ethics. Also, when you were describing how humans, animals, plants, stars, and galaxies are all part of a vast community, I was looking at the trees, the clouds, the sun, the dunes, and the birds circling overhead, and intuitively sensed a harmonious connection between the parts.

Thanks very much; I'm glad that you liked it. The thing that fascinates me is how contemporary science is helping to confirm these ancient understandings—and what you yourself have intuitively felt.

How so?

Well, take for example the idea that harmony, goodness, and beauty coincide. Plato makes this case strongly in the *Philebus*, where he argues that goodness is not a simple essence but arises from proportion, and both proportion and goodness are related to beauty. As he says, "the power of the good has taken refuge in the nature of the beautiful; for measure and proportion are everywhere identified with beauty and virtue."[21] What he is saying is that goodness, beauty, and harmony are not separate from one another.

And how does contemporary science support this?

It proves that various phenomena arise from harmonious, proportional relationships. For example, all living systems embody a proportional harmony between the extremes of stability and change. If a living system becomes too static, it dies; but if it changes too quickly, it falls apart. In the mathematical world, fractal geometry exists on the boundaries between stability and change. In fact, it is at the intersection point between stability and change that the greatest complexity and beauty arises in the fractal domain. By analogy, in the biological world, life itself is an effervescent flowering that exists on the boundaries between stability and change.

That reminds me of Plato's description of the World Soul as a harmony between Sameness and Difference. Aren't Sameness and Difference quite similar if not identical to stability and change?

I would say that they are. We touched upon this when we were talking about the growth of a nautilus shell.

Yes.

Furthermore, contemporary astrophysics has shown that the existence of the entire universe rests upon a host of delicately balanced harmonies. For example, the density parameter of the universe determines the rate of expansion. And if the density parameter was either one-trillionth of a percent weaker or stronger, the universe itself would not hold together.

Talk about the balance of nature!

Christopher reaches inside his bag for further documentation.

Yes. I've been reading this good book by Brian Swimme and Thomas Berry called *The Universe Story*. It contains a beautiful quote, which is very much to the point. Brian Swimme is a mathematical physicist and he writes that:

> The universe thrives on the edge of a knife. If it increased its strength of expansion it would blow up; if it decreased its strength of expansion it would collapse. By holding itself on the edge it enables a great beauty to unfold. The Milky Way also thrives at the edge of a knife. Decrease its gravitational bonding and all the stars scatter; increase the gravitational bonding and the galaxy collapses on itself. By holding itself in the peace of a fecund balance of tensions, it enables planetary structures and living beings to blossom forth.[22]

By the gods! He is describing exactly what Plato was talking about. The universe, by achieving a finely-tuned proportional relationship between expansion and contraction, allows the beauty and goodness of life to blossom forth.

Yes, as Plato said, beauty, goodness, and proportion are tightly interwoven. And perhaps we should also remember that Aristotle identified virtue and goodness with the mean between extremes, which is itself a type of proportional relationship.

If goodness depends upon proportion and good measure, that would explain the dangers and unhappy consequences of too much specialization, which is a one-sided emphasis on the parts without regard for the whole.

Yes, and it would probably be safe to say that emphasis on the part and narrow self-interest—a lack of proportion and justice—are responsible for many contemporary problems, including the ecological crisis. In the words of Marcus Aurelius, we have forgotten that we are members of a cosmopolis—we have become "parts" rather than "limbs."

Unfortunately, these relationships that were so clearly evident to the Greeks have become opaque to the modern outlook. We've become stranded in an mindset that obscures our bond with the world rather than illuminating it.

Who knows? Perhaps the fact that we're able to discuss this is a hopeful sign. In any case, let's get back on the trail.

The two philosophers resume walking.

I'm fascinated by the relationship between goodness, proportion, and beauty. For one thing, it shows how ethical, metaphysical, and aesthetic concerns are all interrelated.

Yes. And while it may be impossible to measure beauty and goodness in a quantitative sense, we can certainly demonstrate how they emerge from harmony and proportion, which is itself a form of good measure. In fact, if you'll hold on for a moment, I'd be happy to show you an example.

He bends down at the side of the trail and snaps off an ivy leaf.

Here, take a look at this. Hold this up to the sun and meditate on the patterns that you see. Look at all the fine details, but also squint and unfocus your vision so you can see the larger, overall patterns.

A few moments pass.

That is amazing. The patterns in the leaf are almost psychedelic, and when I gaze on the relationships my attention shifts back and forth to different levels of scale within the network of capillaries. Whenever I look into the leaf it's apparent that there is a whole–part relationship, in which the larger patterns are reproduced at smaller levels of scale.

Perhaps the leaf *is* psychedelic in some sense. After all, *psychedelic* literally means soul-revealing or mind-revealing, and the patterns in the leaf are certainly a reflection of the plant's life principle, which the Greeks called *psyche*. Similarly, Gregory Bateson described Mind as "the pattern which connects." Or, to tie this all together, we could say that the patterns embodied in the leaf are a reflection of its own life process, and life is a form of intelligence or mind.

What you are saying corresponds with our premise that Mind exists not only within humans, but in the greater world at large. The Stoics would also agree that the leaf embodies a rational, intelligent order. They would say that the leaf is an expression, on its own level, of the all-inclusive Mind of the universe.

Let's return to the question of the whole–part relationship, since this is clearly reflected in the leaf. You said that the same patterns are embodied at different levels of scale. Would it be possible for you to draw what you are talking about in the sand with a stick? That would give me a clear idea of what you mean.

Sure. I'm not much of an artist, but will do my best.

Time passes and a pattern begins to emerge in the sand:

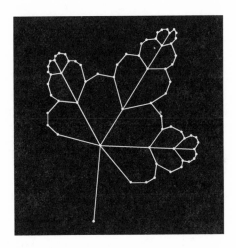

There. How's that?

You did a fine job and I can clearly see what you're talking about. The same basic pattern permeates the entire leaf. And each part is linked to the next through proportion and good measure. As Marcus Aurelius said, living nature is a complex web of relationships.

If philosophy is a practice of relationship, then maybe nature herself is a philosopher!

That's an interesting idea, but not entirely new. Plotinus, the Neoplatonic philosopher, playfully suggested something along those lines when he said that all of nature is engaged in contemplation.[23]

The two pause.

In my understanding, thought is a natural process that is folded back on itself; that's why we speak of thinking as "self-reflection." At the very least, the ivy leaf is engaged in a process of self-reflection, because each part is a mirror image of the next. If I had to explain the plant's decision to employ symmetry and self-reflection, my guess is that it's the most efficient way to deploy structure and integrate the parts within the whole.

Many thoughtful people have reflected on this simplicity and efficiency of nature. For example, Ralph Emerson wrote that

> Beauty rests on necessities. The line of beauty is the result of perfect economy. The cell of the bee is built at that angle which gives the most strength with the least wax; the bone or the quill of the bird give the most alar strength with the least weight . . . There is not a particle to spare in natural structures. There is a compelling reason in the uses of the plant, for every novelty of color or form . . .[24]

That's a fine and very relevant quotation. When he says that "The line of beauty is the result of perfect economy," by "perfect economy" I think that he's talking about the same thing that we've been describing as proportional relationships. Would you agree?

Yes. Perfect economy is realized through a system of the most efficient proportional relationships. Another name for this is elegance.

From this I think that we could conclude that the study of harmony demonstrates *why* the forms of nature are so beautiful. Nature is economical and embodies its organic harmonies of sharing in the most fit, graceful, and elegant patterns. As Plato argues in the *Philebus*, the Good by its very nature radiates the essence of Beauty. But when we work against nature's harmonies and good patterns of sharing, ineffi-ciency, wastefulness, and ugliness result.

This point has a lot of implications not only for ethics, but also in terms of our economic models and business practices. In comparison to living systems where little is wasted, a lot of our industrial systems are quite inefficient.

The Stoics believed that excellence is achieved by "following the path of nature." Interestingly, there is an emerging field of ecological design which is devoted to this very idea. The ecological designers wisely maintain that we need to emulate nature's own patterns of sharing, and intelligently integrate our human activities within the greater systems of the biosphere.

Nature possesses a vast, untapped repository of design intelligence! I'm sure that we have a lot to learn from her, but it all depends on our ability to approach the world with a renewed sense of vision and insight. And also perhaps with a sense of humility, since living systems are so much more efficient than anything we've been able to devise. After all, living systems are able to regenerate and perpetuate them-selves, which is something that no human creation has ever attained.

A moment of silence passes.

During our walk we've considered at least three natural designs that are living reflections of good proportion: the human hand, the nautilus shell, and the capillary system in the ivy leaf. These three examples are very similar because they all achieve a dynamic, functional relation-ship between the part and the whole through the use of harmonic proportion. But now I'm struck by a question. What I'd like to ask is: Do you think that this throws any light on the relationship between the ideal and the useful?

I think that it does, especially if we assume that nature is efficient and does little in vain. After all, we seem to have concluded that the most effective patterns of sharing and relationship radiate goodness and beauty.

And what is the nature of goodness?

Goodness refers to that which is desirable and fit. For example, if I want to pound a nail into a board, a good hammer will help me to do that without falling apart in the process.

If something works well and is desirable, in most cases it possesses some form of value and goodness.

Correct.

And if nature embodies *good* patterns of sharing, we cannot assume that the objective, larger-than-human world is value-free?

That's right, and supports two earlier points from a new perspective. We have already agreed that living things possess intrinsic value, and also that the world embodies beauty, which is a form of value. And now our latest point—the understanding that good proportion gives rise to function and beauty in nature—further establishes the fact that the world embodies goodness, which is the highest form of value.

They proceed in silence for a couple of minutes.

What I'd like to do now is advance further and draw a correlation between the spheres of the ideal and the pragmatic by suggesting that they are not entirely separate, but in harmony with one another.

And how would you do that?

On the one hand, we have to assume that proportions like the Golden Section represent *ideal* harmonic relationships. For as we saw, the Golden Section is the only possible ratio where the small part is related to the larger part as the larger part is related to the whole. But a ratio in itself is not a physical thing.

I see your point. Because the Golden Section is an eternal mathematical relationship that we can study and think about totally apart from anything in the physical world, it seems to be some type of ideal, mathematical principle. In other words, the Golden Section is an Idea rather than an abstraction from some concrete thing.

Exactly. But if we assume that nature does nothing in vain in a pragmatic sense, and if we can see that the Golden Section is used in our fingers and throughout the entire fabric of nature, then we have to conclude that the "pragmatic" and the "ideal" are not totally separate things, but very intimately conjoined in some way.

Agreed. And that goes along very well with what Plato concluded at the end of the *Timaeus*, that the physical cosmos is an image of the ideal or the intelligible.

This also suggests that it is not impractical to philosophize and study ideal relations, because the patterns of nature prove that ideal realities are not separate from pragmatic situations and applications.

That's true. But as we've said, we don't need to pursue ideas and relationships only in a world of pure thought, because nature itself reflects ideas, and ideas are embedded in tangible, living things.

Yes, we don't want to stray too far from the Book of Nature and the world of lived experience. Because if philosophy is going to remain a practice of relationship, it needs to maintain a bond with the embodied world.

They reach the end of the trail, having returned to the beginning.

Look, we're back where we started, and it's almost time for dinner. Thanks for a wonderful outing and the very fine conversation.

Yes, I couldn't have had a better time. My favorite part was our discussion about the relationship between proportion, goodness, and beauty. The examples that we considered were very convincing, and contemplating the forms of nature in this way has allowed me to sense the truth of this relationship in a very deep and nonverbal way.

I am also intrigued by the relationship between goodness and beauty and recently made an interesting discovery along these lines.

What was that?

I was looking into the etymology of the word *beauty* and discovered that the Latin words for beauty and goodness come from the same Indo-European root.

You don't say?

Not only that, but the word *beatitude*, meaning supreme blessedness or happiness, also comes from the same root as the Latin words for beauty and goodness. So in Latin goodness, beauty, and happiness are all related.

It really makes you wonder how these words came into being, especially when you consider that both Plato and Thomas Aquinas concluded that the contemplation of the Good results in a beatific vision and realization of true happiness.

It does make you wonder, but then again, perhaps the relationship between goodness, beauty, and happiness is just built into the nature of things.

That I would not doubt, especially if by happiness you mean the optimal state of human flourishing. For my own part, our conversation has made me very happy.

I have enjoyed it too. And now, off to the restaurant . . .

The two philosophers enter a parked car and drive off, as they take up another theme.

Notes

1. Richard Tarnas, *The Passion of the Western Mind* (New York: Ballantine, 1993), 421.

2. Stephen Rowe, *Rediscovering the West: An Inquiry into Nothingness and Relatedness* (Albany: State University of New York Press, 1994).

3. R. G. Collingwood, *The Idea of Nature* (Oxford: Oxford University Press, 1960).

4. Jacques Monod, *Chance and Necessity*; quoted in Theodore Roszak, *Where the Wasteland Ends* (Berkeley: Celestial Arts, 1989), 106.

5. Alfred North Whitehead, *Modes of Thought* (New York: Macmillan, 1938), 105.

6. Edmund Sinnott, *Matter, Mind, and Man*; quoted in Louise B. Young, *The Unfinished Universe* (New York: Oxford University Press, 1993), 185.

7. Herman Daly and John Cobb, Jr., *For the Common Good: Redirecting the Economy Toward Community, the Environment, and a Sustainable Future* (Boston: Beacon Press, 1994), 364–65.

8. Plato, *Gorgias* 507E.

9. Plato, *Republic* 443D–F.

10. Plato, *Timaeus* 33A.

11. Plato, *Timaeus* 30D–31A.

12. Plato, *Timaeus* 92C.

13. *The Meditations of Marcus Aurelius* 8.52 (Maxwell Staniforth translation, Penguin Books).

14. Cicero, *The Nature of the Gods* 2.20–23.

15. *Meditations of Marcus Aurelius* 4.40.

16. *Meditations of Marcus Aurelius* 7.9.

17. *Meditations of Marcus Aurelius* 5.30.

18. *Meditations of Marcus Aurelius* 9.23.

19. *Meditations of Marcus Aurelius* 7.5.

20. *Meditations of Marcus Aurelius* 7.13.

21. Plato, *Philebus* 64E.

22. Brian Swimme and Thomas Berry, *The Universe Story: From the Primordial Flaring Forth to the Ecozoic Era* (San Francisco: Harper San Francisco, 1992), 54.

23. Plotinus, *Enneads* 3.8, "Nature, Contemplation, and the One."

24. Ralph Waldo Emerson, *The Conduct of Life*, chapter 8. *The Works of Ralph Waldo Emerson* (New York: Charles C. Bigelow, no date), vol. 3, 193.

Cultivating Ecological Design Intelligence: Notes from an Invitational Conference at Esalen, Big Sur, California, October 16–19, 1994

STUART COWAN

DESIGN CONNECTS CULTURE AND NATURE through flows of energy and matter. If we take ecology as the basis for designing our products, buildings, and communities, we can preserve natural capital while meeting human needs.

A new vision of ecological design is emerging, one that brings together architects, planners, engineers, farmers, artists, and many others in a shared search for the nitty-gritty design details of a sustainable culture.

Just as architecture has traditionally concerned itself with problems of structure and aesthetics, or as engineering with safety and efficiency, we need to consciously cultivate an ecologically sound form of design that is consonant with the long-term survival of all species. Ecological design proposes a partnership with nature in which environmental impacts are minimized by carefully integrating designs within wider living systems. Examples include wastewater treatment systems that employ the inherent purifying capacities of artificial wetlands, industrial "ecosystems" in which all wastes become "food" for other processes, and agricultural systems whose structures mimic wild ecosystems. Ecological design provides a coherent framework for redesigning our systems of energy, water, food, shelter, waste, and manufacturing.

This conference was convened to find the next step. Ecological design offers a rich source of solutions and research directions, but its practitioners have lacked a common forum to share their ideas.

The circle of introductory statements raised key themes. How should ecological design be taught, and what kind of jobs can trained students and professionals reasonably expect to hold? How can we garner institutional support for ecological design? How can we create new kinds of accounting, curricula, ecological enterprise, and inter-disciplinary networks? As David Orr emphasized, "We need to drive the definition of ecological design to clarity." There was a consensus that ecological design is not an "alternative" to the dominant forms of technology and design, but the best path for their necessary evolution towards ecological viability.

Introductory Statements

- We need a "Do Tank" to teach and do ecological design.
- What is the institutional base to get ecological design mainstream?
- How can we create opportunities to make a living doing ecological design?
- How do design professionals make ethical choices?
- Create a learning environment that matches the context.
- The insurance industry may provide an opportunity for bio-remediation.
- Find a quality of life to believe in and be nourished by.
- Nature is the standard for design: we need ecological accounting.
- College-age people who "got it" need a place to use it.
- How do we build a constituency for tectonic change?
- Educate and retrain older students and practicing designers.
- What works is taking care of local community.
- The transition is here and we have the time to make it.
- Produce examples that cut across disciplines.
- Design innovative educational institutions.
- Create networks and intellectual family.

- Redesign infrastructure using ecological design.
- Convince sources of power that they need what we've got.
- We need to satisfy people's emotional need for beauty as well as scientific logic.
- Seed pods of change need to come together.
- Establish local enterprise centers for the ecological design arts.

Ecological Design Nodes

To date, ecological design has been carried forward by isolated "nodes"—nonprofit research institutes, individual design practices, and special groups within universities. These nodes are deeply committed to their surrounding communities and bioregions. Their work deals with the essentials: energy, water, food, shelter, waste, ecological accounting, environmental justice, and spirituality. As conference participants described their work, it became clear that a formal network of nodes would be enormously valuable. The following nodes, each run by a conference participant, give a good sense of the range of current work in ecological design:

Bioregional Building—At the Center for Maximum Potential Building Systems in Austin, Texas, Pliny Fisk and colleagues are creating a bioregional design science. They are learning how to build homes with climate-adapted local materials that produce their own energy and water and treat their own wastes. By examining the entire life cycle of materials and products, they are finding ways to add value without leaving the bioregion, turning waste into a resource in the process.

Earth And Spirit—At the Whidbey Institute near Seattle, Fritz and Vivienne Hull and more than a dozen close associates are designing a school that will bring together environmental and spiritual concerns. The campus itself will be a rich learning tool, its very materials and systems embodying the highest aspirations of ecological design. In this place of healing, those deeply involved in the work of creating sustainable culture will find spiritual renewal.

The Ecological Design Institute—Under the leadership of Sim Van der Ryn, the Farallones Institute has been active in ecological design since the 1970s. Its projects have ranged from an environmentally sound demonstration house in Berkeley to experiments in organic farming and solar architecture. Under its new name, the Institute is creating an ecological design curriculum for pre-K–12 at San Domenico School in San Anselmo, California. It will also sponsor an annual workshop for ecological designers.

Habitat And Commons—Chris Desser is organizing the Migratory Species Project, which will bring together communities along the annual migration route of the gray whale from the Bering Sea to Cabo San Lucas in Baja, California. Coastal communities can become aware of the interdependence of life by sharing stories about the whale. Young people will be encouraged to make a pilgrimage along part of the 6,000 mile route, stopping to learn about the significance of the whale to local cultures and ecosystems along the way.

Ecological Accounting—Deserted houses and public buildings in the town of Matfield Green, in Chase County, Kansas, are being lovingly reinhabited in a grand experiment in ecological accounting. Is it possible to live on the prairie without eroding its ecological capital? To answer this question, Wes Jackson and his fellow reinhabitants are quantitatively assessing what they take from the land—in water, soil, nutrients, energy—and what they return.

Presidio Institute—In San Francisco, the Army has recently transferred the Presidio base to the National Park Service. In response to this opportunity, Marty Krasney and the Coalition for the Presidio Pacific Center are working to establish the Presidio Institute for Sustainable Development at the Main Post. This institute will be dedicated to international and cross-cultural cooperation on sustainable development as the prerequisite for global security in the twenty-first century.

The Restoration Of Waters—Ecological wastewater treatment pioneer John Todd and his team at Ocean Arks International build diverse artificial ecosystems with remarkable purifying abilities. These systems replace energy and materials with a resilient living web of bacterial, plant, and animal intelligence. Todd is currently working on a major creek restoration project in Chattanooga, Tennessee.

606 Studio—The final year of the Masters of Landscape Architecture degree at California State Polytechnic University in Pomona. Under the leadership of John Lyle and his colleagues, small teams of students consult for government agencies on ecological planning issues. The 606 Studio has a distinguished history of ecological design pedagogy.

The Big Sur Declaration

Ecological Design reintegrates the needs of human societies within the dynamic balance of nature. It calls for an ecological revolution as fundamental as the industrial revolution.

Conventional forms of agriculture, architecture, engineering, and technology have not proven themselves sufficient to maintain either human health or the integrity of ecosystems.

We call for a regenerative ecological design science that honors the following principles:

1. Trace the ecological footprint: Set up the books for a full ecological accounting. Evaluate designs by their environmental impacts over their complete life cycle.

2. Live off solar income: Increase the renewability of energy production and the efficiency of energy use until we can provide for our needs out of annual solar income.

3. Maintain biodiversity and the locally adapted cultures and economies that support it: We take the preservation of species, representative ecosystems, and ecologically viable landscapes as a self-evident necessity. This can only be accomplished with a diversity of cultures and economies predicated on the uniqueness of place.

4. Waste equals food: Create restorative materials cycles in which all waste from one process becomes food for the next.

5. Work with whole systems: Design in keeping with the greatest possible degree of internal integrity and coherence.

6. Design must follow, not oppose the flows of life: Replace energy and materials with the self-designing capabilities of ecosystems. Allow living systems to unfold in a full expression of their creative capacities. Ecological design occurs in planetary time.

Neoplatonism and the Cosmological Revolution: Holism, Fractal Geometry, and Mind in Nature

DAVID FIDELER

IN THE PHILOSOPHIES of ancient and traditional cultures, the universe was recognized as being all of one piece. Social and religious structures helped maintain the bond between individual, culture, and cosmos, and in traditional societies the universe itself was commonly seen as an organism, a living entity with whom they lived in mutual symbiosis. Plato described the cosmos as a "single Living Creature which encompasses all the living creatures that are within it,"[1] a canonical description quoted time and again by Plotinus.[2] In the body of the living universe, animated by the World Soul, all parts are interrelated through the power of sympathy and by the fact that the manifest cosmos is itself rooted in the *Nous* (Mind/Being), which is a dynamical system of unity-in-multiplicity.

Nothing could be further from the Neoplatonic vision of the living universe than the mechanistic cosmology of the Scientific Revolution, which emerged from the first great cosmological revolution of the Western world. God was portrayed as an engineer and lawmaker who set the atomistic world-machine in motion. The universe was pictured as a giant clock, and all external reality was reduced to two fundamental principles: dead, unintelligent matter, and motion, the efficient cause that powered it. Galileo suggested that only the primary

This paper was given at the conference on "Neoplatonism and Contemporary Thought," Vanderbilt University, May 18–21, 1995.

qualities of mass and motion were essential; secondary qualities like color and beauty, which could not be quantified, were irrelevant in scientific work and perhaps even unreal. Descartes explained that only humans possessed mind; our bodies, animals, and the rest of the world functioned as mere machines. Francis Bacon formulated a philosophy of science in which the worlds of fact and value were sharply divorced, and in which science was seen as a means for the rational control and exploitation of nature.[3] Thus, at its birth, contemporary science was not simply a search for rational understanding as philosophy had claimed to be in earlier times. Science became a way of knowing based on prediction and control of the external world. The picture of God as an engineer was really nothing other than an image of the scientific ethos itself. This "divine engineer" possessed detached, calculating reason; power, prediction, and control over nature; and the godlike wisdom to structure reality in the best possible way. With the rise of capitalism and the explosion of industrial technology, the stage was set for the emergence of the contemporary world. Not only did the scientific worldview sanction the exploitation of nature, but with the rise of economic and factory structures, workers too came to be pictured as cogs in a vast economic machine. Technology, which promised human salvation in the new, milennialistic mythology of progress, also possessed an ambiguous, shadow side, for the very machinery that was supposed to liberate humanity from mundane concerns could itself become an instrument of bondage.

Over the last century the mechanistic view of the universe has started to completely break down. Because the implications of quantum mechanics, chaos theory, and the realization that we inhabit an evolutionary, self-organizing universe are starting to work themselves out, it is no exaggeration to say that we are truly living in the midst of a new Cosmological Revolution that will ultimately overshadow the Scientific Revolution of the Renaissance. And if the mechanistic worldview left us stranded in Flatland—a two-dimensional world of dead, atomistic matter in motion—the emerging cosmological picture is far more complex, multidimensional, and resonant with the traditional Neoplatonic metaphor of the living universe.

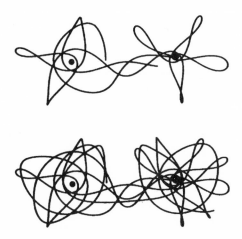

Figure 1. Chaotic behavior exhibited by a dust particle orbiting two equal gravitational centers.

In the basic equations of classical physics, a complexity so great has been discovered that it renders simple natural systems unpredictable and "chaotic." Our awareness of the universe is returning to life with chance, spontaneity, and creativity. The Newtonian model of the solar system as a deterministic, periodic system works quite well when the system consists of only two bodies—the sun and one planet—but as soon as other bodies are introduced, so too is a chaotic, nonlinear dimension.[4] Figure 1 illustrates the path of an imaginary dust particle orbiting between two equal gravitational centers; it exhibits a complexity so great that, beyond a certain point, it is impossible to predict the orbit of the dust particle with classical equations. Astrophysicists now realize that a similar complexity exists within the solar system, and highly chaotic behavior is exhibited by Hyperion, a moon of Saturn. As Hyperion tumbles through space its speed of rotation is in constant flux, exhibiting periods of order in an otherwise chaotic sea of behavior.[5] For the most part, regions of chaotic gravitational turbulence in the solar system are found to exist between the habitual pathways of the planetary orbits, but this is not entirely true; it is possible for planetary orbits to change, and chaotic variations in the

Earth's own orbit account in part for the climactic changes associated with ice ages. Astrophysicists think that Pluto's orbit might some day change suddenly; and, while not as likely, it is possible that the Earth itself could shift into a new orbit. While somewhat unsettling to contemplate, the solar system is stable only in a statistical sort of way.[6]

If mechanistic science had painted a thoroughly deterministic picture of the world, it is now suggested that the indeterminacy of the quantum realm would be inevitably amplified through the sensitive dependence on initial conditions that underlies chaotic, natural systems. Given two planets that were absolutely identical in every respect, it wouldn't be long before they started to exhibit uniquely different behavior in their weather patterns and so forth, thanks to the creative, indeterminate energy boiling up from the quantum level.[7]

By over-simplifying the world, classical physics contained the seeds of its own destruction. In a universe comprised solely of discrete bits of unintelligent matter in motion, it's hard to account for the self-organization of the cosmos and the fact that organisms behave as though they are more than the sum of their individual parts. But the real surprise came as physicists began their descent into the mystery of matter. Matter itself dematerialized and started to look more like dancing patterns of energy; according to the theory of General Relativity, matter and energy are entirely equivalent. Then, with the emergence of quantum physics, the whole apparatus of discrete, either/or categories on which traditional Western logic is based were shown to be inadequate. Paradoxically, light acts like a discrete particle *and* a non-discrete wave in one and the same phenomenon.[8] Recently in 1982, physicists proved by repeatable experiments that "particles" of light that originate from a common source continue to act in concert with one another as a whole system, regardless of how far apart they are—the type of "spooky action as a distance" that Einstein tried so hard to avoid.[9] The tantalizing implication of quantum nonlocality is that the entire universe, which is thought to have blazed forth from the first light of the big bang, is at its deepest level a seamless holistic system in which every "particle" is in "communication" with every other "particle," even though separated by millions of light years. In this sense, experimental science seems to be on the verge of validating the perception of all mystics—Plotinus included—that there is an underlying unity to the cosmos which transcends the boundaries of space and time.[10]

If the emblem of the mechanistic worldview was the Cosmic Clock, a symbolic image which reflects our current cosmological revolution is the Mandelbrot set, a specimen of fractal geometry which first entered public awareness in 1985 and has continued to ripple outward ever since.[11] Fractal geometry provides one of the most powerful cognitive tools available for deeply understanding the complex fabric of nature, and it is a subject that is intrinsically related to the Neoplatonic philosophy of Mind. As we reflect upon the basic characteristics of fractal geometry and the Plotinian description of the Nous, the essential relationship between the two topics becomes immediately obvious.

We'll begin in familiar territory with the Plotinian description of the Nous and move on to fractal geometry.

The Plotinian Description of the Nous

1. The Nous is a Living Harmony of Sameness and Difference, Unity and Multiplicity

Aside from the One which exists beyond Being, the most abstract, universal concept is Being itself. But Being possesses two essential qualities: simultaneous Unity and Multiplicity or Sameness and Difference. In order for something to be, it must first be itself through self-identity or Sameness, and it must also be unique and distinct from everything else through the principle of Difference.

For Plotinus, universal Being is a living, harmonic synthesis of Sameness and Difference, Unity and Multiplicity, the Finite and the Infinite.[12] All of these analogous terms describe the same fundamental relationship, and in his thinking Plotinus is indebted to the Pythagorean and Platonic tradition. For the Pythagoreans, the *kosmos* is a *harmonia* of the Limited and the Indefinite, the perfect image of which is the musical scale: a harmonically differentiated image of Unity.[13] Plato likewise follows this tradition in the *Timaeus* when he describes the generation of the World Soul: The primordial constituent of reality is Being, and its two faces, Sameness and Difference. The demiurge weaves Sameness and Difference together through the mathematical ratios of music, and the resulting harmonic entity is the World Soul, in which every part is sympathetically related to every other part through *logos*, proportion, and resonance.

2. The Nous is Self-Recursive: Intellect–Being is Folded Back on Itself

Another characteristic of the Plotinian Nous is that Intellect and Being is self-recursive or folded back upon itself. Plotinus characterizes the Transcendent Absolute as One, the Nous as a One-Many, and the World Soul as a One-*and*-Many. As a living Unity-Multiplicity, the Nous is folded back upon itself in a circle. Plotinus insists repeatedly that the Nous is a thought that thinks itself: thinker, thought, and the object of thought are one; Intellection or Being is a living vision in which subject and object are identical.[14] Reality is a self-recursive act rooted in the eternal.

3. The Nous is a Holistic System in Which the Parts Contain the Whole and all the Parts are Interimmanent within One Another

There is a total harmony and unity of existence. The manifest universe, rooted in the Nous, is a closely knit organism in which all of the parts are interrelated, for they are parts of a self-sympathetic living unity. The whole is articulated in the parts and the parts holographically reflect the nature of the whole.[15] Moreover, the parts are interimmanent[16] and reflected in one another; in the cosmic fellowship of the universal organism, the far is also near, and every part both receives from the All and gives to it.[17] From an epistemological perspective, knowledge is possible because all beings are rooted in Being and all intellects are rooted in Intellect. As Plotinus states, Mind is not something in us, but we are in Mind, and the very fact that you can understand these words is because we are rooted in a common matrix of Mind which exists between us.

Figure 2. Fractal model of a maple leaf. (© Michael Barnsley, from *Fractals Everywhere* by Michael F. Barnsley, published by Academic Press, 1988, 1993)

Figure 3. Fractal model of a fern in two dimensions.

Figure 4. Fractal model of a fern in three-dimensions. (© Michael Barnsley, from *Fractals Everywhere* by Michael F. Barnsley, published by Academic Press, 1988, 1993)

Figure 5. Fractal model of a branch. (© Michael Barnsley, from *Fractals Everywhere* by Michael F. Barnsley, published by Academic Press, 1988, 1993)

Fractal Geometry, Mind, and the Fabric of Nature

Like Plotinus's description of Mind, the most interesting type of fractal geometry—nonlinear fractal geometry—emerges when a natural or mathematical process is folded back upon itself in a self-recursive loop. Because the existence of computer graphics makes the exploration of fractal geometry possible, the study of fractals is relatively young. But fractal geometry is already changing the way that we look at the world, because it has become obvious that most natural phenomena possess a fractal dimension. As we can see in figure 2, one primary characteristic of fractal geometry is that it possesses self-similarity at different levels of scale. In this computer generated fractal of a maple leaf—and in actual maple leaves—we can see that the pattern of the entire leaf is organically replicated at ever smaller levels. Like the edges of a leaf, coastlines and mountain ranges are fractal and exhibit self-similarity at different levels of magnification. Each tiny leaf on a fern is a model of the branch on which it resides (figure 3). And each branch is a model of the entire fern (figure 4). The same type of self-similarity is seen in many types of trees (figure 5).

As the mathematical study of fractal geometry progressed, it became obvious that the central patterns of fractal geometry—self-similarity, scaling, and feedback—are reflected most organic and inorganic phenomena. In the same way that we exist in Mind, and mind is not something exclusively "in" us, so too are fractals not exclusively "in" the computer: the fabric of the living universe is itself fractal in nature. The fractals are not in the computer, but we are in the fractals.

It is possible to draw a much stronger analogy between the Neoplatonic philosophy of Mind and the nature of fractal geometry. For this we turn to the most famous example of fractal geometry, the so-called Mandelbrot set (figure 6), which is an infinite, artificial fractal that reveals the life and activity of numbers on the complex plane. The Mandelbrot set, which can be explored on a home computer with easily available software, is described by a simple algorithm which harmonically weaves the principles of Stability and Change, Sameness and Difference, the Finite and the Infinite.

If we look at the equation which describes the Mandelbrot set, we

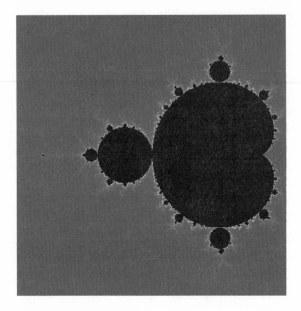

Figure 6. The Mandelbrot set.

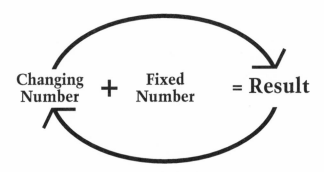

Figure 7. The Mandelbrot set is described by a circular, self-recursive equation that harmonically unites the principles of Stability and Change or Sameness and Difference.

can see how it harmonically unites Sameness and Difference (figure 7). A fixed number provides the foundation of Finite Sameness and Stability, but a changing number contributes the principle of Infinite Difference and Change. Like Plotinus's description of the Nous, the equation is recursive and folds back on itself, and through the circular path of Sameness pulsates an ever-changing informational flow of Difference.

When a computer plots the Mandelbrot set, it tests each individual computer pixel, which represents a fixed number on the complex plane, against the recursive algorithm to see how fast the number is changing. This is represented on the screen in various colors: stable numbers at rest are painted black, while numbers that are rushing off toward infinity are assigned different colors depending on their rate of change. From this simple equation, an entire graphic universe is brought into being.

Because the complex plane is infinite between any two points, it is possible to use a computer as a microscope to explore ever-finer details of the Mandelbrot set at ever-increasing magnifications. The most interesting and complex region appears at the boundary between stability and change. Zooming in along the edges, in different parts of the set we discover a host of organic forms reminiscent of the natural world: rivers, coastlines, flashes of lightning, crystals, leaves, and patterns that look like simple organisms. But the most amazing thing of all is that no matter how great the magnification is increased, the spaceship-like shape of the "mother set" continually reappears. This characteristic is shown in figures 8A–8F, where the highlighted area is enlarged in the following illustration.

Using supercomputers which can magnify the scale billions of times, the haunting visage of the mother set continues to appear at ever-deeper levels like a mandala of tranquillity amidst a sea of change and becoming.

Like the universe now being envisioned by quantum physics, the self-recursive cosmos of the Mandelbrot set—and the cosmos of Plotinus—is a self-contained whole in which every part is related to every other part. And like the axiom of the Hermetic philosophers, "as

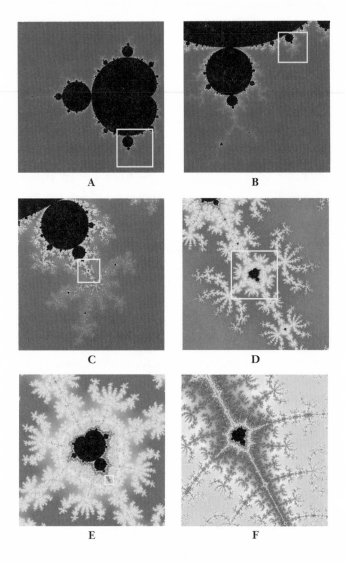

Figure 8. A short voyage into the infinite depths of the Mandelbrot set. Each successive illustration is an enlargement of the highlighted area in the previous illustration. Because the Mandelbrot set harmonizes the Finite with the Infinite in a self-recursive loop, it is infinitely complex but displays a holographic self-similarity at all levels of magnification. (David Fideler)

above, so below," the Mandelbrot set is holographic: a part contains the pattern of the entire whole—the macrocosm is perfectly reflected in the microcosm.

In summary, Plotinus's description of the Nous details how a harmonic union of the Finite with the Infinite, linked in an eternally self-recursive loop of self-reflection, gives birth to a holistic universe—a dynamical system in which the parts contain the whole and are interimmanent within one another. The Mandelbrot set clearly illustrates all these central characteristics of the Plotinian Nous, and gives us a clear idea of what it looks like to gaze into a self-recursive infinity of Sameness united with Difference. Yet beyond the infinite, there is also an elegant simplicity to all of this. Fractal geometry also shows how a simple, repetitive cycle of self-recursion can give birth to very complex structures of organic relatedness, a fact undoubtedly related to the genesis and development of organic life.

Finally, as Plato and the Pythagoreans symbolized the World Soul—the harmony of Sameness and Difference—by the musical scale, the Mandelbrot set offers an even better symbolic image of the World Soul because it shows in a graphic way how the harmony of Sameness and Difference gives birth to the organic relatedness of the natural world.

Revisioning Neoplatonism:
Life and Mind in an Evolutionary Universe

While the implications of fractal geometry and the existence of quantum nonlocality tend to support Plotinus's view of the seamless, holistic interconnectedness of the universe, the findings of contemporary cosmology also undermine several of his premises. Contemporary physics has demonstrated that all classical conceptions of matter are inadequate in the extreme, and if Plotinus was with us today he would surely revision his thinking in this area. Another problem occurs with Plotinus's assumption that the Earth and solar system have existed from eternity and always will,[18] which doesn't reconcile itself very well with our contemporary knowledge of the evolutionary universe. Platonists can still accept the premise that the universe and its beauty are rooted in eternal Being, and that beauty, contemplation, and creativity are gateways to the experience of timeless levels of reality. But the question remains: How does eternity get played out in the flow of time? And how do we bridge the gap between the eternal, noetic realm, and the evolutionary, self-organizing universe?

I believe that an answer might be found in Gregory Bateson's philosophy of Mind. Anthropologist, biologist, epistemologist, and contributor to the theory of cybernetics, Gregory Bateson saw Mind as a metapattern, "a pattern that connects." Bateson described Mind in its simplest expression as "a circular or more complex system of parts in which information flows that makes a difference."[19] From this perspective, Mind is a self-recursive system, and processes like ecosystems can be said to possess Mind. Through varying combinations of negative and positive feedback within a system, minds can grind to a halt, be self-regulating, or spin wildly out of control on a runaway course. In healthy organisms, societies, and ecosystems, there is some type of self-regulating dynamic at work; otherwise, these types of minds would self-destruct or cease to exist. Assuming that such minds can pass on their characteristics through time, the evolutionary unfolding of further complexity becomes possible.

As a biologist and a naturalist, Bateson never fully worked out all the philosophical, cosmological, and metaphysical implications of his conception of Mind, which, as he pointed out, is closely allied, if not identical, with the principle of Life.[20] But these considerations could provide a rewarding area for further exploration. The most unhappy and destructive bias of the modern world is the Cartesian notion that Mind exists only within humans, and that the rest of the world is inanimate, dead, and dumb. However, the epistemology of Plotinus and Bateson points in an entirely different direction. Plotinus, after all, repeatedly affirmed that the entire universe is a single, living, intelligent organism.

Contemporary cosmology also suggests that the universe itself is teeming with life. Galaxies are now described as manifestations of self-recursive fractal geometry, and there are at least 100 billion galaxies, 50 billion of which can be photographed from Earth. Each galaxy

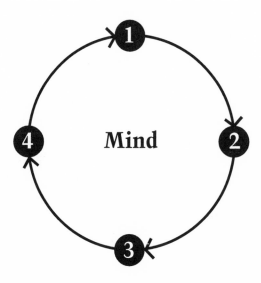

Figure 9. Gregory Bateson's definition of Mind: "A circular or more complex system in which information flows that makes a difference."

contains on average some 100 billion stars and at least that many planets, a certain percentage of which must be inhabited by noetic, contemplative beings. Swimming like vast organisms in the endless sea of space, spiral galaxies appear as beautifully spun, moving, pulsating, evolving, and mutating entities—celestial flowers or starfish—containing billions of individual cells. While Gregory Bateson never advanced the claim, galaxies are certainly "circular or more complex systems in which information flows that makes a difference," and thus are noetic, living systems by his definition. Moreover, if a galaxy is silently humming with the thoughts of beings who wonder about the meaning of existence, how can we assert that the galaxy itself is unconscious? Just as the skeletal system provides a foundation for more complex life processes but in itself does not think, galaxies, stars, and planets should not be hastily dismissed as dead and unintelligent when they are inhabited by intelligent life.

If we continue to investigate Gregory Bateson's definition of Mind and travel in a thought experiment back to the initial conditions of the physical universe, the universe itself could be said to possess a noetic dimension as soon as the fundamental forces of creation were linked together in a circular, mutually-transformative process, which must have been at an unimaginably primordial date. From this perspective, the entire universe can be seen as a circular noetic event progressively unfolding itself in time—"a thought that is thinking itself," to use the terminology of Plotinus. The advantage of this model is that it successfully reconciles the Platonic and process schools of philosophy which are not contradictory, in my opinion, but complementary. On the one hand, all of reality is rooted in the archetypal foundation of eternal Being, but on the other hand there is a genuinely creative evolutionary unfolding of manifestation, which can itself be pictured as a forward-moving noetic event of increasing complexity. Time is thus revealed as "the moving image of eternity,"[21] to quote Plato—a moving image that is not closed, but creative and open-ended. The implication of this view is that the entire universe is noetic, dialectical, and evolutionary in nature; it is also teleological in the sense that it leans very heavily in certain directions. But by the same token, there is creative freedom, for no one specific manifest phenomenon is absolutely predetermined in advance. In this sense, reality is both unfolding Process and Being, an ongoing dialectic between time and eternity, between creative freedom and the confines of Form and universal Necessity. From this perspective, Bateson's view of Mind may be the needed missing link that can unite the Platonists with the process philosophers, the ontologists with the evolutionists, and the philosophers with the cosmologists.

Now that the mechanistic worldview is breaking down, we need a new language, science, epistemology, and ontology that reflects our holistic relation with the living universe more accurately than does the language of classical science. In this sense, the epistemology of Plotinus and Bateson points in a direction that can help us move beyond the subject–object impasse of Cartesian dualism. Physicist

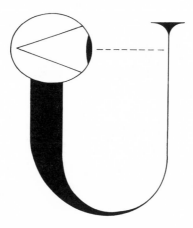

Figure 10. Physicist John Wheeler's concept of the participatory universe.

John Wheeler's concept of the participatory universe also points in a similar direction. In a charming illustration, Wheeler describes the universe—the big "U" in Figure 10—as "a self-excited circuit" that is looking back at itself.[22] Starting with the primordial Flaring Forth,[23] over billions of years the universe expands, cools, and evolves, only to look back at itself in a moment of contemplative self-reflection. Humanity's so-called "dialogue with Nature" is actually the universe's dialogue with itself. In this regard, Plotinus offers some valuable advice:

> All that one sees as a spectacle is still external; one must bring the vision within and see no longer in that mode of separation but as we know ourselves; thus a man filled with a god—possessed by Apollo or one of the Muses—need no longer look outside for his vision of the divine being; it is but finding the strength to see divinity within.[24]

Plotinus, Bateson, and Wheeler each suggest that the psyche is not distinct from the cosmos, but the Mind of the living universe in search of its own nature. In this sense, none of us are detached, isolated observers, but we all belong to a community of beings which is itself a reflection of the entire universe. Because a worldview colors every aspect of human experience, in the aftermath of the Scientific Revolution the focus of life became more one-dimensional and utilitarian as individuals came to be seen as passive, mechanical cogs in systems of social and economic control. In the aftermath of the Cosmological Revolution, the focus of life will become more multidimensional, contemplative, and celebratory as we as individuals come to see ourselves as living embodiments of the-universe-in-search-of-its-own-Being, and as active participants in the ongoing creation of the world.

Notes

1. Plato, *Timaeus* 30D3–31A1.

2. See for example Plotinus, *Enneads* 3.2.6, 3.2.7, 4.4.11, 4.4.32, 5.9.9.

3. On the mechanization of the world order in the Scientific Revolution, see Carolyn Merchant, *The Death of Nature*; Morris Berman, *The Reenchantment of the World*; and Rupert Sheldrake, *The Rebirth of Nature*.

4. This unpredictable complexity was first discovered by Henri Poincaré in his work *On the Problem of Three Bodies and the Equations of Dynamics* (1890). For discussion see Ian Stewart, *Does God Play Dice?*, chapter 4, and the sources cited in note 6.

5. Stewart, *Does God Play Dice?*, chapter 12.

6. For further discussions of chaos in the solar system see Ralph Abraham, *Chaos, Gaia, Eros*, chapters 15–17, and John Briggs, *Fractals: Patterns of Chaos*, 50–54.

7. Some forms of "chaos" are completely deterministic but unpredictable. Other forms, like the "quantum chaos" described here, are indeterminate. For a lucid discussion of the implications of chaos theory in relation to the different concepts of determinism, see Stephen H. Kellert, *In the Wake of Chaos*, chapter 3.

8. This is proven by the famous two slit experiment in quantum physics. For discussion see John Gribbin, *In Search of Schrödinger's Cat*, 163–71; Paul Davies and John Gribbin, *The Matter Myth*, 209ff.

9. On the experimental verification of nonlocality see Fritjof Capra, *The Turning Point*, 82–85; John Gribbin, *In Search of Schrödinger's Cat*, 216–31; Paul Davies, *The Cosmic Blueprint*, 176–77.

10. For a fascinating though sometimes technical discussion of the implications of quantum nonlocality, see Menas Kafatos and Robert Nadeau, *The Conscious Universe: Part and Whole in Modern Physical Theory*.

11. The Mandelbrot set was discovered by mathematician Benoit Mandelbrot and first seen in 1980 on a computer screen at Harvard University. This mathematical object first entered widespread public awareness in 1985 when it was featured in a *Scientific American* cover story. One fractal enthusiast suggests that "It could be thought of as a particularly insidious computer virus in that it not only takes over computers (very computationally intensive) but also the minds of programmers with its fascination."

12. This is encapsulated in Plotinus's Pythagorean-Platonic doctrine that the Nous is a harmonic union of the Monad (Form) and the Indefinite Dyad

(the infinite "Intelligible Matter" of the noetic realm).

13. See my introduction to Kenneth Guthrie, *The Pythagorean Sourcebook and Library*.

14. Plotinus, *Enneads* 2.9.1, 3.8.8., 5.1.5.

15. As is well known, in a holographic image the whole image is distributed in such a way that a part of the hologram contains the entire image. Neuropsychologist Karl Pribram has drawn on the holographic metaphor to explain the nonlocalized, distributed nature of memory in the brain, and physicist David Bohm's theory of the implicate order suggests that the whole of reality is enfolded within every single part. Proponents of holism refer to this principle as *holonomy* and have drawn parallels between the idea of holism in contemporary scientific thought and Eastern mystical traditions. However, the fully-developed philosophical holism of the Greek philosophers seems to have been overlooked in this context. Plato's cosmological holism is clearly reflected in his description of the universe as "One Whole of wholes" (*Timaeus* 33A) in which all the parts fit together in living harmony; the same type of holism is to be found in the writings of the Stoics.

16. By *interimmanence*, I am referring to the idea that parts of a holistic system are so closely interrelated that they can be thought of as being present or immanent within each other. In addition to the cosmological thought of Plotinus, the idea of interimmanence is reflected in the Buddhist idea of *pratitya samutpada* or "interdependent origination." The idea of interimmanence is also found in Stoicism, as for example in the *Meditations of Marcus Aurelius* 4.40: "Always think of the universe as one living organism, with a single substance and a single soul; and observe how all things are submitted to the single perceptivity of this one whole, all are moved by its single impulse, and *all play their part in the causation of every event that happens*" (my emphasis).

17. Plotinus on holism, the harmony of the universal organism, and the interimmanence of parts: *Enneads* 2.3.5, 2.3.7, 3.2.1, 3.3.6, 4.4.32, 4.4.35, 4.4.45, 5.7.2, 5.8.4, 5.8.10, 6.2.20.

18. Plotinus, *Enneads* 2.1.

19. See Gregory Bateson, *Mind and Nature*, chapter 4, for his discussion of the six criteria of mental process.

20. "It is conceivable that we may take the six criteria [of mind] as criteria of life" (Bateson, *Mind and Nature*, 137). Or as Bateson remarked to Fritjof Capra, "Mind is the essence of being alive" (Capra, *The Turning Point*, 290).

21. Plato, *Timaeus* 37D.

22. John Archibald Wheeler, *At Home in the Universe*, 292.

23. I have adopted the term "Flaring Forth" from Brian Swimme and Thomas Berry, *The Universe Story*.

24. *Enneads* 5.8.10 (MacKenna translation).

Bibliography

Abraham, Ralph. *Chaos, Gaia, Eros*. San Francisco: HarperSanFrancisco, 1995.

Barnsley, M. F. *Fractals Everywhere*. Boston: Academic Press, 1988. (Source for slides of plant fractals.)

Bateson, Gregory. *Mind and Nature: A Necessary Unity*. New York: E. P. Dutton, 1979.

Berman, Morris. *The Reenchantment of the World*. Ithaca: Cornell University Press, 1981.

Briggs, John. *Fractals: The Patterns of Chaos*. New York: Touchstone, 1992.

Capra, Fritjof. *The Turning Point: Science, Society, and the Rising Culture*. New York: Simon & Schuster, 1982.

Davies, Paul. *The Cosmic Blueprint: New Discoveries in Nature's Creative Ability to Order the Universe*. New York: Touchstone, 1988.

Davies, Paul and John Gribbin. *The Matter Myth: Dramatic Discoveries that Challenge Our Understanding of Physical Reality*. New York: Touchstone, 1992.

Gribbin, John. *In Search of Schrödinger's Cat: Quantum Physics and Reality*. New York: Bantam, 1994.

Kafatos, Menas and Robert Nadeau. *The Conscious Universe: Part and Whole in Modern Physical Theory*. New York: Springer-Verlag, 1990.

Kellert, Stephen H. *In the Wake of Chaos: Unpredictable Order in Dynamical Systems*. Chicago: University of Chicago Press, 1993

Merchant, Carolyn. *The Death of Nature: Women, Ecology, and the Scientific Revolution*. San Francisco: Harper & Row, 1980.

Plato. *Works*. 12 vols. Loeb Classical Library. Cambridge: Harvard University Press, 1914–1927.

Plato. *Plato's Timaeus*. Translated by F. M. Cornford. Indianapolis: Bobbs-Merrill, 1959.

Plotinus. *The Enneads*. Translated by Stephen MacKenna. Burdett: Larson Publications, 1992.

Plotinus. *The Enneads*. 7 vols. Translated by A. H. Armstrong. Loeb Classical Library. Cambridge: Harvard University Press, 1966–1988.

Sheldrake, Rupert. *The Rebirth of Nature: The Greening of Science and God*. New York: Bantam, 1991.

Stewart, Ian. *Does God Play Dice?: The Mathematics of Chaos*. Oxford: Basil Blackwell, 1989.

Swimme, Brian, and Thomas Berry. *The Universe Story: From the Primordial Flaring Forth to the Ecozoic Era.* San Francisco: HarperSanFrancisco, 1992.

Wheeler, John Archibald. *At Home in the Universe.* Woodbury: American Institute of Physics Press, 1994.

The Green Man of Bamberg
Photo by Clive Hicks

Egos, Angels, and the Colors of Nature

ROBERT D. ROMANYSHYN

Green

Green! Deep, rich, fresh, moist, wet, dripping, morning Green! Blue-green, yellow-green, green-green! A green so green that only the sky could be more blue. Color! Yes, that and the pungent smell of the vegetable body. A heavy, cool, damp odor penetrating the cold corners of the dark interior jungle of life, green swells the vegetable body. Green, a tumescent, throbbing pulsation, a rhythm, a tempo, a pace, a speed, a quivering, a small shudder of the body of creation. A frequency, a vibration, a radiance of the world's consciousness, perhaps even the first vibration of consciousness in creation. Is color a kind of consciousness and is consciousness a frequency of color? Green, yellow, blue, red, purple, orange: variations in the harmonies of consciousness, neighbors, kindred spirits of knowing, of ways of being in the world.

Ensconced in folklore, the Green Man is an icon who reaches out to us from the depths of prehistory. Either as "a male head formed out of a leaf mask," or "a male head disgorging vegetation from his mouth and often from his ears and eyes," the Green Man is the explosive exfoliation of all life, the omnipresence of renewal and rebirth. William Anderson in his study of the Green Man says that he "symbolizes the union of humanity and the vegetable world" and while that is true it is also incomplete.[1] For the greenness of the Green Man is something wholly other before it is ever icon or symbol for human consciousness. The greenness of the Green Man is a pre-human or a proto-human force. It is the iron of the icon, the sap of the symbol, if you will.

The greenness of the Green Man is a vibration of consciousness itself, a punctuation in the multiple frequencies of consciousness which comprise all creation, a moment of consciousness which is older than the frequency of our ego consciousness, a green consciousness which is always there, always present and throbbing at the core of our being, and which often announces itself to us in moments of shipwreck, in those moments of breakdown of ego consciousness, in those vegetative states as we call them when the ego can do nothing else but surrender to its vegetable coffin, when in the midst of some deep loss or terrible tragedy it can do nothing else but lie in its vegetable cocoon. In such moments, green returns and we are beyond symbols and can only wait, listen, and allow ourselves to become green. Green is a frequency of vegetable consciousness, a wisdom of its own. It is what Hildegard of Bingen called *viriditas*, greenness, her name for the cosmic energies of creation. *Viriditas* is an intelligence built into creation and of which we partake as witness, as spokesperson. Through us greenness becomes aware of itself and we, with proper respect and humility, become aware of ourselves as gifted with a wisdom of which we are not the makers.

A Parable: The Cocoon Man

Cast up upon a shore by fate, you are in shipwreck marooned, cut off from the mainland of your daily life. Once the proud captain of your fate, you no longer have in shipwreck an anchor in the world. Cut loose from your moorings by the death of a loved one, or by the loss of health, or by some other tragedy, the shipwrecked you no longer has anything to do. There are no plans to be made, no actions to take, no summonses which reach you from the side of the world. Indeed, in shipwreck you grow deaf, the world grows silent, and the greening begins.

Green consciousness reaches deep into the dark soil of the earth, where all is night. In its vegetable veins "circulate the juices drawn up from the rocks and the realms of the mole, the worm, and the micro-organisms of the soil, to be touched ... by the light of the sun."[2] In this night below the earth, the greening of consciousness begins and you only hear the sound of yourself being enwrapped within a vegetable cocoon. The sound, like that of green leaves being torn from a ripened ear of corn, is the threnody of your transformation into vegetable life, the sound of your becoming vegetable matter itself. The green vegetable force in the dark night of the earth works itself into your flesh, pierces your skin, cracks your bones, and soaks up the blood of your veins. The body, dissolving in shipwreck, is re-made in the deep, slow rhythms of plant life, re-made by the master of the green, the green of creation, the frequency of green consciousness.

> The force that through the green fuse drives the flower
> Drives my green age; that blasts the roots of trees
> Is my destroyer.
> And I am dumb to tell the crooked rose
> My youth is bent by the same wintery fever.[3]

The time of vegetable consciousness is slow. Cocooned in green consciousness, eons can pass, and gradually but inevitably thoughts evaporate, mind stops, and only sensuous awareness remains. The sounds, smells, tastes, textures, and rhythms of the world take place, but it is not *you* who experiences them. On the contrary, green consciousness is identification, participation. You *are* the breeze that only slightly disturbs the leaves of your vegetable tomb. You and that breeze are one. You *are* the warmth that barely penetrates the depths of your vegetable cocoon. You and that warmth are one. You *are* the rain which washes the skin of your vegetable body. You and the rain are one. Light, darkness, warmth, cold, rain, snow, only the cycles of hours and seasons matter. But each ray of morning light is exuberance. That first moment of warmth, of heat after the cold darkness of the night, and every first moment of morning, is all of creation, all of time in that one moment, and in the next one, and in the one after that, each moment the whole. Green consciousness is singular and complete with no horizons of memory or anticipation. Tucked within the rhythm of this consciousness, woven into the vegetable fabric of creation, you who were the weaver disappears.

Re-imagining the Unconscious

From the point of view of the *human* psyche, shipwreck is a descent into the unconscious, that uncharted domain which has been the province of the depth psychologist. But from the point of view of greenness, shipwreck is the epiphany of another kind of consciousness, the breakdown of ego consciousness and the breakthrough of vegetable consciousness, an equally uncharted domain of creation which has been the province mostly of the poet.

We are at an evolutionary point in history where the one great task of exploration is the nature of consciousness, and it is the *pathologies* of the human psyche, its *shipwrecks*, which afford perhaps the best path of exploration. For whatever reasons on the part of creation, the human psyche seems to be the sensitive receiver of the multiple and varied vibrations of consciousness which comprise the universe. In contemporary physics the anthropic principle says that human consciousness is the means by which the universe comes to know itself as ordered and lawful. We do not stand outside creation and through observation and experiment come to know and to control it. On the contrary, we are the self-reflective part of creation, the means through which the consciousness of creation continually realizes itself.

The notion of the unconscious in depth psychology is too limiting. It is an anthropomorphic prejudice inescapably yoked to a definition of ego consciousness as neurotic. It is the product of cultural-historical circumstances which have led to planetary crises and which we can no longer afford. From the point of view of greenness (and the Angel, about whom I will say more later), we need to re-imagine the unconscious as another frequency or range of consciousness. In effect, we need to re-tune the frequency of our ego consciousness so that we might begin to respond to the other vibrations of consciousness which compose all creation. *Our* symptoms, *our* dreams, *our* imaginal musings are *not* the products of *our* unconscious. Indeed, we say that and we think of it in this way only because the range of our ego consciousness has been so limited. On the contrary, symptoms, dreams, and imaginal moments of inspiration are the consciousness of the world. What *we* call the unconscious is the many faceted consciousness of creation. Indeed, the term unconscious is a confession not only of our ignorance but also of our stubbornness. The term unconscious, therefore, needs to be re-imagined as vegetable, mineral, animal, and Angelic harmonies, vibrating at frequencies which heretofore we have imperially ignored. Shipwreck affords one such opportunity. Dreams offer another, and moments of imaginal inspiration a third. As I have written elsewhere, melancholy is the way in which the orphan of ego consciousness is touched by the Angel, and dreams are the voices of creation whispering into our nocturnal ears.[4]

Itzhak Bentov in his remarkable book *Stalking the Wild Pendulum* (1977) offers an approach to consciousness which allows a re-imagining of the unconscious along the lines suggested above. Based in contemporary physics, his work demonstrates how human consciousness as part of the consciousness of all creation is situated within a field of differences. Since the early part of this century, and only slightly after Freud's discovery of the unconscious, we have known from quantum theory that the consciousness of the experimenter is an integral factor in the experiment. Indeed it is appropriate to say that the consciousness of the experimenter and the consciousness of subatomic particles interact. It is true that we are not used to speaking of the consciousness of matter, but that is only because the narrow window of ego consciousness has limited consciousness to the human domain. This limitation is particularly true of the last five hundred years, during which human consciousness has increasingly become a private ego subject, which as a spectator-observer has divorced itself from the world increasingly understood as inert, dead matter. But quantum theory radically challenges that paradigm, and effectively broadens the range of consciousness. Viewed from this perspective, the phenomenon of the unconsciousness is transformed into other frequencies of consciousness, and in this context psychoanalysis might be re-situated as a radical challenge to the paradigm which limits consciousness to the human order.

From the atom through man to other spiritual realities (like Angels, I would say), we have a spectrum or band of frequencies which differentiates types of consciousness. Consciousness is frequency vibrations, a matter of harmonics, and as such it is the capacity to be responsive to one's environment and to be in tune with other and different harmonies. Or, if you prefer, vegetable consciousness compared with our consciousness, greenness compared with ego, is another kind of energy whose frequency range overlaps with, but is not identical to, ours. In fact, Bentov diagrams a series of energy exchange curves which illustrate this overlap among different frequencies of consciousness, different realities. Thus we experience something of vegetable consciousness on one side and of Angelic consciousness on the other. Indeed, might it be that memory is our animal-vegetable-mineral heritage, the way in which rocks and stones, plants and trees, birds and fishes continue in us, and that imagination is our angelic destiny?

However we might answer that question, the symptom, or the experience of shipwreck as I have called it, does seem to put us in touch with these other vibrations of being. The parable of the cocoon man describes how in shipwreck a person descends into and becomes vegetable consciousness. In such moments the symptom heralds not only the breakdown of an ego consciousness, but also the break-through of another kind of consciousness. Along this line Bentov sadly notes that "persons in whom the evolutionary processes of nature have begun to operate more rapidly, and who can be considered as advanced mutants of the human race, are institutionalized as subnormal by their 'normal' peers."[5] Do our diagnostic categories fail to appreciate the *breakthrough* side of our neurotic and psychotic symptoms? Do they attend only to the side of breakdown because they remain enmeshed within a view of ego consciousness which believes that the frequency of consciousness is rare and indeed so rare as to belong only to the human order? Should we not begin to imagine schizophrenic processes, for example, as the consequence of a nervous system finely attuned to other frequencies of consciousness, receptive to multiple and simultaneous transmissions as it were? Then the symptoms of schizophrenia would not merely signal the breakdown of an individual ego consciousness; they would also be an indication of the anthropomorphic prejudices of *all* ego consciousness and of its condition of isolation and separation from the rest of creation. The symptom then would be enlarged beyond its entrapment within human psychopathology.

The dream and our capacity to symbolize it as culture also allows a resonance between us and these other frequencies of consciousness. When we dream, our dreams become the royal road not to our unconscious, as Freud would have it, but to the consciousness of all creation. Moreover, traffic upon this road flows both ways. In dreaming not only are we opened to other vibrations of consciousness, to other realities, to the energies of other beings, they are also opened to us. Bentov says that the animals we encounter in our dreams indicate "that *they* do reach into [our] level of consciousness."[6] Notice his language! Bentov is not saying that we dream the animal. Nor is he saying the animal dreams us. Rather he is saying that dreams are the way in which our consciousness and that of animals *interact*. Dreaming is an attunement of different frequencies of consciousness. The dream no more belongs to us than it does to the animal. On the contrary, the dream is the way in which we meet.

Bentov also adopts a teleological perspective in his book, and from this point of view he argues that "what nature is doing to us during sleep [when we dream] is simply giving us a 'preview of coming events.' "[7] In dreams, nature is preparing us for that expansion of consciousness which will allow us to be in harmony with and to participate in the consciousness of all creation. Depth psychology's discovery of the unconscious was an important step in this direction. The unconscious broke the limited window of ego consciousness. But it is still too limiting a notion, insofar as the unconscious remains tied to human psychology, either as the personally repressed, or as the collective repository of the experiences of our species. *The unconscious needs to be re-imagined as the consciousness of animals and plants, of minerals and stars, of Angels, and atoms.* It needs to be freed from the notion that it describes *our ignorance about ourselves,* and re-imagined as the epiphany of other kinds of consciousness. It needs to be transformed from a way of tuning out all creation to a way of tuning into it. The "common uniting element of all creation is consciousness," Bentov says, "and through this bridge all things are in constant contact."[8] So we need to become comfortable with the thought of the interaction of all creation, and even more comfortable with the insight that minerals dream of animals and Angels, just as plants dream of rocks and of us. Stories help us to become comfortable with these claims.

A Second Parable: The Worm, the Stone, and the Angel

> I died from minerality and became vegetable;
> and from vegetativeness I died and became animal.
> I died from animality and became man.
> Then why fear disappearance through death?
> Next time I shall die
> Bringing forth wings and feathers like angels;
> After that, soaring higher than angels—
> What you cannot imagine,
> I shall be that.[9]

So writes the Sufi poet Rumi. His words describe not only a passage, but also an interconnectedness among all creation witnessed in memory.

But another poet, Heraclitus, has told us that the way up is the way down, and the Angel about which Rumi speaks also lies on the other side of the mineral body, flecks of light released from shattered quartz, crystal, and diamond, and dispersed as radiant points of energy—as stars—throughout the cosmos. The Angel is as deeply below us as it is above us, encountered in descent through the earth as it is an ascent toward the heavens. Yes, the way up is also the way down.

He lay there, lost in the slow rhythms of green. Snow had come and had blanketed the vegetable coffin. The rains of Spring had come and washed it clean. Night had come, so many times, with its frigid darkness. The morning sun had come and had warmed vegetable dreams. How long he had lain there did not matter. He was in vegetable sleep watched over by a mineral wizard, a stone guardian.

The descent was a precipitous fall. The vegetable body itself had begun to rot. Green had turned to spots of brown and yellow. Plummeting deeper and deeper into the soil, the cocoon coffin began to mingle with the dark matter of the earth. Termite and ant, mole and worm feasted on the remnants of the vegetable body. The cocoon above had collapsed. The mineral wizard stood alone.

Deeper, deeper into the blackness of earth, vegetable consciousness slipped away. For stone and rock, pebble and mineral, green was now so far away. Had green always been only a mineral dream? Mineral being: consciousness as form! Only shape and texture, and the awareness of a brittle-hard endurance.

There was only a sound, a terrible wind, and then a shattering explosion. Flecks of mineral, tiny crystals tumbled, twisted, turned, and were swept along on oceans of swirling, streaming energies. Space, vast, dark, and empty was being made. A thunderous, deafening roar continued. A whole universe of light was being born from the hammered fragments of the mineral body.

And then it stopped. As if this universe of stars in a black sea of empty space had always been. As if it had already been there from the beginning of time which had just begun. New and ancient. There was a circle, or maybe a spiral, turning back upon itself at its nadir.

He saw a being of light, an Angel body made of stars. He saw the Angel as the circle turned toward its zenith. Mineral consciousness had exploded into Angelic consciousness. Quartz and crystal, diamonds and coal had become stars.

For a moment and only a moment, for an eternity and all eternity he rested there, on a pivot, on a threshold between worlds. The Angel neither beckoned nor turned away. It neither welcomed nor rebuffed. All was balanced, in place, a perfect harmony of all creation. Perfect, total stillness.

The trembling began, an earthquake of the cosmic soul. The turning of the circle switched directions: deeper and deeper into the dark soil of earth, shattered fragments of stone coming together, worm and mole disgorging vegetable matter, brown tubers pushing through moist soil, a green shoot puncturing the skin of earth, celebrating the sun.

It was morning. The landscape was empty, save for the vegetable womb watched over by the ancient, stone wizard. Womb and wizard were being warmed by the sun. The greenness of the vegetable cocoon was in shiny, wet abundance.

It is not possible to say with any claim of precision what this parable means. Does it describe a descent into the unconscious of its creator? Does it speak of the breakdown of an ego-consciousness? If yes, then so much more too. If yes, then it speaks also of such breakdowns as breakthroughs to other frequencies of consciousness. Beyond acting as witness for this occasion, I must settle for two comments. One comes from the tradition of alchemy. It tells us of this paradox: that the waters of life and the stone, the most solid and dead thing, are one and the same. Plant and stone, rock and star, Angel and worm are one and the same. Punctuations in a field of differences.

The second is from William Wordsworth, fitting perhaps to close this parable as it began, with the wisdom of the poet:

> Our birth is but a sleep and a forgetting:
> The soul that rises with us, our life's star,
> Hath had elsewhere its setting,
> And cometh from afar:
> Not in entire forgetfulness,
> And not in utter nakedness,
> But trailing clouds of glory do we come
> From God, who is our home:
> Heaven lies about us in our infancy![10]

If consciousness is the common element of creation, and if consciousness is a matter of frequency vibrations, then perhaps creation began as a sound. Perhaps it was the creator/creatrix singing or sighing. A sound which already contained within itself all the frequencies to be eventually individuated as a field of differences. Yes, we do come trailing clouds of glory, wisps and puffs of consciousness, melodies of all creation which echo about us in our living and in our dying.

From Psychology to Ecology

In shipwreck there is a greening of consciousness, a moment in which the breakdown of ego consciousness can be a breakthrough to other vibrations of consciousness, a moment when the ego can be opened and attuned, for example, to vegetable, animal, mineral, and angelic frequencies. Such greening happens to individuals who are shipwrecked by grief and despair, by trauma and sorrow, by illness and wound, and to cultures shipwrecked in a moment of radical change. The birth of depth psychology, the creation of psychotherapy, the origins of the therapy room occurred in such a moment.

The therapy room, that place midway between the academy with its education of mind without body, and the clinic with its treatment of the anatomical body without mind, is a culture-historical invention. In Vienna during the last quarter of the nineteenth century, Freud and those who followed him made a place for the symptoms and dreams of their neurotic patients. Those patients who crossed the threshold into Freud's consulting rooms were shipwrecked survivors of a cultural-historical dream. They were the shadow figures of a dream which, as I described elsewhere, began centuries earlier, a dream which, in effect, created our ego consciousness displaced as a spectator from a world transformed into a spectacle for measurement and exploitation, and from a body transformed into a specimen for dissection and exploration.[11] Unconscious they stumbled onto the stage of European consciousness bearing a critical message of change: reconnect with nature and the transcendent, with *its* verdant depths and angelic heights, reconnect with the world, with the earth, with the cosmos. Uncomfortable with the message, however, psychoanalysis "killed" the messengers. It diagnosed, interpreted, and treated the unconscious away. Depth as a matter of human consciousness in partnership with the consciousness of creation, depth as lateral resonance, depth as the principle of relatedness, became an *interior* darkness, a deepening of humanity's isolation and withdrawal from the world and creation. The unconscious became a *psychological* domain, the hidden depths of ego consciousness symptomatically revealed in moments of breakdown. It did not become a moment of breakthrough to other frequencies of consciousness. The unconscious did not become an *eco-cosmological* domain.

James Hillman and Michael Ventura have argued that after one hundred years of psychotherapy the world is getting worse.[12] But that argument gives only half the story. It is not only that things have been and are getting worse. In itself that is true and obvious. It is also that things never could get any better in the first place, because the therapy room in its inception was already divorced from the world, was already isolated from nature and the Angel. Treating the unconscious as only a psychological matter, the greening of consciousness which shipwreck invites could never happen. The neurotic, whose symptoms were indicative of a disconnection from nature and the sacred, whose symptoms were *colorful and awesome*, was imprisoned within the confines of a psychology whose theories of pathology and treatment imagined, and in large measure continue to imagine, psyche, soul, and consciousness as identical with the human. The irony here is that depth psychology, beginning with the profound awareness that psyche is more than ego-consciousness, did not recognize that consciousness is more than human. The consequence is that the unconscious of depth psychology was never green nor angelic. And the tragedy is that today we remain as "colorless" and as profane as our progenitors, those early casualties of shipwrecked ego-consciousness whose symptoms were bleached of their green depths and tamed of their angelic heights. Indeed, does it not seem that today we have become only more adept at these processes of bleaching and taming? Can not "McProzac," for example, kill Angels? Only a deep sense of sadness will suffice here and allow us to recognize that after a hundred years of psychotherapy we are still neither "green" nor "angelic," while our rivers continue to die, and our air becomes fouled with the poisons of a dying, and perhaps already deadened, heart.

What depth psychology achieved in its excavation of the unconscious of the ego is not, however, to be dismissed. The *human* dimensions of the unconscious, its *personal* and *collective* depths, are real in their presence and in their effects. Depth psychology did recover what ego consciousness had lost touch with, in its headlong retreat from the world: time, memory, and history; the child, the body, and sexuality; death, the dream, and the feminine. In all these respects, depth psychology did attend the sufferings of ego consciousness.

That achievement, considerable as it was and is, is, however, not enough, especially today. Simply put, we can no longer afford the price of the term unconscious, because in its genesis and development it is tied to a conception of consciousness that remains specifically and exclusively human. In short, we need to get beyond psychology or face ecological disaster. The logos of psyche (psychology) needs to be placed within the larger logos of the earth (ecology), and even within the larger song of creation. We need to struggle toward a *non-human centered point of view*, which terms like the unconscious and psychology—because of their human, all too human ties—prevent us from doing. We need to see ourselves from the viewpoint of the star and the atom, the animal and the stone, the plant and the angel. We need to acknowledge with a sense of awe and humility these other frequencies of consciousness. We need to begin to listen to *them* before *we* begin to speak.

The Ballet of the Whale

We were walking together on the beach, engaged in meaningful conversation about a patient. Trading fantasies disguised as theory, we went back and forth in a dialogue about dynamics and diagnoses, about treatment strategies and the burdens of psychotherapy. Embraced by the world but rather oblivious to it, we took for granted, as we all usually do, how receptive the landscapes of the world are to human words. Passing rock and shell, bird and wave, we never gave a thought to their impressions of our conversation. Our world had

*in fact closed in on itself. Our words had in fact shaped the space of the
landscape into a place to hold the meaning of our words. Our world had in fact
become rounded, like a bubble in which we moved over and slightly above the
sand and the shells, momentarily cut off from the breeze and the sound of the
waves.*

*Who saw it first is difficult to say, and indeed the experience began as
something less than a vision, and as something more of a feeling. When the
whale's spray spouted above the surface of the water, the bubble of meaning
in which we were encased—should I really say entombed?—was broken, and
it was that shift in the landscape which initially registered the whale's
presence. Like air rushing out of a closed chamber, the whale drew from each
of us only the sound of air escaping from our bodies. Breath so swiftly pulled
from us as an exclamation of the whale's presence escaped being formed into
word. Silenced by the depth of the moment, we stood still, gasping for a word,
gazing in awe. "Look!" was all that finally come out, accompanied by a raised
hand and a finger pointing toward the water. "Look!" A command that felt
as if it was spoken to us rather than by us. "Look!" A single word and a simple
gesture that felt as if it were the command of the whale itself spoken through
us.*

Such moments which silence *our* meaning making in the world can
only be obeyed, and in reply to our obedience the whale began its
ballet. Over and over again it dove and then breached the surface, its
fluke delicately poised in the air, like a dancer at the apogee of her
jump, before breaking the surface of the water. Its dance had *deepened*
the space of our world, re-figured it as a place of joy, and drew each of
us out of the interior depths of our *psychological* spaces into the *aesthetic*
depths of the world. Every Angel, because of its beauty, is terrible,
Rilke says. So too is the whale, a terrible, awe-ful beauty whose
epiphanies explode the narrow chambers of the human mind.

*The whale danced and danced again, and before it departed its ballet had
spread beyond itself to incorporate not only our bodies, but also those of a school
of dolphins swimming nearby. The dolphins joined the water ballet, and in
graceful, sweeping arcs they choreographed an accompaniment to the whale's*

presence. The ballet of the whale had radiated across the landscape, whale becoming dolphin, dolphin becoming ocean, ocean becoming earth, earth becoming sky, sky becoming us, each and all of us becoming mirrors for and echoes of the other, deepening and re-figuring the presence of all. In the epiphany of this moment myriad forms, multiple frequencies of consciousness resonated and embraced. And in this epiphany we were emptied of ourselves, delivered of who we are, and received by the splendors of creation. For a moment it felt as if we had found our way home.

Green is a form, a display of nature's consciousness making its appeal to us. So too is the ballet of the whale, and the breakthrough of an Angel. And in this respect, neither green, nor whale nor Angel are matters of meaning. Rather they are eruptions of Beauty, awe-ful epiphanies of Beauty. The greening of consciousness takes us beyond psychology by taking us beyond meaning into presence, by taking us beyond the activity of meaning making into moments of aesthetic *response-ability.* Green is not just something we see with distant eyes. It is a disposition of our flesh, a way of being in tune with, in love with the world. Green, like the whale was, or like the epiphany of an Angel might be, is a dance, a vibrational intercourse between us and the flesh of the world. Green is a dance which differs from blue, and unless we dance the world in this way we die, and so too does the world. We are neurotic because our egos are colorless. Having no blue sky in our souls we have the blues. Having no green vegetable life, we vegetate in our stuporous addictions.

The greening of consciousness matters, therefore, but not only to us but also for all creation. Whether it be through moments of grief, or awe, or beauty, the imperative of creation is for us to become *aesthetically responsive* to *its* calls. In such moments we will discover that our unconscious is, in fact, our *non-responsiveness* to the consciousness of all creation. And held by such moments we might harmonize and dance our dreamings with the dreamings of stars and atoms, of stones and whales, of plants and angels.

Notes

1. William Anderson and Clive Hicks, *Green Man: The Archetype of Our Oneness with the Earth* (London and San Francisco: HarperCollins, 1990), 14.

2. Anderson and Hicks, *Green Man*, 157.

3. Dylan Thomas, "The Force that through the Green Fuse Drives the Flower," in *The Poems of Dylan Thomas*, ed. Daniel Jones (New York: New Directions, 1971), 77.

4. Robert Romanyshyn, "The Orphan and the Angel: In Defense of Melancholy," in *Psychological Perspectives* 32 (1995), 90–105.

5. Itzhak Bentov, *Stalking the Wild Pendulum* (New York: E. P. Dutton, 1977), 138.

6. Bentov, *Stalking the Wild Pendulum*, 76.

7. Bentov, *Stalking the Wild Pendulum*, 77.

8. Bentov, *Stalking the Wild Pendulum*, 70.

9. Quoted in Reshad Feild, *The Last Barrier: A Sufi Journey* (Rockport: Element Books, 1993), 39.

10. William Wordsworth, "Ode: Intimations of Immortality from Recollections of Early Childhood," in *William Wordsworth: Selected Poetry and Prose*, ed. Philip Hobsbaurn (London and New York: Routledge, 1989), 148.

11. Robert Romanyshyn, *Technology as Symptom and Dream* (London and New York: Routledge, 1989).

12. James Hillman and Michael Ventura, *We've Had a Hundred Years of Psychotherapy—And the World's Getting Worse* (San Francisco: HarperSanFrancisco, 1993).

The Contemporary Christian Platonism of A. H. Armstrong

JAY BREGMAN

THE CHRISTIAN PLATONIST and Neoplatonic scholar A. H. Armstrong is especially well known for his English translation of the *Enneads* of Plotinus, his book, *The Architecture of the Intelligible Universe in the Philosophy of Plotinus*, as the editor of the *Cambridge History of Later Greek and Early Medieval Philosophy*, and other books and numerous articles, many of these gathered in the collections *Plotinian and Christian Studies* and *Hellenic and Christian Studies*. In his works for some sixty years, he has also expressed his personal Platonic religious outlook. Most significant among these are his "apophatic" or "negative theology," a rather unorthodox religious openness combined with Socratic skepticism as well as with traditional religious practice, and a positive view of the cosmos reflected in his sense of the universe, which he envisions as an iconic epiphany of the divine.

Armstrong's scholarship has been well received and has made a major impression on the learned world seriously concerned with Late Antiquity and Neoplatonism. His personal religious ideas are perhaps less well known. In them he presents viable alternatives to rigid, exclusivist orthodoxies, and he builds bridges between East and West: Neoplatonism is the most natural and advantageous point for a Westerner to approach Eastern, especially Indian, thought. He offers living options within the tradition that do not deny or negate historical criticism, modern concerns, or modern science. His feeling for the rhythms of the cosmos, nature, and "the beautiful" speaks to modern

This paper was given at the conference on "Neoplatonism and Contemporary Thought," Vanderbilt University, May 18–21, 1995.

sensibilities, concerns, and problems, while it retains a creative relationship to the tradition, especially to the Hellenic rather than the
Biblical elements of our "inherited conglomerate."

Beginning in the mid-1930s, as a Roman Catholic convert,
Armstrong's works display developments in Neoplatonic scholarship
as well as his own changing religious attitudes and commitments. In
the 1936 "Plotinus and India," still under the influence of Gilbert
Murray and E. R. Dodds, he reflects the the old ideas of late antiquity
as an "age of anxiety" and the "failure of nerve." Even essentially
rationalist Greek thinkers were concerned with ascending beyond the
Fate-ruled cosmos and/or unifying with its inner principle. The
Gnostics prefer the first; the *Hermetica* and especially Plotinus employ
both of these methods of release. There is no sharp distinction
between subject and object and all are deeply influenced by the
Hellenic outlook. Yet despite similarities to Vedanta, Plotinian pan-
theism (as Armstrong then called it) and related phenomena need not
be Indian in origin as E. Brehier thought. The 1937 "Emanation in
Plotinus" takes up the theme of "solar theology"—later so important
to the emperor Julian—in Plotinus and the *Hermetica. Nous* ("divine
intellect") is "*ho ekei Helios*," the Sun of the other world, and Soul is an
intermediary between *Nous* and the visible sun.

During his Roman Catholic period, essentially the 1930s to the
1970s, Armstrong avoided the "party line" of the Christian theological
"de-Hellenizers," who blamed the Greeks—especially the Platonists—
as the main source for contemporary perceived defects of Christianity:
dualism, devaluing of the body and the material world, and non-linear,
non-progressive views of history. Even when he takes the Catholic
side in this debate, he minimizes the differences and even sees
advantages for Christians in the Greek view: "the Christian, like the
Platonist, should apprehend the eternal as present here and now, and
should not reserve his hope for the end of the historical processes, and
the Christian ought to desire as passionately as any Pythagorean or
Platonist to be delivered from coming to be and passing away from the
cycle of death and generation."[1]

Armstrong also perceives common ground for the notions of Platonic *Eros* and Christian *Agape*. The outpouring of the One is not a form of natural automatism; beyond *necessity* the One gives itself. The impulse of *Eros* comes from above, though the One remains impersonal.[2] The Christian emphasizes history and community more than Plotinus. Even the most individualistic Christian mystic expects to enjoy the Beatific vision in the company of heaven. Yet the mystery of how and why the citizen-souls of the City of God are being assembled in history, no Christian interpretation of history can solve. For Plotinus, the beginning of ascent must be the exercise of the civic virtues (*politikai aretai*). He also has a strong feeling for "the visible universe as a community of living intelligences"; it would hardly be going too far to speak of the "mystical body of the cosmos" in Plotinus. Their refusal to recognize *any* community with the gods of the visible universe was one of Plotinus's strongest reasons for hostility to the Gnostics. On *this* doctrine, Armstrong notes, Christians could well learn something from Plotinus, "and our traditional doctrine of angels would enable us to do so within the limits of orthodox belief."[3]

In his Roman Catholic period, then, Armstrong's qualified pro-Plotinian position might be thus summarized: Though Plotinus's description of the unity in diversity of *Nous* may have had a powerful influence on the Christian discretion of the unity-in-diversity of the heavenly city, intellect remains an impersonal universal principal, not a community of beatified persons: "And union with the One is *always* unqualified *monou pros monon*."

To some extent during the 1960s and especially the 1970s, Hilary Armstrong moved more and more in the direction of "Hellenic Christianity." By 1981, he had arrived at a religious position, perhaps best expressed in his "Negative Theology, Myth, and Incarnation,"[4] in which he makes a very sharp distinction between the Hellenic and Biblical, history and myth, and attempts to take the Hellenic side.

This also involved a return to the liberal Christian Platonism encountered in the late 1920s at Cambridge and also a personal transmission from his more conservative father, an Anglican clergyman, who accepted a traditional equation of Platonism and the Bible—a form of liberal Christian Platonism, which, he claims to have abandoned in immature and exaggerated reaction to both its defects and virtues for a more conservative form of Christianity and to have only recently fully consciously returned to it.[5]

Platonic philosophy has been a force against the alienated Gnostic attitude, reinforcing elements in traditional Christianity opposed to Gnosticism and opposed to those Gnostic influences which have persisted in the Christian tradition.[6] The Plotinian view of divine hierarchy opposes the austere monotheistic idea of no degrees of divinity: "it is not contracting the divine into one but showing it in that multiplicity in which God himself has shown it which is proper to those who know the power of God (*theos*), inasmuch as abiding who he is, he makes many gods, all depending upon himself and existing through him and from him."[7] God comes and brings *the gods* with him.

This Henotheistic polytheism as a pure Hellene might conceive it— *inclusive* monotheism for a Christian Platonist—provides a contrast between monotheism in which God communicates divinity, in and through himself, and the "Abrahamic" tradition's exclusive God separated *from His creation.* For the Christians, despite talk of cosmic function of the Logos and the world-animating activity of the Holy Spirit, the saving work of the Logos is through membership in the Church rather than the Cosmos. This difference about the religious relevance of the material cosmos and its multiple self-communication and revelation everywhere and always—the ecclesiastical versus the natural cosmos—allowed Christian anthropocentrism to lead the way for modern technological progress and pollution in a desacralized world. There is no theophany left for the majority, no divine self-manifestation here below. "We had been set free by the Christianity which most of us had abandoned from the superstition and wisdom of the ancients, set free to try to realize our dreams of a wholly man-centered technocratic paradise, which is beginning to look to more and more of us more and more like hell."[8]

The Christian Hilary Armstrong elaborates what he believes are "some advantages of polytheism": "The (Hellenes) did not repudiate the gods for the sake of God, the world is a unity in plurality, a harmony of conflicting opposites and alternating rhythms (seasonal) of a dance, rather than a march to a goal. Plotinus's *On Providence* (the greatest ancient theodicy) remains close to the spirit of the tragedians and in *Enneads* 1.8, Plotinus implies the cosmic choral dance in his adaptation of Sophocles's view of Colonus to the cosmos: 'All the place is holy, and there is nothing which is without a share of soul' (*Enneads* 1.8.14, 36–37). I can only say that awareness of God in the natural world is the heart and foundation of any religion I have."[9]

The notion of God as a Person tends to make him one particular among others; the Good always lies over the edge of our thought. We can only construct a multiplicity of inadequate images . . . the *symbol* for reality. The icon is a *sign*, not a likeness, by which he makes himself present. The true Neoplatonist is an *idoloclast* who opposes idolatry, but an *iconodule* who embraces symbolism.[10] Thus the theologian's formulations are "icons" as much as are the artistic "images" of the church, and neither can be elevated in status.

The important Eranos paper on "The Divine Enhancement of Earthly Beauties"[11] was written in part as a Hellenic response to the disintegration of our inherited conglomerate. "The beauties of Earth and the beauties of the gods, or the divine . . . are apprehended together so that earthly beauties stimulate and provide expression for awareness of divine presence, and in turn, the sense of divine presence enhances earthly beauties";[12] such reciprocal perception is at the root of Neoplatonic aesthetic experience (see Plato's *Symposium* 210A–212B; *Enneads* 1.6; 5.8) In this paper Armstrong discusses: 1) Archaic/ Classical Greek religion, with its ubiquitous but varied sense of concrete omnipresent *numina*; 2) Hellenistic "cosmic piety" somewhat artificially distinguished from 3) Neoplatonic transcendence, which includes and transforms 1) and 2). In the final stages of Hellenism, Platonic and poetic religion had come together. The Neoplatonists of Athens were the last defenders of the old Hellenic ways of recognizing and worshipping the gods as icons. They also went beyond Plotinus in overcoming dualism—the "feminine other," the dyad, is equal to the monad and both proceed from the One. They were well content that the Platonic imagination should be the old Hellenic imagination, and in fact had never ceased to be.[13] On the ladder of the *Symposium*—from beautiful things to the Beautiful—*all stages* remain at *every* stage (*Enneads* 1.3) and at every stage from beginning to end the universal and absolute beauty is present *in* particular beauties and is apprehended as what makes them beautiful.[14] The spiritual enjoyment of earthly beauties was most splendidly celebrated in seventeenth-century England by Armstrong's country neighbor, Thomas Traherne, whose writings he quotes at length.[15] Armstrong then goes on to point out that "it was above all Plotinus who gave Platonism the form in which it has helped most to make us vividly aware of *the divine presence in the beauties of the earth* "[16] (emphasis mine).

In the allegory in *Enneads* 5.5.18–24 about Ouranos (the One), Kronos (*Nous*), and Zeus (*Psyche*), the latter's (as Hadot suggests) preference is for Ouranos. The fact that "he is not satisfied with the contemplation of his father but aspires to, we might say, the active power with which his grandfather established reality in being" is a *hidden preference* in Plotinus for the process of procession, at the root of which is the *bonum diffusivum sui*, the primacy of the generosity of the Good. That even the perfection of Nous—the absolute perfection of Being—is not enough, is a striking development of Platonism.[17] Armstrong points out, however, that Zeus also remains in Kronos, and even if the Hypostases are distinguished, they are never disjoined. Plotinus himself might have let the sharp distinction vanish.[18]

Finally, the later Athenian Neoplatonists went far in overcoming dualism, and in this surpassed Plotinus. Platonic-Pythagorean dualism is never simply a conflict dualism of the Iranian pattern—"light versus dark" in more or less eternal opposition—it is rather in between the Iranian and the Chinese Yang-Yin Circle. The late Platonists, "by rehabilitating" the account of the feminine principle, the "dark other," brought it over to the Chinese side. The negative statements about this principle are abandoned; both monad and dyad are seen as equal, proceeding directly from the One/Good, the father and mother of all that exists, of real being and intelligible cosmos as well as of material cosmos. Though as imperfection "evil" is in a sense a result of the "dark other," she still has a necessary and transcendent function.[19] As Proclus puts it in *Platonic Theology* 3.8, "all unity, wholeness and community of being and all the divine measures depend on the primal limits and all division of generative making and procession to multiplicity come from the supreme unboundedness."[20]

Armstrong summarizes his position as follows:

> The recognition of the "dark other" . . . can clearly do a great deal to remove the Platonic uneasiness, still apparent in Plotinus, about the beauties of the material world . . . the point is that at which cosmic optimism becomes . . . too roseate . . . and world affirmation . . . self indulgent, and there is no longer any call to rise to the higher world of spirit. The doctrine of the Athenian Neoplatonists does not deny the evil of the material world . . . it still preserves something of the ambiguity of valuation inherent in the concept or image. But the image is now very much an icon. It becomes more necessary than ever before for the devout philosopher to be aware of the divine in and through material things and outward observances.[21]

The Athenian Neoplatonists not only practiced Chaldean theurgic rites, but were champions of Hellenic and all pieties and theophanies. Proclus thought that a philosopher should be the "hierophant of the whole world."[22] In the history of Hellenic and Platonic awareness of the divine in the beauties of the Earth, the beginning was present in the end. The last defenders of the primeval theophanies were Platonic philosophers.

Today Hilary Armstrong takes his religious stand with Christians whose piety is becoming "pre-Constantinian" and who have abandoned the "Theodosian model" of universal compulsory Christianity. He has also abandoned religious exclusiveness: "I normally worship

God in a Christian Church . . . But if I came across a Hindu temple, our world's answer to a temple to Graeco-Roman Isis—I should go into it and give true veneration to their holy *images* as *true images* of God"[23] (emphasis mine).

A figure from late antiquity I consider to be comparable is Synesius of Cyrene (*c.* 370–413 C.E.). Synesius was a well connected Greek gentleman from the polis of Cyrene in Libya. According to Gibbon he had the longest pedigree in history. He came to Alexandria in the 390s to study with Hypatia, the Platonic-Pythagorean philosopher. She "initiated" him into Neoplatonic "mysteries." His famous metaphysical hymns, especially the early ones, suggest the fervor of a "convert" to the Neoplatonic philosophy. If Synesius was somehow Christian, for whatever reason, before he encountered Hypatia's teaching—or, as is more likely, he became so shortly after—by all appearances he remained a Hellenic Neoplatonist in the Hypatian sense and probably didn't care much about what orthodox clergy said or thought. But when he accepted an episcopal appointment in 410 C.E., he felt obligated to take a position. In *Epistle* 105 he expresses Platonic reservations concerning Christian dogma: the world was not "created," nor will it ever be destroyed; the human soul pre-exists; the resurrection can only be an allegorical image of a purely spiritual event. After 410, he continued to correspond with and confide in Hypatia, and continued to understand his religion from the perspective of an *inclusive* Hellenic Neoplatonist.[24]

Hilary Armstrong's remarks in correspondence and private conversation clarify the way in which he perceives the religiosity of Synesius in relation to his own. "My religion was never very Jesus-centered—and similar in some ways in my upbringing to Cambridge Platonists like Henry More . . . since the sixteenth century the Anglican Church has tolerated Christian Platonists, who have sometimes had a good deal of influence." On re-reading Synesius's *Epistle* 105, Armstrong writes:

One difference struck me among the many which there are between me and Synesius. Synesius believed there was one true religion, the Platonism he'd learned from Hypatia, as opposed to the myths of the demos. This is why for him the main opposition in religion is between philosophical truth and "myth." The main opposition for me is between people who claim to know too much about God, including all sorts of highly sophisticated people, and those who don't. I am quite addicted to religious "myths" as long as no one tries to impose them officially. I used to light candles to local goddesses all over the place especially in or near the Alps. I'm more like Amelius than either Porphyry or Iamblichus. I'm inclined to think that both Protestantism and Indian "spirituality" (not the religion of India as a whole) make the separation between the "spiritual" world and this one very sharp and hard. This seems to me more like Gnosticism than the Platonic tradition . . . which is why "icons" or "theophanies" are important to me.[25]

In recent speculations published in *Sphinx* 4, he reflects on eschatological themes from the point of view of an almost purely Hellenic Neoplatonist—but also from a critical/modern/revised-perspective. The soul's *experience* of eternity is emphasized, while the traditional idea of immortality is abandoned or left in doubt. The idea of resurrection is avoided for clear critical reasons, in a way not very far from those of Synesius. It seems philosophically incoherent and fantastic.

Thus Armstrong presents a special though non-dogmatic status for the Christian myth.[26] "Diversity, in my opinion, is co-extensive with all conscious thought and reflection on higher reality. I have lately taken to symbolizing this by the late Neoplatonic doctrine of the Peras-Apeiron (see my "Platonic Mirrors"= *H&C* VI) and in general am more devoted to the splendid diversity of the holy images of the unknowable in this world." He accepts negative theology as such, but from an anti-absolutist perspective. Negative theology may suggest a deep, obscure, anonymous faith in something, a dim awareness that there really is something "behind" and "beyond" all the inadequate concepts and expressions. A radically apophatic faith permits the use in a peculiar way of very positive language. Its adherents may thus come to understand the expressions of their traditional religions, not just as "myths" or "icons" made up by men, but as multiple and varied revelation of images through which the Good communicates "iconi-cally" with all of us, of all religious traditions.[27] This "general" or natural revelation—close to Proclus's view of the significance of myth and ritual (see Trouillard, *In Remp.* n.8)—will, of course, include human participation, error and inadequacy. This attitude should also be extended to include the statements of dogmatic and philosophical theology, not only poetic and imaginative myth, icons and so on.

Armstrong's personal background suggests comparisons with Synesius: "Some sort of Christian Platonism or Neoplatonism was a natural growth in the soil of a moderately well-read English country vicarage when I was young, which was my native soil. . . . it's very difficult to explain the ethos in which one was brought up."[28] "Classi-cal" and "Christian" *really comprised* a conglomerate. "I think I love the Inherited Conglomerate, think I belong to it, and even see classical civilization to some extent through it, though I'm conscious of the differences, rather as one would love an old house in a splendid landscape, to which one's ancestors had contributed a great deal, in which one was brought up."[29] On the Classical versus Biblical debate within the Christian tradition: "the only reason why I to some extent believe in and practice unreformed Christianity is that it has been Hellenized enough for me."[30] Armstrong, therefore, is often surprised at the to him somewhat strange penchant for "revived" Classical myths that have been given special significance in the modern world. For example, archetypal psychologists, who see the gods as diseases and/or collective powers of the psyche, often become "enthusiastic" when they invoke Dionysus. His reaction is that "when they talk to me in this manner they don't seem to realize that they are referring to an old friend of mine."[31]

Today the "Platonic Mirrors" of an "implicate order" of the cosmos in which "all things are in all things, but appropriately" (Proclus, *Elements of Theology*, prop. 103),[32] informs the "Procline" physics of

David Bohm and others. For Hilary Armstrong the Plotinian image/ archetype reflections on *all levels* symbolize the idea that the cosmos itself is best characterized as the resulting image of an "effortless contemplation"—an almost natural reflection, rather than the painstaking work of a "craftsman" from a "model." But all of the images are shattered in the One.[33] And the One is the only cause of Matter (*Hyle*). The "highest" and "lowest" are imageless, but only images—or icons—point toward them.

Notes

1. *Plotinian and Christian Studies* (London, 1979), VI, "Salvation, Plotinian and Christian," 136. (Referred to below as *P&C*).

2. *P&C* VI, 127–29. Here Armstrong follows the ideas of Jean Trouillard.

3. *P&C* VI, 138 and n. 23.

4. In *Hellenic and Christian Studies* (London, 1990), VII, 47–62. (Referred to below as *H&C*.)

5. *H&C* Intro. xi, where Armstrong also claims—at the time of writing—to have made too sharp and exclusive distinctions between history and myth, Hellenic and Biblical, in the section I have paraphrased immediately above.

6. *P&C* XXI, "Gnosis and Greek Philosophy," esp. 104–107; *H&C* XII, "Dualism, Platonic, Gnostic and Christian," esp. 34–37.

7. Plotinus, *Enneads* 2.9.9, 37–39.

8. *P&C* XXII, "Man in the Cosmos: A Study of Some Differences between Pagan Neoplatonism and Christianity," 11–12.

9. *H&C* I, "Some Advantages of Polytheism," 184.

10. *P&C* XXIV, "Negative Theology," 189.

11. *H&C* IV, 49–81. This article provides the best summary in print of Greek religiosity from the Archaic and through the Hellenistic era and Late Antiquity from the point of view of a Platonist.

12. *H&C* IV, 51.

13. *H&C* IV, 65.

14. *H&C* IV, 69.

15. *H&C* IV, 71–72.

16. *H&C* IV, 72.

17. *H&C* IV, 73–74.

18. "Aristotle in Plotinus," 127. In *Oxford Studies in Ancient Philosophy*, ed. Julia Annas, Supplementary Volume, 1991; *Aristotle and the Later Tradition*, ed. Henry Blumenthal and Howard Robinson (Oxford, 1991) 117–127.

19. *H&C* IV, 79–80.

20. *H&C* IV, 80.

21. *H&C* IV, 81.

22. Marinus, *Life of Proclus*, 19.

23. Correspondence, January 1993. (All correspondence referred to is personal correspondence.)

24. In his first *Hymn*, Synesius refers to the One as "Unity of Unities,

Monad of Monads" (58–59), which "holds the force of three summits." This is a reference to the Neoplatonic/Chaldean First Intelligible Triad rather than the Christian Trinity which he was later able to assimilate to this Triad. For a review of Synesius's religious ideas, see my "Synesius of Cyrene: Early Life and Conversion to Philosophy" in *California Studies in Classical Antiquity* 7 (1974), 55–88, and "Synesius, the Hermetica and Gnosis" in *Neoplatonism and Gnosticism*, edited with an introduction by Richard T. Wallis and Jay Bregman (Albany: State University of New York Press, 1992).

25. Correspondence, May 1992.

26. See *H&C* VII, passim.

27. *H&C* VII, 52.

28. Correspondence, January 1993.

29. Correspondence, April 1995.

30. Correspondence, June 1995.

31. Correspondence, February 1995.

32. Proclus, *The Elements of Theology*, translated with an introduction and commentary by E. R. Dodds (Oxford, 1963). See p. 254 for some interesting connections of this proposition with earlier and later philosophers: "the Pythagoreans," Plotinus, Porphyry, Iamblichus, Bruno, Leibniz.

33. "We have passed irrevocably, into a climate of opinion in which the more one claims to know about God the less one is likely to be believed" (Correspondence, February 1996).

The Theology of the Invisible

BRUCE NELSON

Quis caelum possit, nisi caeli munere,
Nosse et reperire deos,
Nisi qui pars ipse deorum ist.

Who could know heaven
Save by heavenly grace
Or find the gods if he weren't
Himself part of the gods.

—Manilius

PLATO TAUGHT that there are three things we should always remember about the gods. First, that they exist; second, that they care about this world; and third, that they are always just. Later, Epictetus would add that the gods are the bearers of all good gifts, and that we should be assured they always have our best interests at heart even when we don't.

Unfortunately, while the gods are present to all things, not all things are present to the gods. Where they traverse all paths, discovering even a single path is a delicate and difficult matter for us. Not that we lack freedom—we have complete freedom, but our freedom is of attitude, not of circumstance, and freedom of attitude is a subtle freedom, yet one that constantly shapes our awareness and our appreciation. In fact, it is this unique patterning of our awareness and appreciation that forms our destiny. Destiny is always personal. Each of us has our own labyrinth of dream, desire, and vision to thread, our own Minotaur, and our own Ariadne, a singular mythos whose purpose and ultimate meaning is inexplicable, but where everything is full of divinity.

Awareness of the individuality of destiny is the basis of mutual understanding and sympathy. It is also the basis for discovering our original confidence. Our destiny is always present, although never completely visible until we remember who we truly are, which as Manilius suggests may be somewhat grander than we suppose. Everything bears witness to our remembrance, for remembrance not only recalls our divinity but is the primary expression of it.

The ancients believed that the guardian of our destiny was our personal daimon, the guiding spirit who is our closest link to the gods. Our personal daimon always appears as that which is higher within us. If we live through our senses and our emotions, then it appears to us as reason. If we live by reason, it appears as intuition. And if we live through intuition, it appears as presence. Our daimon is the best of guides because it will both descend and ascend with us. It will not desert us no matter how far we stray, but always remains to show us the first step back. Present even when we aren't, our daimon reveals the intelligence appropriate for each situation. Whether we follow its intelligence is another matter, one that delicately hinges on the depth and clarity of our awareness.

Awareness is developed through contemplation. Contemplation is a way of life, not a specific practice, although certain practices help establish it as a path. It is based on a strong confidence in the sufficiency of providence and the undiminished presence of Goodness. Contemplation is allowing our attention to be inwardly at rest, rather than dispersed outward toward objects or situations we hope will fill or complete some lack within us. Through contemplation we use the assurance of our inner emptiness to communicate with the presence of outer objects, creating a common ground with their invisible nature. In this way objects do not diminish but enhance and extend our mutual inwardness.

This mutual inwardness we share with the world reflects the unity of the invisible as pure experience. The invisible is never separate or in conflict with the logic and physics of everyday reality. That is why contemplation is so powerful. Through continuity of commitment, one can participate in a magical, poetical level of being that illuminates both the visible and the invisible. Although there are many paths, there is no discipline beyond continual availability. The ancient, golden intimacy of gods and men can be recaptured because it is not the gods who have left and become less real, but us. Deities are the highest images of reality, the true mediators between heaven and earth, and rediscovering their presence opens us to the world as it really is.

The world, as it is, exists as contemplation, as pure vision. We exist as part of that contemplation, as vision descended into the visible. As we descend, we take on time as a condition of being. Descent is the color of time, time descending through the plane of moments. When we turn back toward the vision, we ascend and time disperses. There is a natural hierarchy of awareness and a natural hierarchy of incarnation, and the language of this hierarchy is myth. Myth is the story of divine movement, of the always miraculous transmutation of energies. It is an image of a reality that is continually occurring. Free from time, myth is always present event. Expressed in time, myth becomes history, the relative fruition of infinite form. History is a constant outpouring of the timeless into time. Descent always has a history, but ascent is timeless and happens in a moment.

The incarnational hierarchy is also the basis of true cosmology. We cherish the obvious, the literal, and the tangible, but heaven prefers the subtle. That is why invisibility is the natural clothing of the divine, but not the only clothing of the divine. The subtle, pre-conceptual energies of heaven become animated, and take form against the backdrop of matter. The visible, physical world exists as a vibrational emanation stretched between a Goodness whose subtlety is inconceivable, and whose density is equally inconceivable, but whose presence, filtered through a series of levels, is the source of everything that exists. The challenge is to experience this presence, that which animates both the visible and the invisible, not just once or for a moment, but continually without ceasing.

If we are to name this presence, if we are to personalize it as we invariably do, then we are speaking of the gods. The gods are pure presence and, as pure presence, completely intertwined in our lives. They work without signature, always in accordance with the Good, for they are the highest and best reflections of the Good. Those who are ignorant of the gods, who ignore the presence of the gods, descend deeper into matter and create further suffering for themselves. Without turning back, without conversion, there is no end to this suffering. The invisible is primary, yet its primacy does not negate the worth and beauty of the visible, for they are at every point inseparable.

Because our heart lies at the crossroads of the visible and the invisible, there is always ambiguity in our experience of the ineffable. We want both intimacy and distance from our experience. Yet when there is too much distance, when experience becomes reflection, the intimacy is lost. Ego loves the hermetic, the complex and the distant— it is always stepping back, avoiding directness. But the gods have never known ego, only Eros. Eros is the opposite of ego: that which dissolves. Eros fulfills itself through our love of the gods, the deepest love we can feel. It is a love initiated by the gods themselves, for, as Iamblichus said, only they know the spells that can compel their presence. Our discovery of those spells is no accident, but the natural end of our desire. Thus, everything is motivated by our persistent nostalgia for heaven.

The beauty of the natural world is the clearest, most direct expression of divinity. Yet only when the visible becomes invisible do we truly perceive it. The Earth constantly turns towards the invisible, even as we move deeper toward the density of matter, and begin to mistake the hallucinations of matter to be something true and desirable. In these hallucinations a physicality is created disembodied from soul. Yet however clever our artifice becomes, the shadow is still a shadow, and if we lose the physical we also lose the divine. So it is not disassociation from the physical that we need, but release from our incomplete conception of the physical. The perception of the world as full of soulless, separate objects placed here to be used, rather than of living, interconnected entities with inherent destinies of their own is the basis of our current, pervasive nihilism. It is not the problem of a dead world, for the world has always possessed soul, but of a dead vision, one which numbs and deadens us until we extricate ourselves from it.

The ancients knew soul as animation and movement: the self moved. Since soul is movement, loss of soul is experienced as confinement. That is why we imagine hell as claustrophobic, and heaven as spacious. The soul's movement becomes restricted through attachment. Attachment is always to some form of matter—physical objects, ideas, images, whatever is a reflection of reality rather than reality itself. This attachment creates a coloring of the soul's vehicle or subtle body. Because of this coloring, we have a distorted vision of the physical and subtle worlds. The primary symptom of this distortion is confusion about where ultimate value really lies.

There is an unavoidable stain, or distortion of perception caused by our descent into the body. We are born into a tangible interpretive and perceptual matrix, a common referential reality, but from the vantage point of our preexistent state this reality is a type of forgetfulness. Everyone forgets—no one has yet been born who has not submerged themselves in the river Lethe. To be born is to drown, to lose consciousness of what we once were. The body itself is forgetfulness. Because of this stain inherited by birth, there is always a certain imprecision in our knowing. Everything we experience is filtered through appearances. It is both there and not there, like an image in a mirror. Reality is veiled because we are veiled, and yet this veil is also the best possible reflection of the light we once knew face to face. So we should not diminish our present experience. If we cannot find the Good here, it will escape us in any other space or form we may inhabit.

The stain of birth is not removed by affiliation or belief, virtue or action. Nor is it removed by study or reflection, meditation or ritual. It is removed only by remembrance. And remembrance is a form of grace. It is the grace that arises from awareness and experience of the gods. Activity has no other objective than this. Our contemplation and devotion is not a preparation for the experience of grace, nor is it a purification to make us worthy of such experience, but is itself the expression of the very grace we seek. It is through the grace of the gods that we seek the gods, that we discover the path of remembrance that allows us to be reunited with them completely.

Through remembrance we restore our original confidence. With this innate confidence there are no problems—the view and the pattern of events are in alignment. There is no judgment because there is no thought. The world is without blemish, without distinction—clear, limitless, and at peace. Remembrance is recovered through love of the invisible. This love inspires persistence of vision—a deeper commitment to the unfolding reality glimpsed by intuition and confirmed by presence. Perfection of attitude is realized as no attitude, not adhering to any fixed point of view. With this understanding, even vices become virtues for everything is contemplation. The whole world becomes an altar at which incense burns without ceasing.

In the world of true remembrance, being and becoming are inseparable: there is no creation from nothing, and no deity who stands apart from the natural order and on whim fashions the world in seven days or seven aeons. The world as becoming is eternal because it is always one with eternity. It does not reflect its creator; it reflects its primal status as uncreated. This is the source of its abundant creativity. This is also the basis of immortality. The gods know no separation—this is the secret of their being and their becoming. They are the archetypes of original confidence.

Only form sees form as separate. And once that occurs everything is thrown into conflict. Jealousy arises and gods are brought down into demons. For the god who is jealous is the god who knows that he is only one form among many, which is to say that he has no form, and could disappear as easily as he appears. Such a deity could know nothing because it would be removed from the source of its own creative power. That creative power exists in unity and wholeness, not in dispersion. Similarly for us, without participation in the divine, we are only capable of destruction—we can only pull things apart; we cannot bring things together.

Things are brought together by grace, and it is grace that lifts us to our deeper destiny. As Chrysippus said, "Even our thoughts are fate." Hermes the Revealer, the daimon with winged sandals, is always present, never resting in a single image, but appearing in ever new forms for every image is its own iconoclast. For this reason, it is true that almost everything said of the gods is unworthy, for the very reason that it is capable of being said. The infinite by nature transcends all categories, including the subtle categories of intuition and presence. The gods not only transcend their expression, they also transcend any experience we might have of them. They are in flux and they are constant. They are immortal and yet within time. They are traceless, yet they leave traces everywhere.

This is the creative irony of heaven—to hide what is most precious within what is most obvious. Since ultimate reality is not separate from its expression in the present world, there is no place to look for it other than the present moment. The real depth lies on the surface. Once discovered, the primary reality of the invisible overwhelms all speculations and discursions and creates in our souls its own mythos and its own logos. So it is not a matter of accumulating wisdom, but rather realizing the complete insufficiency of our understanding, and thus abandoning any search for wisdom. In fact, every search is a departure, for since the gods have concealed what is most secret in what is most obvious, only the gods can reveal its presence.

As Plotinus says, "We must not look, but must, as it were, close our eyes and exchange one faculty of vision for another. We must awaken this faculty which everyone possesses, but few people ever use . . . for there is no whence, no coming or going in place, now it is seen, and now not seen, we must not run after it, but fit ourselves for the vision and then wait tranquilly for its appearance, as the eye waits on the rising of the sun, which in its own time appears above the horizon—out of the ocean, as the poets say—and gives us our sight."

The Earth Mother
Panel from the Altar of Augustan Peace, Rome, 13–9 B.C.E.

The World Religions and Ecology

JOSEPH MILNE

I WOULD LIKE TO OFFER in this talk a way of exploring the relationship between religion and ecology. We shall try to look at this relationship very simply and directly. What I hope to show is that there is a distinctly religious way of understanding the ecological issues of our time. In fact, I will go a step further and suggest that the ecological crisis, in its deepest sense, is really a religious issue.

This is because our theme invites us to take an all-embracing overview of two great spheres of existence: the sphere of revelation and the sphere of creation. By the sphere of revelation I mean and include all the world religions, and by the sphere of creation I mean the entire created universe.

If we reflect upon these two great spheres for a moment, it becomes evident that they encompass the whole of reality, and so they embrace the full scope of all human concern and responsibility, material and spiritual. For it is as a being in the creation that humanity finds itself wholly dependent upon the abundance of Mother Nature for sustenance and life, and it is only within nature that mankind has the scope to realize all its creative potential. But also it is only as an offspring of the earth that humanity has the power to turn its gaze heavenward towards the spirit, towards the transcendent, and reflect upon the ultimate mysteries of being. For every human soul feels the call of the transcendent, in which lies its ultimate fulfillment and meaning. And so, just as every human being is an offspring of Mother Earth, so every human being is also open to the transcendent. But also, the creation, this material world in which we "live and move and have our being,"

This talk was given at Canterbury Cathedral, March 1994, for the Council of Christians and Jews.

is the setting for revelation; it is the sacred space in which the transcendent spirit reveals itself to humanity.

Thus, for humanity, matter and spirit are, as it were, the two poles of one reality, within which every human action is possible and to which every human being is responsible or answerable. An awareness of the laws of nature on the one side, and of the laws of God on the other, converge in humanity in a quite unique way. No other creature is likewise able to grasp these two orders of law and consider them. No other creature is obliged to bring these two orders of law into harmony within itself or to consciously fulfill them in all its actions and aspirations. It is mankind's unique awareness of these two orders of reality that makes him a religious being.

It is worth reflecting that, as far back as we can gaze into human history we find that mankind has always understood itself to be the offspring of the earthly Mother and the heavenly Father. With the emergence of civilization these concepts have refined and deepened, though in essence they have remained the same. *Homo sapiens* is a religious species. This is what modern archaeology now attests. The earliest remains of humanity are religious sites. The earliest written documents are religious works. The earliest art is religious art. As far back as we can see, humanity has revered the earthly Mother and stood in awe of the heavenly Father, and has sought to bring these two orders of reality together in its way of life. Out of this reverence and awe have arisen all the great religious traditions of the East and the West, and out of these have arisen all the great cultures and civilizations of the world.

Culture and civilization have sprung from this awareness of two orders of reality, the material and the spiritual. It is worth remarking that there has never been a secular civilization, and here I would like to suggest that the current talk we hear about the modern secular society originates in a very narrow perception of the world, and a very shallow understanding of humanity. Such talk does indicate, however, that there is a loss of the sense of the spiritual order of reality in our time, as well as a loss of the sense of the natural order of reality, and this loss is leading to the fragmentation of society. The loss of the

sense of the spiritual order and the natural order is the loss of the sense
of unity, and so it is really an inner crisis of the soul. A conflict has
arisen between the spiritual life and the material life of humanity, a
conflict between the inner and the outer, between the heavenly and
the earthly. The two spheres of revelation and creation have become
dissociated in humanity's general consciousness.

I would suggest that there is a direct link between this inner crisis of
the soul and all the economic and ecological problems of our time—
the problems of pollution and mass starvation, the problems of the
exploitation of nature and the exploitation of human beings. If the
spiritual order is forgotten, then the material order breaks down. If the
natural order is forgotten, then the spiritual order breaks down. This
is something that every great religion teaches, for every religion
teaches that it is the task of humanity to bring the divine order and the
natural order together. This task cannot be evaded.

With the emergence of our complex modern society, which is part
of progress, in which every national economy is related to the world
economy, contemporary humanity is being challenged to reach a new
and deeper understanding of its relationship to nature and to spirit.
This challenge presses on us from all sides. We see the dangers of the
industrial abuses of nature. We see the increasing problem of poverty.
We see racial, ideological, and religious conflict. We see the barren-
ness of materialism. It is surely significant that all these problems have
arisen at a time when individualism, or what has been called enlightened selfishness, is the prevailing social ideology.

I believe that these problems can only be explored properly within
a religious context, because it is only people with a religious vision that
can address them in their full depth and seriousness. This is because
religion alone—and here I mean every great religion—strives for a
total vision of reality, for a view or a perspective which includes every
created thing as well as the Creator of all things. One of the things that
makes any person or any community religious is a deep intuition of the
total unity of everything. We may not directly see that total unity, but
we sense it intuitively. I do not mean a mechanistic unity, such as that
proposed by bad scientists. I mean, rather, a unity such as we find

expressed by the great prophets and mystics of every religious tradition, in which every created thing is seen as meaningful and purposeful, as an expression of the will of God, a unity in which everything exists within a divine order and participates in a divine plan, a unity in which matter itself is seen ultimately as an expression of Spirit.

If this intuition of the total unity of all things, no matter how vaguely it is felt, is at root a religious intuition, then I think we can rightly say that the new wave of concern for the environment—the ecological sense as we might call it—is also at root a religious intuition. Yet, having granted that, I would also suggest that this wave of environmental concern is, in general, still in its infancy. It is only partial. Although positive, it is a limited sense of wholeness. For many this concern is based, not so much upon a deep sense of the unity of the everything, but rather upon a fear of some immanent ecological catastrophe in which the future existence of mankind is threatened. But even for those whose concern is in fact for the whole earth, their focus is mainly upon conservation for its own sake and their proposed solutions are narrowly mechanistic and they tend to exclude humanity. In fact, for many ecologists, the human race is regarded as outside nature and as the enemy of the environment. Therefore their political and economic solutions are rather crude and limited. Because they are based only on a concept of conservation, they leave out of account both the question of the ultimate purpose of nature and the question of the ultimate destiny of humanity. In short, they are only a partial grasp of the natural order, but leave out the divine order entirely.

If I were to put my finger on a single lack in current ecological thinking, it would be its extremely narrow conception of mankind. It has no holistic anthropology. There is an unspoken assumption that the ecosystem does not really require the human species, and that humanity is not an essential part of nature. This assumption springs from viewing mankind merely as a consumer and exploiter of nature, without an integral part in its meaning or destiny—notions which originate in an entirely materialistic and secular view of humanity.

This narrow conception of mankind is obviously profoundly anti-religious, and all religious thinkers are surely called upon to challenge it. For every religion, without exception, perceives humanity as absolutely central to the meaning and destiny of the creation. In Judaism, as also in Christianity, humanity is seen as the crown or completion of creation. In the Chinese religions, in Confucius and in Taoist thought, for example, humanity is understood to be the mediator between heaven and earth, the maintainer of cosmic harmony and equilibrium. In Buddhism the highest aspiration is the liberation of all beings, while in Hinduism humanity is understood to be, in essence, pure spirit and the direct expression of Brahman, the Supreme Lord. But even in the so-called primitive religions, such as those of the Australian aborigines or the Bushmen of the Kalahari Desert, humanity is seen as the guardian of the sacred order of the world. For them, the world of nature and the sky are living manifestations of Spirit.

I suggested a moment ago that mankind alone among all creatures is able to reflect upon the spiritual order and the natural order, and that this power of reflection is what makes the species *Homo sapiens* a religious species. I went on to suggest that the modern ecological sense was a partial awakening to the natural order, but not to the divine order. And I suggested that the main deficiency in current ecological thought lay in its limited view of mankind, in its lack of a holistic anthropology, and in the absence of a vision of human destiny. I would now like to suggest further that the question of human nature is, at this time, the key to the religious approach to ecology. In short, I would suggest that the contribution that religion can make to the current ecological crisis is to offer a sacred anthropology—a sacred and holistic vision of mankind. Strangely enough, religion itself has neglected this question for a long time, especially in the West. So an enquiry into human nature is as important to contemporary religion as it is to the contemporary world generally.

The question of sacred anthropology has been my area of research for several years, and I would like to offer you in simple outline some of my basic findings from a comparative study of the way different religions look at human nature. My findings show most remarkable similarities between the ways different religions address the question of human nature. What we find is a rich set of relationships between three primary senses of existence: the sense of Self, the sense of World, and the sense of Totality. Every human being has a sense of Self, a sense of World, and a sense of Totality. In religious language these three senses are grounded in a threefold relationship between Self, World, and God. These three belong together and cannot be separated from each other. Let us look briefly at each in turn.

First, the sense of Self. Man is a reflective being. That is to say, what first makes us human is the simple fact that we reflect upon our own being, on our own sense of existence. It is this power of self-reflection or self-consciousness that enables us the reflect upon being and existence generally. Thus we may say that man is not only aware of being, he is aware that he is aware of being. As the theologian Paul Tillich puts it, "Every being participates in the structure of being, but man alone is immediately aware of this structure."

Second, humanity has a sense of World. Man alone conceives of a world. Let us look at this sense of world in a little detail. Because he is a reflective being, man cannot help but find himself in a world to which he mysteriously belongs, in which he must act to be himself, and towards which he must act responsibly for the sake of the world. This is the same for man anywhere and at any time. And in the interaction between man and the world lies all the glory and all the tragedy of the human story.

Yet here a question emerges: whence does humanity's sense of world arise in the first place? Every human individual lives and acts according to how they conceive the world to be. Every society lives and acts according to a common notion of a shared world. But more than this, our sense of self arises through our sense of relationship to a structured world. There is no human personhood without a sense of a world to which the human person is related. The autonomy of self, the basis of our sense of freedom and our potential, arises only through a sense of a world in which we can meaningfully act. Self and world are the two poles of being that mutually articulate one another. Without a structured world over against which our sense of self stands, our sense of self would be void of any content or form. Similarly, without our sense of self the world would be void of any content or form. No affirmation of being would be possible. For man, as a self-reflective being, there is an exact correlation between self-consciousness and world-consciousness, a correlation based at once upon man's sense of differentiation from the world and his relatedness to the world. Every human act presupposes this relatedness and affirms a quality of self and a quality of world. Every human act, therefore, expresses a concept of self and a concept of world, and every such concept carries a value-judgment of self and world, either affirming being or denying it, or either realizing the potentiality of being or negating it. Any action that affirms both the being of the self and the being of the world deepens the relatedness of man to the world, while any action that negates either the being of the self or the being of the world isolates man from the world and from himself. We do not have to look far to see that alienation from self and from the world is a common feature of our time.

If we look at this more closely we begin to see that humanity's sense of world manifests on three broad levels. The first and most rudimentary level, the level which humanity shares with all other living beings, is the environment, that is, the given natural conditions that sustain man as a biological species. Here humanity interacts with its surroundings simply through the necessity to survive. At this level humanity encounters itself, in common with every animal species, simply through necessity. To this level belong all environmental, biological, and behavioristic concepts of man's existence in the world.

The second level, which is peculiar to man alone, we may broadly call the social level. On this level humanity interacts conceptually and dialogically with the world. It is only at this level that we may properly speak of humanity as participating in a world as distinct from environment. For World is not merely the conditions in which man finds himself placed by nature, it is the structured realm that man conceives as the totality made up of all beings and which he in part creates for himself. For example, he creates a human culture at this level. And so it is at this level that man emerges specifically as a reflective being, as a being that shapes his own conception of being and existence, and who creates his own relationships with his surroundings and so transforms them from environment to world, or from conditions to cosmos.

The third level we may call the sacred. This is where the world is perceived as exemplifying or intimating transcendent Being, or what theology calls the Ground of Being, which is the origin of all beings. This is the level of religion, in which the world becomes the creation in the theological sense of that word.

This third level brings us to man's sense of totality. It is only through this sense of totality that humanity comes upon the mystery of God. However, this sense of totality, the sense that everything is ultimately unified and grounded in a single principle, has a complementary aspect. This is the human capacity of participation, that is, the power in every human individual to fully engage with all that exists about him and to enter into creative relationship with all things. And this capacity of participation, the sense of relatedness to everything, deepens man's power of self-reflection. This circular motion of participation and deepening self-reflection may be formulated into a principle: The greater man's sense of relatedness to the modes of being that stand over against his own being, the greater his self-consciousness. To put that more simply: the more deeply man engages in the totality of reality the more deeply he engages in his own being. Man finds himself through going out of himself.

Now these three senses of Self, of World, and of Totality tell us something else very important about human nature. Man's consciousness of existence extends in three directions: first, outwardly, potentially embracing the universe in its totality; second, inwardly, potentially embracing the self in its totality; and third, vertically, potentially embracing Transcendent Being in its totality. In religious terms, these are the acts of total self-giving, total self-recollection, and total self-transcendence. These three modes of conscious being may be found represented in the life of Christ, who gave himself to the world in total service, who recollected himself in the Father, and who transcended himself through the Passion. But these same qualities may also be found exemplified in Abraham, in the Buddha, or in Krishna.

We are not equating these three directions of consciousness with the three levels of man's experience of being. The three levels are a broad hierarchy of the modes of being, while the three directions of man's consciousness signify the non-hierarchical threefold structure of human consciousness. What is clear, however, is that there is a correspondence between the three levels and the possible extension or depth of the three directions of consciousness. At the level of environment, the reach of consciousness is limited simply to the conditions of existence. Here participation is confined to dependency. But at the level of world, the reach and depth of consciousness is immensely expanded, but yet it is confined finally within the manifest world of created things. Only at the third level, the level of totality, is consciousness open to the infinite or transcendent, or to the Ground of Being Itself in Itself. Traditionally these three levels are spoken of as the physical, the psychological, and the spiritual. They exist both inside and outside man.

Now, I realize that these are large concepts to grasp all at once, so let me briefly summarize them. We said that there is a threefold relationship between Self, World, and God. Through his power of self-reflection we said that mankind was distinguished from all other creatures because he can reflect on his own being and the being of all things. Then we observed that, because of this gift of self-consciousness, man was able to discern three levels of existence: the environment which he shares with all creatures, then the world as an ordered whole in which he participates creatively, and, finally the transcendent ground of Being Itself which is God. We further observed that human consciousness extends in three directions: inwardly through self-consciousness, outwardly through participation, and vertically towards the Creator and origin of all things.

I am sure that you see that this has enormous implications. We can see, for example, that the outward direction of human consciousness opens the way to man's fullest creative participation in the world, as well as to philosophy and art, but also to what has been called nature mysticism in which the divine presence is found in every creature. The inward direction of human consciousness likewise opens the way into the human soul and heart, to psychology and to anthropology. But this also opens the way to what is called soul mysticism, which we find in Buddhism, Hinduism, and Jewish Kabbalah as well as in Christian mystics such as Meister Eckhart. The vertical direction of consciousness opens the way to metaphysics, theology, prayer, to the search for the ineffable, and to the various forms of theistic mysticism which we find in most religions.

But above these specific things, this view of man shows us his potential both as a being within the creation whose creativity can transform the world and participate in its unfolding story—its eschatology or divine history—and as a being with a destiny beyond the world in the heart of God. It shows us that through self-knowledge man can unlock his hidden inner potential, that through full participation in the creation he can discern his deep relationship with all created things, and that through his devotion to the transcendent he can arrive at the divine ground of Being which is the end of all created beings. It shows us that there is no inherent conflict between humanity and the world, nor between human potential and the world of nature. In fact, it shows us that they complement one another. This is because only if man goes out of himself by seeking through all his actions the wholeness and interdependence of everything is he able to arrive at true knowledge of the world and of himself. And this is because, as every religion teaches, the true being of everything actually exists in the mind of God. Let me quote one of the great Christian theologians of the ninth century, John Scottus Eriugena, who until quite recently had been almost forgotten. Speaking of the relationship between God and the creation, he says:

> We should not therefore understand God and creation as two different things, but as one and the same. For creation subsists in God, and God is created in creation in a remarkable and ineffable way, manifesting Himself and, though invisible, making Himself visible, and though incomprehensible, making Himself comprehensible, and although hidden, revealing Himself, and, though unknown, making Himself known;

though lacking form and species, endowing Himself with form and species; though superessential, making Himself essential . . . though creating everything, making Himself created in everything. The Maker of all, made in all, begins to be eternal and, though motionless, moves into everything and becomes all things in all things.

We find in all religious traditions that the knowledge of God and the knowledge of the world belong together. For example, in Judaism the Zohar says:

God made this (terrestrial) world in the image of the world above; thus, all which is found above has its analogy below . . . and everything constitutes a unity.

The idea that all is a unity, and that this unity is to be found through participation in the creation, is to be found in every religious tradition. The creation exists in God, and God exists in creation. But also it is said that everything exists in man, who is the image of God. Thus, again in the Zohar, we read "Man is an image which comprises everything." In the Christian tradition this idea is expressed in the conception of man as the microcosm. Thus Nicholas of Cusa, an important Christian theologian of the fourteenth century, says:

human nature it is that is raised above all the works of God and made a little lower than the angels. It contains in itself the intellectual and sensible natures, and therefore, embracing within itself all things, has very reasonably been called by the ancients the microcosm or world in miniature.

These ancient traditional religious ideas are perhaps finding new expression in some of the advances of modern science, in which the long-held notion that there must be an objective separation between man the observer and the world he studies is now being challenged. It is now being established by modern science that even the most detached scientific investigation involves a mysterious interaction between the observer and the observed, between human consciousness and the world. Leading scientists are suggesting to us that scientific method is gradually being forced to acknowledge that the world is not an inert and purely mechanical object, but is living and permeated with an extraordinary intelligence. For example, Glen Schaefer, a leading mathematical physicist, writes:

> in the last few years, out of the very details of cosmic evolution and the details of the genetic code, and so on, has come the realization, but only to the minds of the few leaders of these fields, that there is an essentially perfect order and perfect design, demanding an intelligence behind evolution. . . . A new paradigm is required. . . . I believe that the new paradigm will come out of the Western tradition.

If there is indeed to be a new paradigm of the cosmos, that will include a new paradigm of man and of human nature, and a new understanding of the central place of humanity in the universe. The Christian evolutionist Teilhard de Chardin, whose writings were published after his death during the sixties, says that it is through man that the universe is coming to know itself, because humanity is the conscious element in the universe. Human destiny and the spiritual destiny of the universe are bound together.

Let me draw to a close by indicating some of the spiritual and the ecological implications of the ideas we have looked at.

As I suggested earlier, the ecological crisis of the modern world reflects modern man's limited worldview and his limited anthropology. It reflects in an obvious physical sense the disjunction that has arisen between man and the creation. Humanity's world has become, in Hamlet's words, "an unweeded garden." But this unweeded garden is not so much the environment, but the psychological world of community and culture, and the ways in which humanity sees itself as participating in the world. The root of this disjunction lies, I would like to suggest, in the spiritual estrangement of man from the very ground of his own being. The real problem for modern man is, in fact, the most ancient problem of all: the problem of inner alienation. This is not an ethical problem, even though it has ethical implications. It cannot be solved by the imposition of laws, by declarations of human rights or duties, or by claims of the rights of the biosphere, well-intentioned as such moves may be. At a more fundamental level what is needed is a fresh understanding of the tripartite relation between God, Man, and Creation which fully accords with God's will, which fully embraces the totality of all beings and the universe, and which opens up to man the depth of his own being and the possibility of realizing his full potential as a physical, psychological, and spiritual being. What is remarkable about the religious vision of nature we have briefly glanced at is that it affirms all these criteria simultaneously and at a stroke. Creation is God's disclosure of Himself, and man is the one being in whom the totality of all being is contained. That is to say, man is that being who may comprehend the structure of all being through his unfettered openness to the world, his openness to self, and his openness to the transcendent.

The sacred view of nature is informed by a critique of total participation. This, I would like to suggest, is the genuinely religious or sacred view of man living in the world. Participation is transformative of both humanity and the world. Only through participation does man come to know experientially the mysterious nature of the world, and only through participation does he come to know the mystery of himself. Man is not the conqueror of the world, as the nineteenth century conceived him, nor is the world the conqueror of man, as some ecologists would tell us. Such a perspective reduces the world to a mere thing. Nothing could be further from any religious cosmology. Rather, the world and humanity are modes of being in mutual dialogue with one another, mutually disclosing one another. Through this interaction being becomes conscious of itself at all its levels, in differentiation and in unity. That is to say, the greater man's engagement in the world, the more he discovers and becomes himself. And the more he becomes himself the closer he comes to God. That seems to be the mystery that evolutionary theory is gradually indicating to us. Humanity's sense of cosmos, its sense of structured totality, is not a redundant remnant from a previously limited worldview, but rather a primary religious intuition that at once moves mankind towards participation in totality and reminds us of the provisionality or inadequacy of anything less than totality. It is in proportion to this totality that every problem of man's life in the world has its place and its resolution. It is only in terms of this larger vision of humanity and the universe that we can find a truly constructive perspective from which to view our present ecological crisis. But the ecological problems we face, as I suggested at the beginning, are only the physical reflection of modern man's inner fragmentation. We have only to look at the way society in every nation is splitting up into hundreds of separate so-called special interest groups to see this fragmentation. We have only to see how many people are searching for a sense of identity to see how alienated modern man is becoming from himself, and from community, or from the universe. These are psychological manifestations. But some of the religions also are getting drawn into this wave of fragmentation, as we see in so many new cults and in growing fundamentalism. At the same time, and on the positive side, a growing number of people—scientists, artists, scholars, philosophers, and religious people generally—are feeling their way towards a more integral and harmonious vision of the world and of humanity, a vision that does not de-nature the world or de-humanize mankind, a vision that rediscovers, perhaps in a greater way than ever before, the essential sacredness of all that exists, a vision that perceives the entire cosmos as a spiritual event in which God is disclosing Himself and making Himself known through all things.

The Information War

HAKIM BEY

HUMANITY has always invested heavily in any scheme that offers escape from the body. And why not? Material reality is such a mess. Some of the earliest "religious" artifacts, such as Neanderthal ochre burials, already suggest a belief in immortality. All modern (i.e. post-Paleolithic) religions contain the "Gnostic trace" of distrust or even outright hostility to the body and the "created" world. Contemporary "primitive" tribes and even peasant-pagans have a concept of immortality and of going-outside-the-body (*ek-stasis*) without necessarily exhibiting any excessive body-hatred. The Gnostic Trace accumulates very gradually, like mercury poisoning, until eventually it turns pathological. Gnostic dualism exemplifies the extreme position of this disgust by shifting all value from body to "spirit." This idea characterizes what we call "civilization." A similar trajectory can be traced through the phenomenon of "war." Hunter/gatherers practiced— and still practice, as amongst the Yanomamo—a kind of ritualized brawl (think of the Plains Indian custom of "counting coup"). "Real" war is a continuation of religion and economics (i.e. politics) by other means, and thus only begins historically with the priestly invention of "scarcity" in the Neolithic, and the emergence of a "warrior caste." (I categorically reject the theory that "war" is a prolongation of "hunting.") World War II seems to have been the last "real" war. Hyperreal war began in Vietnam, with the involvement of television, and reached full obscene revelation in the "Gulf War" of 1991. Hyperreal war is no longer "economic," no longer "the health of the state." The Ritual Brawl is voluntary and hon-hierarchic (war chiefs are always temporary); real war is compulsory and hierarchic; hyperreal war is imagistic and psychologically interiorized ("Pure War"). In the first the body is risked; in the second, the body is sacrificed; in the third, the body has disappeared. (See P. Clastres on war, in *Archaeology of Violence*.) Modern science also incorporates an anti-materialist bias, the dialectical outcome of its war against Religion—it has in some sense become Religion. Science as knowledge of material reality paradoxically decomposes the materiality of the real. Science has always been a species of priestcraft, a branch of cosmology; and an ideology, a justification of "the way things are." The deconstruction of the "real" in post-classical physics mirrors the vacuum of irreality which constitutes "the state." Once the image of Heaven on Earth, the state now consists of no more than the management of images. It is no longer a "force" but a disembodied patterning of information. But just as Babylonian cosmology justified Babylonian power, so too does the "finality" of modern science serve the ends of the Terminal State, the post-nuclear state, the "information state." Or so the New Paradigm would have it. And "everyone" accepts the axiomatic premises of the new paradigm. The new paradigm is very spiritual.

Even the New Age with its gnostic tendencies embraces the New Science and its increasing etherealization as a source of proof-texts for its spiritualist worldview. Meditation and cybernetics go hand in hand. Of course the "information state" somehow requires the support of a police force and prison system that would have stunned Nebuchadnezzar and reduced all the priests of Moloch to paroxysms of awe. And "modern science" still can't weasel out of its complicity in the very-nearly-successful "conquest of Nature," civilization's greatest triumph over the body.

But who cares? It's all "relative," isn't it? I guess we'll just have to "evolve" beyond the body. Maybe we can do it in a "quantum leap." Meanwhile the excessive mediation of the Social, which is carried out through the machinery of the Media, increases the intensity of our alienation from the body by fixating the flow of attention on information rather than direct experience. In this sense the Media serves a religious or priestly role, appearing to offer us a way out of the body by re-defining spirit as information. The essence of information is the

Image, the sacral and iconic data-complex which usurps the primacy of the "material bodily principle" as the vehicle of incarnation, replacing it with a fleshless ecstasis beyond corruption. Consciousness becomes something which can be "downloaded," excised from the matrix of animality and immortalized as information. No longer "ghost-in-the-machine," but machine-as-ghost, machine as Holy Ghost, ultimate mediator, which will translate us from our mayfly-corpses to a pleroma of Light. Virtual Reality as CyberGnosis. Jack in, leave Mother Earth behind forever. All science proposes a paradigmatic universalism—as in science, so in the social. Classical physics played midwife to Capitalism, Communism, Fascism, and other Modern ideologies.

Post-classical science also proposes a set of ideas meant to be applied to the social: Relativity, Quantum "unreality," cybernetics, information theory, etc. With some exceptions, the post-classical tendency is towards ever greater etherealization. Some proponents of Black Hole theory, for example, talk like pure Pauline theologians, while some of the information theorists are beginning to sound like virtual Manichaeans.[1] On the level of the social these paradigms give rise to a rhetoric of bodylessness quite worthy of a third-century desert monk or a seventeenth-century New England Puritan—but expressed in a language of post-Industrial post-Modern feel-good consumer frenzy. Our every conversation is infected with certain paradigmatic assumptions which are really no more than bald assertions, but which we take for the very fabric or urgrund of Reality itself. For instance, since we now assume that computers represent a real step toward "artificial intelligence," we also assume that buying a computer makes us more intelligent. In my own field I've met dozens of writers who sincerely believe that owning a PC has made them better (not "more efficient," but better) writers. This is amusing—but the same feeling about computers when applied to a trillion dollar military budget, churns out Star Wars, killer robots, etc. (See Manuel de Landa's *War in the Age of Intelligent Machines* on AI in modern weaponry). An important part of this rhetoric involves the concept of an "information economy."

The post-Industrial world is now thought to be giving birth to this new economy. One of the clearest examples of the concept can be found in a recent book by a man who is a Libertarian, the Bishop of a Gnostic Dualist Church in California, and a learned and respected writer for *Gnosis* magazine:

> The industry of the past phase of civilization (sometimes called "low technology") was big industry, and bigness always implies oppressiveness. The new high technology, however, is not big in the same way. While the old technology produced and distributed material resources, the new technology produces and disseminates information. The resources marketed in high technology are less about matter and more about mind. Under the impact of high technology, the world is moving increasingly from a physical economy into what might be called a "metaphysical economy." We are in the process of recognizing that consciousness rather than raw materials or physical resources constitutes wealth.[2]

Modern neo-Gnosticism usually plays down the old Manichaean attack on the body for a gentler greener rhetoric. Bishop Hoeller, for instance, stresses the importance of ecology and environment (because we don't want to "foul our nest," the Earth)—but in his chapter on Native American spirituality he implies that a cult of the Earth is clearly inferior to the pure Gnostic spirit of bodylessness:

> But we must not forget that the nest is not the same as the bird. The exoteric and esoteric traditions declare that earth is not the only home for human beings, that we did not grow like weeds from the soil. While our bodies indeed may have originated on this earth, our inner essence did not. To think otherwise puts us outside of all of the known spiritual traditions and separates us from the wisdom of the seers and sages of every age. Though wise in their own ways, Native Americans have small connection with this rich spiritual heritage.[3]

In such terms (the body = the "savage"), the Bishop's hatred and

disdain for the flesh illuminate every page of his book. In his enthusiasm for a truly religious economy, he forgets that one cannot eat
"information." "Real wealth" can never become immaterial until
humanity achieves the final etherealization of downloaded consciousness. Information in the form of culture can be called wealth meta-
phorically because it is useful and desirable—but it can never be wealth
in precisely the same basic way that oysters and cream, or wheat and
water, appear as wealth in themselves. Information is always only
information about some thing. Like money, information is not the
thing itself. Over time we can come to think of money as wealth—as
in a delightful Taoist ritual which refers to "Water and Money" as the
two most vital principles in the universe—but in truth this is sloppy
abstract thinking. It has allowed its focus of attention to wander from
the bun to the penny which symbolizes the bun.[4] In effect we've had
an "information economy" ever since we invented money. But we still
haven't learned to digest copper. The Aesopian crudity of these
truisms embarrasses me, but I must perforce play the stupid lazy yokel
plowing a crooked furrow when all the straight thinkers around me
appear to be hallucinating.

Americans and other "First World" types seem particularly susceptible to the rhetoric of a "metaphysical economy" because we can no
longer see—or feel or smell—around us very much evidence of a
physical world. Our architecture has become symbolic, we have
enclosed ourselves in the manifestations of abstract thought (cars,
apartments, offices, schools), we work at "service" or information-
related jobs, helping in our little way to move disembodied symbols of
wealth around an abstract grid of Capital, and we spend our leisure
largely engrossed in Media rather than in direct experience of material
reality. The material world for us has come to symbolize catastrophe,
as in our amazingly hysterical reaction to storms and hurricanes (proof
that we've failed to "conquer Nature" entirely), or our neo-Puritan
fear of sexual otherness, or our taste for bland and denatured (almost
abstract) food. And yet, this "First World" economy is not self-
sufficient. It depends for its position (top of the pyramid) on a vast

substructure of old-fashioned material production. Mexican farm-workers grow and package all that "natural" food for us so we can devote our time to stocks, insurance, law, computers, video games. Peons in Taiwan make silicon chips for our PCs. Towel-heads in the Middle East suffer and die for our sins. Life? Oh, our servants do that for us. We have no life, only "lifestyle"—an abstraction of life, based on the sacred symbolism of the Commodity, mediated by the priest-hood of the stars, those "larger than life" abstractions who rule our values and people our dreams—the mediarchetypes; or perhaps mediarchs would be a better term. Of course this Baudrillardian dystopia doesn't really exist—yet.[5] It's surprising, however, to note how many social radicals consider it a desirable goal, at least as long as it's called the "Information Revolution" or something equally inspir-ing. Leftists talk about seizing the means of information-production from the data-monopolists.[6] In truth, information is everywhere—even atom bombs can be constructed on plans available in public libraries. As Noam Chomsky points out, one can always access information—provided one has a private income and a fanaticism bordering on insanity. Universities and "think tanks" make pathetic attempts to monopolize information—they too are dazzled by the notion of an information economy—but their conspiracies are laugh-able. Information may not always be "free," but there's a great deal more of it available than any one person could ever possibly use. Books on every conceivable subject can actually still be found through inter-library loan.[7] Meanwhile someone still has to grow pears and cobble shoes. Or, even if these "industries" can be completely mechanized, someone still has to eat pears and wear shoes. The body is still the basis of wealth. The idea of Images as wealth is a "spectacular delusion." Even a radical critique of "information" can still give rise to an over-valuation of abstraction and data. In a pro-situationist 'zine from England called *NO*, the following message was scrawled messily across the back cover of a recent issue:

As you read these words, the Information Age explodes . . . inside and around you—with the Misinformation Missiles and Propaganda bombs of outright Information Warfare.

Traditionally, war has been fought for territory/economic gain. Information Wars are fought for the acquisition of territory indigenous to the Information Age, i.e. the human mind itself . . . In particular, it is the faculty of the imagination that is under the direct threat of extinction from the onslaughts of multi-media overload . . . DANGER—YOUR IMAGINATION MAY NOT BE YOUR OWN . . . As a culture sophisticates, it deepens its reliance on its images, icons, and symbols as a way of defining itself and communicating with other cultures. As the accumulating mix of a culture's images floats around in its collective psyche, certain isomorphic icons coalesce to produce and to project an "illusion" of reality. Fads, fashions, artistic trends. U KNOW THE SCORE. "I can take their images for reality because I believe in the reality of their images (their image of reality)." WHOEVER CONTROLS THE METAPHOR GOVERNS THE MIND. The conditions of total saturation are slowly being realized—a creeping paralysis—from the trivialisation of special/technical knowledge to the specialization of trivia. The INFORMATION WAR is a war we cannot afford to lose. The result is unimaginable.[8]

I find myself very much in sympathy with the author's critique of media here, yet I also feel that a demonization of "information" has been proposed which consists of nothing more than the mirror-image of information-as-salvation. Again, Baudrillard's vision of the Commtech Universe is evoked, but this time as Hell rather than as the Gnostic Hereafter. Bishop Hoeller wants everybody jacked-in and downloaded—the anonymous post-situationist ranter wants you to smash your telly—but both of them believe in the mystic power of information. One proposes the pax technologica, the other declares "war." Both exude a kind of Manichaean view of Good and Evil, but can't agree on which is which. The critical theorist swims in a sea of facts. We like to imagine it also as our *maquis*, with ourselves as the "guerilla ontologists" of its datascape. Since the nineteenth century the ever-mutating "social sciences" have unearthed a vast hoard of information on everything from shamanism to semiotics. Each "discovery" feeds back into "social science" and changes it. We drift. We fish for poetic facts, data which will intensify and mutate our experience of the real. We invent new hybrid "sciences" as tools for this process: ethnopharmacology, ethnohistory, cognitive studies, history of ideas, subjective anthropology (anthropological poetics or ethno-poetics), "dada epistemology," etc. We look on all this knowledge not as "good" in itself, but valuable only inasmuch as it helps us to seize or to construct our own happiness. In this sense we do know of "information as wealth"; nevertheless we continue to desire wealth itself and not merely its abstract representation as information. At the same time we also know of "information as war";[9] nevertheless, we have not decided to embrace ignorance just because "facts" can be used like a poison gas. Ignorance is not even an adequate defense, much less a useful weapon in this war. We attempt neither to fetishize nor demonize "information." Instead we try to establish a set of values by which information can be measured and assessed. Our standard in this process can only be the body. According to certain mystics, spirit and body are "one." Certainly spirit has lost its ontological solidity (since Nietzsche, anyway), while body's claim to "reality" has been undermined by modern science to the point of vanishing in a cloud of "pure energy." So why not assume that spirit and body are one, after all, and that they are twin (or dyadic) aspects of the same underlying and inexpressible real? No body without spirit, no spirit without body. The Gnostic Dualists are wrong, as are the vulgar "dialectical materialists." Body and spirit together make life. If either pole is missing, the result is death. This constitutes a fairly simple set of values, assuming we prefer life to death. Obviously I'm avoiding any strict definitions of either body or spirit. I'm speaking of "empirical" everyday experiences. We experience "spirit" when we dream or create; we experience "body" when we eat or shit (or maybe vice versa); we experience both at once when we make love. I'm not proposing metaphysical categories here. We're still drifting and these are ad hoc points of reference, nothing more. We needn't be mystics to propose this version of "one reality."

We need only point out that no other reality has yet appeared within the context of our knowable experience. For all practical purposes, the "world" is "one."[10] Historically, however, the "body" half of this unity has always received the insults, bad press, scriptural condemnation, and economic persecution of the "spirit"-half. The self-appointed representatives of the spirit have called almost all the tunes in known history, leaving the body only a pre-history of primitive disappearance, and a few spasms of failed insurrectionary futility.

Spirit has ruled—hence we scarcely even know how to speak the language of the body. When we use the word "information," we reify it, because we have always reified abstractions—ever since God appeared as a burning bush. (Information as the catastrophic decorporealization of "brute" matter.) We would now like to propose the identification of self with body. We're not denying that "the body is also spirit," but we wish to restore some balance to the historical equation. We calculate all body-hatred and world-slander as our "evil." We insist on the revival (and mutation) of "pagan" values concerning the relation of body and spirit. We fail to feel any great enthusiasm for the "information economy" because we see it as yet another mask for body-hatred. We can't quite believe in the "information war," since it also hypostatizes information but labels it "evil." In this sense, "information" would appear to be neutral. But we also distrust this third position as a lukewarm cop-out and a failure of theoretical vision. Every "fact" takes different meanings as we run it through our dialectical prism[11] and study its gleam and shadows. The "fact" is never inert or "neutral," but it can be both "good" and "evil" (or beyond them) in countless variations and combinations. We, finally, are the artists of this immeasurable discourse. We create values. We do this because we are alive. Information is as big a "mess" as the material world it reflects and transforms. We embrace the mess, all of it. It's all life. But within the vast chaos of the alive, certain information and certain material things begin to coalesce into a poetics or a way-of-knowing or a way-of-acting. We can draw certain pro tem "conclusions," as long as we don't plaster them over and set them up on altars. Neither "information" nor indeed any one "fact" constitutes a thing-in-itself. The very word "information" implies an ideology, or rather a paradigm, rooted in unconscious fear of the "silence" of matter and of the universe. "Information" is a substitute for certainty, a left over fetish of dogmatics, a super-stitio, a spook. "Poetic facts" are not assimilable to the doctrine of "information." "Knowledge is freedom" is true only when freedom is understood as a psycho-kinetic skill. "Information" is a chaos; knowledge is the spontaneous ordering of that chaos; freedom is the surfing of the wave of that spontaneity. These tentative conclusions constitute the shifting and marshy ground of our "theory."

Notes

1. The new "life" sciences offer some dialectical opposition here, or could do so if they worked through certain paradigms. Chaos theory might have been able to deal with the material world in positive ways, as might Gaia theory, morphogenetic theory, and various other "soft" and "neo-hermetic" disciplines. Elsewhere I've attempted to incorporate these philosophical implications into a "festal" synthesis. The point is not to abandon all thought about the material world, but to realize that all science has philosophical and political implications, and that science is a way of thinking, not a dogmatic structure of incontrovertible Truth. Of course quantum, relativity, and information theory are all "true" in some way and can be given a positive interpretation. I've already done that in several essays. Now I want to explore the negative aspects.

2. Stephan A. Hoeller, *Freedom: Alchemy for a Voluntary Society* (Wheaton: Quest, 1992), 229–30.

3. Hoeller, *Freedom*, 164.

4. Like Pavlov's dogs salivating at the dinner bell rather than the dinner— a perfect illustration of what I mean by "abstraction."

5. Although some might say that it already "virtually" exists. I just heard from a friend in California of a new scheme for "universal prisons"— offenders will be allowed to live at home and go to work but will be electronically monitored at all times, like Winston Smith in *1984*. The universal panopticon now potentially coincides one-to-one with the whole of reality; life and work will take the place of outdated physical incarceration— the Prison Society will merge with "electronic democracy" to form a Surveillance State or information totality, with all time and space compacted beneath the unsleeping gaze of RoboCop. On the level of pure tech, at least, it would seem that we have at last arrived at "the future." "Honest citizens" of course will have nothing to fear; hence terror will reign unchallenged and Order will triumph like the Universal Ice. Our only hope may lie in the "chaotic perturbation" of massively-linked computers, and in the venal stupidity or boredom of those who program and monitor the system.

6. I will always remember with pleasure being addressed, by a Bulgarian delegate to a conference I once attended, as a "fellow worker in philosophy." Perhaps the capitalist version would be "entrepreneur in philosophy," as if one bought ideas like apples at roadside stands.

7. Of course information may sometimes be "occult," as in Conspiracy

Theory. Information may be "disinformation." Spies and propagandists make up a kind of shadow "information economy," to be sure. Hackers who believe in "freedom of information" have my sympathy, especially since they've been picked as the latest enemies of the Spectacular State, and subjected to its spasms of control-by-terror. But have hackers yet "liberated" a single bit of information useful in our struggle? Their impotence, and their fascination with Imagery, make them ideal victims of the "Information State," which itself is based on pure simulation. One needn't steal data from the post-military-industrial complex to know, in general, what it's up to. We understand enough to form our critique. More information by itself will never take the place of the actions we have failed to carry out; data by itself will never reach critical mass. Despite my loving debt to thinkers like Robert Anton Wilson and Timothy Leary, I cannot agree with their optimistic analysis of the cognitive function of information technology. It is not the neural system alone which will achieve autonomy, but the entire body.

8. Issue 6, "Nothing is True," Box 175, Liverpool L69 8DX, U.K.

9. Indeed, the whole "poetic terrorism" project has been proposed only as a strategy in this very war.

10. "The 'World' is 'one'" can be and has been used to justify a totality, a metaphysical ordering of "reality" with a "center" or "apex": one God, one King, etc., etc. This is the monism of orthodoxy, which naturally opposes Dualism and its other source of power ("evil")—orthodoxy also presupposes that the One occupies a higher ontological position than the Many, that transcendence takes precedence over immanence. What I call radical (or heretical) monism demands unity of One and Many on the level of immanence; hence it is seen by Orthodoxy as a turning-upside-down or saturnalia which proposes that every "one" is equally "divine." Radical monism is "on the side of" the Many—which explains why it seems to lie at the heart of pagan polytheism and shamanism, as well as extreme forms of monotheism such as Ismailism or Ranterism, based on "inner light" teachings. "All is one," therefore, can be spoken by any kind of monist or anti-dualist and can mean many different things.

11. A proposal: the new theory of Taoist dialectics. Think of the yin/yang disk, with a spot of black in the white lozenge, and vice versa—separated not by a straight line but an S-curve. Amiri Baraka says that dialectics is just "separating out the good from the bad"—but the Taoist is "beyond good and evil." The dialectic is supple, but the Taoist dialectic is downright sinuous.

For example, making use of the Taoist dialectic, we can reevaluate Gnosis once again. True, it presents a negative view of the body and of becoming. But it is also true that it has played the role of the eternal rebel against all orthodoxy, and this makes it interesting. In its libertine and revolutionary manifestations the Gnosis possesses many secrets, some of which are actually worth knowing. The organizational forms of Gnosis—the crackpot cult, the secret society—seem pregnant with possibilities for the TAZ/Immediatist project. Of course, as I've pointed out elsewhere, not all gnosis is Dualistic. There also exists a monist gnostic tradition, which sometimes borrows heavily from Dualism and is often confused with it. Monist gnosis is anti-eschatological, using religious language to describe this world, not Heaven or the Gnostic Pleroma. Shamanism, certain "crazy" forms of Taoism and Tantra and Zen, heterodox Sufism and Ismailism, Christian antinomians such as the Ranters, etc., share a conviction of the holiness of the "inner spirit," and of the actually real, the "world." These are our "spiritual ancestors."

Philosophical Counseling

KATHLEEN DAMIANI

PHILOSOPHICAL COUNSELING is a term applied to a wide variety of activities which involve dialogue and interaction between two or more people. It focuses on the practice or application of philosophical methods to examine and unravel—not necessarily solve—the concrete problems facing individuals or groups. Philosophical counselors desire to bring philosophy—the process, that is, not the theories—to bear upon problems and life situations such as mid-life crises, questions of meaning or about death, family problems, or occupational dissatisfaction. The subject matter of philosophical counseling is "the philosophical questions posed by life. Thus, philosophical counseling seeks to bring philosophy closer to everyday life. It holds that philosophical ideas are not disconnected from the individual's concrete living moment, as they are commonly treated in academic philosophy."[1]

The American Society for Philosophy, Counseling, and Psychotherapy (ASPCP), was founded in 1992 as an affiliate of the American Philosophical Association. Dr. Paul Sharkey from the University of Southern Mississippi and Dr. Elliot Cohen from Indian River College in Florida co-founded the ASPCP. According to Sharkey, the ASPCP "promotes the philosophical examination of the theory and practice of counseling and psychotherapy and of philosophy as a private practice profession. It hosts annual program sessions at each of the divisional meetings of the American Philosophical Association. The

This paper was given at a panel on "The World Soul and the Soul of the World: Philosophy, Cosmos, and Culture," organized by the *Alexandria* journal, at the fifteenth annual conference on Ancient and Medieval Philosophy and Social Thought, State University of New York at Binghamton, October 25–27, 1996.

ASPCP represents the internationally growing trend to promote philosophy as an independent practice profession. To this end, it has a code of ethical practice and standards for the certification of professional practitioners." Sharkey contends that "for most of this country's history, philosophy has been confined primarily to academies of higher learning where its relevance to the everyday lives and concerns of ordinary people has largely been either ignored, overlooked, or unappreciated. The ASPCP is dedicated to promoting increased awareness of philosophy's importance to the concerns and issues affecting our everyday personal and professional lives."[2]

The preamble in the "Standards of Ethical Practice" developed by the ASPCP defines the role of the philosophical counselor and articulates the context of the relationship between counselor and client:

> A philosophical practitioner is a trained professional in the ancient calling of philosophy. As philosopher, a philosophical practitioner helps clients to clarify, articulate, explore, and comprehend philosophical aspects of their belief systems or "worldviews." These include epistemological, metaphysical, axiological, and logical issues. Clients may consult philosophical practitioners for help in exploring philosophical problems related to such matters as mid-life crises, career changes, stress, emotions, assertiveness, physical illness, death and dying, aging, meaning of life, and morality. In addition to individuals, clients may also include hospitals, businesses, and other institutions that seek the guidance of a philosopher. The practice of providing philosophical assistance to others is at least as ancient as Socrates who, in the fifth century B.C., made such a practice of philosophy.
>
> While individual philosophical practitioners may differ in method and theoretical orientation, for example, analytic or existential-phenomenological, they facilitate such activities as: (1) the examination of clients' arguments and justifications; (2) the clarification, analysis, and definition of important terms and concepts; (3) the exposure and examination of underlying assumptions and logical implications; (4) the exposure of conflicts and inconsistencies; (5) the exploration of traditional

philosophical theories and their significance for client issues; and (6) all other related activities that have historically been identified as philosophical.

Although several other helping professions have also incorporated some of the aforementioned ancient, philosophical activities into their therapeutic practices, they should not thereby be confused with the private practice of philosophy as defined by the performance of distinctively philosophical activities for which philosophical practitioners have uniquely been educated and trained.[3]

The Roots of Philosophical Counseling in Ancient Times

A common complaint about philosophy is that it is irrelevant and abstract, far removed from the everyday affairs and problems that concern the average person. (There is a cartoon in which a character says "My brother is a philosopher." The other character says, "My brother doesn't do anything, either.") Although philosophers deal with abstract and subtle issues that may bear little significance for everyday life, there is a rich tradition of thought that has directly addressed the question, "How should we live?"

The desire to live wisely—to apply thinking and self-reflection to character, fate, and the problems of life—is rooted deep in the earliest teachings of sages to students, found in the wisdom traditions in the ancient Near East. Long before the word *philosopher*—lover of wisdom—was coined by Pythagoras, the cult of wisdom flourished in the ancient Near East. Wisdom, Sophia, has been interpreted as the World Soul by philosophers and visionaries throughout the Western world. Feminine wisdom figures—such as Maat in Egypt, Rita (Rta) in India, Tao (Tien) in China, a deified feminine Wisdom figure in Mesopotamia and Syria, and Themis in early Greece—personify world order, justice, and law. These figures were not mother or fertility goddesses. Although deified, they were not related to or worshipped like other deities. For instance, you would not worship *maat*; rather, you would "keep" *maat*. Teachings from Egyptian sages to their sons or to students resemble a kind of philosophically-oriented counsel. The object of these Egyptian instructions (*sboyet*)—

which span over twenty-five centuries, from the Fifth Dynasty in the third millenium B.C.E. to the Ptolemaic period—was to teach the student to conform to *maat*, a word usually translated as "justice" or "order." Maat, like Sophia as world soul, was created before the world "at the beginning of time" and it was through her that creation came about.[4] The ideal behavior of one who harmonizes with *maat* is patience, calm, and self-control. Passion, hot-headedness, and lack of discipline lead to ruin. The teachings admonish the student to "hear" or obey—to not only memorize these rules but to put them in practice. Wisdom here is not mystical or abstract but of the utmost practical concern: attention to character and self-discipline must be applied to daily life in order to mold the character to adjust to this natural order. Successful application lessened the blows of fate and led to happiness and well-being.

In Mesopotamia, a collection of Sumerian sayings was discovered, called the "Instructions of Suruppak"—believed to be older than 2,500 years before the Common Era. Similar in style is the "Counsels of Wisdom" which teaches proper speech and the avoidance of bad companions. "The Dialogue about Human Misery" (also called "The Babylonian Theodicy") sounds much like a modern day discussion that might arise in a philosophical counseling session. It records a conversation between a suffering man and his sympathetic friend. The man asks questions such as: Why does crime pay? Why should the firstborn be favored ahead of later children? Why do the gods not help orphans?[5]

In the early history of Western philosophy, various schools developed theories, techniques, and visions of cosmic order that addressed the problem of life and humanity's relation to the world, establishing communities to manifest their ideals in practical life. Pythagoreans sought to actualize a life of integrity and harmony with the cosmos through purification techniques, mathematics, music, and harmony. Pythagorean liberation from the "hard and deeply-grievous circle" of incarnations "is obtained not through religious rite, but through philosophy, the contemplation of first principles. Hence, *philosophia* is a form of purification, a way to immortality." Unlike the Eleusinian and Orphic Mysteries based on revelation or a religious way of life, "Pythagoras offered a way of life based on philosophy."[6]

The Cynic school of philosophy in fifth and fourth century B.C.E. Greece advocated self-sufficiency, independence, and abstinence from pleasures and material possessions. The Cyrenaic school (fourth century B.C.E.) taught that material pleasures lead to happiness. The Stoics in fourth-century Greece and later in Rome before the rise of Christianity, taught that the cosmos follows a harmonious course of events governed by fate. The proper behavior for a person is to be in harmony with the cosmos and with its natural course of events, exercise self-control, and accept every mishap peacefully, indifferently, or "stoically." The philosophy of the Epicurean school argued that a life of pleasure, free of anxiety, passion, and sex was the best life.[7]

Today, philosophical counselors do not offer theories, purification techniques, or the adoption of certain lifestyles, but rather encourage the use of thinking skills to arrive at understanding—or, acceptance of uncertainty and the capacity to relate to the unknown. An environment of safety is created in which the client can ask the questions forbidden or ridiculed by society. The method employed by Socrates is generally held to be worthwhile, a standard of sorts toward which the modern philosophical counselor aims. In the book *Essays on Philosophical Counseling*, the midwife analogy employed by Socrates and described in Plato's *Theaetetus* (150C–151B) is used as an exemplary technique for modern philosophical counselors to assist the client in the exploration of assumptions and care of the soul:

> The criticism that's often made of me—that it's lack of wisdom that makes me ask others questions, but say nothing positive myself—is perfectly true. Why do I behave like this? Because the god compels me to attend to the labours of others, but prohibits me from having any offspring myself. I myself, therefore, am quite devoid of wisdom; my mind has never produced any idea that could be called clever. But as for those who associate with me—well, although at first some of them give the impression of being pretty stupid, yet later, as the association

continues, all of those to whom the god vouchsafes it improve marvelously, as is evident to themselves as well as to others. And they make this progress, clearly, not because they ever learn anything from me; the many fine ideas and offspring that they produce come from within themselves. But the god and I are responsible for the delivery... There's another experience which those who associate with me have in common with pregnant women: they suffer labour-pains. In fact, they are racked night and day with a far greater distress than women undergo; and the arousal and relief of this pain is the province of my expertise (Waterfield translation).[8]

Philosophical Counseling Today

The modern form of philosophical counseling was first introduced by the German philosopher Gerd B. Achenbach, who opened his practice in Bergisch Gladbach, near Cologne, in 1981. The following year, he founded the German Association for Philosophical Practice (*Gesellschaft fur Philosophische Praxis*), consisting of ten members. In 1987, the first edition of *Agora*—the association's journal—appeared, publishing articles and discussions, mainly in German. The association now consists of about 125 members from around the world, including fifteen practicing philosophical counselors.

The new vision of philosophy quickly spread to Holland. In 1984, students at the University of Amsterdam, interested in applying philosophy to life, started a working group. Influenced by Achenbach's writings, they trained themselves in philosophical counseling, examining and discussing theory, methods, and techniques. Ad Hoogendijk, a member of the original group, opened the first philosophical practice in Holland in 1987. Others soon followed him and received much attention from the media. In the same year the group started to publish the journal *Filosofische Praktijk*. *Hotel de Filosoof* (The Philosopher Hotel) was opened in Amsterdam the next year. Ida Jongsma, also a member of the original group, is a co-owner of the hotel, which hosts many of the group's activities. In 1989, the Dutch Association for Philosophical Practice was founded. It provides introductory courses for beginning philosophical counselors, training workshops, and lectures. It now numbers more than 130 members, more than twenty of whom are active practitioners.

In recent years, groups of practitioners have formed in other countries besides the ASPCP in the United States. At the University of Calgary, Canada, Petra von Morstein, a practicing philosophical counselor, has organized a working group on the topic. In Paris, France, an organization called *Le Cabinet de Philosophie*, which organizes Sunday discussions of practical philosophy at a local cafe and publishes a newsletter titled *Philos*, is involved in counseling. In Israel, the Organization for the Advancement of Philosophical Counseling was founded recently. In South Africa, Steven Segal and Barbara Norman have formed The Institute for the Art of Thinking, designed to help individuals to develop philosophical self-examination.

In July of 1994, the First International Conference on Philosophical Counseling took place at the University of British Columbia, with more than one hundred in attendance from eight countries. University courses on philosophical counseling and related topics can already be found in several countries.[9]

Three Practitioners' Interpretations of Philosophical Counseling

According to the current president of the ASPCP, Maria daVenza Tillmanns, philosophical counseling starts from experience, not theory. It is

> the art of hearing through experience. Philosophical counselors listen to the "truth" of the client directly through the client's own frame of reference—not mediated by theories or conceptual analyses. Thus, the client's own worldview, or "theory of life," serves as the guideline for both philosopher and client in their dialogue. In articulating and restructuring the frame of reference, problems . . . often dissolve. . . . Philosophers realize that we cannot merely "philosophize" (rationalize) difficult situations away; rather, we need to understand that our problems contain real opportunities when attended to thoughtfully. This is what philosophical counselors are for: they assist people in finding ways to

wrestle with their "problems" as well as the frame of reference which creates and perceives them as such. In this way, the client can move on with her life, without feeling dominated by forces she cannot handle, even when such forces are beyond her control.

In philosophical counseling, it is important that the client come to terms with her problems on her own terms (not on psychological, religious, or other imported theoretical terms). Problems are considered within the person's own theoretical structure; thus, the client can take direct responsibility for her issues and feel true to herself in the process. The philosopher assists in establishing agreeable terms for the mutual acceptance of problems and mindsets.

Petra von Morstein, mentioned earlier, claims that "philosophy must be practical and experimental. If the practice of philosophy rests on any assumptions, it must be this: that lived experience is the origin and foundation of philosophy. Thus, the practice of philosophy requires both full and unprejudiced attention to lived experience and commitment to philosophical scholarship. Given the immediacy of intensely lived experiences and thus their indeterminateness, appropriate methods of understanding have to be generated on their basis: there can be no independent criteria for the appropriateness of such methods. Thus, there can be no explanation fully to represent such experience."[10]

Barbara Norman, co-founder with Steven Segal of The Institute for the Art of Thinking in South Africa, uses the term "ecological thinking" to describe her interpretation of philosophical counseling. She sees philosophical counseling as "a means towards releasing persons from the captivity of immovable ways of understanding the world in which we live." Ecological thinking is an attitude that seeks to develop the arts of relationship and interpretation. It is a way of being in the world which is ready and willing to continually interpret and reinterpret cultural and personal beliefs, values, and attitudes through which we relate to the world. Ecological thinking recognizes the importance of caring rather than confrontational interactions with others. It is a way of being in which relationships, particularly that of counselor and client, are remembered and interpreted as mutually interdependent.[11]

The Art of Philosophical Practice

Within this revival of philosophy, there is dispute about what to call it: some say the word counseling is too suggestive of therapy. Some call it philosophical practice. Barbara Norman calls her practice "ecological thinking." Jon Borowicz at the Milwaukee School of Engineering prefers the term "philosophical colloquy." Many feel that the term counseling is too restrictive in that it excludes or limits the possibilities of philosophy to fertilize education, health care, corporate structures, and groups.

Then there are the many professionals within the field of psychology who have stood up, claiming they have been "doing this kind of philosophy" for decades. Even some academic philosophers are giving voice to a long-held secret desire to bring philosophy to bear on the crises facing individuals and the planet. Whatever the name we choose to give it, what is arising is the living, creative power of philosophy. Revitalizing lives and careers, philosophy rooted in the soil of lives is being expressed, longed for, and deeply felt around the world, in and out of the academy.

What this phenomenon might be is not only unnamed but undefined. It is not only difficult to define because it is new, but even seems to resist definition. Perhaps the philosophical counselor fits the description made by Richard Rorty as "'one who makes things new,' ... who is typically unable to make clear exactly what it is that he wants to do before developing the language in which he succeeds in doing it. His new vocabulary makes possible, for the first time, a formulation of its own purpose."[12]

Most practitioners, however, do agree—in fact, insist upon—their right to dismiss the request for a conceptually defined turf, especially the invitation to deliver philosophical "products," that is, theories, insights, strategies, solutions that would assist other fields in boxing philosophical practice as distinct from themselves. Gerd Achenbach states emphatically that *if there is anything which characterizes philosophy, it is that it does not accumulate insights, knowledge, or stores of truths which only wait to be called up when needed.* . . . it is precisely this model of division of labor and responsibilities which is designed to grant traditional philosophy entry into scientific discourse, which sterilizes the discipline. The result is that philosophy is pushed into boundaries within which it is supposed to manufacture thought-products . . . This amounts to getting rid of the only philosophical element of which there is something to be afraid: the insistence on the freedom of uncensored philosophical reflection which does not produce solutions but rather questions them all.[13]

The practice of philosophy, it seems, is more of an art than an academic or professional discipline. The study of art history teaches the student about periods and styles of artists but is not itself the creative activity of painting or sculpting. So, too, philosophy as practice is similar to *doing* art. Rather than learning about theories and systems of other philosophers and then applying them to people's problems, *doing* philosophy is a process that occurs outside conceptual boundaries.

On the other hand, practitioners agree that a sound knowledge of philosophy is essential. Most of us students who are passionate about philosophy eventually realize how the profound thinking of great philosophers disengages the mind from contentment and sleep. The process of philosophy—thinking, reflection, questioning, and doubt—undermines foundational theories and systems, leaving us in an unsettled state, a kind of no-man's land outside the periphery of conventional beliefs. "Philosophy," Achenbach reminds us, "does not lighten the burden, but rather makes it more difficult. . . . we know that our worries do not come to an end through philosophical discussion . . . Instead, the worry of the unknown deepens."[14]

It is in this space of the unknown, the peculiar state of being expelled from ordinary certainties that is the creative medium, so to speak, of the philosophical practitioner. It is here, outside of boundaries and definitions, that the healing power of philosophy reveals herself in the person of the philosophical counselor as mediator. What lives in this space that seeks expression or nourishment? The question that cannot be asked is exiled in this space. The need to inquire, ignited by the contradictions of life, rots and dies here if not nourished. The passion to understand life, a passion not honored by the education system, is banished to this place. The search for soul, for purpose, for the sacred, for the meaning of cruelty, death, and suffering withers here or longs for its awakening. The vital soul, desperate to escape the coffin of socially conditioned personas, waits here for its release.

The counselor is both mediator and Other. An Other is needed, claims Achenbach, in order that the lonely thought can be brought forth. *"This is the point,"* he says, *"at which philosophical practice becomes a real need: The merely subjective and lonely thought that is being abandoned by others, the completely subjective personal feeling that is being excluded from all interactions with, or acknowledgment by others, either kills or drives us into madness."* He calls this philosophical practice "an Orphic, underworld philosophy." Philosophy, he says, is a "suffering from normality," and "resides in those very purgatories and hells which would not have existed had there not been a rational 'heaven' from which everything that does not fit into its holy regiment is expelled." Achenbach asks, but leaves unanswered, this question: "How is it possible to descend into the underworlds without falling victim to them, without becoming like the many who are treated in the psychiatric clinic?"[15]

Perhaps the answer can be drawn from the comments of the three counselors mentioned earlier: reliance on experience, the attempt to grasp the moment, to hear beyond the language of social conditioning and theory, to care for the Other and the relationship. Perhaps what enables survival in the underworlds and what ignites the process of healing lies in the hands of the Other, *each* other: both counselor *and* client. Perhaps it is the shift of attention, of feeling, to Other—what Martin Buber calls *teshuvah*, turning—that dissolves the barriers between worlds and brings to fruition and beauty the art of philo-Sophia.

Notes

1. Ran Lahav and Maria daVenza Tillmanns, eds., *Essays on Philosophical Counseling* (Lanham, Maryland: University Press of America, 1995), x.

2. Paul W. Sharkey, "About the Society," *ASPCP Newsletter* 1.1 (April 1996), 2.

3. "Standards of Ethical Practice, Preamble," *ASPCP Newsletter* 1.1, 4.

4. Gerhard von Rad, *Wisdom in Israel* (Nashville: Abingdon Press, 1972), 153 and note.

5. Raymond E. Brown, Joseph A. Fitzmyer, Roland E. Murphy, s.v. "Introduction to Wisdom Literature," in *The New Jerome Biblical Commentary*, second edition, (Englewood Cliffs: Prentice Hall, 1990), 451.

6. David Fideler, "Introduction," in K. S. Guthrie, *The Pythagorean Sourcebook and Library* (Grand Rapids: Phanes Press, 1987), 31.

7. Ran Lahav and Maria Tillmanns, *Essays in Philosophical Counseling*, x.

8. Ran Lahav and Maria Tillmanns, *Essays in Philosophical Counseling*, xii.

9. Ran Lahav and Maria Tillmanns, *Essays in Philosophical Counseling*, xii–xiv.

10. Personal communication from Petra von Morstein.

11. Barbara Norman, "Philosophical Counseling: The Arts of Ecological Relationship and Interpretation," in Ran Lahav and Maria Tillmanns, *Essays on Philosophical Counseling*, 50.

12. Richard Rorty, *Contingency, Irony, and Solidarity* (New York: Cambridge University Press, 1989), 13.

13. Gerd B. Achenbach, "Philosophy, Philosophical Practice, and Psychotherapy," in Ran Lahav and Maria Tillmanns, *Essays on Philosophical Counseling*, 68.

14. Achenbach, "Philosophy, Philosophical Practice, and Psychotherapy," 68.

15. Achenbach, "Philosophy, Philosophical Practice, and Psychotherapy," 71, 73.

Further Information

For more information about philosophical counseling and the ASPCP, contact: Dr. Kenneth F. T. Cust, Editor, *ASPCP Newsletter*, Department of English and Philosophy, Central Missouri State University, Warrensburg, MO 64093.

The first book in English on Philosophical Counseling is *Essays on Philosophical Counseling*, edited by Ran Lahav and Maria Tillmanns (Lanham, MD: University Press of America, 1995).

Novelty, the Stop, and the Advent of Conscience

DAVID APPELBAUM

TO EACH EPOCH of the spirit, there corresponds a chief problem. Once recognized, the problem—"thrown out in front" to block the way to spiritual wholeness—becomes primary material for the ascent to understanding. Until that time, we repeatedly bump up against it like blind men a wall. The *prima materia* of our day, and the prime sustenance for inner growth, is not (as it was for other days) the idea of potentiality, integrity, or time. It is newness.

Novelty: the new, the fresh, the creative, the original, the not-yet-done, the just-now-manifesting. A philosophy, cosmology, or spiritual exploration that cannot furnish an account of newness *that is new* fails to meet the prime need of our time. That primary need is for renewal. Unless a body of knowledge provides for renewal, we are bound to suffocate under an ever-growing weight of the known.

What criteria are there for a new account of newness? An account that is repetitious recounts only the known and omits the direction to origin. A new account, by contrast, innovatively bares the originary signature in a never-seen-before disclosure. Furthermore, it differs with what has come before it and is able to account for the difference. There is an analogy with awareness. An increase in awareness adds an element to the old awareness by means of which an understanding arises of how the new awareness differs from the old. Awareness involves discernment of difference—without loss of a sense of the whole. A greater intensity of differentiation allows transformation to proceed to an ever higher level. Whitehead's vision of emergent newness conforms to these criteria in that, for him, "God's purpose in the creative advance is the evocation of intensities."

* * *

Another implication of the search for a new account of newness is implicit in what I have just said. Novelty entails a break with old, fixed, established, accepted, tradition-bound forms. Unless a pattern of sameness is disrupted, it persists, and persists in a dismissal of a newness that differs from the same. In a strange way, denial is *wary* of awareness, that sensitivity to differentiation as such. It arrays itself against in ways that are fascinating, creative, and new! Yet the sameness cloaks itself in suits that conceal its novelty and that require unconcealment to reveal the new disguises. A dismissal of newness, made conscious, contains the very differentiation that breaks it from a past of denial. The gates of heaven lie right beside the blackest lie to self.

In any event, novelty appears in its own discontinuous fashion. Given the discontinuity of newness (*and* a newness of discontinuity), a new account of newness must break with all previous accounts, completely, shockingly, abruptly, stunningly. It must feature a break-through consciousness, as Meister Eckhart did. Novelty is a force. The force of an account of novelty must be *felt*. To use Gabriel Marcel's words, it must have the sting of truth.

When we look to our lives and times, it seems undeniable that the force of newness is lacking. Surrounded as we are by "new" products, images, and ideas, we rarely feel wonder and awe, feelings evoked by newness. The tyranny of the same, in the various forms it takes, dissipates the force before it can register in our awareness. A new account of newness has to address this kind of totalitarian rule over experience: that we are not free to meet the new even when before us.

* * *

Opposed to creative advance, the energizing crest of innovation that breaks open entrenched positions, is retreat. Retreat is the principle that governs the formerly new but now old. Such forms are diminished, shrunken in intensity, and depreciated. Losing vivacity and suppleness in form, they suffer rigidification. British empiricism from Hobbes and Locke to the present has noticed the enervation of experience that results from this principle. Multiplicity and ambiguity give way to fixity and definition. The loss is tantamount to a shift from dynamism to mechanism. Lawfully, consciousness—the flux of life itself—decays and we are left with automatism.

For Hume, "force and vivacity" belong to an impression, the experience of immediacy. He writes, "The most lively thought is still inferior to the dullest sensation." The inferiority is in terms of energy. Cognitive life represents a net energy loss in its gain of knowledge. The inevitability of the equation drove Hume to a deep pessimism concerning the implications of his own research. We are still today affected by his mood.

Hume's discovery that a cognitive mode deenergizes experience serves to localize the pattern of sameness. The kind of concepts used in cognitively interpreted experience—thought—are of the past. While their worth in organizing experience is invaluable, their use tends to be in denial of the unity they draw from. Any concept unifies different experiences under one and the same idea. Yet, by the workings of an unseen automatism, we see only the sameness. The difference is dismissed. If we cease to be carried by a pessimistic mood, the question presents itself, can this automatism be neutralized?

Neutralization means that differences inherent in cognitive experience would again become apparent. Uniquenesses and specificities that make impressions so energizing would then also belong to thinking. Thinking would be living, not dead. Using Hume's approach, recovery of an ascending path is quite possible. That pathway, from decay to rejuvenation, complements the descending path that he dwells on. It is comprised of those missing phases of receptivity that complete a cycle of energy from unitary source to differentiated outlet. It is the cycle of hope, effort, and will.

* * *

In the stop can be found an authentically new account of the appearance of newness. In the stop, a creative breakthrough of novelty into time is allowed to manifest. The stop, therefore, cannot be considered an ordinary event but rather a vehicle for the extraordinary. When Ouspensky speaks of it (having learned from his spiritual master, Gurdjieff), he writes that "the 'stop' exercise is considered sacred in schools." Its sacred character lies in a secret ability to usher in the new. At the same time, that quality is concealed by its utter simplicity:

> at a word or sign, previously agreed upon, from the teacher, all the pupils who hear or see him have to arrest their movements at once, no matter what they are doing, and remain stockstill in the posture in which the signal has caught them.

What could be more simple an idea than a cessation of outward activity in the form of physical movement? The matter of the stop's action—arrest—remains concealed by the dismissive attitude of cognitive experience. That mind's ceaseless, aimless movement is endangered by the stop. Thus, the first condition supplied by the stop is confrontation with inner disquiet. One meets with a restless ebb and flow of involuntary interior movement, predominantly as inner commentary.

Ouspensky's idea is more specific and more potent. The stop is an invitation to the awareness ordinarily throttled by automatic functions of thought, feeling, and sensation. He says, "the character of the movements and postures in every epoch, in every race, and in every class is indissolubly connected with definite forms of thinking and feeling." There is a deep and habitual interdependence uniting ordinary ways of being. "In ordinary conditions," he continues, "we have no conception how much our thinking, feeling, and moving functions depend upon one another, although we know, at the same time, how much our moods and our emotional states can depend upon our movements and postures." Habits (or subjective necessities) of physical movement, far from being isolated from those of mind and emotions, bear an intimacy to cognition and feeling. To stop a physical movement in the frame of illumination is to disclose an aspect of the entire individuality. This gives the second condition of the stop. It is to reveal the stance of automatism in all its dimensions.

In its call to the awareness, the stop brings light to old, usual, customary, tired ways of ourselves. The conveyance of light itself is a new element—*the* new element—in the configuration. In light's presence, a habitual closure to awareness (the force of denial) is disclosed and thereby opposed. The aim of stopping—"to oppose this automatism and gradually to acquire control over postures and movements"—is creation of conditions of impartially viewing one's wholeness. Nothing in the automatism is changed. Its fragmented functioning remains intact. Only a vision—*the new* element—is added. In Whitehead's words, "The many are increased by one, and become one."

Disclosure of the old as old is a channel of the new. The decay of energies, once explosive, wondrous, and vivid, to habits continues while the restitution of energies from stale, worn, tired particles proceeds parallel to it. As a dynamic bridge between these two streams, the stop allows the new to make its appearance within the tyranny of habit. A current of life mingles momentarily with that of death. In the exchange, a delicate cosmic balance is maintained.

In a paradoxical way, the stop does not stop the automatism, but an attitude toward it. Once denial, as habit, is opposed by an affirmation, the conditions for novelty are recreated. The automatism, once seen, is an object of novelty. The object, the automatism itself, once seen is seen through the source of novelty. That object thereby becomes a vehicle for newness.

* * *

"Nobody," Ouspensky writes, "except the principal teacher or the person he commissions has the right to command a 'stop.'" That the sacred right resides in an external agent results from absence of an inner authority, one whose command is independent of the automatism. That person is initial administrator of "school discipline," the study of which gradually teaches an ability to give the stop to oneself. The achievement coincides with the advent of conscience.

School discipline in reality is a study of absence. It strives to understand that which usurps authority and speaks in the name of the "I" of presence. That which would substitute personal preference for impartiality has put forward the whole scheme of automatism in order to remain concealed. That something operates by virtue of the force of denial. As absence is gradually disclosed and longing for authentic presence is increased, the stop becomes practicable. Its practicability is a measure of will.

*   *   *

Conscience is an awareness of the obligation to become whole. The obligation is objective in the sense that one is obligated before doing anything to incur obligation. The obligation resides in the fact of selfhood rather than any consequence of the fact. Feeling obligated, one is aware of an ever-present incompleteness of being human. To respond to the need to finish and perfect that which is presently undone is to respond with conscience. Ordinary compulsions of morality or the utilitarian calculations of the intellect do not emanate from a source of feeling. They serve to distract one from the purpose of recognizing the imperfect state of automatism and the subsequent need of self-perfection. They leave one forgetful of the stop—the call to awareness.

The continuing emergence of the new, in the form of fresh material about one's state, requires a sense of being obligated. Otherwise, a force of affirmation attenuates and is overcome by denial, the selfsame denial that maintains the automatism. Novelty disrupts. The new can be profoundly disturbing. Ouspensky, a man not given to emotional expression, says of his first meeting with his spiritual master Gurdjieff that it

> produced the strange, unexpected, and almost alarming impression of a
> man poorly disguised, the sight of whom embarrasses you because you

see he is not what he pretends to be and yet you have to speak and behave
as though you did not see it.

The uncanny, not to be anticipated, unforeseen, awakening power of
the new excites old, established reactions with renewed strength.
There are many ingenious analgesics against the sting of truth. To feel
an ethical command to accept the facts, come what may, can alone
open one to novelty.

The creative advance destroys as it creates. Newness destroys
illusions as it creates a presence to the actual Presence. The former
involves conscience in suffering, though I do not mean the ordinary
suffering of unfulfilled expectations. The pain of ego has nothing to
do with the acquisition of self-knowledge unless blockages have to do
with the springs of creative expression. To remain available in the face
of disturbing revelations of self is to cultivate an attitude of conscience.
Vulnerability to a pained discovery is a preparation for conscious
suffering.

It would not be useful to overemphasize the payment for over the
action of conscience. Conscience, the other, as act is absolute disruption. It intercedes in everyday functioning of thought and feeling like
an alarm, to use Ouspensky's image, that shocks one to wakefulness.
Imperatively, it has nothing to do with right and wrong, good and bad.
In fact, it is as liable to interfere with deliberations on these matters as
readily as with other matters. Conscience breaks up the linear continuity of functioning with a call to recognize the mechanical nature of
that functioning as such. The level on which that call arises is one not
governed by laws of linear or causal succession, a time-space continuum, or methods of representational expression. Conscience arises
on a level other than that of samsara, and relative to samsara, is the
absolute other—uncontainable by a logic of sameness. And if we agree
that novelty is a valuation (even, *the* value of valuation), then conscience, the disruptive force of novelty, is also the source of value.
Perhaps, of all value.

Life, Lindisfarne, and Everything: William Irwin Thompson Speaks Out

INTERVIEWED BY JOHN DAVID EBERT

ONE OF WILLIAM IRWIN THOMPSON'S primary concerns throughout his career has been how the human imagination creates historical "reality." Narratives of human history are as old as myth itself, and historiography proper at least as ancient as Zoroaster, who imagined the drama of the cosmos unfolding in three acts: the primordial fall of Light into Darkness was followed by the arrival of Zoroaster onto the stage of history itself, and at the end of time, the Great Man, Saoshyant, would come to restore Light to its state of original purity. This trifold schema reincarnated itself in the imaginations of Augustine, Joachim of Floris, and even the German aesthetician Lessing, but it has played counterpoint to the much older quaternary myth of the Eternal Return as articulated, for example, in Hesiod's cycle of the Four Ages of Man. And it was this Classical species of the cyclical idea that migrated into the imagination of the eighteenth-century Italian philosopher Giambattista Vico in his fourfold cycle of Gods, Heroes, Men, and Chaos. These four great vertebrae, then, evolved into the skeleton of Joyce's Puranic classic *Finnegans Wake*, which was published in 1939. Goethe, meanwhile, had picked up the idea from Vico, and in his 1817 paper entitled "Epochs of the Spirit," had designated the four stages of culture as the Poetic, Theological, Philosophical, and Prosaic. Oswald Spengler, then, in his 1918 masterpiece *The Decline of the West*, amplified Goethe's libretto into an operatic magnum opus of cultural history, to which Arnold Toynbee, in *A Study of History*, responded with his equally brilliant English version of the rise and breakdown of civilizations.

The point at which the trunk of this great tree of historiography bifurcates into the philosophy of the evolution of consciousness is the publication in 1949 of the first volume of Jean Gebser's *Ever Present Origin*. Gebser picks up where Spengler leaves off, seeing in the disintegration of the modern world during the nineteenth century not merely decay, but the genesis of a whole new structure of human consciousness, which Gebser termed the "Aperspectival." But this transformation of consciousness, with its shift from the Renaissance Perspectival Space—in which a world of three dimensions was created by the human eye—to one of Aperspectivity—in which three-dimensonal space was relativized to a larger context of multiple spaces, multiple times, multiple points of view—has much in common with Marshall McLuhan's observation of the shift from the Gutenberg Galaxy of print-based literacy and mechanics to the creation of electronic culture, with its sense of "everything all at once" completely shattering the old linear grid system of the Cartesian analytical worldview.

It is out of this tradition of grand historical meta-narratives that William Irwin Thompson's vision of human culture draws its inspiration. Thompson's mind inhabits the very Aperspectival Space which Gebser articulated, wherein he shifts around the various ways in which men have imagined the great patterns of history with the apparent effortlessness of moving icons in a Macintosh. Indeed, already in his undergraduate days, he was freely inhabiting this space, while his professors were still constrained by the myopia of Perspectival Space. As Thompson puts it, "I played my own Vico," and "in a mere two hundred pages of an undergraduate honors thesis that my professors derided as my Summa Anthropological-Philosophica . . . I tried to show that the evolution of styles in ancient Greek statuary, Middle American Mayan architecture, and English poetry, all revealed the same structural pattern."

Thompson's first book, *The Imagination of an Insurrection* (1967), in direct counterpoint to his honors thesis, specialized by focusing on a single event that took place in "one week in one city." But again, the main theme of the book was "the role of imagination in the construction of historical reality," as Thompson chronicled the unfolding of

Irish culture through the restoration of Celtic mythology in the decades preceding the famous uprising.

During this period, Thompson had been teaching English at MIT, but, having become impatient with its cult of technocracy and the paradigm of materialism informing its basic principles, he left and went north to Canada, where he taught for a time at York University, and in 1971 published *At the Edge of History*. In this book, Thompson's restlessness becomes evident, as he roams from Los Angeles to Esalen to MIT, sifting through the cultural detritus of history's burnt-out civilizations for clues to the creation of his own mythology.

In his next book, *Passages About Earth* (1973), Thompson articulated the vision of that mythology. The creation of the counterfoil institution in the mid-'60s as an alternative to the dismal hijacking of the university by the defense industry after World War II, inspired Thompson to undertake a kind of Volkerwanderung over the Earth, visiting as many of these institutions as he could. The result of this "withdrawal and return" was Thompson's creation of Lindisfarne, an intentional community originally set up in Southampton, New York, where people of all faiths could come to recognize common ground, and in the process, cultivate ecological skills. Lindisfarne was eventually moved to Colorado, where a beautiful chapel was designed by architect Keith Critchlow, based upon the classical principles of Pythagorean geometry. But, as Thompson later wrote in a poem:

> No wife or child could stand
> near the structure's forbidding,
> Platonically absolute tyranny,
> only a constructed crew of single men,
> filled with a lust for masculine abstractions
> that blinded them to the real trash
> that piled up beside their sacred temple.

Thompson's New Age idealism had begun to disintegrate as he realized that Lindisfarne, as a cultural magnet, had attracted too much culture, for a series of ontological conflicts began to be evident to him in the various projects in which he had become involved. Thompson realized that the sacred mystery school of Platonic geometry, though concerned with aesthetic values, was elitist and reactionary, afraid of embracing the transformations of modern culture; meanwhile, the ecological content of the counterculture, with its concern for energy efficiency and recycling of waste products was intensely democratic, though not much attuned to the soul's need for the harmonious proportions of Pythagorean geometry. Ultimately, Thompson turned the chapel over to a group of Zen monks and then moved on, taking Lindisfarne with him.

This epistemological shift in Thompson's imagination—from the static world view of Platonism to the dynamics of "processual morphology," as he terms it—is embodied by a trilogy of books which he wrote during this period: *The Time Falling Bodies Take to Light* (1981), *Blue Jade from the Morning Star* (1983), and the novel *Islands Out of Time* (1985). With his next book, *Pacific Shift* (1985), he invented a new mythos for himself in what is perhaps his best essay, "The Four Cultural Ecologies of the West," in which he imagines that the history of mathematics, literature, and ecology has undergone four basic transformations: from the Riverrine-Arithmetic of the Sumero-Babylonian world to the Mediterranean-Euclidean of Platonic geometry; and from the Atlantic-Cartesian or dynamical to the post World War II Planetary-Processual. The shift from the Industrial nation state, based on ownership of land—the economic creation of the third mentality—to the Planetary Society, with its emphasis on ecology, the biosphere, the atmosphere, and dynamical systems theory—the creation of the fourth mentality—is the fundamental transformation of culture which Thompson bases his entire worldview on.

Thompson at this point refocused Lindisfarne's energies toward healing the schism between "the two cultures" of the sciences and the humanities. Accordingly, Lindisfarne became something of a refuge for maverick scientists interested in amplifying the dimensions of their science with a fresh spiritual resonance. A new group of poets, philosophers, and scientists began to migrate to Lindisfarne, and Thompson's *Imaginary Landscape* (1989) celebrates its rebirth in this period, and expresses his gratitude to scientists James Lovelock, Francisco Varela, Lynn Margulis, and Ralph Abraham, who assisted him in the creation of the new interface between science and spirituality which has become the primary focus of Lindisfarne.

Thompson's new book *Coming into Being*, based on a series of talks which he delivered in New York at the Cathedral of Saint John the Divine, is simultaneously an overview of the evolution of human consciousness and a recapitulation of the main stages in the development of his career as a visionary. It is a "conscious summing up," in which all the strands which have preoccupied his imagination—myth, science, philosophy, anthropology, and literature—are taken up and woven into a tapestry of living ideas.—*John David Ebert*

JOHN EBERT: Your first book, *The Imagination of an Insurrection*, seems to be somewhat atypical of your writings in that it's more of a specialized account of a single historical event, the Easter Rebellion in Ireland in 1916. Tell me how that book evolved in your imagination and what impelled you to write it.

WILLIAM IRWIN THOMPSON: I've always wanted to go to Ireland, and being American-Irish I had—as many American-Irish have—a kind of desire for a fantasy landscape of returning to the old sod and finding a culture that had tradition and roots and something deeper than the highway strips of America when I was growing up in L.A. So Ireland and the Celtic spirit in general—especially the Irish writers, like Yeats and Dylan Thomas—were always adolescent heroes of mine.

When I was an undergraduate, I wrote a long honors thesis on a philosophy of history, much to the chagrin of all my professors, who believed that you should just do a specialized thing on one poem or one writer. I did a whole theory of cultural history and played my own Vico and they didn't like that. I had to fight them very hard to do it, and I was majoring simultaneously in anthropology, philosophy, and English literature. The book represented my tying up together all the strands of my three different majors. And then when I went to graduate school—it's even more intensely specialized at Cornell—I became interested in AE and Yeats and the Easter Rebellion and their different poems on it. I wrote a term paper for Robert Martin Adams at Cornell on the Easter Rising, and then suggested that there was enough material there for a doctoral dissertation. They said "OK," though there was no one in Irish studies there. Adams was really only a Joyce scholar.

Because I had already published a dissertation-length thesis as an undergraduate, and had already published a couple of articles, I wanted to skip the whole dissertation exercise and just simply write a book. If it were an academic dissertation, you would drag out Chapter One for 200 pages and lots of footnotes. And then in your first year as a professor you would have to boil that long 200 pages into just one introductory chapter, and then add on all the other stuff to make it a book. So I said, "Why don't we just skip this exercise, and I'll simply go to Dublin and write a book?" So I did that, and it was always under the constraints of academe, which is nothing if not specialized. I was interested in combining the anthropological studies of a nativisitic movement, and historical studies, and the literary studies of the Irish Renaissance in ways that no scholar that I knew of combined, or even knew, those areas of discourse. I found a lot of resistance from academics who were specialists; they have a visceral contempt and suspicion of big ideas. They're primarily postal clerks: they live in a bureaucracy and they receive stamped opinion and then pass it on. And that's their job.

Even when I was doing the book, the Irish historian at MIT, Emmitt Larkin, really disliked my generalizations on imagination and history at the end. And he said with scathing contempt, "If I wanted Open End, I would listen to David Suskind"—a television talk show of the '60s.

And I said, "No way, I've done the research to give myself license to make these generalizations about imagination and history. That's what I'm interested in, and I'm going to put it in, anyway." And he really didn't like that kind of thing because he was a historian of very detailed studies of the role of the church in nineteenth-century

Ireland.

But Oxford University Press liked the book and published it as a university press book, so it was not a trade book. So it's very much a work of history and not a work of what would now be called trade non-fiction. And that was in the old days when I was a professor at MIT.

JOHN EBERT: In your next book, *At the Edge of History*, you talk about your disillusionment with the university. Can you discuss what the intellectual atmosphere was like at MIT in the late '60s?

WILLIAM IRWIN THOMPSON: It was extremely polarized between World War II warriors who were believers in modernizing the world through American corporations, and believed in high-tech solutions to all things, and were basically captured by the behavioral sciences and a kind of modernizing political science; and then the New Left, who were inspired by Marxism under the leadership of Noam Chomsky and the Chair of the Humanities and Literature Division, Louis Kampf. They basically were the mirror opposites of the technocrats. But they were technologists who believed in technological rationality, and they believed that philosophy and ideology were just simply the superstructure of the means of production, and that reality was economic and technological. Either way, you had a choice between a materialism of one variety or another, and there was nothing resembling the tradition that I was attracted to, that was expressed by more mystical poets like Yeats and Blake and Whitman, with a kind of power of mysticism to empower the individual to create a kind of democratic vision, especially with people like Blake and Whitman. Yeats was a little more conservative, so I was attracted more to Yeats's poetry than to his politics.

Basically, there wasn't any room for what I wanted to do. So I just decided to quit and I went off to Canada with McLuhan in Toronto. Canada was just coming into it own, it was no longer the kind of sleepy province of England forgotten by America. It was beginning to be an interesting, exciting place in its own right. And Toronto remains one of my favorite cities.

JOHN EBERT: Did you study with McLuhan for a time?

WILLIAM IRWIN THOMPSON: No, not at all. I was already an

associate professor when I went up to Toronto and I had already published *At the Edge of History* when I met McLuhan. I had attended a lecture of his when he came to visit MIT, and I had, of course, always read his work in the '60s and used it in all my books. I always liked his free intellectual style because he seemed to be able to live an imaginative intellectual life, even within academe. He was, in that sense, a positive role model. But I'd never studied under him.

Then, when I went to his coach house, I was a little distressed because it was like a temple filled with all his disciples and followers. And they were all weak xeroxes of him, weak clones. They weren't actually taking his ideas imaginatively and individualistically doing original work with them in the way that I thought I was doing.

And you couldn't, with people like Bucky Fuller or Joseph Campbell or Marshall McLuhan, actually be around them except in the form of a disciple kissing their ring. I just wasn't comfortable in that mode, so I thought, well, the best way to get the best of these gentlemen was to read them in my study, and integrate what I think is valuable in my own writing, and just ignore the personality and the ego, and the ego-dynamics of a cult of followers.

I went to see him once, and McLuhan was very defensive and threatened by me because a reporter had said the intellectual center of Toronto had shifted from the South with McLuhan at the University of Toronto, to the north of the city, to York University and to me. Of course, that wasn't the way I felt; that was just journalistic packaging. But he felt like I was after his turf.

So I went to the coach house as a way of honoring him and saying, no, this is not the case, this is just an irresponsible journalist, and I respect your work and I'm not after your bishopric. But he basically was a highly autistic individual: he couldn't really listen, he could only recite—*brilliantly*—his aphorisms and insights. I mean, he was undoubtedly a genius, and the media tends to exaggerate that in people. Whenever I would meet people like Alan Watts or Bucky or Joseph Campbell—very much so—the media magnified their egos and put them into a kind of celebrity status and so they didn't have the ability to listen or exchange thought or ideas. They only had the ability to play the tape recording of their ideas. And it's better to get that just by reading a book instead of hanging around the person. So I left and I went elsewhere.

JOHN EBERT: Wasn't it about that time that you founded Lindisfarne?

WILLIAM IRWIN THOMPSON: Yeah, I was getting restless because York was becoming a suburban drive-in university, and was trying to basically duplicate the technocratic vision of post-industrial society that had been pioneered by MIT. And so I took a sabbatical and went around the world—and that became *Passages About Earth*. I was looking at alternatives, because when I was in Canada, I went to a summer conference, and Ivan Illich gave the opening address. He was a *very* charismatic speaker, one of the more charismatic lecturers I've ever heard, actually. He articulated the whole vision of the counter-foil institution, and had set up his own center for intercultural documentation in Cuernavaca.

I decided to look at these places around the world. I had already gone to Esalen in '67 and been very impressed by Michael Murphy, who remains a very close friend. So I decided to look at Arcosanti and the Center for Eastern Wisdom and Western Science in Starnberg, Germany, and Auroville in the Sri Aurobindo ashram in India, and Findhorn in Scotland. So I took off and just went around the world and tried to understand the new planetary culture that was emerging, and was talking to people like Aurelio Peccei and the Club of Rome, and people in the World Order Models Project, and the Institute of World Order in Tokyo.

Out of all that wandering I wrote that book, and from the inspiration of Findhorn and my meeting with David Spangler, I decided to get up my courage and not go back after the end of my sabbatical. I was promoted to full professor, and thank you very much, but I was not going back, and I quit and set up Lindisfarne.

JOHN EBERT: Has your vision of Lindisfarne changed any over the years?

WILLIAM IRWIN THOMPSON: Oh, yeah, it has to, because Lindisfarne dies every year. It's twenty-four-years old, and it dies every year for lack of money. So one has to be a *bricoleur* and be flexible. You can only be rigid and inflexible if you have an endowment and that makes you an institution, like Princeton University. Lindisfarne has no endowment, it just has little tactical funds that donors and individuals give from time to time for a program, and that'll do the program, and when the money's gone, you're broke and you have to start all over again. I've done that for twenty-four years, and so Lindisfarne has changed.

In the first wave, in the '70s, because of the wonderful idealism of the '70s—I miss it in this kind of materialistic '90s—there was the influence of the intentional community as a way of getting out of the suburbs. Since I'd grown up in L.A., it was attractive, and Findhorn and Auroville and the intentional community dynamic like Zen Center and Tassajara, California were interesting. So I set it up as a kind of institute that was run by a communal staff. We were involved with the usual kind of return to nature of organic gardening and alternative medicine, and then a lot of the agenda of the '70s.

Then, as it evolved, it became more of a fellowship of artists and scientists and poets, and it was the fellowship that became really charismatic and dynamic, more than the intentional community. And that began to take us into the interface between spirituality and science. So, in the '70s, it started with Gregory Bateson and the astronaut Rusty Schweickhart, and it just kept growing with Francisco Varela and the physicist David Finkelstein, and then Jim Lovelock in atmospheric chemistry, and Lynn Margulis in biology. Our program in biology and science began to be the strongest and most original thing about Lindisfarne because Findhorn is very heart-centered but is *intensely* anti-intellectual. And Auroville is just kind of a yogic New Age ashram, or community. It has no scientific component.

What was unique to Lindisfarne was this fellowship of scientists re-imagining a new kind of science, in which art, science, and religion collaborated in a more interesting ecology of consciousness than was the case at MIT. I tried to set up such an interface *at* MIT, but they wouldn't let me do it, so that's why I got restless and quit.

JOHN EBERT: Could you describe what you mean by a shift from an

Industrial society to a Planetary society, and what the new social and cultural structures might entail with that?

WILLIAM IRWIN THOMPSON: Well, the Industrial nation state arose in the eighteenth century—England being the charismatic example—and it was a shift away from a feudalistic empire with all value based on land, and an aristocracy and a church, to capitalism, with a basis on industrial productivity and a new economic exchange of value. The Industrial nation state created the international world system we have now, and the world economy, which is, of course, creating all the problems that we face now with the industrialization of the biosphere and the greenhouse effect and the ozone hole. Which gives us crazy things like hurricanes in July when they used to come in September, and thirty of them instead of three, and the inability of schoolchildren to go out and play in the sun in Australia.

The interface between an industrial economy and the biosphere is what the industrial nation state can't handle. So the new culture isn't based on nation state turf; it's based on biological, ecological processes, so the atmosphere is more the model than the land. And the science that would describe the processes of the atmosphere are more the new complex dynamical sciences, chaotic systems of clouds, rather than the clods.

The old Romanticism wanted to go back *to* nature, and you got a kind of Romantic attempt to achieve the pre-industrial world of folk culture, Romanticism in Germany and England. But I'm more interested in going forward *out* of Industrial society, so I use the word "planetary" to distinguish between "international," because "international" is what I had at MIT. That's basically the relationship between the G-7 and commitment to technological modernization and industrial development. And that, of course, just exacerbates the problems we have now.

Also, we're polarizing as we create a new economy in which the rich get richer and the poor get poorer, and the ultimate effect of this new form of post-modern capitalism is the peculiar meltdown of middle-class industrial society, as the middle class is getting pushed back down into the lower class again. So you're getting a fabulous amount of wealth with a smaller and smaller group of people. And the lower middle class that used to live in tract houses and had cars and were reasonably well off and had labor unions and could send their kids to college, they're getting forced back into being post-industrial serfs. And so industrial society is coming apart at the seams in more ways than one.

My efforts in *Passages About Earth* and *Darkness and Scattered Light* and *Evil and World Order* were attempts to articulate the shift from economics as the governing science of society to ecology as the governing science. It's a shift away from an ideology in which there is a ruling elite, whether it's a Chomskyesque Leftist elite, or a Jerry Wiesner technocratic elite, to a new diverse ecology of difference in which there is no single elite articulating one simple ideology. That's why Lindisfarne was always a fellowship and not a followership, and why we had very diverse people who shared an ethos—but they definitely did not share an ideology, and I was not a leader articulating an ideology seeking followers.

JOHN EBERT: You mention very often in your writings that you see the cultural and social structures of the middle ages reemerging in our new electronic society. Could you describe what those structures are?

WILLIAM IRWIN THOMPSON: Part of it is disliterate, in the sense that you're going back to a culture that's not based on the Gutenberg galaxy of the middle classes having access to information through books and paperbacks. You're going through television and channels and cable TV and the Internet, and this is creating a kind of disliterate Internet chatter where people certainly don't write Jeffersonian eighteenth-century letters on the Internet. So you get a culture which is a meltdown of civilized literacy.

You get a meltdown of the nation state and this meltdown of the middle class, and a return to aristocrats and serfs. And you get global noetic polities that are very much like the church and the religious orders in the middle ages—like the Knights Templar—that extend across boundaries and are not wed to any particular nation state ideology, whether these are Microsoft or Pepsi or science, or pop music, or Greenpeace. There are many different versions that are meta-national configurations where identity isn't coming from nationalism.

The return to the breakup of religious consensus to religious orders is also a medieval thing, where you have fanatical groups like Aryan Nation, or cults, or charismatic leadership, or some fanatical saint. That's a very medieval pattern, and all of these involve the breakdown of any kind of civilized literate consensus. You know, there's no *New York Review of Books* or one single intelligentsia, in New York or at Harvard, articulating what civilization is all about for the rest of us. And that's very much a kind of medieval diversity. So it's a raggle-taggle system of fools and scholars and knights and their electronic capitals, and aristocrats—not in land, but aristocrats in vast resources of money in a Bill Gates kind of way.

The other medieval thing is the way in which information is being controlled by these vast, what I call, electronic latifundia. Latifundia were these huge colossal slave plantations that came at the end of the Roman Empire before the collapse. And when you have CNN and Capital Industries and Disney and Time Warner and all these vast informational processing units coming together to control books and publishing, and Barnes and Noble Bookstores, satellites and software and the Internet and all of these things—America Online—you're getting a kind of dumbing-down homogenization where the people are sort of collectivized in these feedlots like cattle and they're just fed this techno-swill. When I had Prime Star on my backyard satellite dish in Colorado, I had like fifty channels, and it was all garbage—The Golf Channel, the Faith and Values Channel—and there was no intellectual content whatsoever. And PBS wasn't an alternative because it was an Oklahoma PBS that thought educational television was Lawrence Welk and a concert where you photograph the pianist's hands, which is a travesty of music. So that kind of dumbing-down of America in creating this techno-swill is very much turning people into serfs. They're not citizens who are reading pamphlets and philosophy and coming to empowerment of philosophical discourse and voting for their representative in Washington, they're just voting for the celebrity of their choice. So that's a medieval formation, where everybody becomes a techno-peasant.

And that's going to continue. It's very hard for an intellectual such as me to live in that world, because it's very hard for anyone to find my books in a bookstore, because in Barnes and Noble the publisher has to be a large, rich publisher and he has to bribe and rent the shelf space. The publisher has to pay a fee if the book is turned out—face out—and if the shelf is in the front close to the window, they have to pay more. And since intellectual publishers can't afford to pay those rates, intellectuals such as I won't be represented; you just won't find us in Barnes and Noble. You'll just find O. J. Simpson or a movie star or some guy who'll pretend to be a philosopher—maybe a human potential sound-biter with the latest gadget on how to fix your life. And that's a medieval formulation, too.

It means that literacy—you know, in the time of Kant there are probably about twelve philosophers—it means that intellectuals are going to be very few and far between. And the masses are not going to be going to college and being smart, they're just going to be . . . They'll probably go to college, but they'll read textbooks that will be produced by Time Warner that will have ads for Nike and Pepsi in the end pages. And you know, they'll be sitting in class with their baseball caps with another commercial on their foreheads. So, we're already there.

JOHN EBERT: You see your writings as an example of a new literary genre which you term *wissenskunst*. Could you define what that's all about?

WILLIAM IRWIN THOMPSON: Well, I tried to find a word for it in English and couldn't. I had just come back from a meeting with Werner Heisenberg at the Max Planck Institute and was reading some poetry of Rilke, and my mind was more in the German language, and I was thinking of the German word for "science," *wissenschaft*, and thought, well, what I'm looking for is something not quite "*schaft*," but "*kunst*." So I thought, "Well, why don't I just call it *wissenskunst*?"

But I'm not alone in this. I once had lunch with Lewis Thomas, who won the National Book Award for *Lives of a Cell*, and I said to him, "You know, all your little short essays that you write for the *New England Journal of Medicine* have the structure of Romantic poems of description and meditation." Since I wrote my master's essay on that genre, I was sensitive to it. And he said, "Yeah, I love poetry, and I write poetry, and I consciously tried to make these little essays poetic in that form." And so that kind of genre—Tom Wolfe has raised non-fiction to a novelistic art-form—I think it was something that was peculiar to my generation. A lot of us just got bored, and reality was so fascinating. As I was running around the world, the thought of trying to invent a make-up reality like a novelist was not as fascinating as writing about what was coming on down. So I shifted in and just tried to make non-fiction an art form.

JOHN EBERT: During the mid-'80s you seem to have had a kind of epistemological shift from a Platonic New Age worldview based on static geometries to a kind of a more post-modern vision of shifting grounds and uncertain horizons. Can you talk about what happened, what was going on in your imagination?

WILLIAM IRWIN THOMPSON: That was basically coming to the shadow side of the whole European school of sacred geometry and discovering that, unbeknownst to me, Schwaller de Lubicz was an anti-Semitic fascist and had been a member of a fascist group in France. And that René Guénon was basically an Islamic fundamentalist who hated the modern world. And Keith Critchlow wasn't a fascist, but he was totally in love with rigid geometry and the cult of the leader and the follower and did not like projective geometry or anything that was multi-dimensional. And so what happened was that the school of sacred geometry just became a male-dominant primate band with followers. It was very rigid and there was no place for women or children and it was very esoteric in a kind of nasty, superior anti-democratic spirit.

I became very restless and unhappy with that, and at the same time in the complexity of the fellowship of Lindisfarne, separate from all that European group was the scientific group of Lynn Margulis and Jim Lovelock and Francisco Varela and then later Ralph Abraham and mathematics. And I just began to understand we were at a critical quantum leap in culture, and we were moving into a new mentality, and that the people like Critchlow were actually regressing to the old one, to the medieval Platonic one, pre-Galilean in orientation. And I wanted, again, to go forward into the post-Galilean, and move into the new fourth mentality instead of going back to the second. So that's when I developed the whole theory that there was an evolution of literature and mathematics through history. That it went through the Arithmetic; the Geometric, which is the Platonic and the Critchlovian; and the Galilean dynamical one, which is the modernist, Cartesian-Galileo; and then the new one, which we're in now, that starts around '72 with Rene Thom, *Structural Stability and Morphogenesis*, and gets developed into chaos dynamical theory.

I don't like the phrase "post-modern" because it means different things in different disciplines. I always use "planetary" to distinguish. But I made up this phrase "planetary culture" twenty-five years ago, but now it's gotten a little co-opted by the New Age movement so the word seems kind of like a buzzword instead of a technical term, as I would like it to be. But "post-modern" is an even worse term, because it means one thing in literature and another thing in architecture, so I just don't like the phrase. And it also means nihilistic, amoral, no center—and that's the opposite of my own contemplative sensibility.

My 1985 novel, *Islands Out of Time*, was an effort to write myself free of the charisma and influence of Keith Critchlow—and then redesigning the chapel and moving it away from being a temple to Platonism, and making it a much more post-historic, archaic, simple, Quaker, minimalist architectural form, as it is now. So I had to redesign the building.

JOHN EBERT: How did you become acquainted with Ralph Abraham's work?

WILLIAM IRWIN THOMPSON: The other Lindisfarne fellow who founded International Synergy Institute and publishes *IS Journal*, Andra Akers, the actress, asked me to come out and give a lecture at the L.A. Film Institute on Sunset Boulevard. I did, and she then had a party that evening and introduced me to Ralph Abraham. And then Ralph sent me in Bern a copy of his essay "Mathematics and Evolution," and that was the seed form of my taking the idea and developing it fully into the chapter, "The Four Cultural Ecologies of the West" in *Pacific Shift*; I developed it further in *Imaginary Landscape*, that theory that there are these four mathematical mentalities. Since then, Ralph and I have lectured together and designed a curriculum for a girls' school, an elementary school K through 12 in East Hampton, New York. So we're collaborating all the time.

JOHN EBERT: In your new book *Coming into Being*, you compare the work of Jean Gebser with Ken Wilber. Can you discuss the differences that you see in the approaches of both of these men to the evolution of consciousness?

WILLIAM IRWIN THOMPSON: Oh, it's almost classic European versus Midwestern American. You know, I think people like Terence McKenna and Ken Wilber just grew up in Eastern Colorado and Nebraska, in such culturally deprived areas, that they get captured by a kind of abstract construction of what they imagine the big European thinker to be, or the psychedelic hero in the case of McKenna. And Wilber, as I say in *Coming into Being*, is just very abstract and Gebser is an artist. He has an incredible insight, for example, into the role of adjectives in Rilke, and what it means when you use language in a particular way to create an imaginative landscape that's more *processive* and less prospective of composed objects nailed down into perspectival space. So, in Gebser, there's an amazing sensitivity to art and poetry and painting and the richness of European culture. But when I was teaching temporarily in San Francisco, the students didn't like it because they can't remember a painting of Cezanne, they don't read Rilke, they're just into drugs and taking Ecstacy, and looking for some kind of psychotherapy technique. And so Wilber is their hero because he just gives them all these maps and charts, this Michelin guide. He's a control freak. There's no sense of humor, there's no sense of art, it's just sterile and masculine in a very dry and abstract way.

I don't want to be an egomaniac and say, well, my cultural history is better than Wilber's—I don't want to get into that. But I went out of my way to use Ken Wilber's *Up from Eden* as a textbook, and had everybody read it in my Lindisfarne symposium at the cathedral. But when I did that, and went out of my way to give equal time and to really be open to it, and read the book, and underlined it, I just thought, God,

the difference between this and *The Time Falling Bodies Take to Light*—
they cover exactly the same turf—it's the difference between a textbook and a work of art!

And then I went back because I wanted to be fair, because I knew
Treya Wilber, and was corresponding with her when she was going
through the crisis, and she was also a friend of my wife's, and I've had
cancer, and so Treya and I were talking a lot about cancer. I've never
met Ken face to face, but I knew Treya before she married Ken, and
I wanted to go out of my way to be fair to Ken, so I got the new book—
Sex, Ecology, Spirituality—and I thought, God, this is ridiculous! Three
thousand pages that are going to explain everything. You know, that
kind of German nineteenth-century scholarship, that's over. I don't
have the time to read 3,000 pages! And then when he kept having this
little slogan from his literary agent, John White, put on all his books—
"the Einstein of the consciousness movement"—I was revolted by the
vulgarity of it. And then when he went beyond that and put his picture
on the front of a book and called it *A Brief History of Everything*! Ken
Wilber explains the entire universe to you, everything you wanted to
know . . . and I thought, this is just inflation, this is an ego that's just
suffering from a hernia.

Jung and the Myth of the Primordial Tradition

Andrew Burniston

AFTER THE IRREVOCABLE BREAK with Freud, Jung knew that he could no longer adhere to the myth of psychoanalysis. As he found it impossible to return to the Christian myth, he had no option but to confront a crisis of identity. Here is how he recalled the dilemma in his autobiography, *Memories, Dreams, Reflections*:

> About this time I experienced a moment of unusual clarity in which I looked back over the way I had travelled so far. I thought, "Now you possess a key to mythology and are free to unlock all the gates of the unconscious psyche." But then something whispered within me, "Why open all the gates?" And promptly the question arose of what, after all, I had accomplished. I had explained the myths of people of the past, I had written a book about the hero, the myth in which man has always lived. But in what myth does man live nowadays? In the Christian myth, the answer might be. "Do *you* live in it?" I asked myself. To be honest the answer was no. For me it is not what I live by. "Then do we no longer have any myth?" "No, evidently we no longer have any myth." "But then what is your myth—the myth in which you live?" At this point the dialogue with myself became uncomfortable and I stopped thinking. I had reached a dead end.[1]

There was only one way out of this impasse for Jung, a descent to the source of all mythologies in the depths of the unconscious psyche. His inner journey took him beyond the personal unconscious which "ends

Delivered as a lecture for a conference on "Jung in the Light of the Perennial Philosophy" held at the Canonbury Academy, London, on April 23, 1994.

at the earliest memories of infancy" to the transpersonal or collective
unconscious that constitutes the "pre-infantile period" or the "residues of ancestral life." In the *Two Essays on Analytical Psychology*, he
describes the outcome of his experience:

> When ... psychic energy regresses, going beyond even the period of early
> infancy, and breaks into the legacy of ancestral life, the mythological
> images are awakened: these are the archetypes. An interior spiritual
> world whose existence we never suspected opens out and displays
> contents which seems to stand in sharpest contrast to all our former
> ideas.[2]

Regression to the pre-infantile period does not lead to chaos and
dissolution for Jung, but to a coherent spiritual world.[3] This world is
ruled by the archetypes which are the ordering principles of the
collective unconscious and pervade every aspect of psychic life.[4] If
Jung is correct and these archetypes are structures that coincide with
myth-motifs, then even psychology is an abstract kind of myth. Jung's
psychology has the merit of being a myth that is conscious of itself, a
point he develops in his contribution to the *Essays on a Science of
Mythology*:

> Psychology as one of the many expressions of psychic life operates with
> ideas which in their turn are derived from archetypal structures and thus
> generate a somewhat abstract kind of myth. Psychology therefore
> translates the archaic speech of myth into a modern mythologem—not
> yet of course recognised as such—which constitutes one element of the
> myth "science."

Jung does not elaborate on his provocative expression "the myth
'science,'" but he does indicate that the kind of myth he has in mind
is not merely a product of the intellect. He concludes:

> This seemingly hopeless undertaking is a living and lived myth, satisfying
> to persons of a corresponding temperament, indeed beneficial insofar as

they have been cut off from their psychic origins by neurotic dissociation.[5]

Jung's psychology is a "living and lived myth," and like all myths it refers back to primordial times. In the Prolegomena to the *Essays*, Kerényi explains how myths are concerned with the *archai*, that is with "primary states that never age, can never be surpassed, and produce everything always." Whereas the philosopher treats these states as concepts, the teller of myths "without any digression or searching on his part, without any studious investigation or effort . . . finds himself in the primordiality that is his concern in the midst of the *archai* of which he is speaking."[6] Similarly, a Jungian analysis enables the analysand to find his way back to his own primordial time, and, by telling his story, renew his connection with the archetypes of the collective unconscious.

An unprecedented decline of religious authority in our culture has left many people dissociated from their spiritual origins. The French metaphysician and esoterist René Guénon (1886–1951) sought to counter this trend. His extensive writings cover Vedanta, Taoism, Sufism, Christianity, and the Hermetica, and present these traditions as so many aspects of a unanimous, perennial philosophy. This is not an exercise in comparative religion nor is it syncretism. Guénon aimed to reverse the collapse of religious certainty in the modern West and to reinstate traditional spirituality. The task of restoration that he initiated has been taken forward by a group of scholars who include Frithjof Schuon, Titus Burckhardt, Martin Lings, and S. H. Nasr. Their studies in metaphysics, cosmology, alchemy, sacred art, rites, symbols, and myths are based on the premise that the essential principles of all religions are identical. Every revelation has its source in one plenary revelation and each tradition is a branch of the one primordial tradition. This impressive synthesis, however, could only have been accomplished in an age of global communication. Despite its constant appeal to tradition, the perennial philosophy is but another way of "translating the archaic speech of myth into a modern mythologem."

S. H. Nasr's book *Knowledge and the Sacred* is an excellent introduction to the perennial philosophy or traditionalist school. In it he expounds the myth of the primordial tradition like this:

> From a certain point of view there is but one Tradition, the Primordial Tradition, which always is. It is the single truth, which is at once the heart and origin of all truths. All traditions are earthly manifestations of celestial archetypes related ultimately to the immutable archetype of the Primordial Tradition in the same way that all revelations are related to the Logos or the Word which was at the beginning.[7]

Whereas Jung's psychological myth takes us back to the foundations of psychic life in the collective unconscious, the myth of the perennial philosophy returns to the origin of religion in the primordial tradition.

Guénon has shown how the archetype of the primordial tradition is symbolized by the Holy Grail. In *The Lord of the World* he tells us that the Grail was originally entrusted to Adam in the terrestrial paradise only to be lost when he was banished from Eden. Later Seth obtained permission to return so as to recover the Grail and restore the primordial order that was destroyed by the Fall. There are no legends that can tell us who kept the Grail until the time of Christ. Guénon mentions the Celtic sources of the myth and suggests that "the Druids had a part in it and should be counted amongst the regular guardians of the primordial tradition."[8]

The terrestrial paradise is the true center of the world and is traditionally represented as a mandala with the tree of life at the central point and the four rivers flowing towards the cardinal points.[9] In the human microcosm the corresponding center is the heart, a symbolic equivalent of the Grail. Both the heart and the Grail signify the true center in man, namely the sense of eternity that was displaced by the Fall.[10] Whoever regains this center in himself restores the primordial tradition. Wagner must have intuited the connection between the Grail and the sense of eternity. As Gurnemanz is leading Parsifal to the Grail ceremony, the following dialogue is sung:

Parsifal: Scarce have I moved a pace
          and it seemeth that I am already far.

Gurnemanz: See, my son
          here time doth change to space.

Parsifal's quest for the treasure hard to obtain is a variant of a universal myth-theme. It involves the task of reversing the consequence of the Fall and thereby regaining the primordial tradition. For Jung it is symbolic of the individuation process, the inner work of restoring the wholeness of the psyche that is lost with the fall into ego-consciousness. Although this wholeness is inexpressible, it can be intuited through a multiplicity of symbols, e.g. the mandala, quaternity, sphere, lapis, microcosm, etc. Both Jung and Guénon studied these traditional symbols from the standpoint of their respective disciplines.[11]

Jung and Guénon draw upon a common vocabulary of symbols for the wholeness of man. Yet neither side would be inclined to credit the other with a viable method of attaining this wholeness. The mutual suspicion between representatives of both schools is such that no one has attempted to look at their ways of psycho-spiritual development from a phenomenological standpoint. What follows is merely a first step towards a comparative study of two "technologies of the self."[12]

In 1925 Guénon gave his only public lecture on *Oriental Metaphysics*. He presented a model of metaphysical realization that was applicable to a wide range of spiritual disciplines, e.g. Yoga, Sufi, or Taoist meditation. There are three stages of development involved. The first does not exceed the human domain and leads as far as the attainment of "integral individuality" which Guénon defines as the "realization or development of all the potentialities that are contained in the human individuality and that . . . reach out in diverse directions beyond the realm of the corporeal and sensible." Whoever realizes this state escapes the inexorable flow of time so that "the apparent succession of events is transformed into simultaneity."[13] In other words, the sense of eternity associated with the primordial tradition has been regained.

Guénon calls this first stage the "primordial state" because it entails the re-establishment of man's condition before the Fall. "He who fully 'owns' the primordial tradition," says Guénon in *The Lord of the World*, "who has reached the degree of effective knowledge implied by this possession is . . . effectively reintegrated in the fullness of the primordial state."[14]

At the second stage of metaphysical realization the human condition is fully transcended. Guénon denotes this level "the supra-individual state" which he describes thus:

> Here the world of man . . . is completely and definitely exceeded. It must also be said that what is exceeded is the world of forms in its widest meaning comprising of all individual states; it is that which determines individuality as such. The being which can no longer be called human has henceforth left "the flow of forms" to use a Far Eastern expression.[15]

Even though the supra-individual state transcends the flow of forms, it is still a conditioned mode of being and is therefore transitory. Beyond this level there is "the absolutely unconditioned stage free of all limitation." This is the third stage of metaphysical realization which is called the Supreme Identity in the Sufi tradition. It is only at this level that final Deliverance is attained.[16]

I will be examining the structural correspondences between the first two stages of metaphysical development and Jung's individuation process. But before that something must be said about the antithetical attitudes of Guénon and Jung.[17] Whereas Freud and Jung worked to extricate men from the authority of the past,[18] Guénon sought to reinstate traditional spirituality in the modern world. If he had no compunction about declaring psychoanalysis to be a satanic masterstroke, it is unrealistic to expect him to have been sympathetic to analytical psychology.[19] Schuon and his circle, who cannot differentiate between the two schools, have denounced Jung as the prophet of a subversive pseudo-spirituality.[20]

Few if any of my Jungian friends and colleagues are inclined to be ecumenical towards Guénon or his successors. But is it asking too much of psychologists to differentiate between Guénon's paranoid reactions to the modern world and the compelling metaphysical insights he formulated so lucidly? The experience of reading Guénon at his best confronts one with a vision that penetrates down to the *archai* of the world and beyond to its unfathomable ground. As both Guénon and Jung drew upon the great Gnostic tradition, a dialogue between perennial philosophy and analytical psychology could have important cultural consequences.

Jung's anti-metaphysical stance is not exactly helpful in this respect. He adhered rather doggedly to Kant who had argued that there were *a priori* limits to knowledge and that metaphysics was impossible.[21] For Guénon, any philosopher who followed this line simply displayed his incapacity for metaphysical thinking. According to the perennial philosophy, true metaphysics derives from direct spiritual realization. It does not deal in empty abstractions and proceeds from "immediate supra-rational knowledge." As Chuang Tzu put it, "If you have insight you use your inner eye, your inner ear to pierce to the heart of things and have no need of intellectual knowledge." Incidentally, I found this quotation in Jung's *Synchronicity* essay. He interprets it as an instance of "the absolute knowledge of the unconscious" and of "the presence of the microcosm in macrocosmic events."[22] I will have more to say about the microcosm in the next section.

Guénon is emphatic that the metaphysical states that are his concern must not be regarded as psychological. In *Oriental Metaphysics* he maintains that:

> By definition psychology can only be concerned with human states, and further, what it stands for today is only a very limited part of the potentialities of the individual, who includes far more than specialists in this science are able to imagine.[23]

However, according to Jung's understanding of the scope of psychology, this science is by no means confined to the "human all too human":

> The indefinite extent of the unconscious component makes a comprehensive definition of the human personality impossible. Accordingly, the unconscious supplements the picture with living figures ranging from the animal to the divine, as the two extremes outside man, and rounds out the animal extreme, through the addition of vegetable and inorganic abstractions, into a microcosm.[24]

Whereas the psychology Guénon has in mind is confined to the ego, the subject of waking consciousness, Jung's model of the psyche is centered on the self, a totality that encompasses the unconscious and conscious, the animal and the divine in man. Individuation is a method of psycho-spiritual development that leads to the relativization of the ego and the realization of the self. An existence that is bound to ego-consciousness can only actualize a limited range of a person's potentialities—in a word, getting and spending. In the self, all the possibilities immanent in the person are actualized. Jung calls this condition "wholeness" and equates it with "life in God."[25]

For Jung, the emergence of ego consciousness in the first half of life is a *felix culpa*. It confines the personality to profane time, which, of necessity, places a limit on the possibilities that can be actualized. Individuation in the second half of life strives to overcome the privations of finitude and restores the sense of eternity. Jung describes this process in his little essay *On Resurrection*:

> Through the progressive integration of the unconscious, we have a reasonable chance to make experiences of an archetypal nature providing us with the feeling of continuity before and after our existence. The better we understand the archetype the more we participate in its life and the more we realize its eternity or timelessness.[26]

In the next paragraph Jung follows on with a quotation from the Mithraic Liturgy, "I am a Star following his way like you." Wholeness and the sense of eternity are fused in this evocative image. The star is an exemplary symbol of the self, and Jung goes on to confirm that "The realization of the self means a re-establishment of Man as the microcosm, i.e. man's cosmic relatedness."[27] This statement is consistent both with logic and the perennial philosophy. The person who attains integral individuality and thereby actualizes all the possibilities inherent in his being becomes a microcosm and a mirror of the totality of states in the macrocosm.[28]

The self, the microcosm, and the endless circular way of the stars are all symbols for a mode of being we can intuit but never grasp with the intellect. Once in a foolhardy moment, I put the proposition to a former disciple of Guénon that Jungian individuation was a way of restoring the primordial state. He found this deeply offensive and said that the wholeness Jung spoke about was "pitifully relative." In mitigation, it should be said that Jung's robust anti-metaphysical stance invites an attack like this.

Whereas Guénon's three stages of realization unfold within an orthodox religious tradition, Jung's individuation process does not depend on this context. For a traditionalist, any technique of transcendence without the sanction of spiritual authority is *prima facie* invalid. Yet a phenomenological comparison has disclosed significant correspondences between psychological wholeness and the primordial state. Both modes of being are characterized by the actualization of totality and the restoration of the sense of eternity. This can hardly be dismissed as "pitifully relative."

If the primordial state is still confined to the human domain, there is nothing inherently contradictory in the claim that it can be attained by way of a psychological method. The second stage of metaphysical realization, the supra-individual state, is, however, beyond the range of psychology by definition. But Jung exceeded the normal limits of psychology in the theories of the last phase of his working life. From the mid-'40s he began to formulate a metapsychology that encompassed transpsychic reality. This in turn led him to revise his model of the individuation process and take it to a new level of being.

Jung's paradigm shift occurred when he found it necessary to redefine the concept of the archetype to take account of synchronistic

phenomena. For the sake of brevity I will compress the history of
Jung's archetypal theory into three stages:

(i) Archetypes manifest themselves in one dimension, as images in the
    psyche. Initially Jung defined the archetype as an innate disposi-
    tion in the unconscious to form an image. Such a disposition is
    analogous to instinct and universal in the human species.

(ii) Jung had experiences that suggested an archetype could manifest
    itself in two dimensions: in the interiority of the subject as an
    image and as a corresponding configuration of events in the
    external world. He conjectured that in these instances the arche-
    type "transgressed" the boundary between inner and outer. Such
    an archetype could no longer be described as psychic, but as
    "quasi-psychic" or "psychoid." The theory of synchronicity is
    based on this premise and finds empirical confirmation in the
    clinical experience of all Jungian analysts.

(iii) The second formulation, however, presupposes the inner-outer
    dualism of ego-consciousness and also implies that somehow the
    psychoid archetype "causes" a synchronistic event. But
    synchronicity is an acausal category and the connection between
    the inner and outer event is one of meaning, not cause and effect.
    Eventually Jung came to see that the experience of synchronicity
    contradicted our dualistic habits of thought. The presence of
    acausal orderedness or "the latent rationality of all things" points
    towards a unitary reality that is neither inner nor outer but
    transcends both dimensions. In *Mysterium Coniunctionis* Jung
    designated this implicate order "the unus mundus."

Jung derived the term *unus mundus* from the sixteenth-century
alchemist Gerhard Dorn and traced the source of this idea back to the
Logos doctrine expounded by Philo of Alexandria (20 B.C.E.–50 C.E.).
According to Philo, God initially conceived the creation of the world
in his mind just as an architect conceives the blueprint of a city before
it is built. The totality of divine ideas or archetypes constitute the
intelligible world and the intelligible world in the act of creation is the

Logos.[29]

While Dorn called the intelligible world the unus mundus, Jung spoke of "the transcendental psycho-physical background to our empirical world." He described it as "a potential world insofar as all the conditions which determine the form of empirical phenomena are inherent in it."[30] The doctrine of the unus mundus enabled Jung to view psyche and matter as two sides of the same coin and made him a metaphysician despite himself.

For Jung the idea of a transcendental background to the world was no armchair speculation. He may well have experimented with Dorn's method of alchemical meditation which he described at length in chapter six of *Mysterium Coniunctionis*. If so, he would have gone beyond psychological individuation. Whereas this process reaches its goal in the realization of the self as the totality of the psyche, Dorn's alchemical meditation goes a step further to the union of the whole man with the unus mundus.[31] At this stage the human condition is exceeded.

We are now better placed to discern the correspondences and divergences between Jung's model of psycho-spiritual development and Guénon's three stages of metaphysical realization. The first stage is that of integral individuality or the primordial state. It entails the actualization of all the possibilities inherent in the person and the restoration of the sense of eternity. I have suggested that the psychological experience of wholeness or the realization of psychic totality displays the same features. Both wholeness and the primordial state are represented by the microcosm, but neither Jung nor Guénon see this as symbolizing the final developmental stage. In Guénon's scheme the next level of realization is the "supra-individual state" where the being passes beyond the "flow of forms." Could he not be said to have merged with the unus mundus that contains everything in a state of undifferentiated potentiality? Just as the primordial state is a return to the situation of man before the Fall, so is union with the unus mundus a reversion to the first day of creation.

The correlations between Jung's metapsychology and Guénon's metaphysic continue up to the second stage of metaphysical realization, namely the supra-individual state. But because psychology is confined to conditioned states of being, it is unable to encompass the third and final stage of realization, the Supreme Identity. As Guénon points out, this state can only be spoken of in the language of metaphysics:

> The highest objective is the absolutely unconditioned state, free from all limitation; for this reason it is completely inexpressible, and all that one can say of it must be conveyed in negative terms by divestment of the limits that determine and define all existence in its relativity.[32]

In his commentaries on the Eastern traditions, Jung equates this state with one of sheer unconsciousness. For example, in his commentary on *The Tibetan Book of the Great Liberation*, he states:

> It is psychologically correct to say "At-one-ment" is attained by withdrawal from the world of consciousness. In the stratosphere of the unconscious there are no more thunderstorms because nothing is differentiated enough to produce tensions and conflicts.[33]

If this is correct psychologically, it is almost certainly incorrect metaphysically. Jung's conflation of pre-subject-object with trans-subject-object vitiates his commentaries on oriental doctrines and spiritual disciplines.[34] Here the Guénonian metaphysicians have a legitimate critical grievance. However, this is not a valid pretext for dismissing Jung out of hand or for attempting to refute his psychology after a cursory and narrowly selective reading of the Collected Works.[35]

Jung's psychology has been aptly described as a myth of reflective consciousness.[36] Such a myth must of necessity be at variance with the non-dualism advocated by Guénon. An extinction of the conscious subject in the undifferentiated ground of Being contradicts the premises upon which Jung's model of individuation rests. The goal of this process is to enable God to become conscious in man, not to bring about the reabsorption of man in the Godhead. That said, Jung's willingness to endorse the possibility of attaining the union of the whole man with the unus mundus indicates that he did not confine his vision of individuation to the psychic domain.

We began with Jung's admission that his psychology is a modern myth and suggested that the same applied to the perennial philosophy. Both myths are equally compelling, but in the end one is obliged to make a choice between them. Jung's myth of consciousness must, by its own logic, acknowledge that it is a myth. By contrast, Guénon and his successors are convinced that there really was a Golden Age and that, when the present Iron Age or Kali-yuga has run its course, the primordial tradition will be reinstated in all its fullness.[37] Their myth is born out of a deep hostility to the modern world and carries the imprimatur of their spiritual authority. I need hardly emphasize the sinister totalitarian shadow that tends to be constellated when these doctrines are taken seriously.[38]

As a modern myth-maker, Jung was not immune to such shadow contamination. Fortunately, he preferred "the precious gift of doubt" to the certainties of Guénon or Schuon.[39] A dream he had prior to writing *Answer to Job* is an eloquent testimony to his position. He dreamt of his long deceased father, who had been a Lutheran pastor but was now custodian of a spacious eighteenth-century house. Father and son go up to the second floor and enter a vast circular room, a mandalic structure like the council hall of Akbar that Jung had seen during his visit to India. A ladder leads up to a door set in the wall behind which "the highest presence" resides. Paul Jung is to take his son up there, but before ascending the ladder he prostrates himself Muslim style. Carl Jung then does the same, but he is unable to bring his forehead all the way down and leaves just a millimeter of space above the floor.[40]

A psychology that places such a high premium on reflective consciousness cannot be reconciled with a spirituality that requires unconditional submission to authority. Guénon and his disciples are all Muslim converts and regard complete obedience as the sine qua non for spiritual development. For this reason, they would regard the dream as evidence of individualism on Jung's part and the work it anticipated as a revolt against transcendence.

To conclude I will suggest that *Answer to Job* should be read in the light of a statement that Guénon once made. He remarked that the historical religions were "so many heresies" compared with "the primordial and unanimous tradition."[41] From this perspective, the iconoclasm of *Answer to Job* could be seen as preparatory to the restoration of the primordial tradition by the most radical means possible. Jung could never have undertaken this task without first distancing himself from spiritual authority, and therefore he could not bring his head all the way down to the floor. Guénon, by contrast, had no such mental reservations in the face of divine decrees. But while he remained in a state of projection and anticipated the return of the primordial tradition as a literal fact, Jung regarded this event as an imaginal reality. Their myths come to meet each other at this point, separated by only a millimeter of space.

Notes

1. C. G. Jung, *Memories, Dreams, Reflections*, recorded and edited by Aniela Jaffé, trans. Richard and Clara Winston (London: Fontana Paperbacks, 1983), 194–95.

2. C. G. Jung, *Two Essays on Analytical Psychology*, Collected Works 7, ed. Herbert Read, Michael Fordham and Gerhard Adler, trans. R. F. C. Hull (London: Routledge and Kegan Paul, 1966), para. 118.

3. This claim has been severely criticized by Ken Wilber who maintains that the pre-personal and the transpersonal are conflated in Jung's psychology: "not only does Jung occasionally end up glorifying certain infantile mythic forms of thought, he also frequently gives a regressive treatment of Spirit" (Ken Wilber, "The Pre-Trans Fallacy," in *Eye to Eye: The Quest for the New Paradigm* [New York: Archer Books, 1983], 211).

4. Jung likens the archetypes to "the logical categories which are always and everywhere present as the basic postulates of reason" (C. G. Jung, *Psychology and Religion West and East*, Collected Works 11, ed. Herbert Read, Michael Fordham and Gerhard Adler, trans. R. F. C. Hull [London: Routledge and Kegan Paul, 1969], para. 845).

5. C. G. Jung and C. Kerényi, *Essays on a Science of Mythology*, trans. R. F. C. Hull (Princeton: Princeton University Press, 1969), 98–9.

6. Jung and Kerényi, *Essays on a Science of Mythology*, 7–8.

7. S. H. Nasr, *Knowledge and the Sacred*, The Gifford Lectures 1981 (Edinburgh: Edinburgh University Press, 1981), 74. For Nasr the "archetype of the Primordial Tradition" has nothing to do with the collective unconscious in Jung's psychology. He understands the terms in "the strict Platonic sense," i.e. as an unmanifest idea in the mind of God.

8. René Guénon, *The Lord of the World*, trans. Carolyn Shaffer and Olga de Nottbeck, revised by Anthony Cheke and Anthony Blake (Moorcote, Yorkshire: Coombe Springs Press, 1983), ch. 5. See also, Caitlin Matthews, "The Voices of the Wells: Celtic Oral Themes," in *The Household of the Grail*, ed. John Matthews (Wellingborough, Northamptonshire: Aquarian Press, 1990).

9. See: C.G. Jung, *Psychology and Alchemy*, Collected Works 12, ed. Herbert Read, Michael Fordham and Gerhard Adler, trans. R. F. C. Hull (London: Routledge and Kegan Paul, 1968), figs. 62, 197. Here Christ or the Lamb replaces the Tree at the center.

10. René Guénon, "The Sacred Heart and the Legend of the Holy Grail," in *Studies in Comparative Religion* 16.2–3 (Bedfont, Middlesex: Perennial

Books, undated), 234–41. In this essay Guénon explains the correspondence between heart and Grail like this: "The terrestrial Paradise was in fact the true 'Center of the World,' which is everywhere symbolically assimilated to the Divine Heart. Can one not say that Adam, by the fact he was in Eden, truly lived in the Heart of God?"

11. For Jung's important Grail dream which occurred while he was in India, see: C. G. Jung, *Memories, Dreams, Reflections*, 310–12. See also: M. L. von Franz, *C. G. Jung: His Myth in Our Time*, trans. W. H. Kennedy (London: Hodder and Stoughton, 1975), ch. 14, "Le Cri de Merlin," and Pedro-de Salles P. Kujawski's "In Service to the Psyche" in *The Household of the Grail*, ed. John Matthews.

12. This term was coined by Foucault. See, for example, *Technologies of the Self: A Seminar with Michel Foucault*, ed. Luther H. Martin, Huck Gutman and Patrick H. Hutton (London: Tavistock, 1988).

13. Guénon, "Oriental Metaphysics," in *The Sword of Gnosis*, ed. Jacob Needleman (London: Routledge and Kegan Paul, 1986), 49–50.

14. Guénon, *The Lord of the World*, 28.

15. Guénon, "Oriental Metaphysics," 50–51.

16. According to Ananda Coomaraswamy, "The ultimate reality of metaphysics is a Supreme Identity, in which the opposition of all contraries, even of being and not-being, is resolved" (Coomaraswamy, "The Vedanta and Western Tradition," in *Coomaraswamy 2: Selected Papers, Metaphysics*, ed. Roger Lipsey [Princeton University Press, 1977], 6).

17. Guénon came from a background of conservative French Catholicism, Jung from one of Swiss Protestantism. For a short biography of Guénon in English, see Robin Waterfield, *René Guénon and the Future of the West* (Wellingborough, Northamptonshire: Aquarian Press, 1987).

18. I have taken this phrase from Philip Rieff. See *Freud, the Mind of the Moralist* (Chicago: University of Chicago Press, 1979), ch. 6, "The Authority of the Past." Rieff, however, maintains that only Freud is a genuine liberator; Jung represents a conservative, revisionist form of psychoanalysis of dubious merit.

19. Guénon, *The Reign of Quantity and the Signs of the Times*, trans. Lord Northbourne (Baltimore, Maryland: Penguin, 1972) ch. 34, "The Misdeeds of Psychoanalysis." See also, "Tradition and the Unconscious," in *Fundamental Symbols: The Universal Language of Sacred Science*, trans. Alvin Moore; ed. Michel Válsan and Martin Lings (Cambridge: Quinta Essentia, 1995). Here Guénon presents a critique of the collective unconscious that anticipates Ken

Wilber's "pre-trans fallacy."

20. For a reply to this dreadful polemic, see my "Pneuma and Psyche: A Reply to a Gnostic Critique of Jung," in *Spring* 54 (Putnam, Connecticut: Spring Publications, 1993), 56–70.

21. Wolfgang Giegerich suggests that Jung did his work a disservice by insisting he was an empiricist: "Whenever he exercised conscious control over his theorizing and intended to be critical, he wanted to freeze his amazing psychological insights on the logically lowest level, the ontic level of 'empirical findings'" (Wolfgang Giegerich, "The Rescue of the World: Jung, Hegel, and the Subjective Universe," *Spring* 1981 [Dallas: Spring Publications, 1981], 108).

22. C. G. Jung, *The Structure and Dynamics of the Psyche*, Collected Works 8, ed. Herbert Read, Michael Fordham and Gerhard Adler, trans. R. F. C. Hull (London: Routledge and Kegan Paul, 1969), para. 923.

23. Guénon, "Oriental Metaphysics," 52.

24. C. G. Jung, *The Archetypes and the Collective Unconscious*, Collected Works 9 (i), ed. Herbert Read, Michael Fordham, and Gerhard Adler, trans. R. F. C. Hull (London: Routledge and Kegan Paul, 1968), para. 315.

25. In a dialogue with the theologian H. L. Philp, Jung described individuation as "the life in God." See: C. G. Jung, *The Symbolic Life*, Collected Works 18, ed. Herbert Read, Michael Fordham, and Gerhard Adler, trans. R. F. C. Hull (London: Routledge and Kegan Paul, 1977), para. 1624.

26. C. G. Jung, *The Symbolic Life*, para. 1572.

27. C. G. Jung, *The Symbolic Life*, para. 1573.

28. Guénon examines the relationship between the primordial state and the microcosm in *The Symbolism of the Cross*, trans. A. Macnab (London: Luzac and Co., 1958/1975), ch. 2., "Universal Man."

29. Philo, *De Opificio Mundi*, in *Works*, vol. 1, trans. F. H. Colson and G. H. Whitaker (Harvard and London: Loeb Classical Library, 1929).

30. C. G. Jung, *Mysterium Coniunctionis*, Collected Works 14, ed. Herbert Read, Michael Fordham, and Gerhard Adler, trans. R. F. C. Hull (London: Routledge and Kegan Paul, 1963), para. 769. For a comparison between Philo's Logos and the unus mundus of Jung and the alchemical tradition, see my essay "A Word Conceived in Intellect," in *Temenos* 6 (London, 1985), 195–206 (published under my former name, Andrew Mouldey).

31. C. G. Jung, *Mysterium Coniunctionis*, para. 760.

32. Guénon, "Oriental Metaphysics," 51.

33. C. G. Jung, *Psychology and Religion: West and East*, para. 799.

34. To concede that Wilber's "pre-trans fallacy" is applicable in this particular context is not to endorse his critique of Jung's psychology as a whole. See note 3.

35. As does Titus Burkhardt in "Cosmology and Modern Science," in *The Sword of Gnosis*, 167–78.

36. This myth is expounded in Edward F. Edinger, *The Creation of Consciousness: Jung's Myth for Modern Man* (Toronto: Inner City Books, 1984).

37. Guénon advances this thesis in his apocaplyptic book, *The Reign of Quantity and the Signs of the Times*. This compelling work reads like science fiction in parts, and like the best science fiction it may well have correctly anticipated the future. For an exposition of the Hindu Doctrine of the yugas on which Guénon's claims are based, see Heinrich Zimmer, *Myths and Symbols in Indian Art and Civilization*, ed. Joseph Campbell (Princeton: Princeton University Press, 1946), ch. 1:2, "The Wheel of Rebirth."

38. The reports of alleged cultic abuses at the Tariqah presided over by Schuon in Bloomington, Indiana are now too numerous to disregard.

39. "I for my part prefer the precious gift of doubt, for the reason that it does not violate the virginity of things beyond our ken" (C. G. Jung, *Psychology and Alchemy*, para. 8).

40. C. G. Jung, *Memories, Dreams, Reflections*, pp. 244–47. Curiously, Jung gives a very different version of this dream in a letter to Victor White dated 30 January 1948. C. G. Jung, *Letters Vol. 1: 1906–50*, ed. Gerhard Adler and Aniela Jaffé (Princeton University Press, 1973), 490–93.

41. Frithjof Schuon cites this remark in his "Note on René Guénon" in *Studies in Comparative Religion* 17.1–2 (Bedfont, Middlesex: Perennial Books, undated), 5.

The Lost Spirit of Hellenic Philosophy

CHRISTOS EVANGELIOU

THE APPELLATION "Western" is inappropriately applied to Ancient Hellas and its products, especially Hellenic philosophy. For neither the spirit of free inquiry and bold speculation, nor the quest for human perfection via autonomous, virtuous activity and ethical excellence survived, in their Hellenic form, the imposition of inflexible Church doctrines and practices upon Europe with the coming of Christian faith and the theocratic proclivity of the Church, especially the hierarchically organized Catholic Church. Yet, these noble ideals had been embodied in the lives, and expressed in the theories, of genuine Hellenic philosophers for many centuries, from Pythagoras to Plato, to Plotinus, to Porphyry, and beyond. Since the Renaissance, several attempts, primarily by Platonists, to revive the free spirit, and other virtues of Hellenic philosophy, have been invariably frustrated by violent reactions from religious movements, such as the Reformation, the Counter-Reformation, and the bloody wars which followed them.

While modern science succeeded, to a certain extent and after much struggle with the Catholic Church, in freeing itself from the snares of medieval theocratic restrictions, and thereby managed to reconnect itself with the scientific spirit of late antiquity and its great achievements—especially in the fields of cosmology, physics, mathematics, and medicine—which enabled it to advance, the mainstream philosophy in the West has as yet failed to do so. For, as in the Middle Ages, so in modern and post-modern times, "European philosophy" has continued to play the undignified and servile roles of *ancilla theologiae*,

This paper was given at the conference on "Neoplatonism and Contemporary Thought," Vanderbilt University, May 18–21, 1995. The complete version of the paper, including footnotes, will be published in the conference proceedings.

ancilla scientiae, and, with the coming of Marxist orthodoxy of "scientific socialism," *ancilla ideologiae*. In this respect, "Western philosophy," as it has been historically practiced in Europe, especially Northern and Eastern Europe, is a very different kind of product from the autonomous intellectual activity which the Ancient Hellenes named *philosophia* and honored as "the queen of arts and sciences" to which it gave birth.

Consequently, as we stand at the end of the twentieth century and at the beginning of the post-cold war era; as we witness the collapse of Soviet-style socialism and the coming of the post-modern era; as we look at the dawn of a new millennium and dream of a New Global Order, the moment would seem propitious to stop and reflect upon our philosophical past as exemplified in the free spirit of Ancient Hellenic philosophy and its many misfortunes—"its passion," if you like—in the West in the last two millennia. From such a vantage point, it would seem imperative that the philosophic freedom and its concomitant religious tolerance, as experienced in the Hellenic and pre-Christian era, be revived and fostered in the post-modern world of today and tomorrow, if our global, fragile, and culturally diverse community is to be preserved and allowed to flourish in the dawning new millennium.

In my view, Neoplatonism, as a form of successfully revived Platonism in late antiquity, has much to contribute to the goal of common cultural preservation and global flourishing. Representing, as it does, the last phase of activity of the spirit of Hellenic philosophy in late antiquity, and having played a key role in nobly defending Hellenism against various forms of barbarism, Platonism may become again the avant-garde of a new movement to restore philosophy to its ancestral dignity and glory. This task it can accomplish by reviving the Hellenic spirit of freely theorizing about nature and culture, and by acknowledging no other authority but human reason (in both its forms, as Hellenic *logos* and *nous*, that is, discursive reasoning and intellective or intuitive seeing) and human virtuous action in both its aspects, as ethical and intellectual activity in accordance with Hellenic excellences.

I should add parenthetically that, as a student of the history of

Hellenic philosophy, I have been puzzled for a long time by the facility with which the Northern European historians of philosophy attempt to appropriate the heritage of Hellenic philosophy as exclusively their own, and to make it part of what they call "Western philosophy," which they oppose to Eastern philosophies. More recently, in my trips to Greece and to India, I was surprised to discover that even these non-Western and remote peoples have uncritically accepted this European claim with its artificial division between East and West, with Ancient Hellas (as distinct from Modern Greece) and its glorious philosophy placed firmly, but unfairly, as we will see, in the West. Unexpectedly, I encountered strong resistance from Greeks and Indians, when I tried to discuss the falsity of the unhistorical Northern European exclusive claim to the heritage and glory of Ancient Hellenic philosophy.

I would like, therefore, to take this opportunity to express some of my novel views regarding the question of the so-called "Western philosophy" and its alleged connection to, and continuity with, the free spirit of inquiry of genuine Hellenic philosophy. In what follows I shall provide evidence in support of the thesis that the appellation "Western" is a misnomer, when it is uncritically applied to Ancient Hellas in general, and to Hellenic philosophy in particular which—in the artificial balance of "West versus East" conventional division—has historically and with good reason inclined towards the spiritually more refined East.

I shall also argue that the reason for which Christian and theocratic Western Europe, as a matter of historical fact, did not develop any schools of genuine philosophy comparable to the many and diverse schools of ancient, humanistic Hellas, is related directly to a terrible misfortune which befell Europe and from which it has not, as yet, completely recovered. By this I mean the coming into being of what may be called aberrations of Judaism, namely Christianity and Islam. These two monotheistic religions have been, by their own dogmatic theologies and theocratic proclivities, historically intolerant, not only of other divinities (both gods and goddesses), but also of genuine Hellenic *philosophia* as the Ancient Hellenes envisioned this discipline, that is, a free and unfettered inquiry into the nature of all things including truth, beauty, goodness, and human and divine beings.

A note of clarification is called for here, and I wish to be clear on this important point. The expression "genuine philosophy" is intended to capture, I repeat, the original sense in which *philosophia* was understood by Hellenic philosophers during the millennium of free philosophic activity from Pythagoras to Proclus. There is no doubt that the Ancient Hellenes practiced philosophy in at least two essential ways which have been conspicuously absent from Western Europe: First, philosophy as a free and unfettered intelligent search for truth regarding the nature of Nature and the nature of Man; and secondly, philosophy as an authentic way of life which is ethically self-sufficient and active in accordance with both kinds of Hellenic excellences, intellectual and ethical.

In this respect, it would seem, to an objective observer, that these two revealed religions of "the Book," as they are called, have been primarily responsible for two sins against Hellenic philosophy which can perhaps be identified briefly as follows: First, the strangulation of that unrestricted and free spirit of inquiry and that kind of autonomous ethical life, which had given birth to genuine Hellenic philosophy as it developed in the pre-Christian and pre-Islamic Mediterranean world, by introducing the alien authority of "sacred books" and scriptural revelations, accompanied by the claim that such revelations be accepted on faith as "the word of God"; and secondly, the fact that, like the Islamized world, Christian Europe, including Orthodox Christian Greece, has failed to produce any philosophy comparable to the genuine Hellenic philosophy, in its autonomy, its dignity, and self-sufficiency, as opposed to simple pseudonyms and "homonyms" of philosophy which are dogmatic or scholastic theologies in disguise, and invariably in the service of theocratic tyrants such as the Pope, the Caliph, the Holy Emperor, or the Turkish Sultan.

I think that this larger problem of the relation between *philosophia* as the Hellenes understood it, and the homonymous term "philosophy" as has been used and abused in the Christian West during the long Dark Ages, the Middle Ages, and further on, clearly relates to the issue of the West's claim to "cultural hegemony," and has important implications for the emerging character of our global cultural community which needs above anything else religious tolerance, cultural diversity, and philosophical enlightenment. At the end of the twentieth century, the time seems right for a revival of genuine philosophy, especially the revived Platonism which, as the last representative of Hellenic philosophy, was able to preserve in some measure its autonomy, its dignity, and its diversity. It can, therefore, serve as a linkage for our world to reconnect with the Hellenic roots of its great philosophic past.

The Ambiguity of "Western" as Applied to Hellenic Philosophy

In the expression "Western philosophy" two ambiguous terms are connected closely and repeated so frequently that the confusion generated by such infelicitous juxtaposition almost cries out for clarification. Regarding the first term "Western," one would be taxed to point out, in the globe which revolves round the sun and makes day and night, where on Earth the East stops and the West begins. Even if we follow the conventional wisdom and allow that Iceland and England are definitely in the West, while Korea and Japan, for example, are definitely in the East, where shall we rightfully place countries like Greece and India? Both are to the East of the first pair, but to the West of the second pair. Hence the problem. One may think that the problem can be easily solved by comparing the two countries directly to each other, in which case it can be said that India is definitely in the East and Greece is definitely in the West relative to each other. But perhaps the situation is more complex than it appears to be at first glance.

For, even if the Indians were to go along with this solution, I suspect that the Greeks would have great difficulty accepting it for the following reason: geographically, Greece belongs to "Eastern Mediterranean"; as in ancient times, Greece occupies the tiny peninsula and the Aegean sea where three continents meet: Africa, Asia, and Europe. This fact perhaps explains why the Ancient Hellenes conceived of the strange notion that the center of the world, "the navel of the Earth" as they used to say, was right there in the middle of Hellas, at one of the peaks of Parnassus. It was there, at the holy shrine of Delphi, where Dionysus, the god of music and dance, rested from his long journey from India through Asia and Africa, according to ancient legend, and was welcomed by his brother Apollo, god of light and reason. In this symbolic way, the conventional "East and West" came together harmoniously, and from their harmonious union the Classical Hellenic civilization emerged as a ripe fruit of the human spirit and took its rightful place among the other ancient civilizations of the great rivers: the Nile, the Euphrates, the Indus, the Ganges, and the Yangtze.

In terms of geography, then, the Modern Greeks, like their ancestors or like any other sensible people, may think of themselves as Westerners when they face towards the rising sun, but when they turn around and face the setting sun they consider themselves as Easterners or, at least, as non-Westerners. Even if we turned to history for assistance, we would find that it provides no greater help than geography for the correct characterization of the place of Hellas and its philosophy: Western or Eastern? Historically speaking, from the time of the rise of Rome to political power in the third century B.C.E. to the Italian Renaissance in the fifteenth century C.E., the Hellenic and the Hellenistic Hellas—and even the Byzantine and Christian Greece—had invariably identified itself with the culturally more refined East, in conscious opposition to the Latin West which to the Hellenic minds and eyes of that time, as opposed to modern times, appeared as a synonym of barbarity.

Thus, when the Roman Empire was divided into two in the end of the fourth century (in 395 C.E.), the division created the Latin (Western) and the Greek (Eastern) Roman Empires. Ironically, as it would seem, history was to repeat itself in the eleventh century, when a schism occurred in Christendom between the Catholic Church which was, not surprisingly, Latin and Western, and the Orthodox Church which was, again not surprisingly, Greek and Eastern. These historical considerations seem to tip the balance of placing both Ancient Hellas and Christian Greece definitively toward the East in the artificial division between East and West.

But this is not the end of the story. Since the Crusades, and more so with the rise to prominence of such Western European powers as France, England, and Germany, the ex-barbarians of the West and the North thought that they would gain some respectability if they presented themselves as inheritors of the classical world and its brilliant culture. Thus they boldly claimed as their own not only the Latin, but also the Hellenic, classical heritage which they began, at that specific time, to characterize as "Western" and oppose it to the Eastern Orthodox as well as the Islamic world.

It may be true that intellectually awakened people have always remained skeptical about the applicability of the appellation of "Western" to the Ancient Hellenic philosophy and culture, and about the truthfulness of the European claim of having an exclusive right to classical inheritance. However, the Northern Europeans have been successful in persuading almost the entire world that there is no real difference between themselves, in the role of builders of colonial imperialism, and the creators of classical civilization and Hellenic philosophy. Unfortunate and sad as it may seem to some of us, the result of these activities of the Europeans has been that the Ancient Hellenes are uncritically identified as Westerners now, and they are placed in the same basket with the British, French, Dutch, and German colonialists of Africa and Asia, not only by the Northern Europeans themselves and their propaganda, but also by many African and Asian peoples as they struggle for ethnic identity, national recognition, and social reconstruction. This outcome is certainly unfair to the Ancient Hellenes; but it is also unjust to scholars in the African and Asian nations who, as a result of the European claim to the Hellenic heritage, do not readily perceive the falsity of such claims at their own expense. They thus deprive themselves of a valuable ally, the treasure of Hellenic culture and philosophy, in their pedagogical, political, intellectual, and cultural endeavors.

This is truly a tragic irony. The European claim is a monopoly of the worst possible kind. The fraud should be exposed, I think, and the truth should be told: The achievements of the Ancient Hellenes, especially Hellenic philosophy, do not belong exclusively (or even primarily) to the Christian European West or the Islamic Asiatic East; rather, they belong to the World at large and to mankind as a whole, especially to those remnants of pre-Christian and pre-Islamic traditions and cultures, with which the Ancient Hellenes had many affinities including the love of human and undogmatic wisdom, as opposed to the dogmatic and divine "wisdom" to be found in some sacred books; and the tolerant worship of many divinities (gods and goddesses), as opposed to the monomaniac folly of masculine monotheism, and its concomitant bigotry and religious fanaticism. By working diligently together, all those who value these old traditions could bring about a revival of philosophy of the genuine kind, perhaps here in America, this great land of the free and the brave, whose democratic institutions have been characterized by tolerance and diversity.

So much, then, about the ambiguity and the perplexities of the appellation "Western" as applied to Ancient Hellas and to Hellenic *philosophia*. It is time now for us to try to provide perhaps a more precise definition of genuine Hellenic philosophy and its ideal representatives as they function in theory and in practice.

Hellenic Philosophy Delineated

Since the previous observations have shown that Ancient Hellas and the West have, historically and geographically, stood at opposite poles, and since philosophy is legitimately connected with Ancient Greece, it follows that the expression "Western philosophy" as used by Northern European historians of philosophy, becomes problematic. Besides, if we were to grant the Northern Europeans their wish to remove Classical Hellas from the middle place which it has historically, geographically, and culturally occupied between the East and the West, the South and the North, as a beacon of bright light available to every part of the world which seeks philosophical enlightenment—and, furthermore, if we were to allow the Northern Europeans, especially the British and the German, to claim as exclusively their own the Hellenic Classical heritage, especially Hellenic philosophy which, by its very nature, has an ecumenical value and pananthropic appeal—then we would be doing a disservice, as I said earlier, to our students and our children who deserve a better future, a life with more genuine humanistic *paideia*, and with less racial or religious intolerance and hatred.

From these considerations the following central question arises: Has the Christian West, impartially seen as an entity separate and different from Ancient Hellas, and narrowly defined as the barbarized Western part of the divided Roman Empire, in its millennial history produced any philosophers or philosophical schools which are comparable to the schools of Hellenic philosophy or to Indian and Chinese schools of philosophy for that matter? This is an important and complex question which cannot be answered with a simple and short answer. The nature of the answer depends on the meaning to be assigned to *philosophia* which, like the word *demokratia*, is a very attractive Hellenic concept and, thus has been much used and abused by many in the European West who, as Plato said, would like to appear rather than be philosophers.

What, then, is philosophy? What is this wisdom with which great minds, the authentic philosophers, are said to fall in love? What exactly did the Ancient Hellenes mean with this beautiful word *philosophia*, and how did they distinguish the genuine from the seeming philosophers of their time whom they called Sophists? In a broad sense, there is nothing mysterious about the inborn and burning human desire to learn by opening the eyes and the mind to the natural and the cultural world around us, by asking difficult questions both as teachers and as students, and by trying to the best of our ability to articulate reasonable, responsible, and honest answers to such questions.

But if we were to isolate any specific criteria by which an authentic philosopher would be distinguished from his "homonyms," then in the light of the long history of Hellenic philosophy we would not be far off the mark if we specified the two kinds of Hellenic excellence, intellectual and ethical, as such criteria. According to this delineation of genuine Hellenic philosophy, one can say that a genuine philosopher is both a noetically self-sufficient and an ethically autonomous human being, which means that he or she has accomplished two important philosophical tasks.

First, he has thoroughly examined himself; he has, for a long time, carefully observed the natural and the cultural world around him; he has diligently studied the works of other great minds and has freely discussed with his friends the great questions of life; and after prolonged and serious thinking, he has likely formed a cosmo-theory and/or a bio-theory, which articulates his insight into the nature of things and his own nature, the human nature, so that he can give a reasoned account of it and can teach those who may wish to listen and learn from him.

Secondly, the genuine philosopher does not only teach his wisdom, but also, and more importantly, he practices his teaching in his own daily life; for he is ready and willing to hold himself to higher ethical standards than the ones which his society demands of the majority of the people, and he is prepared to set the value of his philosophic freedom higher than life itself, and much higher than wealth and material goods of any kind. By so doing, the genuine philosopher naturally sets his lived philosophy as a model way of living for his pupils and others fellows who may wish to follow. Like Socrates and Plotinus, he has become an enlightened man, a passionate lover of truth, a gentle teacher by word and by deed, and a beacon of light for those who might desire philosophical enlightenment.

This is, briefly, the noble portrait of the ideal philosopher as envisioned and occasionally realized by many of the Ancient Hellenes and other non-Western people who were able to look at the cosmos, at their political institutions, and at their inner souls and minds as free human beings, without the fetters of any dogma, least of all any ecclesiastical dogma backed by the rhetoric and the sophistry or, even worse, by the fear and the terror of some entrenched Theocracies. This being so, the crucial question arises: What happen to this noble philosophical ideal in the West?

From Hellenic Philosophy to "Western Philosophy"

Judging by the two specified standards, as set by the Ancient Hellenic philosophers, I doubt seriously that one will be able to find many or any of the so-called "European philosophers" who would be able to meet the above mentioned criteria, especially the second. Let me explain my skeptical pessimism on this important point. By the criterion of noetically self-sufficient inquiry, anyone who takes divine revelations on faith, though they may be found in books of uncertain origin, and then uses "philosophy," that is, philosophical terminology and arguments, to justify religious dogma on behalf of some established theology or theocracy, as Christian and Moslem theologians, jurists, and orators have traditionally done, is clearly disqualified from being called a genuine philosopher, as the Ancient Hellenic philosophers understood and used this honorable name. Such a devout person may be a good writer or a sharp advocate of the cause of his respective sect, but a philosopher he cannot be, according to our first specified criterion.

Similarly, by the second specified criterion of autonomous, exemplary, and self-sufficient life of ethical excellence, anyone who seriously believes in the efficiency of divine grace by baptismal ablutions in holy waters, and other sacraments of this kind, to produce and sustain a life of integral philosophic virtue, as (Catholic, Protestant, and Orthodox) Christians, Jews, and Muslims traditionally have believed, cannot be called a genuine philosopher. Again, such a person may be a good man or even a saint, but a philosopher, in the original sense of this Hellenic word, he will never be, for a genuine philosopher is expected to rise to human perfection by human means only, that is, by virtuous activity at each case and under any adverse conditions.

In this light, then, and considering the fact that Western Europe, in the last two millennia, has been forced to serve various authorities under the double yoke of Catholic scholastic dogmatism and Protestant puritanical fanaticism, it is not surprising that philosophy, in the Hellenic sense and purity of the word, has not flourished there, and that genuine philosophers are conspicuously absent from the "theater" of so-called "Western philosophy."

Now, some may find it perhaps amusing, but it is sad to see how cautious the philosopher-theologians, and other so-called "philosophers" of the Western European type, have been in their writings, lest they contradict the received dogma of the respective sect and, thus, upset the ecclesiastical authority and hierarchy. The list of such persons is long and cannot be covered here in any detail. But it would surely include not only Augustine, Aquinas, Bonaventure, and other theologians and church fathers, but also modern "philosophers" such as Descartes, Berkeley, Leibniz, Hegel, and many more European thinkers whose purpose for "philosophizing" seems to have been to either, explicitly, provide support by using dialectical and rhetorical techniques for the Church doctrines or, implicitly, to "make room" for the practice of faith, especially in its Protestant and Catholic formulations which have dominated Western Europe.

It is true that in the last four or five hundred years several attempts have been made to revive the Ancient Hellenic spirit of free, autonomous, and self-reliable inquiry but, philosophically, as opposed to scientifically, they have invariably failed. For example, the hope that the opening of the Florentine Academy, during the Italian Renaissance in the fifteenth century, would lead to the rebirth of "Platonic philosophy" in its Hellenic version, as opposed to its Christian and Islamic versions, was cut short by the coming of the Protestant Reformation, not surprisingly, from the North. Moreover, "the Age of Reason" of the late seventeenth and early eighteenth centuries, on which the French *philosophes* had build their dreams for a Europe freed from religious oppressive dogma, ended up with the formation of the Holy Alliance and the coming of Romanticism and German Idealism, and their concomitant obfuscations. Thus, once again, "Western philosophy" was turned into a handmaid of Lutheran Protestantism, as it had been of Catholicism in the Middle Ages.

These historical examples clearly indicate that up to the nineteenth century no genuine school of philosophy in the specified sense had appeared in the horizon of the Western world. But the situation, significantly, has not changed since that time, in spite of the multiplication of "isms" coming out of Northern Europe in rapid succession:

Marxism, Existentialism, Phenomenalism, Nihilism, Deconstructionism. The protagonists of these movements make much noise, but they seem as ephemeral phenomena passing away. They can be fairly classified into five categories, none of which can pass the two tests of genuine philosophy as specified above.

If we were to categorize the "European Philosophers" in descending order, according to the honesty which they exhibit in their "philosophical" and literary writings, we would obtain the following scale: First, there are the rebellious European thinkers from any ecclesiastical establishment, who demand the right to absolute freedom of thought and expression (Nietzsche, Russell, Sartre, and Kazantzakis perhaps belong in this category); second, there are the players of the familiar old role of so-called "Western philosophers" as providers of philosophical justification or respectability to the Church dogmas and practices (theist existentialists and phenomenologists perhaps belong in this group); third, there are others who prefer to play the novel role of providing philosophical foundations for the grounding of the scientific method and its discovered "truth" (logical positivists and many language analysts belong perhaps in this category); fourth, there are the players of a more radical role, who serve the political ideology of the so-called "scientific socialism" and its issue "the dictatorship of the proletariat" (all faithful Marxists, if there are any left, and Maoists fit into this category); fifth, there are the experts of the old sophistical game of words, whom the Ancient Hellenes called "sophists," but they pass as "philosophers" in Western Europe (deconstructionists, like Derrida, and neo-pragmatists, like Richard Rorty, would fit nicely here).

Be that as it may, the recent collapse of communism and the discrediting of Marxism; the disillusion that science will find the ultimate "truth" by chasing the Platonic "Great and Small" which becomes smaller or greater without apparent end; and, above all, the end of the Cold War and the coming of a New Global Order, has given some hope for the possibility of philosophy's rebirth. The friends of Plato and Plotinus, and all true lovers of wisdom, are called upon to try once again to restore philosophy to its ancestral autonomy, dignity, and glory. The task is a noble one. May they be more fortunate than the Platonists of the Florentine Academy or the Cambridge Platonists for the common good of mankind as it prepares itself to live in and to share the global village of the future.

Conclusion

In conclusion and in philosophical terms, the Western terrain looks today like the thing that it has always been, a wasteland. For, as we have seen, the nobility of Ancient Hellenic philosophy, as it was expressed in the unrestrained freedom of inquiry and in the self-sufficiency of authentic ethical life for the genuine philosopher, was lost in the West with the coming of the revealed religions of "the Book," with their restricting dogmatic theologies and oppressive hierarchical and theocratic religious and political structures. It is, therefore, benighted to present the history of "philosophy" in the West as if it were a continuity.

The gap which separates the Hellenic philosophers from the "Western philosophers," whether Medieval theologians, Modern positivists, Marxist/Leninist theorists, or the post-modern deconstructionists, is too wide to leap over and too glaring to be overlooked. In the hands of the "European philosophers," what for the Hellenes had been the "the Fair Queen" of arts and sciences was turned shamelessly, one may say, into a handmaid of divinely revealed theology, methodical technocratic epistemology, and revolutionary political ideology, respectively. These three "Masters" constitute the unholy trinity which Hellenic philosophy has been forced to serve for almost two millennia in the West. That is a long time, you may think, and I would agree. The time, then, would seem right to try to set free—perhaps in America, the land of the free and the brave—the enslaved and abused Lady Philosophy.

Hence the urgent need for the philosophically minded to return to their genuine philosophical roots, which are pre-Christian and pre-Islamic, in search for a new inspiration for a new beginning of philosophical humanism in the new millennium. The lesson to be learned and the conclusion to be drawn, by any person with an open mind and a sensitive soul, is that Hellenic philosophy in general, and the Platonic tradition in particular, do not belong exclusively to the Northern Europeans despite of their arrogant claim to it. Rather, it belongs to the global world and to mankind as a whole by reason of its perennial and pananthropic virtues, including the freedom to theorize and the responsibility to perfect ourselves.

I am inclined to believe that, perhaps if we dig deeply enough in our human souls and cultural traditions, we shall discover that the roots of genuine philosophy, whether they are Hellenic and Mediterranean, Indian and Asian, Egyptian and African, or Native American, somehow connect in a common underground and point to the ascent to the common ideal of philanthropic diversity, polytheistic tolerance, and political civility as the necessary preconditions of an authentic life with philosophic freedom and human dignity. Now, it would seem, more than ever before, such a noble ideal is within reach and needed for our global world and its fragile civility.

Lamentation of the Muses
Woodcut by Georg Pencz, 1535.

The Muses declare that they are going to leave Germany, where
their arts are not honored.

Drinking with the Muses

Thomas Willard

THE MUSES have had a bad rap in the late twentieth century, partly
from women who would rather be poets than muses, partly from men
who like their muses silent and sexy. David Fideler's call for a revival
of the *Academiae Musarum* is especially welcome because it reminds us
that the ancients placed education "under the patronage of the Muses,
the nine goddesses of inspiration who preside over the sciences, arts,
and humanities."[1] As our culture struggles with new systems of information storage and retrieval, it would do well to recall that these
goddesses provide an image of how knowledge was organized at the
origin of Western culture.

These are the traditional nine, with their etymologies, roles, and
symbols:

Urania	Heavenly	Astronomy	Celestial Globe
Polyhymnia	Rich in Hymns	Sacred Song	Veiled
Calliope	Fair Voiced	Epic Poetry	Pencil & Wax Tablet
Melpomene	She Who Sings	Tragedy	Tragic Mask
Thalia	Flourishing	Comedy	Comic Mask
Euterpe	She Who Gladdens	Lyric Poetry & Music	Double Flute
Terpsichore	Dancing	Song & Choral Dancing	Lyre
Erato	The Passionate	Erotic Song & Mime	Small Lyre
Clio	She Who Extols	History	Scroll[2]

Here we have celestial knowledge and human history set off against
one another, with seven varieties of poetry in between. The Homeric
hymn is closest to the gods; the dithyramb, though associated with a
divine sexual release, is closest to the merely human. Between these

come the extremes of song in pure auditory and visual movement (music and dance), followed by the three major genres: epic, tragic, and comic poetry. Epic tends to be concerned with Magna Graecia, with the people as a whole; while Greek tragedy concerns just three royal houses; and Greek comedy concerns typical citizens. The Muses are said to be the daughters of Zeus (Bright Sky) and Mnemosyne (Memory), whose love affair lasted nine nights.

In this division of labor, there is a genre for each type of story, and all story is transmitted in verse to make it memorable. The division is implicit in the Muses' names, first listed this way by Hesiod in the eighth century B.C.E., although the specific offices and symbols evolved over the next few centuries.[3] The Muses not specifically concerned with verse, Urania and Clio, are closest to the patrons of mathematics and letters, respectively. Astronomy leads to calculations of angles; historical records such as land transactions are the first data to get recorded in writing. Eric Havelock did not name his muse when he wrote *The Muse Learns to Write*.[4] Our list of properties shows Calliope as a writer and Clio as a reader. But the evidence in Egypt and Asia Minor, where the business writing outnumbers the creative writing by a large distance, suggests Clio was a writer, too, and perhaps the first.

The Muses of Helicon

From the beginning, when the nine danced into Greek poetry in Hesiod's *Theogony*, they offered an ambiguous knowledge:

> They once taught Hesiod this goodly song,
> While he was herding sheep on Helicon;
> The goddesses first gave this word to me,
> Olympian Muses, daughters of lord Zeus:
> "Shepherds afield, rude boys, mere appetites,
> We can speak many falsehoods that ring true,
> And, if we want to, we can sing the truth."[5]

The "word" which the Muses give Hesiod is a myth (*mythom*). The

word *mythos* has many overtones in Greek, including the wiles of
Odysseus, the "many-mythed" (*polymythos*), and the dramatic plots
(*mythoi*) of Aristotle's *Poetics*. Myth can seem true and be false, or it can
be true. Hesiod is the first to talk of myths in terms of many falsehoods
(*pseudea*) and the one unforgettable truth (*aletheia*). This may be part
of his claim for moral poetry as the highest form of epic—part of his
famous contest with Homer, where the crown goes to the man who
sings of peace, that is to Hesiod, rather than to him who sings of war.
In any case, it asks the audience to give a special status to what Hesiod
says. In a book with the provocative title *Did the Greeks Believe in Their
Myths?*, the French classicist Paul Veyne remarks:

> In order to shake his contemporaries out of this lethargy, Hesiod will be
> obliged to create a stir and proclaim that poets lie; for he wishes, for his
> own benefit, to constitute a realm of truth, where one will no longer say
> just anything about the gods. . . . Hesiod received his knowledge from the
> Muses—that is, from his own reflections. By pondering all that had been
> said about the gods and the world, he understood many things and was
> able to establish a true and complete list of genealogies. . . . Hesiod knows
> that we will take him at his word, and he treats himself as he will be
> treated: he is the first to believe everything that enters his head.[6]

Hesiod believes in his myths, Veyne suggests. He considers himself
chosen by the Muses he chooses to praise, and his myth of bemusement
on Helicon is easily deconstructed. Here is a deconstructionist reading by Pietro Pucci:

> this gift of the Muses should enable the poet to recover a lost privilege,
> divine memory, and truth: yet it is unsolicited and uncontrollable; it can
> lead to truth or the worst fallacy; it establishes the origin of poetry in a
> territory that lies beyond the control of man.[7]

The comments of Veyne and Pucci are both quite modern. We love
our musings, Veyne seems to say, and want to give them a privileged
position; we may indeed love them because they seem to carry a special

truth. But we are most easily deceived, Pucci seems to add, by what we love most dearly. The Muses take us into a realm where our scientific criteria of truth and falsehood no longer apply. Nietzsche put it most succinctly: "The Muses of the arts of illusion pale before an art which speaks the truth in its intoxication."[8] If we still have the critical impulse to distinguish truth from falsehood, it must be something like Keats's truth of the imagination that we seek. That search is part of Hesiod's *mythos*.

The Muses give Hesiod a myth from which all other myths proceed:

> Thus spoke the fluent daughters of lord Zeus,
> Then plucked a laurel bough, gave it to me,
> Miraculous rod, and breathed the divine voice
> Into me so that I could sing of past and future:
> Sing, as they urged, of the eternal gods,
> But always, first and last, sing of the Muses.[9]

This is literal inspiration: divinity goes into the poet with the breath, so long as the breath comes from the Muses. Divinity comes out with the breath, so long as the poet is singing what he has mused upon. The rod helps that miracle of transformation to occur, for it comes from the laurel tree, sacred to Apollo, a memento of his Daphne. It marks Hesiod as a son of Apollo, who was sometimes called his father. In late antiquity, the laurel bough seemed a mere allegory for book learning; so Proclus claimed,[10] though the claim seems anachronistic in light of recent research on Greek literacy and orality. Hesiod takes us back to the beginnings of Greek literacy, and his Muses may well give us a glimpse into the oral culture of Homeric Greece.

Hesiod likes to make lists, and calls Muses by name:

> Thus sang the Muses, the Olympians
> Begotten by great Zeus, the daughters nine:
> Clio, Euterpe, Thalia, Melpomene,
> Terpsichore, Erato, Polyhymnia,
> Urania, and Calliope first of all,

Who serves the much-sung rulers.[11]

Hesiod's arrangement is determined by verse rhythm, among other things. There are four names in one line, four in the next line (in the Greek text), and one name in the third. The first two hexameters each break in half, at the transitional word "also" (*te*), so that we have four pairs of Muses:

Clio (history)	Euterpe (lyric)
Thalia (comedy)	Melpomene (tragedy)
Terpischore (dance)	Erato (erotic song and mime)
Polyhymnia (sacred song)	Urania (astronomy)

Calliope comes last in the procession, but she is not the least. Plato follows tradition when he pairs Calliope and Urania as the two oldest muses and the most helpful to the philosopher.[12]

Other arrangements are possible, of course, and it was natural to group the Muses in threes. "Never fewer than the Graces nor more than the Muses" was the oft-quoted advice to Roman hostesses: at least three, at most nine.[13] If the Muses are to be grouped in threes, Calliope would presumably join Urania and Polyhymnia; Clio and Euterpe might have to separate.

Thalia is later listed as one of the three graces, daughters of Zeus and Ocean.[14] It may be just a pleasant name, like Erato, who is said to be the granddaughter of Ocean.[15] Hesiod specifies that the Graces live near the Muses on Mount Olympus. The Graces are in the business of love, and the gracious Thalia's gaze is said to be so erotic that it makes a man's legs wobble; the Muses are devoted to song. The proximity of *Charites* and *Musai* may refer back to the ritual practices at temples throughout the pagan world, where ritual prostitution was often close to religious ceremony.[16]

An old problem for Hesiod's readers is what the Olympian Muses are doing on Mount Helicon, considerably to the south. They could be on vacation, or could be running a branch campus. One possible solution is that Hesiod, a real youth from a family in real financial straits, stumbled into a real academy of the Muses. David Fideler notes that Pausanias, a traveller in late antiquity, saw the statues of the Muses at a temple on Mount Helicon; he adds that the temple floor exists to this day as the floor of a church.[17] Could the Muses have served as schoolmarms for the Greeks' daughters? Could their specialties have been job descriptions, in a day when few jobs for women existed outside the family unit? Could one have taught astronomy, another hymns, and others stories of epic, tragic, or comic dimensions? Could there have been teachers of song, dance, even *ars amatoria*, as well as history?

Mary Barnard, one of Sappho's best modern translators, thinks that she was very likely the music teacher of a girls' school run in the name of Aphrodite.[18] Sappho is a transitional figure, performing a sacred role but aware of her secular identity. Her musical art is a temple art of song and accompaniment on the lyre. Where she is least personal, in her epithalamia or wedding songs, she is closest to the goddess:

> O Bride brimful of
> rosy little loves!
>
> O brightest jewel of
> the Queen of Paphos!
>
> Come now
>   to your
> bedroom   to your bed
>   and play there
> sweetly   gently
> with your bridegroom.[19]

This may be a choral song, to be sung by a group of bridesmaids. If the bridesmaids are students in the school of Aphrodite, they are preparing for the life which they celebrate in song.

The Origin of Eloquence

As the lead Muse, Calliope has the role of making mortal leaders (*basileusin*) eloquent:

> Thanks to the Muses and long-shot Apollo
> The Earth has singers and has zither-players.
> But leaders must thank Zeus, and he is lucky
> Whom the nine love. Speech from his mouth is sweet.[20]

Eloquence is power in the Muses' world. The poet has one sort of power, the power of song. The leader has the power of public speaking. Hesiod mixes speech and song when he has the Muses say, literally:

> "We can speak many falsehoods that ring true,
> And, if we want to, we can sing the truth."[21]

The distinction between public speech and song is only starting to open up in Hesiod's time, and we should not push it too hard. In these lines, "speak" (*legein*) is the newer word, related to *logos*; "sing" (*gerusasthai*) has geriatric overtones, associated with the formal ways of the elders. Indeed, the power of words and music is still closely connected for Hesiod. The myth of Orpheus brings together the power of poetry, which Orpheus had from his mother, Calliope, and the power of music played on the tortoise-shell lyre, invented by Hermes and given to Apollo and later to Orpheus. All poets were "sons" of Orpheus, even reincarnations, and both Homer and Hesiod were said to trace their ancestry back to Orpheus, eight generations earlier.[22] If Hesiod is dated to the eighth century B.C.E., then Orpheus and the tradition of Orphic song would date back to the tenth century, not long after the heroic age of the Trojan War. The other great master of lyric—Musaeus, whose name marks his devotion to the Muses—is placed in the second generation after Orpheus.[23]

Orpheus and Musaeus were understood to later antiquity as both leaders and poets, who civilized mankind and founded cities by the power of their song. Horace, in his verse essay *On Poetic Art*, writes:

> Orpheus, sacred prophet of the gods,
> Deterred the woodsmen from their vicious acts;
> Thus he is said to tame fierce lions and tigers,
> And thus Amphion, founder of Thebes, is said
> To move stones with the sound of lyre and chant
> And place them where he wishes. This was wisdom:
> To separate the public and the private,
> The sacred and profane, make marriage rites,
> Build towns, carve laws in wood. Thus honor came
> To poets and their songs, and thus the name
> Of the divine.[24]

As a poet, Horace considers himself "the Muses' priest."[25]

Cicero, as a famous orator and a writer on oratory, attributed the same civilizing powers to his art:

> It seems impossible to me that a tacit, helpless knowledge could suddenly turn men from their old ways and introduce them to different lifestyles [lit. 'reasons of life']. And truly, when cities were established, how could people learn to keep the faith and to observe justice, to become accustomed to the common will and not only work for the common cause but even value the lost time, unless they could use eloquence to persuade others what they discovered through reason.[26]

Granted, Cicero's history of rhetoric dates the practice to Corax and Tisias, paralegals in Sicily in the fifth century B.C.E.[27] He has this on the authority of Aristotle; what he does not know is that Aristotle, in a lost book on the Sophists, traces rhetoric back further to the philosopher Empedocles.[28] Long slighted on the ground that no prose of his survives,[29] the claim for Empedocles is revived in the recent work of Richard Leo Enos.[30] From Empedocles there is but a short step forward to his student, Gorgias of Leontini, who brought rhetoric to Athens.[31] And there is but a short step back to Empedocles's teacher,

Pythagoras, who, though a vegetarian, would sacrifice an ox to the Muses while working on a problem in geometry.[32]

Empedocles broke with Pythagoras, claiming that the founder of philosophy so named was hypocritical to shun meat himself and not call for everyone else to do so.[33] The Pythagoreans banished him, in turn, for disclosing secrets to non-initiates, hoi polloi. Enos lists Pythagoras as an influence on Western rhetoric, by which he means an influence on Empedocles. But it seems possible that Pythagoras learned more from the sons of Orpheus than the doctrine of reincarnation. Like Orpheus, Pythagoras deterred the Samians from vicious acts and, when he could not deter the tyrant, built his own city and framed his own laws of conduct, his hexameter *Symbola*.

Classical Music

Greek etymology suggests that the Muses and their arts derived from music (*mousike*), though Plato suggests further that both "Muses" and "music" are related to the word for philosophizing or musing (*mosthai*).[34] Socrates says his father gave him "an education in music and gymnastics," meaning the intellectual and physical disciplines.[35] Then too, the schools of Pythagoras and Plato are both dedicated to the Muses,[36] as is the great center of learning at Alexandria, the Musaeum. The ten categories of books in the library, as reconstructed by one modern scholar,[37] can be readily identified with the Muses and Apollo:

Epic	Calliope
Drama	Melpomene
Laws	Terpsichore
Philosophy	Polyhymnia
History	Clio
Oratory	Euterpe
Medicine	Erato
Mathematics	Urania
Natural Science	Thalia
Miscellanea	Apollo

Oratory and law deserve more than a song and a dance, but Apollo keeps a watchful eye on each.

Cicero associates the Muses with the beings one would wish to see first in the afterlife:

> Isn't this a journey we'd gladly undertake? Truly, to speak with Orpheus, Musaeus, Homer, Hesiod, what price could you place on it? Myself, I'd died a dozen deaths, were it possible, for the opportunity to speak with them.[38]

With Orpheus as the son of the eldest Muse, Musaeus as his follower, and Homer and Hesiod as his descendants, the *peregrinatio* of his dreams is a journey to the Muses. It becomes a cosmic quest. The Academician Proclus, for all his doubts about the "allegory" in Hesiod's report on the Muses, still asks the assistance of Zeus's nine daughters:

> Goddesses, free me from sad ignorance
> And make me understand the wise men's myths.[39]

(*Mythoi* here has the force of sayings and stories.) Macrobius adds the Muses to the dream ascent in the otherwise lost *Republic* of Cicero.[40] There are faint echoes of the ascent in the medieval *gradus ad Parnassum*, where the learned poet or orator can court the Muses. Muses and monotheism coexisted for centuries, perhaps because the nine sisters became symbols of liberal education. In a late set of poems about the Muses, Michael Maier has them describe the virtues to be found in the "College of the German Philosophers of the Rosy Cross."[41]

Apuleius, writing in the second century of our era, offers a wonderful reflection:

> A wise man's celebrated dictum about the table: The first cup of wine quenches the thirst, the second leads to hilarity, the third to voluptuosness, the fourth to madness. *Vice versa*, surely, with the Muses' cups: the more

we drink, the purer the drink and the healthier for the soul. The first cup, from the school master (*litterator*), takes away rudeness; the second, from the grammarian (*grammaticus*), builds knowledge; the third, from the orator (*rhetor*), arms with eloquence. Most are content to drink from these cups. But I drank from the cups in Athens: the deep wine of poetry, the clear wine of geometry, the sweet wine of music, the austere wine of dialectic, and the nectar of universal philosophy that is never in excess.[42]

Apuleius is a deeply learned person, said to be the author of a book of logic, the inventor of the square of opposition,[43] and, less probably, the translator of the Latin *Asclepius*, an important source of Hermetic lore.[44] He is also an eloquent man, an orator, a poet, and author of the greatest prose fiction of antiquity, the *Metamorphoses* or *The Golden Ass*. His novel amplifies an old fiction with a story based on his own initiation into the cult of Isis. It impressed C. G. Jung and Jung's protégée M-.L. von Franz as having an especially well balanced views of matter and the feminine.[45] In the *Asclepius*, Hermes Trismegistus teaches that the Muses have been sent to bring harmony to earth:

> Divinity sent the assembled chorus of Muses to man, not because of any merit but because earth would have been uncultured without their sweet measures; so instead, the music of men's songs adore the father of all, and the pleasant harmonies of earth echo the praises in the heavens.[46]

This Egyptian wisdom fitted well with the Roman lore of Cicero on the origins of civilization from the Muses and Calliope's son, Orpheus. Small wonder, then, that Apuleius should sum up his formal education as a drinking party, where the male experts serve the wine but the wine comes from the Muses.

Muses and Monotheism

So what would a modern Academy of Muses look like on paper? It would have students of all ages and both genders. With the number of teachers fixed by statute, it would be small enough that the teachers know one another and get along together reasonably well, and know all the students too. It would have cross-appointments and specializations, with the faculty chosen to represent nine information requirements of society:

> Astronomy and Cybernetics: Urania
> Biology and Health: Erato (head), Thalia
> Dance and Fitness: Terpsichore (head), Erato
> Drama: Melpomene (head), Thalia
> History and Civics: Clio (head), Calliope, Polyhmnia
> Literature: Thalia (head), Erato, Euterpe, Calliope, Melpomene,
> Polyhymnia
> Music and Art: Euterpe (head), Calliope, Erato, Terpsichore
> Psychology and Religion: Polyhymnia (head), Calliope, Urania
> Rhetoric and Communication. Calliope (head), Clio, Urania

Philosophy, though a specialty of Urania, is not restricted to any one department, since the whole education is directed toward the universal philosophy of Apuleius, for which one's thirst never slakes. There would still be room for majors and minors, depending on which Muses the student takes after most; and there would certainly be no attempt to fashion all students in a single mold. In addition to Zeus or God (*Dios*), there would be Memory (*Mnemosyne*) and their nine daughters as well as their grandchild Orpheus and the "moonlighting Muse, Apollo," as one modern scholar has called him—all models of godly living. This may sound like the "Day Dream Academy for Bards" that W. H. Auden liked to imagine, but there would be "writing across the curriculum" and the college would therefore produce a variety of articulate citizens.

The catalogue would seem to have "elite private school" written all over it, even "denominational," and indeed the hillside campus would seem preferable to the downtown site favored by local business interests. Nevertheless, the Olympian model suggests it could serve the state, even serve the world, while public funding for the arts continues.

Notes

1. David Fideler, "Reviving the Academies of the Muses," *Alexandria* 3 (1995), 215.

2. Etymologies follow Robert Graves, *The Greek Myths*, 2 volumes (Baltimore: Penguin, 1955). Roles and symbols follow Oskar Seyffert, *A Dictionary of Classical Antiquities*, translated and revised by Henry Nettleship and J. E. Sandys (1891; Cleveland: World Publishing, 1956).

3. Hesiod's list does not agree with Homer, but became canonical. For other early Muses, including the nine Pieirides, see Cicero, *De Natura Deorum* 3.54. Also see the excellent chapter on "The Muses" in E. R. Curtius, *European Literature and the Latin Middle Ages*, translated by Willard R. Trask (New York: Pantheon, 1953), 228–46.

4. Eric Havelock, *The Muse Learns to Write: Reflections on Orality and Literacy from Antiquity to the Present* (New Haven: Yale University Press, 1986).

5. Hesiod, *Theogony* 21–28. All translations are mine unless noted otherwise.

6. Paul Veyne, *Did the Greeks Believe in Their Myths?: An Essay on the Constituitive Imagination*, translated by Paula Wissing (Chicago: University of Chicago Press, 1988), 28–29.

7. Pietro Pucci, *Hesiod and the Language of Poetry* (Baltimore: Johns Hopkins University Press, 1977), 3.

8. Friedrich Nietzsche, *The Birth of Tragedy*, section 4.

9. Hesiod, *Theogony* 29–34.

10. Robert Lamberton, *Hesiod* (New Haven: Yale University Press, 1988), 4.

11. Hesiod, *Theogony* 75–80.

12. Plato, *Phaedrus* 259D.

13. Varro, *Menippean Satires* 13.11.

14. Hesiod, *Theogony* 907–11.

15. Hesiod, *Theogony* 246.

16. Nancy Qualls-Corbett, *The Sacred Prostitute: Eternal Aspects of the Feminine* (Toronto: Inner City Books, 1988).

17. Fideler, "Reviving the Academies of the Muses," 222 and n. 11.

18. Mary Barnard, *Sappho: A New Verse Translation* (Berkeley: University of California Press, 1958), 97–100.

19. Barnard, *Sappho*, 31.

20. Hesiod, *Theogony* 94–97. The same lines appear in the Homeric hymn "To the Muses and Apollo," 2–5.

21. Hesiod, *Theogony* 27–28.

22. *Of the Origin of Homer and Hesiod, and their Contest*, in *Hesiod: The Homeric Hymns and Homerica* (Loeb Classical Library,1914), 570–71.

23. *The Manual of Harmonics of Nicomachus the Pythagorean*, translated by Flora R. Levin (Grand Rapids: Phanes Press, 1994), 189.

24. Horace, *De Arte Poetica* 391–401.

25. Horace, *Carmina* 3.1.1.

26. Cicero, *De Inventione* 1.2.3.

27. Cicero, *Brutus* 46.

28. Diogenes Laertius, *Lives of the Philosophers* 8.57. See *The Presocratics*, edited by Philip Wheelwright (New York: Macmillan, 1966), 149.

29. M. R. Wright, editor, *Empedocles: The Extant Fragments* (New Haven: Yale University Press, 1981), introduction.

30. Richard Leo Enos, *Greek Rhetoric Before Aristotle* (Prospect Heights, Ill.: Waveland Press, 1993), 57–69.

31. George A. Kennedy, *Classical Rhetoric and its Christian and Secular Tradition from Ancient to Modern Times* (Chapel Hill: University of North Carolina Press, 1980), 29–30.

32. Cicero, *De Natura Deorum* 3.88.

33. Quoted in Aristotle, *Rhetoric* 1373B (1.13).

34. Plato, *Cratylus* 406A.

35. Plato, *Crito* 50D.

36. Pierre Boyancé, *Le culte des Muses chez les philosophes Grecs: Études d'histoire et de psychologie religieuses* (1936; Paris: Bocard, 1972).

37. Edward Alexander Parsons, *The Alexandrian Library: Glory of The Hellenic World* (London: Cleaver-Hume, 1952), 210.

38. Cicero, *Tusculun Orations* 1.98.

39. Quoted in Boyancé, 295, n. 1.

40. Macrobius, *On the Dream of Scipio* 2.3.

41. Michael Maier, *Symbola Aureae Mensae Duodecim Nationum* (1617; Graz: Akademische Druck-u. Verlagsanstalt, 1972), 296–301.

42. Apuleius, *Florida* 20. The wise man may be Anacharsis; see Paul Vallette, editor, *Apulée: Apologie, Florides*, 3rd edition (Paris: Belles Lettres, 1971), 168, n. 2.

43. *The Logic of Apuleius, Including a Complete Latin and English Translation*

of the *Peri Hermenias of Apuleius of Madura*, edited and translated by David Londey and Carmen Johanson (Leiden: Brill, 1987).

44. *Hermetica: The Greek Corpus Hermeticum and the Latin Asclepius in a New English Translation*, edited and translated by Brian P. Copenhaver (Cambridge: Cambridge University Press, 1992), 214; Garth Fowden, *The Egyptian Hermes: A Historical Approach to the Late Pagan Mind*, corrected edition (Princeton: Princeton University Press, 1993), 198–99 and n. 19.

45. Marie-Louise von Franz, *The Golden Ass of Apuleius: The Liberation of the Feminine in Man*, revised edition (Boston: Shambhala, 1992).

46. *Ascleplius* 1.9.

Philosophy and the Seven Liberal Arts
School of Strasbourg, twelfth century.

Claiming a Liberal Education

STEPHEN ROWE

THOSE OF US ALIVE TODAY inhabit a world of unprecedented options, possibilities, choices. One such choice is that for a liberal education. But despite the fact that "liberal education" is a term people like to use, very few students or institutions today are clear about the meaning of this term, and how it is connected to what they actually do in the name of education. In the absence of some clear understanding, liberal education is not a real possibility. The point is that, without knowing it, most students at most institutions have an option: they can simply go to school, get a degree, and miss a liberal education, or they can spend the same time and money and become liberally educated. But they cannot exercise this option unless they know a choice exists. And they cannot exercise that option wisely unless they see the significance of what is at stake in it: the possibility of their own personal transformation. For the aim of a liberal education is nothing less than that: a transformation that enables us to achieve our full human potential, gives us access to what is great and sustaining in the Western tradition, and moves us to participate directly and positively in the drama of emerging world civilization.

* * *

Our world of expanded choices is deceptive, such that access to liberal education and other options of real substance is difficult in a subtle way. For the amazing choices we have today are embedded in a powerfully seductive culture of consumerism, psychic numbing, and skepticism. One of the chief characteristics of our society might be called the irony of availability. We have access to massive amounts of information, the riches of myths and traditions other than our own, and instant access to forms of communication that had not even been imagined in the past. But at the very same time there is distance, especially—and most ironically—from the visions and vitality of our own tradition. Robert Heilbroner has captured the essence of this characteristic when he describes our society as "dazzlingly rich in every aspect except that of the cultivation of the human person."[1]

The chances of our having access to a liberal education today are slight, even in the world of colleges and universities (some would say especially here). This is peculiar, since liberal education is associated closely with the traditional Western vision of arriving at full human actualization, of becoming an adult in the genuine and deeply gratifying sense of the term. But in the university today liberal education is just one among many options. And it exists in the shade of the specialized career training that is essential to the culture of consumerism, with its obsessive material aspiration and diminished expectation about what is possible in a human life.

One reason for the neglect of persons and the traditions out of which they might emerge is that we live in a society of clashing worldviews. In the background and still in our official language is the older worldview represented by liberal education, humanism, and democracy, with the associated concerns for meaning that is religious, value that is ethical, and social arrangement that is just. But this traditional worldview is being eclipsed by another, one that is not much concerned with "cultivation of the human person." Rather, this post-traditional worldview is represented by three quite different concerns: specialization, such that meaning in any large sense becomes irrelevant; technique, such that value becomes whatever works; and materialism, such that society becomes a unit of consumption (where one of the materials of consumption is experience itself). Hence the subtle problem of availability, where the more we "see" of other cultures by way of media images and entertainment the more we are numbed to and distanced from transformative engagement with any of them—including our own. The new worldview engenders a skepticism about the possibility of any real cultivation of the human person within a maze of options and choices, some of which appear to be "about" this very cultivation, but none of which is actually engaged; they remain at the level of information and images to be consumed passively, rather than actively transforming engagement.

So it is that we find ourselves in an ironic situation, where at the very same time that a higher education is available to many people, a liberal education is improbable. Let us begin the work of overcoming this irony and making liberal education a real choice by becoming clear, at first in a very general way, about the nature of a liberal education. There is one essential point on which virtually all the traditional cultures agree, and that our post-traditional culture of consumerism and instant gratification systematically neglects: cultivation of the human person requires transformation of that person. Adult human beings do not simply unfold out of the natural process, like birds or flowers or other forms of life we know. Some intervention is necessary, some discipline—some educating, educing, leading out or drawing forth of our own real self. Adult humans do not appear without strenuous relationship with other humans, relationship that centers on who we really are and who we might become. In Western culture liberal education has been a most distinctive and persistent form of this relational intervention.

Even in the best of circumstances a liberal education is never going to just happen to us; there is always resistance in one form or another. It requires real work and overcoming obstacles of both society and self. It is the kind of thing we must choose, claim, make our own. Liberal education, like other modes of human transformation, requires a very specific kind of effort and discipline, one of reading, writing, and conversing (it sounds simple; we will need to encounter the complexity of it soon). What it promises in return is large: an encounter with the reality of the world; a relationship with that which is profoundly "other" from ourselves; access to our own real self; and discovery of the vital point of intersection between self and world in both vocation and recreation.

Liberal education is a practice and a way of being, not just a theory or a way of thinking. It is the practice of an "examined life" as taught and modeled by Socrates, the original parent or "midwife" of liberal education: "I tell you that to let no day pass without discussing goodness and all the other subjects about which you hear me talking and examining both myself and others is really the very best thing that a man can do, and that life without this sort of examination is not worth living."[2]

* * *

We need a more specific, more full understanding of just what is envisioned by this enterprise called liberal education. Sorting through the various and sometimes conflicting claims, we find three levels of understanding: one of content, another of method, and a third that claims we do not come into practice of the examined life until we achieve the synthesis of content and method.

The third level of synthesis is challenging, perhaps especially for people today, because it involves paradox: the simultaneous presence of two qualities which appear on the surface to be in contradiction. In reality, however, the paradoxical relation is such that the two qualities involved—in this case content and method—can only exist in their completeness when they are copresent. Maybe "synergy" is a contemporary word that communicates this copresence that is impossible to grasp in a mechanistic or merely informational frame of mind. At its root, the paradox of liberal education is a subset of the paradox of the fully human relationship: in order to develop myself I must learn to forget myself and attend to the other (to "content"), and in order to be present with the other I must actualize my genuine self (my "method"). This means that the synthesis of content and method in the deep understanding of liberal education actually occurs only in the fully human relationship itself, the relationship that is created by the art of genuine teaching and learning.

Below I seek to describe each of the three levels of understanding liberal education, in their essential characteristics and in terms of the benefits associated with each. It is important to note that these three levels frequently function as *alternative* understandings, and it is already clear that the third level is difficult to articulate (perhaps impossible from the outside, such that you and I can only understand it insofar as we are already engaged to some degree in practicing the way of being and relating that is comprehended by liberal education).

1. Content

At the first level, a liberal education means that the student becomes a generalist, rather than only a specialist, though it does not necessarily preclude some career preparation during the college years. Liberal education in this understanding has to do with coverage, becoming familiar at least to some degree with all areas of human knowledge. Beyond this it means that the student also considers the interdependent unity of knowledge in the broad context of the human historical drama. Whether the institution has a "core curriculum" or not, a liberal education implies awareness of the core of common ideas, problems, and aspirations which have been at the center of human cultures throughout history.

The benefits of a liberal education at this level of cultural literacy are several. First, the student acquires broad familiarity with the workings of the world as a basis for informed action in work and in life as a citizen, as well as a personal sense of being at home in one's time and place in history. Second, this "common knowing" provides a basis for communication and a sense of significance that can be shared with others; it makes entrance into a common world possible.

Finally, a liberal education empowers. Most people think and act in a secondary way, assuming that ever shifting current opinions and fashions provide adequate guidance in life. A liberal education gives students direct access to the roots of their culture, its basic sources, its energizing ideas and values. And this has the consequence of empowering them to move from the secondary to a primary attitude. For direct knowledge of root visions and authorities makes it possible for the liberally educated person to live and act out of contact with these primary sources, rather than being at the mercy of what Plato refers to as "the opinions of the many." The student has been enabled to cross a critical educational threshold, from the passive to the active stance.

2. Method

At the second level, to be liberally educated means that the student has learned how to learn, that the art of learning on an ongoing, life-long basis has been developed and fully incorporated. From this perspective, students attend classes, complete assignments, and receive academic guidance until they no longer need these structures. Once educational independence and the rootedness of learning as a basic human function has been established, they become independent learners and are ready to graduate.

This involves not only "book learning" and academic work in the narrow sense, but also nurturing qualities beyond the classroom as it is usually envisioned. In fact, the classroom is understood as a sort of greenhouse where basic critical faculties can develop. In this environment, students learn to "read" not just books, but life experience and situations in the world. Students learn the skills of conversation and thereby the arts of critical discernment, analysis, interpretation, and integration. And students learn to write, to fully and fairly articulate both what someone else has said and their own response.

The benefits of this approach, in a time of rapid social and techno-logical change (when the average person undergoes several career changes over a lifetime), are evident. We live in a world where static bodies of knowledge are rapidly rendered obsolete, and where the skills required for success are primarily those of adapting and relating in the midst of ever changing conditions. But at a level deeper than survival and success on the job, the truly distinguished person is the one who exhibits the quality of practical judgment or wisdom. This is precisely the quality that develops from the repeated practice of liberal inquiry.

3. Synthesis of Content and Method

At the third level liberal education requires a synthesis of content and method, each balanced with the other and related to the transfor-mation of the student. Content without method degenerates into rote learning that makes no real contact with the person, while method without content devolves into mere technique divorced from any consideration of depth. (In fact, most of the educational and cultural history of this century can be understood as an oscillation between these two levels, accounting for much of the frustration in our continual efforts at educational reform.) The key to the third level of synthesis is that content and method can each be effective only in the presence of the other, and that their synthesis occurs when they are related to the development of the mature human being.

The tradition of liberal education, as a distinctive Western form of transformative practice, maintains that some materials, some "classics," have the power not only to inform but also to transform. In these materials, insight about the human condition and the nature of reality occurs at a high level, and in a way that can induce positive growth toward becoming fully human. But these materials cannot be merely asserted or applied to the student; they must be approached and handled in the proper way. First, the materials of a liberal education must be read openly and deeply, independent of the biases and assumptions we inevitably bring to them and through which we initially view them. Second, our own response to them is necessary. Having seen what is there we must then formulate what we think in response, helping us fulfill the Socratic injunction, "Know Thyself." It is through practice of this dialogue between the materials of a liberal education and our responses that we are able to discover both the truth and ourselves, and the point of coincidence between the two.

Liberal education, then, moves between phases of reading and response, each time at a higher level. The classroom consists primarily of the intervening stage of discussion, which formally begins in reading and ends in response, but which actually works the art of separating the two, since any discussion of materials begins with an amorphous mix of inadequate reading and superficial response and proceeds to the fullness of each in dialogue with the other. Here lies the challenge of teaching and the joy of real learning.

The essential benefits of this approach are nothing less than formation of the fully human person. Taking its rise from Socratic encounter, the practice of dialogue or dialectic can be seen as both the method and the goal of liberal education. The method, engaging in successively higher levels of reading and response, is described above. The goal can be expressed from the standpoint of either reading or response, content or method: on one side it is well captured by Thoreau's statement that the ability to give "a true account of the actual is the rarest poetry;"[3] on the other side stands "Know Thyself."

Paradox is inescapable in this, the basic human paradox of openness and definiteness. In order to be fully human we need to be open, to have "an open mind," a clear mind, to fairly and fully hear what others are saying—without being so open that we are non-existent or protean. Yet we also need to be definite, to take a stand or a position, to be committed and able to work toward the achievement of ends in which we passionately believe—without taking a position in a way that is doctrinaire or fanatical. The paradox is that openness and definiteness come into their proper function only when each is engaged in the presence of the other, within the essential dynamic of the fully human encounter. This dynamic is at the root of both the Greek vision of public life and the Hebrew notion of right relationship. The aim of a liberal education is to make this kind of engagement possible.

Perhaps another way to understand paradox is in terms of "vision." The vision of a liberal education cannot be grasped from a detached, merely theoretical perspective. It can only be apprehended from the inside, as an undertaking, an activity. For vision is more than theory; it is that subtle vitality which underlies and embraces the tension between theory and practice. It unifies, so that "theory" indicates a way of being rather than merely a way of thinking, and "practice" becomes a doing, nourished and disciplined by an encompassing sense of meaning and vivid value. Awareness of the nature of vision enables us to understand the problem with the neoconservatives and others whose strategy is to merely assert what they take to be the content of a liberal education, against their frustrations with the relativism and career-orientation of contemporary students (as well as against those contemporary forms of education divorced from vision or theory, where practice degenerates into mere technique or vocationalism). But this strategy fails to attend to practice and method, and thus misses the deeper meaning of liberal education as a vision of human transformation—even if it succeeds to some degree in having students "learn the classics."

The fullness of a liberal education becomes accessible when we enter into that practice which is dialogue. The paradox of liberal education, again, is that we can only know fully and deeply what others think when we inquire as to what we think as part of the same process; conversely, we can only discover where we really stand, who we really are, not in isolated introspection but when we are in right relationship with others. Becoming liberally educated can then be spoken of as coming into the radiance of full participation in the conversation about the meaning and nature of that complex entity which is full human adulthood. For it is the conversation itself, the way in which it gives us ourselves as we give to others, that energizes. At this point the paradox of a liberal education is unlocked, so that it becomes a live ideal and transformative practice, rather than either a collection of inert concepts or an invitation to do whatever one wants.

Here also we come to the essential connection between liberal education and the traditional Western vision of civilization itself. For civilization consists neither in the maintenance of certain positions or "substances" as doctrine, nor in the undisciplined "process" of disparate individuals and groups. Rather, it is the vital interplay between the substance of positions from the past and present, each brought to bear on the process of coming into full humanity as it occurs in the present and future. It is in this way that civilization both requires and produces the liberally educated person. Perhaps it is not too much to hope that, as we begin to become liberally educated, we may find it possible to address the constraints that ensnare society now, enabling us to move closer to a civilized world.

*   *   *

Bringing to light the deep significance of a liberal education requires that we be as clear as possible about the constraints we face today. For the true meaning of a liberal education emerges out of dialogue about existing conditions, the real issues of our lives; it is not an ideal of detachment and purity that stands on a mountaintop above the world, but rather a way of being vigorously present in the world.

First, as has already been mentioned, we live in an age of specialization, where inducements and immediate rewards are geared to expertise in narrowly defined fields. Many educational institutions reflect this structuring in their attempt to prepare students for what they call "the real world" (thereby, ironically, distancing themselves from the real). The danger is that in the attempts of institutions to make education relevant, it degenerates into training. With this orientation it is inevitable that "the liberal arts component"—general education, distribution, or core requirements—comes to be regarded as a series of meaningless hurdles to be gotten out of the way before the student can get on to the important work: the major. Liberal education becomes invisible or, worse, an obstacle.[4]

A second constraint is economic insecurity, the concern of students to find employment upon graduation and of institutions to find and retain students. Insecurity causes both students and institutions to become market-responsive, to merely reflect, without the critical perspective which is essential to the liberal arts, whatever is being demanded (and promised) by the society at any given time. The danger here was succinctly expressed by the Nazi architect Albert Speer, when he confessed that the horror of the Third Reich would not have occurred had Germany not abandoned the liberal arts and become a society of "technological barbarians."[5]

At a deeper level, one which seems to be both a result and a cause of the above two constraints, lies the unwillingness or even inability of present society to recognize and support certain kinds of realities. Liberal education is similar to realities like love, justice, goodness, and beauty in that it is what might be called a "complex entity," an entity about which there is more than one right answer, the kind of entity that cannot be quantified or reduced to any one final formulation. Problems in addressing or even recognizing complex entities result in liberal education being largely invisible to students as an option. Not even the well-documented career advantages of pursuing a liberal education are made available.

One final and perhaps inclusive constraint remains: relativism. This term refers to the post traditional cultural condition in which there is no commonly shared agreement on matters of ultimate value and depth. Lack of such agreement leaves individuals alone in relation to these matters, and places them in a social context where there is very little in the way of support, interpretation, authority, or discipline. As an understandable protective-defensive response to living in this condition, most individuals adopt a posture of skepticism in which they conclude that since little is certain it is safest to doubt all, or even cynicism in which they effectively cut themselves off from questions of belief or doubt altogether. People find ways to numb that part of themselves that longs for ultimate value and deep meaning. The ways of doing this are myriad in our society, but one of the most widespread forms is to remain incessantly busy in pursuit of bureaucratic procedure and material gain.

The combined consequence of these constraints, again, is that liberal education is generally not visible or available to students (and one could make the same case for many faculty members and institutions). The situation is complicated by the fact that students pursuing a baccalaureate degree have to deal with terminology, requirements, and structures *related* to liberal education. But because of the constraints that I have discussed, students never really cross the critical threshold whereby they have direct *experience* of the benefits of this discipline; they never really enter the practice of it. Their institutions do not communicate with them effectively; they are too concerned with specialization and employment; they are too skeptical or well-defended against the possibility of investing themselves in an ideal which will later disappoint them. In the presence of vague requirements and promises having to do with a liberal education, and in the absence of direct engagement, we enter a situation which breeds a gloomy mood of generalized resentment.

* * *

No treatment of liberal education today would be complete without addressing the larger world context. For surely one of the major facts of life in our time is the emergence of world community and the pressing question of global civilization.

We sometimes see liberal education discussed negatively in this larger frame: has it not been associated with sexism, ideas of racial exclusivity and superiority, species chauvinism and other Western values that have become ecologically suicidal, and a logocentrism that excludes too much of what it means to be human? Without denying these difficulties, either in education or in Western culture generally, I want to suggest that practicing liberal education in the larger world context presents a positive side also. It allows us to achieve perspective and hence understanding of our limitations and difficulties, and also to gain access to that which has been and remains great and vital in the Western tradition. I am proposing that liberal education is at the center of this greatness, and thus can play a key role in relation to an item that must be very high on our cultural agenda: enabling the West to identify and reclaim its own greatness, its deep sources of zest and direction, its vision or guiding aspiration.

I have argued that in essence liberal education is a mode of transformation, a practice (praxis), a way of facilitating the development of the fully human person. But one of the first things that the larger world perspective of our era enables us to see is that there has been great difficulty in the Western tradition with maintaining, supporting, or even speaking about the dignity of practice. Our tradition has fallen into an assumption that theory must always be prior to practice, such that practice and action are seen as merely the application or implementation of that which is essentially settled elsewhere in purely intellectual construction. William James refers to this assumption as "vicious intellectualism," and claims it is the reason that "philosophy has been on a false scent since the days of Socrates and Plato,"[6] since intellectualism both reflects and generates insensitivity and even violence in relation to the actuality of lived experience. Alfred North

Whitehead points to the same assumption with his phrase "the fallacy of misplaced concreteness."[7] Again, the actuality of life is missed and violated in the name of conceptual order, in what becomes a sort of idolatry of the intellect that has taken hold in the West. More recently, Sissela Bok has been helpful in coming to terms with this distortion in her description of the "epistemology prior" assumption—that knowing as a purely mental function must be prior to and separate from doing—and in her corrective efforts in the development of "applied ethics."[8]

The assumption Bok describes clearly has enormous significance in every sector of our culture, in ethics, politics, religion, childrearing. In the realm of education in particular, this assumption has led us to attempt to solve our various problems by withdrawing into exclusively intellectual considerations. Our attempt is to construct a better theory, but somehow this never seems to work; in fact, it only serves to remove us temporarily from the immediacy of the educational encounter that has become problematic. Operating somewhat like addictive behavior, our tendency, when confronted with difficulties in practice, is to withdraw into the intellect by appointing yet another commission or study group, which keeps the problem at bay for a while. Of course, this activity generates many reports and pronouncements, quite a few of which seem to be right on the mark, at least conceptually. But then nothing really happens—until another point of crisis arises and the next study is commissioned. Eventually the frustration level, especially for students and teachers who are closest to the educational event, becomes intolerable, and frequently cynicism or some other form of withdrawal is the result.

Some teachers do address problems in education at the level of practice, in ways that are supportive in relation to excellence in the immediacy of the educational encounter with students. Joseph Axelrod, Wayne Booth, and Ken Macrorie provide significant examples of this effort to speak about practice, from practice, in ways that identify and nurture its creativity, rather than abandon it in the rush to the theoretical.[9] But such voices are rarely heard; the "epistemology prior" approach *seems* to be easier. This is perhaps all the more true in our time, or more deeply true, as the epistemology prior mindset operates not just in individual behavior but has become institutionalized in the form of "organizational dynamics," "management by objectives," and the assessment of "outcomes." These, though usually well-intended, engender a blindness to excellence as a function of concrete practice, and thus also an intensification of frustration with our educational dilemmas.

The work of the Japanese scholar of the Kyoto School, Masao Abe, provides a good example of how our new world situation enables us to understand and come to terms with these Western difficulties. In his *Zen and Western Thought*, Abe says that the West has been locked into an "objectification approach" since the time of Aristotle.[10] The insistence in this approach on the subject-object distinction and deductive certainty has caused Western culture to become alienated from Being and to forget higher orders of knowing and relating. This helpful criticism gives perspective on our difficulties, as well as a new or renewed way of seeing (and *living*) the meaning of such figures as Socrates and Jesus (as opposed to the later orthodox interpretations *about* them).

The first essay in Abe's book is entitled "Zen is Not a Philosophy, But . . . ." Here he insists that "For the realization of Zen, *practice is absolutely necessary*. Nevertheless, Zen is neither a mere anti-intellectualism nor a cheap intuitionism nor is it an encouragement to animal-like spontaneity. Rather, it embraces a profound philosophy."[11] Something very similar is true of liberal education (I recall the exclamation of an Asian student once, after wrestling with a difficult passage from Plato: "Oh, so the function of professor and Zen master are much the same!"). As a practice, a mode of human transformation like Zen, there is a sense in which *any* theory could cause us to miss the point. The point is the complex and concrete encounter of the student with a teacher and other students, with a substantial text, and with their own personhood, in an educational situation of speaking and writing that leads to higher levels of insight, integration, and action. This encounter requires "theory" as an essential element of support and discipline, such that attempts to deal with our intellectualism by flipping into irrationalism or "going with the flow" always lead to trouble. Yet the essential encounter is missed or violated if it is conceived of as simply a function of the application or implementation of any single theory or even combination of theories. The educational encounter is not only too complex to be embraced by any theory, but also—and more basically—that encounter is an act which specifically entails movement beyond theory and the intellect.

Liberal education, then, can be thought of as an art in that it requires going beyond the intellect, into the domain of human action, transformation and creativity to which the intellect can only point. William James is especially helpful on this utterly delicate matter of achieving the proper function of the intellect—neither clinging to it rigidly and exclusively, so that it usurps personhood and encounter, nor throwing it out altogether:

> The return to life can't come about by talking. It is *an act*; to make you return to life, I must set an example for your imitation. I must deafen you to talk, to the importance of talk, by showing you, as Bergson does, that the concepts we talk with are made for purposes of *practice* and not for purposes of insight . . . . [A]n *intellectual* answer to the intellectualist's difficulties will never come.[12]

The intellect must serve a way of being and relating which is ultimately beyond its grasp. And yet there is no way around the intellect. In the fullness of its vision, liberal education enables us to bring the intellect into the service of transformation in the direction of the human.

* * *

Perhaps it is fitting to conclude with a direct report on practice, an experiential perspective on what I mean by liberal education and Socratic inquiry as a mode not only of information but also transformation, and even as a way out of our current cultural paralysis and decline.

I teach in a public institution, one that is ambitiously committed to liberal education. In the classroom there is a general pattern to encounter. My more cynical colleagues are correct that in any given class of students most initially appear to be asleep, in a stupor of superficial and ineffective self-concern, oriented to media immediacy and unexamined images of career and leisure; and they are suspicious of any big claims about meaning and value. Frequently students—and, sad to say, quite a number of teachers as well—reflect a pervasive condition within contemporary society: a low-level and unconscious nihilism that is perhaps best captured in Robert Jay Lifton's phrase "psychic numbing."[13]

It is out of this situation that the work begins.

First there is resistance to the practice of liberal education, usually in the form of students trying to force the demands of the course into the format that is familiar to them: read the textbook, listen to the professor (especially on what will be "on the test"), passively take notes, prepare to repeat what has been "learned." But within the discipline of liberal education, we continue to insist that inquiry is what is needed: students actively taking hold of the material, their identification and choice of those sources that are most significant in relation to their work, their own thinking and writing on the issues at hand in dialogue with that of the sources.

As the expectation is turned back on practitioners of liberal education, a deeper discomfort begins to be apparent. The Socratic kind of questioning about relationship between self and sources leads initially to an abyss, a sort of death. In a sense the students' worst fears are confirmed; they confront that which they have been seeking to avoid. Like Meno in the Socratic dialogue of the same title, they come face to face with the fact they do not know what they thought they knew; they arrive at the frustration of what is sometimes referred to as Meno's paradox: "a man cannot inquire either about that which he knows, or about that which he does not know; for if he knows, he has no need to inquire; and if not, he cannot."[14] In terms that are more familiar in twentieth-century articulation, the experience of nihilism—of Nothingness—becomes manifest: the awareness that underneath the various psychological or ego protections we use to control and keep our lives in order, and underneath our opinions and assumptions concerning issues of importance, there is an infinitely vast sea of arbitrariness and indifference, an endless confounding of any effort we might make, a sense that anything we do is even less than insignificant. At this point the low-level nihilism becomes explicit and conscious.

If the practitioner is able to withstand this experience, through the support, discipline, and direction of the classroom, as well as through the strength of her own character, something wonderful begins to happen. A new kind of order and control begins to emerge, a sort of rebirth. It is as though the student begins to learn to draw on the energy of the Nothingness itself, to trust it, to trust herself in the same act. In the terms of Robert Pirsig's popular philosophical work, students come into contact with "the silence that allows you to do each thing just right."[15] At this crucial point we see the emergence of a different kind of person, one who is able to both drop the cloak of cynicism and be serious in ways impossible before, while simultaneously being relaxed, even playful in ways that up to now could not be permitted. These students learn to draw increasingly on the "human wisdom" of Socrates' "not knowing," the kind of awareness that enables one to remain in touch with her "prophetic" inner voice.[16] They begin to flourish, moving beyond the psychic numbing of their original condition; being able to be themselves more fully at the same time they become more responsive to others, to be both definite and open.

This scenario from the classroom underscores what some of the major diagnosticians of Western culture have identified as essential to the revitalization of this culture. Karl Jaspers, for example, has said, "If man is not to be allowed to founder in the mere persistence of life, it may seem essential that in his consciousness he shall be confronted with Nothingness; he must recall his origin."[17] Stanley Rosen, speaking of the Western tradition in philosophy, has said, "If philosophy is to be preserved . . . it must come to terms with the *nihil absolutum*" which was articulated and ironically even popularized by Nietzsche.[18] Much of the feminist upheaval of our era can be seen in terms of the positive recovery of Nothingness or silence, as, for example, in the following statement from Adrienne Rich:

> We begin out of the void, out of darkness and emptiness. It is part of the cycle understood by the old pagan religions, that materialism denies. Out of death, rebirth; out of nothing, something.
>
> The void is the creatrix, the matrix. It is not mere hollowness and anarchy. But in women it has been identified with lovelessness, barrenness, sterility. We have been urged to fill our "emptiness" with children. We are not supposed to go down into the darkness of the core.
>
> Yet, if we can risk it, the something born of that nothing is the beginning of our truth.[19]

Pirsig, Jaspers, Rosen, and Rich, like Socrates, and like Abe and some of the other Eastern coparticipants in the larger dialogue of our era, point to a Nothingness that is not oblivion. It is not even negative. Rather, it is like that Nothingness out of which the God of the Old Testament created everything; it is that Nothingness that is paradoxically the source of everything, including human beings who are created, in their full presence, "in God's image"—as creators.

Notes

1. Robert L. Heilbroner, *An Inquiry into the Human Prospect* (New York: Norton, 1974), 77.

2. Plato, "Socrates' Defense," in *Plato: The Collected Dialogues*, ed. Edith Hamilton and Huntington Cairns (Princeton: Princeton University Press, 1985), 23.

3. Henry D. Thoreau, *A Week on the Concord and Merrimack Rivers* (Boston: Houghton Mifflin, 1929), 347.

4. For a complete analysis of the contemporary university, see Bruce Wilshire, *The Moral Collapse of the University: Professionalism, Purity, and Alienation* (Albany: State University of New York Press, 1990).

5. Cited by Sydney J. Harris, in *Detroit Free Press*, Dec. 1975.

6. William James, *Essays in Radical Empiricism and a Pluralistic Universe* (New York: Dutton, 1971), 150, 260.

7. Alfred North Whitehead, *Process and Reality* (New York: Free Press, 1969), 10.

8. Sissela Bok, *Lying: Moral Choice in Public and Private Life* (New York: Vintage, 1979), 6–11.

9. Joseph Axelrod, *The University Teacher as Artist* (San Francisco: Jossey-Bass, 1973); Wayne C. Booth, *The Vocation of a Teacher* (Chicago: University of Chicago Press, 1988); Ken Macrorie, *Twenty Teachers* (New York: Oxford University Press, 1984).

10. Masao Abe, *Zen and Western Thought* (Honolulu: University of Hawaii Press, 1985).

11. Abe, *Zen and Western Thought*, 4.

12. James, *Essays in Radical Pluralism and a Pluralistic Universe*, 260.

13. Robert Jay Lifton, *History and Human Survival* (New York: Vintage Books, 1971), 376.

14. Plato, *Meno*, trans. Benjamin Jowett (Indianapolis: Bobbs-Merrill, 1949), 36.

15. Robert Pirsig, *Zen and the Art of Motorcycle Maintenance* (New York: William Morrow, 1973), 242.

16. Plato, "Socrates' Defense," in Hamilton and Cairns, ed., pp. 8, 24. For more full presentation of this understanding of Socrates, see my *Rediscovering*

the West (Albany: State University of New York Press, 1995).

17. Karl Jaspers, *Man in the Modern Age* (Garden City: Anchor Books, 1975), 193.

18. Stanley Rosen, *The Ancients and the Moderns: Rethinking Modernity* (New Haven: Yale University Press, 1989), 188.

19. Adrienne Rich, *On Lies, Secrets, and Silence* (New York: Norton, 1979), 64. The essay in which this statement appears, "Women and Honor: Some Notes on Lying," is also included in my anthology, *Living Beyond Crisis: Essays on Discovery and Being in the World* (New York: Pilgrim Press, 1980), 71.

How to Host a
Philosophical Banquet

PLUTARCH

PLATO, dear Sossius Senecio, once got Timotheus, the son of Conon, away from the sumptuous officer's messes he frequented, and entertained him at dinner in the Academy with simplicity and respect for the Muses. It was the sort of table that Ion called "unfevered," a table that is followed by undisturbed sleep and only light dreams, because the body is in a state of calm and tranquility. In the morning Timotheus was conscious of the difference and observed that Plato's dinner guests felt well even on the day after. It is truly a great contribution to our health and happiness to have our bodies in a good state of balance, not sodden with wine, but light and ready unhesitatingly for any activity.

Another and not less valuable privilege guaranteed to Plato's guests was that of recalling afterwards what had been said over the drinks. Remembering past delights in food and drink is an ignoble kind of pleasure and one that is, besides, as unsubstantial as yesterday's perfume or the lingering smell of cooking. On the other hand, the topics of philosophical inquiry and discussion not only give pleasure by remaining ever present and fresh to those who actually recall them, but they also provide just as good a feast on the same food to those who, having been left out, partake of them through oral report. In this way, it is even today open to men of literary taste to enjoy and share in the Socratic banquets as much as did the original diners. Yet if pleasure were purely physical, the proper thing would have been for

From Plutarch's *Table-Talk*, book 6. Translated by P. A. Clement and H. B. Hoffleit. Loeb Classical Library.

both Xenophon and Plato to leave us a record, not of the conversation, but of the relishes, cakes, and sweets served at Callias's house and Agathon's. As it is, they never deign to mention such matters, for all the expense and efforts these presumably involved; but they preserve in writing only the philosophical discussions, combining fun with serious effort. Thus they have left precedents to be followed not only in meeting together for good conversation over wine, but in recording the conversation afterward.

Words of the God:
Ancient Oracle Traditions of the Mediterranean World

LEE IRWIN

THE HISTORY AND INFLUENCE of the various oracle traditions of the ancient and classical Mediterranean world is long and complex. This history, extending over several thousand years, from the Eighteenth Dynasty of Egypt (c. 1550 B.C.E.) through the rise and fall of Greek and Roman culture (c. 500 C.E.), expresses one of the great interconnective spiritual traditions that provided a direct, positive means for communication with higher divinities. Each oracle center, of which there were many, was dedicated to the solicitation and invocation of one or more specific deities whose response was mediated through specially trained and prepared human intermediaries. Surrounding these intermediaries were a select group of assistants and overseers who helped to maintain the sanctity and formalism of the process of invocation. Subsequently, oracle centers and their resident communities became highly influential in both the public and private lives of all those who turned to them for assistance and advice. This influence, radiating from the divinity through the oracle (Latin, *oraculum*) and out into the community at large, acted as a constant affirmation of the influence of the gods and goddesses in human affairs. That the various communities involved valued this influence and guidance is attested to by the long, enduring history of the oracle centers and the constant reference to them in the writings and inscriptions concurrent with their most active phases.

Many of these oracle centers became the foremost examples of religious activity, divination, healing, and worship. In doing so, they became not only places where worship to specific divinities was carried out, but also places where the words of the god might be heard (or indicated) and where human needs and uncertainty might be given new direction and impetus. At the classic Greek oracle centers, the *prophetes* (a male prophet) and the *prophetis* (a female prophet) spoke forth divine words and carried out their religious obligations while the *promantis* (one seized with inspiration) gave the oracle (Greek, *chresmos*) that proclaimed the response of the divinity. Each center had its own traditions and unique practices. Each evolved over many generations their own particular techniques and procedures often undergoing various periods of activity, decline, and resuscitation. Yet, underlying the various fluctuations of popularity and political influence, they remained central to the convergent influences of a shared symbolic and religious worldview that highly valued access to the *pneuma* (spiritual influence) of the divinities, persons, and precincts of the various centers.

Further, while these centers did not maintain highly visible or formal relationships, they did participate in informal connections between those holding various temple offices and those who participated in both oracular sessions and temple festivals in different locales. The main oracle temples were highly visible and well known and many individuals made special pilgrimages to these temples as part of their ongoing religious activities. The inscriptions on many temples show clearly that the range of persons visiting these oracular sites was highly varied and cut across all social classes—from highly formal visits of political emissaries to the everyday concerns of ordinary people troubled by uncertainty and anxiety or illness. While it is possible to see an increase in popular concerns or questions in the later history, nevertheless, concerns of success or failure, of victory or defeat, of doing or not-doing, of the support or non-support of the god or goddess, are paramount in all questions asked out of the 800 or more inscribed and literary oracles presently available for study.

Even the most rarefied political emissary asks very human, very existential questions directed to solving problems in the most immediate circumstances. Future prediction, in the literal sense, plays a very small role in the classic oracle traditions. Primarily, questions and answers engage present needs and issues whose outcomes are relatively immediate and whose consequences bear directly on those whose projects are circumscribed by an indeterminable present or the risky, unknown, normal circumstances of diverse human motives, conflicts, or ambiguities. The oracle, as well as the precinct and personnel of the temple, acted to provide a means for addressing these anxieties by offering a service through which the individual was able to establish a direct sense of communication with the most potent deities of the religious world. The communication might be a terse and concise "yes" or "no" response or more elaborate and symbolic— the response was often suited to the type of question asked. In turn, the answer also depended on the technique used to solicit the response; in most oracle centers there were a variety of ways that the divinity could be addressed or an answer solicited. Oracular responses cover a wide range of solicitations and few indicate the means by which an answer was attained.

While many oracular and divination techniques were practiced in the Mediterranean world, such as various types of lot divination, the examination of animal sacrifice in entrails or liver, the flight of birds or the behavior of animals, omens derived from sounds or unsolicited utterances (*cledones*), dreams, or incubation oracles, it is the inspired oracle-speaker who transmits the words of the god that is my primary concern. Both Plato and Cicero note a difference between two basic types of solicitation. Plato, in the *Ion* (534C), writes of one type: "The god uses diviners and holy prophets as his ministers in order that we who hear them may know them to be speaking not of themselves . . . but the god himself is the speaker and that through them he is conversing with us." Cicero, writing considerably later in *De divinatio* (1.6.12), distinguishes between "technical" divination (*technike mantike*), based primarily on the ability to read and interpret various signs seen in the everyday world or in its inhabitants, and "natural" or "intuitive" divination (*adidaktos mantike*) through inspired states, trance, or vision. It is this second type, the inspired oracle traditions, those often referred to as "prophetic" utterances transmitted through a human intermediary, well known and most highly admired in the classical Mediterranean world, that is my primary focus. Secondarily, I will also explore the use of lot oracles and dream oracles which were so common and so anciently followed in many temples and oracle centers.[1]

Egyptian Oracle Traditions

While it is beyond the scope of this paper to thoroughly explore the Egyptian oracle tradition, nevertheless, this is a rich and complex tradition that was very old and active long before the rise of the classic Greek oracle centers. One of the earliest recorded oracle traditions from Egypt dates to the Eighteenth Dynasty (New Kingdom) at the time of Queen Hatshepsut (1503–1482 B.C.E.). Cut into the walls of the temple at Deir el Bahari, it states: "A command was heard from the great throne, an oracle (*ndwt-r'*) of the god himself, that the ways to Punt should be searched out, that the roadways to the myrrh-gardens should be opened." This is a paradigmatic reference as it gives in concise form the "words of the god" as they issue from his place of enthronement, either from within the temple or from his portable shrine carried in religious festivals. The command is to send trading expeditions into the coastal region of southeast Egypt along the southern end of the Red Sea for myrrh and frankincense trees. Another tradition relates that when the queen was elevated to pharaoh, it was the oracle of the god Amun who proclaimed her king at Karnak, where she received her crown.[2]

Hatshepsut's young co-regent, Tuthmose III (1504–1450 B.C.E.), had recorded the event that as a young boy the sacred procession carrying the image of the god Amun in the hypostyle hall "noticed him and halted," signifying the god's support and recognition. This was interpreted as an oracular event. On a stele found at the Temple of Karnak, an inscription reads: "The king himself commended to be put in writing, according to the statement of the oracle, to execute monuments before those who are on earth." This was a command from the god for Tuthmose III to carry out the many temple building projects and restorations for which he is so famous. Amenophis II

(1450–1425) received an oracular dream from the god Amun who appeared in the form of a cult image (*shawabti*) "to give valor to his son" and to provide "the magical protection of his person, guarding the ruler."[3] Near the temple of Phillae, cut into a rock by order of Tuthmose IV (1425–1417), is a narrative of how the pharaoh went to the temple to make offerings and to consult the oracle when he learned of a revolt in Nubia.[4] He also recorded a famous oracular dream he had as a youth near the great Sphinx when Harmachis, the deity of the Sphinx, appeared to him and prophesied that he would one day be pharaoh. When he was crowned Tuthmose IV, he had the Sphinx cleared of sand and erected a stone stele commemorating the event.[5]

The primary Egyptian technique for consultation with the god was based on the public festival procession of the deity, in both the temple and in the local town. The cult image of the deity was concealed within a portable shrine of gilded wood, similar to a processional boat of the pharaoh, on two long wooden poles carried by approximately twenty "pure ones" (*wee'eb*) or "carriers of the god," dressed in white linen, who had undergone a special ceremonial purification. With the procession walked priests (*hom-neter*) or "servants of the god," at least one of whom waved a long-handled ostrich fan, while others carried sunshades over the shrine. Such a procession would be made, for example, during the Festival of Opet at Thebes in the second month of the inundation season when the god Amun was carried from Karnak to Luxor to renew his union with his divine mother (Mut) in the Luxor temple. During the procession, the god made oracular pronouncements.[6] Questions were asked of the god by either those upper class members invited into the temple, such as the pharaoh and his entourage, or by the populace during the public procession. The god was believed to compel the *wee'eb* toward various persons whose questions when asked were answered by either a forward motion or "nodding" toward the petitioner (*hmn*, affirmative) or a withdrawal or "recoiling" (*n'ynh'*, negative). If the god spontaneously stopped before an observer, such as in the case of Tuthmose III, it was regarded as a special oracular indication of future events.[7]

An example of this technique is given in a papyrus that tells how a priest of Amun, Harsiese, asked his son to address the image of the god carried by twenty "pure ones" in the Hall of Review in the temple of Amun. When the portable shrine stopped before him, the son asked if his father might renounce his obligations to Amun to serve at the temple of Re-Horakhty. The god indicated his answer by moving forward, toward the petitioner.[8] This oracular process usually involved a male divinity; however, female divinities, such as Isis, were also consulted for oracular decisions in this manner. In one procession, the shrine of the goddess Isis brought "an architect in the house of Ramses II" to a halt before an a commander of the local militia signifying the architect's election to a new office. A later Twenty-first Dynasty text mentions that the goddess Mut, "Mistress of the Great Throne," declared, regarding the propriety of transferring some ancestral burials: "It is good before me and there is no fault in it if they [the bodies] are taken out from their tomb, where they are, and moved."[9] Thus, not only were the oracles able to give negative and positive responses, but also more complex commands covering a wide range of subjects.

Not all the oracles, however, involved the Egyptian royalty or priest-classes. There are many fragments of pottery from Egyptian villages, such as Deir-el-Medina, recording questions or answers given to common workmen and their wives who also sought oracular advice. Every village had its small sanctuary or shrine containing an image of the god Amun and the local image would also be carried in procession and questions addressed to it. When five garments were stolen from a warehouse, the guard asked the god to help him recover them. The god agreed and the guard read to him a list of the entire population of the village and when he read a particular name, the god "moved" indicating the guilty party. Questions written on fragments of pottery or stone (*ostracon*) usually recorded in Egyptian hieratic were also presented to the god, who gave a response. Such questions involved everyday concerns such as lost property, boundaries, ownership of tombs, requests for protection or healing, after death protection, whether a child would live (often asked shortly after its birth), the health of friends or absent relatives, and so on. Normally, the petitioner spoke aloud the question and the god responded with an affirmative or negative response. Letters dating from the Twentieth-Dynasty period make frequent references to oracles made at small shrines or local temples over simple things such as when to cultivate a field, quarrels with neighbors, issues regarding pregnancy, as well as questions related to matters of state including the election of a new pharaoh.[10]

At the temple of the lioness goddess Sekhmet at Denderah, an adjoining building housed the sick and those in need of healing. These individuals would petition the goddess for an oracular response or a solution to their illnesses through "therapeutic dreams." Through a process of isolation, silence, purification, and the use of special lamps, the sick would be induced into a state of identification with Nun, the primordial ocean preceding creation, from which state the goddess would communicate with the dreamer regarding his or her illness.[11]

Dreams were considered highly significant and were interpreted as a fundamental means for communication with many different types of Egyptian divinities. The Chester Beatty III papyrus (Nineteenth Dynasty) gives a list of dreams and their oracular interpretations as a reference manual for priestly use. Bad dreams were countered by a spell appealing to Isis for aid in driving away the "terrible things which [the god] Set has made." These spells were first written on strips of papyrus and laid before the god for his approval.[12] Many oracular dreams are recorded in Egyptian literature and inscriptions like those previously mentioned or the dream of Merneptah (1236–1223 B.C.E.) who dreamed of the god Ptah, in the form of a sacred statue, handing him a sword and foretelling his forthcoming victory over the Libyans. Oracular dream traditions abound in late Egyptian lore, especially at such sites as the temples of Isis, Seti at Abydos, or at the temples of Saqqarah outside the burial grounds of the Apis bull, whose behavior while alive was regarded as giving oracular signs to the priests of Memphis and whose aid could be sought in dreams.[13]

Even though a present or past pharaoh could become a medium for oracular revelations, like the deified pharaohs Ahmose at Abydos or his son Amenhotep I in the villages of Thebes where oracular questions on pottery fragments have been found addressed to him at his shrine, it was the god Amun who prospered as the great god of late Egyptian oracular tradition. This old, primeval god, called the Hidden One, the god that was said to abide as the "soul" (*ba*) within all things, is constantly referenced as a primal source of oracular revelations. United with the old solar divinity Re, Amun-Re became the great god of the sacerdotal precincts of Thebes (with the goddess Mut and the god Khons), and by the Twenty-first Dynasty (*c.* 1050 B.C.E.) all decisions of import were brought before the god for an oracular response. The high priest of Thebes interrogated the god on all legal transactions, such as inheritance and property, and many issues of state as well as a wide range of religious questions, such as the care and protection of the dead. From Thebes, the cult of Amun spread to other centers as far as Ethiopia and, more famously, to the desert of Libya.[14]

To the oasis of Siwa, over 500 miles far to the west of the Nile, the god was transported and a temple built in Libya that became famous as an oracle center in the classic Greek and later Roman world. Established no later than the time of Pharaoh Amanis (570–526 B.C.E.), this is the site of Alexander's pilgrimage, during his conquests of Egypt, to question Amun (Greek, Ammon) concerning his future and which gods he should serve. According to Kallisthenes, the god was carried in a gilded boat around the temple by eighty priests ("pure ones"), followed by young girls and women chanting hymns, while the responses were given not in words, but "mainly by nods and tokens" which the temple prophet interpreted.[15] This certainly reflects the older tradition of the god's processional and shows how enduring the pattern of consultation was in Egypt. This pattern of consultation spread far beyond the Egyptian borders and lasted into the late Greco-Roman period. In Syria at Bambyce, Lucian recorded that the Syrian Apollo

> stirs on his throne when he wishes to speak, whereupon the priests at once lift him down, for if they fail to do so he becomes more and more agitated and starts sweating. Then as they bear him on their shoulders, he makes

them change direction and carry him from place to place. Presently the high priest appears and addresses all kind of questions to him. If the god disapproves he withdraws; if he approves, he makes his bearers move forward, as though he were driving them with reins.[16]

Herodotus in his *Histories* (2.83, 2.155) also notes the popularity of Egyptian oracles, particularly those of the goddess Edjo, a protectress of Horus, in the great Delta temple at Bujo.

In reviewing the Egyptian materials, we can see the role of the high priest or prophet as an interpreter of the gods' actions or motions. Though some evidence exists that strongly suggests the god or goddess as "speaking," primarily the technique was to present a petition, question, or even list of individuals read aloud, while waiting for a responsive signal or motion. Often the form of consultation was that of a lot oracle. A question would be written indicating a positive response on a fragment of pottery or a strip of papyrus, then the same questions would be written with a negative response. The petitioner then invoked the local god, explained the circumstances and asked for a reply. Both questions would then be placed before the shrine of the god or goddess, for approval or disapproval, the response indicating one or the other of the questions—sometimes these questions were placed in an urn and only one drawn out indicating the will of the god. Such requests are also found in Demotic and Greek (from Oxyrhynchus and the Fayyum), dated into the Roman period as late as the fifth and sixth centuries C.E. and containing, remarkably, oracular questions addressed to the Christian God—asking about such things as the advisability of traveling or not traveling to a particular place. Two addressed to "Lord God Almighty and Saint Philoxenus," one phrased in positive and another in negative terms, asked if the petitioner should or should not go into the banking business.[17] However, the issue of one who spoke directly for the god, as the medium of the god, is less evident in the Egyptian context and appears more normative in the Hebrew and Greek context.

Greek Oracle Traditions

In reviewing the complex and diverse sources of the Greek oracle traditions, through inscriptions and literary references, it is clear that these traditions were associated with specific oracle centers. The number of such centers is quite large and ranged from the more famous great temples such as Dodona or Delphi to smaller and less well known temples, to country or local town shrines—all sites for petitioning a god or goddess to receive an oracular reply. However, only at certain of these sites was it possible to hear the words of the god directly, as transmitted through a chosen individual dedicated to being the spokesperson of the divinity. It is these sites that most clearly express the "prophetic" nature of Greek religious tradition. Historically, these sites can be conveniently demarcated into three groups: the early oracular temples of Zeus (Dodona, Olympia, and somewhat remotely, Siwa), the great oracular, mainland Greek temple of Apollo in the classic period (Delphi), and the late Greek Apolline oracular sites across the Aegean in Asia Minor (Didyma and Klaros). There are also several others worthy of note, particularly the oracle of Trophonius, the Sibyl at Cumae, and the temples of Asclepius.[18]

Among the Greeks, the concept of *prophetes* is as old as that of the early Hebrew prophets (*nabi'*) such as Amos or Hosea (*c.* 750 B.C.E.) or the Assyrian oracle texts of a similar period (*c.* 650 B.C.E.). The Greek concept of *prophetes* means a person who "speaks forth," usually under divine influence (like the Latin *vates*, an Italo-Celtic concept of one who sings as a consequence of divine possession).[19] Another Greek concept is that of the *mantis* of which Plato in the *Phaedrus* (244A) writes:

> There is a mania which is a divine gift and the source of the chief blessing granted to men. For prophecy is a mania and the prophetess at Delphi and the priestesses at Dodona when out of their senses have conferred great benefits on Hellas, both in public and private life, but when in their own senses few or none.

Plato equates the prophetic ability with a state of *mania* or "divine possession" which radically transforms the individual and makes them a *mantis*, one who is divinely possessed, or a *chrestes*, a speaker of oracles or inspired words. The "divine gift" was highly regarded and recognized in only certain select men or women whom the Greeks regarded with respect and some awe. In early Greek literature, the poet (*poietes*) or the wise philosopher (*sophistes philosophos*) was regarded as inspired with holy words. Hesiod in the *Theogony* (1.1 ff.) writes of the prophetic power of the Muses, daughters of Zeus, who "breathed into me their divine voice" after giving him the symbol of inspiration, the *skeptron*, a rod of "sturdy laurel."

In Homer's *Iliad* (1.43, 62), the *mantis* already appears as a developed religious type in the figure of Kalkhas, son of Thestor, "who knew what is, and what is to come, and what has been before." In this same passage Achilles differentiates the *mantis* from the ritualist (*hiereus*, "priest") and the dream interpreter (*oneiropolos*). Kalkhas, as *mantis*, is specifically a "bird-augur" who reads the flight and cries of birds, and a speaker of oracles, one who knows the mind of Apollo, a role identified by Homer (750 B.C.E.) as contemporary with the Trojan War (*c*. 1200 B.C.E.) and linked to the prophetic inspirations of the god Apollo. In the *Homeric Hymn to Apollo*, after Apollo's birth on the island of Delos, the god exclaims, "My wish is to hold the dear lyre and the curved bow and to prophesy to men the unerring will of Zeus."[20] Thus in early Greek literary traditions, Apollo is identified as one of the preeminent gods of prophecy. In the *Odyssey* (10.492, 11.90), Tieresias the blind *mantis*, holding the golden rod of prophecy, is invoked from the realm of the dead by Odysseus to foretell his future wanderings. Tieresias has his gift of prophecy at the will of the goddess Persephone, indicating that the inspiration of the *mantis* may be linked to a diversity of divine figures, either male or female. Homer in the *Odyssey* (20.351) also writes of hereditary prophetic abilities (or "second sight") in the figure of Theoklymenos, who inherited his prophetic gift from the legendary seer Melampus, and who foretells the death of the suitors of Odysseus's wife Penelope, but is mocked and disbelieved. Disbelief in prophecy (even when true) is a counter theme in much Greek writing.

The raising of the dead to give prophetic guidance is also found in the *Persae* (619F) written by Aeschylus (*c.* 475 B.C.E.) where the ghost of Darius is raised through invocations to Ge (Earth) and Hermes, to advise the Persian queen after the Greek victory at Salamis. Aeschylus gives many examples of early prophetic figures, including the "house prophets" (*prophetai domon*) of Agamemnon, probably interpreters of omens attached to wealthy Greek households. The foremost description of early Greek prophecy is also given by Aeschylus—the climactic, prophetic mania of the fated prophetess Kassandra, Priam's daughter, given her gift of prophecy by Apollo, but doomed to never be believed because she refused Apollo's sexual advances. In the *Agamemnon* (1072–1354) is recorded a remarkable scene of prophetic possession in which the *prophetis* foretells the violent death of Agamemnon at the hands of his betrayed wife, Clytaemnestra. Possessed by Apollo's prophetic gift, Kassandra speaks her terrible vision of betrayal and foretells also her own death. Perhaps the most dramatic of all prophetic descriptions in Greek literature, this scene epitomizes the mania that seizes the prophetess and compels her to speak, even when it means her death. This clairvoyant prophetic ability seems more characteristic of particular Greek literary figures than, as we shall see, the actual oracular traditions of the great temples.

The Oracles of Zeus

Dodona, located in Epirus, in northwest Greece, about 1,600 feet above sea level near Mount Tomaros, is perhaps the oldest and certainly the most famous oracular temple of Zeus. In the *Odyssey* (14.327–28; 19.296), Homer mentions the temple: "He [Odysseus] has gone to Dodona to listen to the counsel of Zeus from his high foliaged oak, how he should return to the rich land of Ithaca." Herodotus (2.54–58) records that Dodona was the "most ancient" of all Greek temples and was, according to the priests at Thebes, founded by one of two abducted Egyptian priestesses, the other of which founded the oracular temple of Zeus-Ammon in Libya. Herodotus also mentions a legend, told to him directly by three priestesses of

Zeus at Dodona, that these same two temples of Zeus-Ammon were founded by two black doves released from the temples of Ammon in Thebes. One flew to Libya and the other to Epirus and the one, landing in an special oak tree, spoke to the local inhabitants, who then built the temple with the oak at the center. Herodotus also notes that the methods of consultation are "similar in character" at both Thebes and Dodona. In a classical note (*scholia*) to the above Odyssey reference, a story is recorded that a dove spoke to an "oak-cutter" and told him the tree was sacred to Zeus. Sophocles in *Women of Trachis* (171–72) wrote concerning the fate of Hercules, "At Dodona he heard the ancient oak declare on the lips of the twin Doves, the priestesses." The Greek term for dove (*peleia*) may refer to several specially chosen priestesses who interpreted or sang the oracles of Zeus around the sacred oak tree. Pausanius in his *Guide to Greece* (10.12.5) claims that the "rock-pigeons" of Dodona preceded the Pythia at Delphi and were the first women singers of sacred songs to the god.[21]

In Homer's *Iliad* (2.750; 16.233–35), there is another reference to Dodona: "Lord Zeus, of Dodona, Pelasgian, dwelling afar, ruling over hard-wintered Dodona and around dwell the Selloi, your interpreters of unwashed feet, sleeping on the ground." This prophetic group of "interpreters" (*hypophetes*), or those who spoke under the compulsion of the god, are only mentioned in the early literature. It is not known how the god communicated through the oak tree, though an account in Apollodorus's *Library* (1.9.16) tells that the keel of the great ship Argo was made from an oak at Dodona fitted by the goddess Athena, which, under certain circumstances, spoke to the Argonauts. Aeschylus, in the *Prometheus Bound* (829), writes of "steep-ridged Dodona where is the oracular seat of Thesprotian Zeus, and, unbelievable miracle, talking oaks." Further, Plato records in the *Phaedrus* (275B), "There was a tradition in the temple of Dodona that the oaks first gave prophetic utterances." The interpreters of this speaking, the Selloi (possibly a hereditary clan), apparently lived an ascetic life at the temple listening for signs of the god. Much later, a Roman priest of Jupiter, the Flamen Dialis, along with other prohibitions, slept on a bed "smeared with a thin layer of mud"—a practice reminiscent of the unwashed feet of the Selloi. Perhaps the precinct of the god's tree was holy and earth from around the tree (or sacred grove) could not be simply washed off.[22]

The three priestesses of Dodona, as interviewed by Herodotus, reflect the normal practice for consultation. Lead strips excavated from Dodona, dated to around the sixth century and lasting as late as 250 B.C.E., contain questions that could be answered with a "yes" or "no," indicating the use of lot oracles at the site, most likely under the direction of the priestesses. A fragment of Euripides reads, "at the holy seat of Dodona beside the sacred oak women convey the will of Zeus to all Greeks who desire it."[23] One technique may have been that the questions (negative and positive) were written on thin lead strips, folded in half, placed in a vessel and, after the appropriate rites, a strip would be drawn out by a priestess to indicate the will of the god. This would be a practice in perfect consonance with the older Egyptian tradition. The strips were kept by the priestesses, smoothed over and then used again (many times) for oracular inquiry—thus the strips can be read as layered with numerous questions. Most questions recorded were those asked by individuals from western Greece and Peloponnesus.[24]

Pindar, in his *Olympian* poem (6.65), speaking of Iamus, writes that "the god endowed him doubly in prophecy: first the gift of hearing the voice immune to falsity; secondly, the right to establish an oracle at the highest altar of Zeus." This altar was the temple of Zeus at Olympia, a city in Elis, the one known throughout Greece for its famed Olympic Games. The tradition of inherited prophecy involved two families after the fifth century—those of Iamus and those of Klytia, with the post of *mantis* being shared by both families. According to inscriptional records extending over 300 years, the prophetic office was held for life and in this listing no mention is made of any priests (*hiereus*) of the temple. The function of the prophets was to make sacrifices (*empyra*) on the altar of Zeus and, in burning them, to read the signs displayed in the flames by the god. After the fifth century B.C.E., the majority of oracles given related to the possibility of victory and/or recognition of athletes in the Olympic games. However, this was not the only kind of question, as many other types were asked and the answers sought through sacrificial burning.[25] The family of the Clytiadae prophets is linked to the legendary sage and seer, Melampus (also linked to Theoklymenos, see above). According to Apollodorus, Melampus received his oracular and prophetic power through young snakes he rescued from an oak; after they were grown, two of them licked his ears while he slept—afterwards, he was able to understand the language of the birds, and the "art of divination through sacrifice."[26]

However, there is an earlier tradition at Olympia of an altar dedicated to goddesses of Earth, Ge or Demeter. Pausanius (5.14.10) says explicitly: "At what they call the Earth-sanctuary, there is an altar of Earth and this also is made of ash: they say that in even more ancient times there was an oracle of Earth there. The altar to Themis is built at what they call the Mouth." Themis is the goddess of order, peace, and justice; she is also an oracular goddess, daughter of Ge, who called the assembly of the gods and took the first cup at their feasts. Further, the goddess Hera was also worshipped early at Olympia as her large temple was built (late seventh century B.C.E.) before the temple dedicated to Zeus; only the ash altars of Ge and Hera have the association with oracular sacrifice. There was also an early shrine to the goddess Demeter Khamyne preceding Zeus, with attendant priestess overseers, possibly dating from the founding of the Olympic games (776 B.C.E.). The earlier practice would likely involve a qualified and specially trained woman *mantis* entering a cavern (like the "mouth") after ritual preparation to seek an oracular inspiration. With Zeus came the advent of two male prophetic patrilines whose prophets sought to honor not Ge, but the sky god Zeus at the newly built sacrificial stone and ash altar which only men could ascend. It was from this high altar that, as Pindar writes in his *Olympian* poem (8.2), "men of prophecy divine the word of Zeus, white lightning's source, in sacrificial fires and learn what plans he has for men."[27]

Pausanius (5.15.11) also notes that the Eleans offer sacrifice every month at the many altars of the gods and goddesses of Olympia, but also "they pour wine not only to the Greek gods but to the Libyan god

... [for] they appear to have used the Libyan oracle from a very early period, and there are altars in Ammon's sanctuary which are inscribed with the Elean's questions and the god's prophetic replies." Thus there were links between both the oracle temples of Zeus at Dodona and Olympia with the Zeus-Ammon temple in the oasis of Siwa in Libya, which Pausanius visited to give an eyewitness account of the Olympian inscriptions. Certainly the Greeks knew of and used the Egyptian oracle of Ammon at Siwa and Plato in his *Laws* (5.738) notes that in the religion of his ideal state, there be "no change in anything which the oracle of Delphi, Dodona, or the god Ammon . . . has sanctioned in whatever manner." By mid-fourth century, the Zeus-Ammon oracle was held in very high regard and equal in authority with the most valued oracle centers in mainland Greece. It is no wonder that Alexander journeyed there to receive the god's oracular replies, as it was regarded as one of the foremost centers for the prophetic revelations of the most high god of Greeks and Egyptians alike.[28]

The Oracles of Apollo

There is one Homeric reference to the Delphic oracle in the *Odyssey* (8.79) which states: "Phoebus Apollo had spoken to him [Agamemnon] in prophecy in holy Pytho when he crossed the stone threshold to consult the oracle." This sets the activity of Delphi into the period of the Trojan war and certainly indicates activity in the time of Homer. In the Homeric *Hymn to Apollo* (391 ff.), the poet sings of the island of Delos as the first oracle center of the god and of the first Cretan caretakers (*orgeones*) of the temple at Delphi, a tradition strengthened by the furniture and symbols of the oracle chamber.[29] Further, the goddess snake cult of Crete was well developed and may have been an origin for the early female oracular tradition at Delphi. In Aeschylus's *Eumenides* (1–5), we read the Delphic Pythia's invocation: "First in my prayer before all other gods I call on Earth (Ge), primeval protectress. Next, Themis sat on her mother's oracular seat, so men say. Third, by unforced consent another Titan, daughter too of Earth, Phoebe." According to Euripides in *Iphigenia in Tauris* (1247 ff.), it was a "ruddy-faced serpent" at ancient Delphi who "ministered the oracle of the earth goddess," but Apollo dispossessed Themis and slew the female serpent. Out of revenge, mother Earth, Ge, sends prophetic night-dreams to human beings, but Apollo petitions his father, Zeus, who commands Earth to cease these prophetic dreams so the Greeks will come to his son at Delphi. As a result of his blood-guilt in slaying the Python, Apollo had to suffer nine years of exile. No doubt, the Earth goddess and her female prophets were revered and original to the site, as symbolized by Athene Pronaia before the temple and by the sanctuary beneath the temple dedicated to Ge.[30]

The ascendancy of Apollo at Delphi, like that of Zeus at Olympia, did not, however, displace the female Pythia, who remained the *promantis* of Apollo and the primary spiritual link to the god. Apollo, as son of Zeus and thus the god of prophecy, was linked with a variety of inspired or ecstatic women who, like Kassandra, spoke the words of the god. According to Pausanius (2.24.1), the sanctuary of Apollo Pythaeus at Argos had a female *prophetis* who "kept from the beds of men" and who "once each moon tasted the blood of a sacrificed ewe-lamb and the god possessed her." Herodotus (1.182) records that the temple of Apollo at the Lycian town of Patara also had "a woman who delivered the oracles" after she was shut up for the night in Apollo's temple. On the Greek mainland, this tradition of a woman who spoke for the god was continued at Delphi. According to Diodorus Siculus in his *Library* (16.26), the original Pythia was a young virgin who was carried off and raped by a Thessalian who came to consult the oracle, after which the Delphians made a law that the Pythia must be over fifty years of age but still wear the dress of a virgin—a reference to the chaste vows of the Pythia. She may also have been a member of a guild of holy women who had renounced sexual relations and who cared for the sacred flame of the temple, feeding it laurel and pine.[31]

Diodorus (16.26) also notes that it was a goatherd who discovered the "chasm" from which emanated a vapor or exhalation that caused "possession" in both the goats and the herder, after which he foretold the future. The local Delphians then appointed a woman to act as a prophetess and to sit on a tripod over the chasm.[32] This site then became the inner sanctuary of the late temple at Delphi. This ratio-

nalized theory, quite common in classical literature, was modified by
Plutarch when he wrote, "the Pythoness herself has the part of her soul
which is affected by the exhalation in different states and dispositions
at different times." For Plutarch, every soul had the potential for
prophetic revelation but the Pythia was especially gifted and sensitive
to inspirations from the god. This inspiration was not a physical vapor
as much as an instrumental, inspiring breath initiated by Apollo, "a
breath like the most delicious and costly perfume" that on occasion
filled the hall of those waiting for consultation in the temple. The
sensitivity of her response was like that of a musical instrument that
was highly crafted but needed careful attunement. He also narrated
that when the Pythia was once forced into the oracle chamber after
receiving ill omens, she gave out harsh cries and rushed with a shriek
to the entrance, frightening away the questioners and the *prophetes*,
and who, after throwing herself on the ground, died a few days later.[33]
Like the moon reflecting the light of the sun, the Pythia reflects the
light of the god, in diminished form, "showing his thoughts aloud" but
mixed with the mortality of her body and the agitations of her soul.
Such a state required the utmost care and purity of mind, as well as
various ablutions. During certain seasons, the demand for consultation was shared by two Pythia with a third who "was appointed as
reserve."[34]

The normal consultation proceeded as follows: at dawn on the
special days of consultation, usually the seventh day of each month
dedicated to Apollo, a preliminary sacrifice was held outside the
temple where the priests sprinkled cold water on a goat; if it failed to
tremble and stood gazing straight ahead, the day was deemed inaus-
picious and no oracle was held. If the goat trembled, the consultation
proceeded. The Pythia then purified herself with fresh spring water,
perhaps drinking, and, passing through the *pronaos* or vestibule,
entered the central building of the temple, accompanied by devotees
(*hosioi*) of Apollo and Dionysus, the male *prophetes* and priests, various
Delphians chosen by lot, and the clients. There an offering was made
at the sacred fire, perhaps of laurel leaves (sacred to Apollo) and barley
meal. The Pythia then entered the most sacred area, the *manteion*, the

place for consulting the god, an area that contained a golden statue of Apollo, the tomb of Dionysus, the tripod on which she sat, and an ancient, round *omphalos* said to represent the center of the earth and to be a funerary monument to the slain serpent. Only the Pythia was allowed to enter this special chamber which was perhaps of untiled, bare earth (not stone), on a lower level than the rest of the temple—here she became truly sacred to the god.[35]

Each consultant or client was required to offer a sacred meal cake before entering the temple and then to make additional animal sacrifices at the sacred flame in the main building (*cella*) under the supervision of the priests. The inquirer was then led to a small room adjoining the *manteion* where he was admonished to "think pure thoughts and speak well-omened words" while he waited. The *prophetes* took the question, either written or oral, which he then recited to the Pythia who may not have been visible to either him or the client. The Pythia then received the words of the god and spoke them aloud. The nature of this inspiration was explicitly described by Plutarch as "the god shut in a mortal body once a month," and Iamblichus writes of the Delphic Pythia, "she becomes wholly possessed by the god" and "entirely gives herself up to a divine spirit and is illuminated with a ray of divine fire."[36] Speaking in a state of trance, possessed by the god, the Pythia spoke prophetic words in oracular form which were then either heard by the client or repeated by the *prophetes*. On special occasions, the inspired Pythia might draw forth names from a special vessel or select among lots in the form of dried, colored (sometimes inscribed) beans in a bowl. Also she might be asked to chose between identical questions written in a negative or positive form, similar to the Egyptian lot oracles.[37]

While later Neoplatonists debated the exact nature of the Pythia's possession as perhaps a "daimon" who was under the direction of the god, early sources attribute such possession to the god himself. Further, Plutarch's own writing clearly supports the idea that the psychic disposition of the Pythia must be calm, centered, and attuned to the moment of possession so as not to distort or diminish the pronouncements through excessive emotional agitations. Thus the late Greek theories of possession involved three elements: the active, divine cause of the god; the instrument of inspiration or earth exhalation (vapor); and, finally, the Pythia's attunement or purified, receptive psychic condition. This response, nevertheless, was impassioned and deeply rooted in an *eros* of soul that sacrificed normal sexuality for union with the god. Virginity and self-mastery were a means for a deeper receptivity and the possession of the Pythia was a form of "spiritual fullness" (*pneuma enthousiastikon*) whose consequent impregnation of soul gave birth to holy words.[38] In such a condition the concept of "possession" takes on an erotic character that allows for merging and union, yet, some sense of individual identity. In its most intense forms, it became a power and presence that overwhelmed, a mania whose intensity was of divine origin and whose outward manifestations were holy words, the oracular pronouncements of the god. This speaking was charged, cryptic, and at times more poetic than didactic—as the famous statement by Heraclitus noted, "The god whose oracle is in Delphi neither speaks out nor conceals but gives a sign."[39] Yet, many of the oracles were clear commands or directions spoken by the Pythia to the inquirer, as an immediate, direct response to their questions.

Strabo notes that the Pythia "received the *pneuma* and speaks oracles in both verse and prose, and these too are put into verse by certain poets who work for the sanctuary."[40] These men, some of whom became well-known collectors of oracles (*chresmologues*), were most likely not priests or attendants on the Pythia, but men who may have made an income from reciting, adapting, and collecting oracular verses. The *prophetes* was most likely a priest—two were continually appointed for life at Delphi after 200 B.C.E.—who assisted the Pythia during her oracular sessions and who may also have presented questions for an envoy sent by an absent client and then put them into writing for the envoy. Such a priest-prophet would act as a guide to the clients and buffer the Pythia from inappropriate requests or intrusions. Many of the oracle responses (after 450 B.C.E.) were sanctions of laws, proposals, often of a religious nature, and prescriptions for cultic activities. These were often down-to-earth answers to immediate questions involving the sanction or approval of Apollo, while enigmatic statements about the future were fewer and mostly associated with literary traditions. A question asked by Xenophon is typical: "To what god should he sacrifice and pray to make his journey successful, to fare well upon it, and to return in safety?" To which the Pythia responded by conveying the words of Apollo as to which gods he should sacrifice. Simple commands by the god were the most common type of response to individual requests, including a fair number of clear predictions, only a few of which are obscure or ambiguous.[41]

While the temple at Delphi flourished in the sixth and fifth centuries, in 373 B.C.E. an earthquake struck near Delphi and a catastrophic landslide led to the near destruction of the temple and a large part of the sacred grounds. The reconstruction required many years of effort on the part of the Delphic Amphictyony in charge of the temple. During this long period, two sacred wars were fought involving Delphi (c. 356 and 339) and it was not until about 330 B.C.E. that the temple was reconsecrated. Further, the Amphictyony was by then under the control of Philip of Macedonia and somewhat estranged from the rest of the Greek mainland. Significantly, at this time other oracle temples of Apollo began to revive and flourish across the Aegean Sea on coastal Asia Minor, particularly the temples of Didyma and Klaros. The temple of Apollo Didymeus, near the city of Miletos, was certainly long in existence before this but, after 334–331, the oracle was reestablished with the title of *prophetes* given to the primary head of the temple.[42]

While originally the temple had been known by the name of the Branchidai, a family that had held a hereditary title for carrying out the rites, the new *prophetes* was elected by lot to office for a one-year term. These were usually from wealthy families of Miletos, and later included three Roman emperors—Trajan, Hadrian, and Julian.[43] The *prophetes* at Didyma was the head magistrate and lived in a special house on the temple grounds; he presided over all rites, sacrifices, feasts, and oracular sessions, speaking all the prayers during the rites. He was expected to entertain and share his wealth with the many visitors, embassies, and other temple holders of sacred office. Two annually appointed stewards (*tamiai*) assisted him in overseeing the management of the entire sanctuary. There were also scribes (*grammateis*) who recorded the oracles and put them into writing for clients. The *chresmographeion* or "oracle writing place" was a special building where oracular inquiries and/or responses could be written. The *neokoroi* were those responsible for cleansing the temple and sprinkling those who came for inquiry with holy water (*sacristans*). There were also manual laborers and slaves who helped to maintain the grounds and the sacred groves (*alsos*) of laurel.[44]

The mantic session at Didyma was carried out by a holy woman who, as at Delphi, was the spokesperson of the god. The *prophetes* led the session by directing clients to the east portal of the temple at dawn on the appointed day. The *promantis* had been fasting for three days previous to the consultation and had purified herself; she was then escorted from her sleeping chambers to the oracle chamber (*adyta*) in which there was a pure spring. During this time ritual offerings and sacrifices were carried out that also required the singing of special hymns by choirs of singers who had journeyed to the temple especially to perform. The *prophetes* then collected the previously written questions of each client and proceeded with several other temple officials down the vaulted corridors to the chamber of the *promantis*, who would then answer each question according to the inspirations and guidance of the god. Under the compulsion of the god, the *promantis* might, on rare occasion speak "spontaneously" (*automatismos*) before the question was asked, thus giving an oracle on matters other than those intended to be asked by the inquirer. In at least one case, the prophetess was a woman from a very wealthy and respected family.[45]

In *De Mysteriis Aegyptiorum*, Iamblichus writes explicitly on the oracle at Didyma (3.12.127–128):

> The prophetic woman too in Branchidae [Didyma] whether she holds in her hand a wand, which was first received from some god, and becomes filled with divine splendor, or whether seated on an axis she predicts future events, or dips her feet or the border of her garment in the water,

or receives the god by imbibing the vapor of water; by all these she becomes adapted to partake externally of the god . . . the baths of the prophetess, her fasting for three whole days, her retiring into the *adyta*, and there receiving the divine light and rejoicing for a considerable time—all these evince that the god is entreated by prayer to approach, that he becomes externally present and that the prophetess, before she comes to her accustomed place, is inspired in a wondrous manner.

Thus through various rites and ritual objects or actions, the *promantis* was able to enter into a state of communion with the god and thereby receive appropriate answers to the questions asked. Over many generations, the questions at Didyma underwent a change from the most practical, from such as whether one city should engage in piracy against another city, to the most metaphysical in the later Imperial age, such as the nature of the soul, its future existence, or questions on the nature of God. Most responses involved clear commands, expressed often in verse, including the foundations of festivals and temples, or for carrying out sacrifices and offerings; other are about religious laws, customs, doctrines. Alexandra, priestess of Demeter Thesmophoros, was disturbed because of certain signs and sacred manifestations in Miletos and she asked the *promantis* whether these phenomena were positive or not. Apollo tells her that the gods meet with mortals on earth to tell men their will and the offerings they should make.[46]

At the temple of Apollo at Klaros, the Roman historian Tacitus recorded in his *Annals* (2.54) that during a visit by Germanicus (18 C.E.) the oracles were given by a man, a *prophetes* chosen from a select group of families who, in mantic sessions, obtained the name and number of the temple inquirers only and took these to the oracle chamber, drank from the sacred spring, and, thus inspired, produced oracular verse on each question. Iamblichus also uses the term for a male prophet and writes in *De Mysteriis Aegyptiorum* (3.11.124–126):

It is acknowledged then by all men that the oracle in Colophon [Klaros] gives its answers through the medium of water. For there is a fountain in the subterranean dwelling from which the prophet drinks; and on certain established nights, after many sacred rites have been previously performed, he drank of this fountain, he delivers oracles, but is not visible to those that are present . . . he neither being any longer master of himself, nor capable of attending to what he says, nor perceiving where he is. Hence after prediction is he scarcely able to recover himself. And before he drinks the water, he abstains from food for a whole day and night; and retiring to certain sacred places, inaccessible to the multitude, begins to receive in them the enthusiastic energy.

The *prophetes* is spoken of as a man of little learning and untaught in literature or poetry. Inscriptions from the reign of Hadrian list the offices at the Klaros temple as the priest (*hiereus*), the *prophetes*, and singer of oracles (*thespiodos*) along with one or two recording secretaries. The priest and the singers were appointed for long periods of life but the prophet changed annually. The *prophetes* would undergo the fast and after drinking from the sacred spring, give the oracles of the god.

Inquiry was held at night at Klaros; those who had questions gathered together under the direction of the priests after undergoing certain restrictions in food, drink, or sexual relations. They were then led in a torchlight procession, as part of the mysteries of the temple, down one of two temple halls to a low tunnel that turned seven times and was roofed in blue marble, before reaching a lamp-lit room—the waiting room outside the oracle chamber, containing an navel stone (*omphalos*) also of deep blue marble. The inquirers sat on stone benches and gave their name and number (but not the question) to the *prophetes*, who then entered the second chamber containing the sacred spring. His responses would then be repeated by the *thespiodes* or singers who would chant the verses inspired by the god. The inquirers would then be led out, to return back up to the main floor temple through a second passageway. A copy of the oracular answers would then be given to the inquirer, written out by the secretaries. Clearly, the evidence supports the notion that the oracle centers were still highly active even in the late Roman Imperial period and some 300 texts inscribed on the temple walls make Klaros a highly visible center for Greek indigenous religion in the developing Christian world. Many envoys came to the city from the Mediterranean world accompanied by choirs of young boys and girls as well as from the borders of Scotland, the highlands of Lycia, from Sardinia to Banasa and Cuicul in Africa. Many other Apolline oracle centers also continued: at Abae in Phocis, in Boeotia at Tegyra, on Mount Ptoion, at Corope in Thessaly, and the Ismenian Apollo at Thebes.[47]

The Roman Oracles Tradition

The Roman connection with Delphi and the oracles of Apollo or Zeus was tenuous at best. Through the Second Punic War, relations were cordial but distant. Roman ambassadors sent to Delphi brought gifts of silver and a golden crown after the victory at Metaurus—the Pythia responded by predicting many more Roman victories. Not long after this consultation, the Pythia was asked for approval of a plan to bring the Mother of the Gods (Magnus Mater) to Rome, which was affirmed by consultation with the god. However, with increasing Roman military strength and victories, there was a dramatic decline in seeking Greek oracular support for Roman actions. By the end of the Third Macedonian war, and the annexation of Greece and Macedonia by the Romans (c. 147 B.C.E.), the Pythia at Delphi no longer played a significant role in the religious life of the Greco-Roman world. The brutal destruction of the oracle of Zeus at Dodona by the Romans (c. 189 B.C.E.) also terminated the influence of other oracle centers on the Greek mainland, though Didyma and Klaros continued to thrive and be highly active in Asia Minor. King Perseus of Macedonia was the last Greek king to consult the oracle at Delphi.[48]

Nevertheless, prophecy was highly active in the Roman Imperial period and there were a multitude of oracle centers. At the shrine of Demeter at Patai, visitors dipped a small mirror on a cord into the sacred spring of the goddess and after burning incense and praying, gazed into the mirror to see there a sick person "either living or dead." Egyptian prophecy was recorded at Memphis in the play of children in the courtyard of the temple to Apis. The Egyptian god Bes gave oracles to Greek and Roman visitors to the Valley of Kings through written requests which he answered with a negative or positive reply. In the coastal city of Alexandria, at the Temple of Isis and Serapis, dream oracles were given. In the many temples of Asclepius, dream oracles were also given, for example at his great temple in Pergamun. At Praeneste, some twenty miles southeast of Rome, was the great temple to Fortuna Primigenia, the Roman goddess of fortune, at whose sanctuary wealthy Romans could receive oracles from the goddess. The method involved the drawing of lots or *sortes* written on oak tablets, not simply indications of "yes" or "no," but whole sentences which required interpretation, often of a didactic or epigrammatic character in a style similar to archaic verse. The college of augurs in Rome read the flights of birds, or designated a special area for observation (*templum*) and determined divine approval or disapproval by events occurring therein. The Etruscan *Haruspices* read the entrails of sacrificial victims in conjunction with the movements of the stars.[49]

A famous Greek oracle center at this time was that of Trophonius at Lebadeia in Boeotia. This site was visited by Pausanius (*c*. 150 C.E.) who described in detail the oracular consultation. The shrine was on a wooded hillside surrounded by a five foot high circular platform wall of white stone, with bronze posts linked together by a chain on top of the wall. A doorway led through it to the center of the walled circle where there was a man-made chasm about twenty feet deep. The supplicant first spent several days purifying himself, bathing in cold water from the river and making many sacrificial offerings, the entrails of which were read by priests to see if the god would accept the inquirer. After a special bathing and anointing with olive oil, the supplicant was then taken to a spring where he drank from the "water of forgetfulness" to clear the mind and then from the "waters of memory" to retain everything seen or heard. He then worshiped before the image shown only to those about to descend, while wearing a white linen robe, ribbons, and heavy boots. He was then taken to the sacred enclosure and climbed down a ladder into the kiln-shaped pit, with honey-cake offerings in his hands. There, before an opening several feet wide and a foot or so high, he laid down, pushing his feet into the opening. Pausanius writes (9.39.4): "The rest of his body immediately gets dragged after his knees, as if some extraordinarily deep, fast river was catching a man in a current and sucking him down. From there on, inside the second place, people are not always taught the future in one and the same way: one man hears, another sees as well. Those who go down return feet first through the same mouth." On return from the pit, the priests took the supplicant to the "throne of memory" and he then repeated everything he heard or saw while in the possession of the god.

However, the most famous oracle of the Roman world was the Sibylline oracle and the well-known writings attributed to her from an early period. The history of the Sibyl is long and complex and originates as a legendary Greek prophetess of whom Heraclitus (c. 500 B.C.E.) wrote, "But Sibylla with frenzied mouth speaking words without smile or charm or sweet savor reaches a thousand years by her voice on account of the god." References to the Sibyl in Greek literature are mostly in the singular in the fifth and early fourth centuries B.C.E., but after that the term (as a title of respect) is used to refer to many different women who gave oracles verses in hexameter at various centers, often in association with Apollo. The origins of the Sibylline "tradition" seems most likely to be Asia Minor, the most famous sites of which were Marpessus and Erythrea, where inscriptions on a statue of the Sibyl record an autobiography.[50] The relationship between the Sibyl and the god Apollo was ambiguous, much like his relationship with prophetess Kassandra. Ovid, in his *Metamorphoses* (14.132), tells how the god would give her immortality if she would surrender herself to him sexually. She asked for as many years as grains of sand in her hand, but refused the god's sexual advances. Apollo then granted her wish but only allowed her to live as a very old woman— thus, the archetypal image of the aged Sibyl. The Roman polymath Varro (c. 120 B.C.E.) drew up a list of ten Sibyls, including the Pythia at Delphi, but omits Hebrew, Egyptian, and Assyrian oracles from the list. Pausanius (c. 150 C.E.) also drew up a list of only four Sibyls: the Libyan, Hermophile of Marpessus, Demo of Cumae, and the Hebrew Sibyl Sabbe (or Sambethe) whom he calls the "Babylonian Sibyl."[51]

Cumae, south of Rome on the Italian west coast, was the site of a Greek settlement (757 B.C.E.) which was an early oracular site under the supervision of an aged Sibyl. In the *Antiquities* (4.62) of Dionysus of Hallicarnassus, he tells the story of how an aged woman came to an early Roman king, Tarquinius Superbus (*c.* 525 B.C.E.), and offered him nine volumes of prophecies for a high price, which he rejected. The woman then burned three volumes and returned to offer him the remaining six at the same price; when he refused, she burned three more volumes and returning with the three remaining offered them again for the same price. At this point, the king realized the import of her actions and purchased the volumes. This is the legendary account of the origins of the *Sibylline Books* which were then housed in the temple of Jupiter under the supervision of two honored patricians and later (*c.* 348 B.C.E.) by a board of ten and then fifteen patricians and plebeians especially elected to one of the highest and most sacred offices in Rome. In 83 B.C.E. the temple of Jupiter Optimus Maximus was burned down and the original *Sibylline Books* were destroyed. When the temple was rebuilt, several years later, oracles were collected from many different oracle centers, especially from the one in Erythrea; Caninius Gallus contributed one such Sibylline collection as late as 32 C.E. These texts were highly regarded and referred to in times of great crisis and then only interpreted by those elected to the sacred office.[52]

As for the Cimmerian Sibyl at Cumae, there is a Greek source, that of Euphorus of Cyme in Asia Minor, referring to an oracle center near Cumae, "deep below the earth" where they "come and go by certain tunnels" to consult the oracle—a possible reference to oracular consultation with the dead. Of the Roman writers, Vergil's *Aeneas* (6.42 ff.; also 3.444) gives a classic description of the aged prophetic woman. She is a prophetess of Apollo, whose use of second sight foretells future war and the Tiber River "foaming with blood." The poet also describes the rocks at Cumae cut into a cave with many doorways. In 1932, Amedeo Maiuri excavated the site and found a cavern with a 450 foot long trapezoid passageway eight feet wide and sixteen feet high through solid rock ending in a room with windows on the right and left leading into an inner oracle chamber. On each side of the doorway are stone cut benches where petitioners would sit. The Sibyl, after ablutions, would pass down the corridor to the inner chamber, accompanied by clients and other temple officials, enter the inner chamber, and, seated on a chair on a high platform, give her oracles to the guests in the outer chamber. Though the site was used in Roman times, after the conquest of Cumae (334 B.C.E.) during which the temple was thoroughly plundered, there is no evidence of a Sibyl in residence, nor of any oracle tradition active at the site. The origins of the *Sibylline Books* may have come from the early period and been collected by various rulers at Rome to guide state policy. Roman accounts trace the origins of the Cumae Sibyl to Erythrae and to the Greek isle of Samos where she may have served the goddess Hera.[53]

The present day *Oraculum Sibyllina* were assembled by Byzantine scholars in the sixth century C.E. and consist of twelve books in Greek hexameter, of which volumes nine and ten are lost. The texts consist of various short oracles strung together with prophetic commentary by a wide variety of unknown authors—containing materials from mid-second century B.C.E. to late seventh century C.E.—and are highly influenced by both Jewish and Christian polemics emphasizing the threat of world destruction, usually by fire. "Foreseeing on behalf of men hardships difficult to bear," the oracle foretells of divine wrath evoked by ritual impurity, ignorance, or ethical violations. They also contain polemics against idolatry, sexual offenses, and an insistence on monotheism as well instructions for carrying out cult activities. They focus dramatically on political upheavals, prodigies, and portents which led the Emperor Augustus (12 C.E.) to burn over 2,000 such oracle collections which he found politically subversive. Many such collections of oracular verse (*chresmologoi*) were found in the late Greek and later Roman periods, attributed not only to gods but increasingly to intermediary spirits (*daimones*). The fading of the oracle tradition was attributed by some to the eventual death of the *daimones*, who were identified as servants of the gods and goddesses of various temples.[54]

About 180 C.E., the pagan author Celsus wrote *The True Word*, which was an attack on Christianity and in this work he relied heavily on oracles as proof of the divinity of the pagan gods. At about the same time Porphyry (c. 230 C.E.) wrote an early book entitled *The Philosophy to be Derived from Oracles*, also attributing oracular insights to various types of *daimones*. In turn, these works led to Christian counter-attacks, such as Origen's *Contra Celsum*, that identified the sources of oracles as coming from "demons" or seductive spirits that took on the appearance of a "god" to mislead human beings. The possession of the Pythia was due to "an evil spirit" acting against the one true god of Christianity. Correct prediction or even good advice was recognized as a way of misleading to better tempt pagans away from true revelations as found in the Jewish and Christian writings. Though some oracular traditions were admired by early Christians, as assimilated into the late Sibylline corpus as overt expressions of Christian belief, oracle writings were not part of the Christian genres. Some Christian writings interpreted the oracles of Didyma as confirming the idea of the demonic origins of oracles, testifying to the end of the oracle tradition. With the increasing dominance of Christianity, oracle centers and pagan temples were attacked and many destroyed as dwelling places of demonic spirits and false gods. With the death of the emperor Julian (c. 360 C.E.), the oracle centers fell silent except for the ancient echoes of far off Siwa in Libya, still active in the time of Justian (547 C.E.).[55]

Notes

1. See also Plato, *Phaedrus* 244A; David Aune, "Oracles," in *Hidden Truths: Magic, Alchemy, and the Occult,* 207–208; Robert Flaceliere, *Greek Oracles,* 4.

2. Jaroslav Cerny, "Egyptian Oracles," 35; Bob Brier, *Ancient Egyptian Magic,* 212; for Amun's oracle proclaiming the queen as pharaoh, see the *Encyclopedia Britannica* (1996), under "Hatshepsut."

3. John A. Wilson, *The Culture of Ancient Egypt,* 200.

4. Cerny, "Egyptian Oracles," 35; Brier, *Ancient Egyptian Magic,* 211–12.

5. Anthony and Rosalie David, *A Biographical Dictionary of Ancient Egypt,* 161.

6. Wilson, *The Culture of Ancient Egypt,* 217; Cerny, "Egyptian Oracles," 36, 40 (where Isis is mentioned); Brier, *Ancient Egyptian Magic,* 205–06, 209, see figures 69 and 70; T. G. H. James, *Introduction to Ancient Egypt,* 142.

7. Cerny, "Egyptian Oracles," 43–44; Wilson, *The Culture of Ancient Egypt,* 170.

8. Brier, *Ancient Egyptian Magic,* 209.

9. Cerny, "Egyptian Oracles," 39–40.

10. James, *Introduction to Ancient Egypt,* 94, see figure 35; Cerny, "Egyptian Oracles," 43–45.

11. A. Rosalie David, *The Ancient Egyptians: Religious Beliefs and Practices,* 141–42.

12. Joseph Kaster, *Wings of the Falcon: Life and Thought in Ancient Egypt,* 153–58; Cerny, "Egyptian Oracles," 40.

13. Brier, *Ancient Egyptian Magic,* 215–17; *Encyclopedia Britannica* (1996), under the entry "Oracles."

14. Cerny, "Egyptian Oracles," 39.

15. Kalisthenes's work as the original biographer is lost and only retained in fragmentary form: Strabo, *History* 814C, and Didorus Siculus, *Historical Library* 17.50.6–7; for dating of the Siwa temple, H. W. Parke, *The Oracles of Zeus: Dodona, Olympia, Ammon,* 196–97.

16. Lucian, *De Syria Dea* 36; see also Curtius Rufus, *History of Alexander the Great* 4.7.23.

17. David Potter, *Prophecy and History in the Crisis of the Roman Empire,* 27–29; Cerny, "Egyptian Oracles," 47.

18. For a classical overview, see J. S. Morrison, "The Classical World," 87–114.

19. Potter, *Prophets and Emperors: Human and Divine Authority from Augustus to Theodosius*, 10.

20. Apostolos Athanassakis, trans., *The Homeric Hymns* 19, lines 131–32.

21. H. W. Parke, *The Oracles of Zeus: Dodona, Olympia, Ammon*, 40–43; Morrison, "The Classical World," 97.

22. H. W. Parke, *Greek Oracles*, 23; Morrison, "The Classical World," 96–97.

23. Morrison, "The Classical World," 97.

24. Parke, *Greek Oracles*, 92–93.

25. Parke, *The Oracles of Zeus: Dodona, Olympia, Ammon*, 184, 186–89.

26. Apollodorus, *Library*, 1.9.11.

27. Parke, *The Oracles of Zeus: Dodona, Olympia, Ammon*, 180–83.

28. Parke, *The Oracles of Zeus: Dodona, Olympia, Ammon*, 218–22; 233.

29. Morrison "The Classical World," 98–99; Parke, *Greek Oracles*, 34, 94.

30. Parke, *Greek Oracles*, 36, 62.

31. Parke, *Greek Oracles*, 74.

32. See also Strabo, *Geography* 9.3.5; Pausanius, *Guide to Greece* 10.5.7.

33. Plutarch, "The Cessation of Oracles," 48–51 (*Moralia* 438A).

34. Plutarch, "On the Pythian Responses," 21 (*Moralia* 414B).

35. Plutarch, *Moralia* 292E; Flaceliere, *Greek Oracles*, 43–45; Giulia Sissa, *Greek Virginity*, 13.

36. Plutarch, *Moralia* 398A; Iamblichus, *De Mysteris Aegyptiorum* 3.11.127.

37. Joseph Fontenrose, *The Delphic Oracle*, 220; Flaceliere, *Greek Oracles*, 49; Parke, *Greek Oracles*, 86.

38. See Sissa, *Greek Virginity*, 41–52, for a good overview; also Parke, *Greek Oracles*, 84–85; Fontenrose, *The Delphic Oracle*, 204 ff.

39. Sissa, *Greek Virginity*, 25.

40. Strabo, *History* 9.3.5; see also Plutarch, *Moralia* 407B.

41. Fontenrose, *The Delphic Oracle*, 218, where Plutarch refers to Nikandros as both a *hiereus* (priest, *Moralia* 386B) and as *prophetes* (prophet, *Moralia* 483B); for oracle responses see p. 42 ff.

42. Parke, *Greek Oracles*, 110–16; Fontenrose, *Didyma: Apollo's Oracle, Cult, and Companions*, 50–51.

43. Robin Lane Fox, *Pagans and Christians*, 201.

44. Fontenrose, *Didyma: Apollo's Oracle, Cult, and Companions*, 36, 52–53, 59–62; Parke, *Oracles in Asia Minor*, 198–99.

45. Fontenrose, *Didyma: Apollo's Oracle, Cult, and Companions*, 78–80, 103;

Parke, *The Oracles of Apollo in Asia Minor*, 218; Fox, *Pagans and Christians*, 183, 224.

46. Parke, *Oracles in Asia Minor*, 200–201; Fontenrose, *Didyma: Apollo's Oracle, Cult, and Companions*, 89–90, 97.

47. Fox, *Pagans and Christians*, 175–78, 195; Parke, *The Oracles of Apollo in Asia Minor*, 139, 223; Parke, *Greek Oracles*, 94,125.

48. Parke, *Greek Oracles*, 131–32.

49. Fox, *Pagans and Christians*, 205–07; Parke, *Greek Oracles*, 132–133.

50. David Potter, *Prophets and Emperors: Human and Divine Authority from Augustus to Theodosius*, 80.

51. Parke, *Greek Oracles*, 50–51; James H. Charlesworth, ed., "The Sibylline Oracles," 317–18 (3.809 f.); Pausanius, *Guide to Greece* 10.12.1–9.

52. Potter, *Prophecy and History*, 112–113; Charlesworth, "Sibylline Oracles," 319–20; Tacitus, *Annals* 6.12.

53. Parke, *Greek Oracles*, 53–54; Parke, *Sibyls and Sibylline Prophecy*, 76–89.

54. Charlesworth, "Sibylline Oracles," 320–23; Parke, *Greek Oracles*, 133–35; Potter, *Prophets and Emperors*, 88–95.

55. Parke, *Greek Oracles*, 144–48; Potter, *Prophets and Emperors*, 87–88.

Bibliography

Aeschylus. *The Oresteia*. Translated by Robert Fagles. New York: Viking Press, 1977.

Apollodorus. *Gods and Heroes of the Greeks: The Library of Apollodorus*. Translated by Michael Simson. Amherst: University of Massachusetts Press, 1976.

Athanassakis, Apostolos, trans. *The Homeric Hymns*. Baltimore: The Johns Hopkins University Press, 1976.

Aune, David. "Oracles." In *Hidden Truths: Magic, Alchemy, and the Occult*, edited by Lawrence Sullivan, 206–16. New York: Macmillan, 1989.

Brier, Bob. *Ancient Egyptian Magic*. New York: Quill, 1981.

Cerny, Jaroslav. "Egyptian Oracles." In *A Saite Oracle Papyrus from Thebes*, edited and translated by Richard Parker, 35–48. Providence: Brown University Press, 1962.

Charlesworth, James H., editor. "The Sibylline Oracles." In *The Old Testament Pseudepigrapha*, vol. 1, 319–472. New York: Doubleday, 1983.

David, A. Rosalie. *The Ancient Egyptians: Religious Beliefs and Practices*. London: Routledge & Kegan Paul, 1982.

David, Anthony and Rosalie. *A Biographical Dictionary of Ancient Egypt*. Norman: University of Oklahoma Press, 1992.

Flaceliere, Robert. *Greek Oracles*. New York: W. W. Norton, 1965.

Fontenrose, Joseph. *The Delphic Oracle*. Berkeley: University of California Press, 1978.

―――. *Didyma: Apollo's Oracle, Cult, and Companions*. Berkeley: University of California Press, 1988.

Fox, Robin Lane. *Pagans and Christians*. San Francisco: Harper & Row, 1986.

Herodotus. *The Histories*. Translated by Aubrey de Selincourt. New York: Penguin, 1972.

Hesiod. *Theogony*. Translated by Norman O. Brown. Indianapolis: Bobbs-Merrill, 1953.

Iamblichus. *On the Mysteries (De mysteriis Aegyptiorum)*. Edited by Stephen Ronan with translations of Thomas Taylor and Alexander Wilder. Hastings: Chthonios Books, 1989.

James, T. G. H. *Introduction to Ancient Egypt*. New York: Farrar Straus Giroux, 1979.

Kaster, Joseph. *Wings of the Falcon: Life and Thought in Ancient Egypt*. New York: Rinehart and Winston, 1968.

Morrison, J. S. "The Classical World." In *Oracles and Divination*, edited by Michael Lowe and Carmen Blacker, 87–114. Boulder: Shambhala, 1981.

Parke, H. W. *The Oracles of Zeus: Dodona, Olympia, Ammon*. Cambridge: Harvard University Press, 1967.

———. *Greek Oracles*. London: Hutchinson University Library, 1967.

———. *The Oracles of Apollo in Asia Minor*. London: Croom Helm, 1985.

———. *Sibyls and Sibylline Prophecy in Classical Antiquity*. Edited by B. C. McGing. London: Routledge, 1988.

Pausanius. *Guide to Greece*. Translated by Peter Levi. 2 vols. London: Penguin, 1984.

Pindar. *Pindar's Odes*. Translated by Roy Swanson. Indianapolis: Bobbs-Merrill, 1974.

Plato. *The Dialogues of Plato*. Translated by B. Jowett. 2 vols. New York: Random House, 1937.

Plutarch. "On the Cessation of Oracles" and "On the Pythian Responses." In *Plutarch's Morals: Theosophical Essays*, translated by C. W. King. London: George Bell and Sons, 1908.

Potter, David. *Prophecy and History in the Crisis of the Roman Empire*. Oxford: Clarendon Press, 1990.

Potter, David. *Prophets and Emperors: Human and Divine Authority from Augustus to Theodosius*. Cambridge: Harvard University Press, 1994.

Sissa, Giulia. *Greek Virginity*. Translated by Arthur Goldhammer. Cambridge: Harvard University Press, 1990.

Wilson, John A. *The Culture of Ancient Egypt*. Chicago: University of Chicago Press, 1965.

From Henry Hawkins, *Parthenia sacra*, 1633

Hermeticism and the Utopian Imagination

JOHN MICHAEL GREER

> It was [Hermes], too, who in the east of Egypt constructed a city twelve miles long within which he constructed a castle which had four gates in each of its four parts. On the eastern gate he placed the form of an Eagle; on the western gate, the form of a Bull; on the southern gate the form of a Lion, and on the northern gate he constructed the form of a Dog. Into these images he introduced spirits which spoke with voices, nor could anyone enter the gates of the City except by their permission.... Around the circumference of the City he placed engraved images and ordered them in such a manner that by their virtue the inhabitants were made virtuous and withdrawn from all wickedness and harm. The name of the City was Adocentyn.[1]

THE STORY OF ADOCENTYN in the Latin version of the *Picatrix*, a standard text for the Hermetic magi of the Renaissance, provides a first point of contact between Hermeticism and the utopian tradition. These two movements of the Western spirit, the inner quest for transcendence and the outer quest for the good society, both have a place as powers of the hidden side of history, the skeleton-realm of ideas and visions which gives shape to the flesh of dates, times, events; and like most such powers these two have contacted and influenced each other at times. Adocentyn itself is a utopia, and an inspiration for other utopias; it has been echoed in other aspects of the Hermetic tradition, and some of those have taken on utopian aspects as well.

We live in a time in which ideals have become all but extinct in the collective life of Western society, a time in which pedaling in place and moment-by-moment crisis management have usurped the role of serious discussions about where we are headed and whether any sane person would want to go there. In such an age, the attractive power of the utopian imagination can be real, and those of us who turn for insight to Hermeticism and related systems of Western esoteric thought may be drawn to seek images of a better future by using these as a basis for utopian explorations.

There's much to be said for a project of this sort. At least once before in the history of the West, during the late Renaissance, utopian ideas with roots in the Hermetic tradition seized the Western imagination and took a significant role in shaping the collective destiny of society. Futurologist Frederick Polak has suggested that the waning of utopian thought may be one of the more worrisome signs of our own age, reflecting a broader failure to conceive any positive image of the future at all.[2] If he's right, utopian visions based on the current revival of Western esoteric thought just might have an unexpected influence over our common fate.

As with anything else, though, these positive potentials have their downside. The history of the connections between Hermeticism and utopian thought is anything but straightforward, and is made even less so by the fog of partisan rhetoric and plain confusion which always seems to surround the coasts of Utopia. Nor are the risks involved wholly abstract. Utopian thinking, to put the matter with maximum bluntness, has proven to be a fertile source of disasters as well as hope—a point we'll return to later—and Hermetic wisdom doesn't seem to grant any particular immunity to the consequences. The journey to Adocentyn may be worth making, but if history is any judge the road there may not be easy to find.

Some Pitfalls of Language

The first obstacle that has to be faced in this doubtful journey comes out of the terms of the discourse itself. Several centuries of journalistic usage have reduced the word "utopian" to little more than a synonym for "very good," "improbable," or—wistfully—both at once. Even taken in a more precise sense, the utopia is too often confused with two other, older images of the ideal society in Western thought: the

Arcadian tradition, which grounds human happiness in a flight from the social realm into a world governed wholly by Nature, and the millenarian tradition, which looks to a final irruption of the transcendent into the world of social experience as a solution to the problems of suffering and evil. Over against these is the utopian tradition proper, which envisions human society as perfectible on its own terms, through human action and understanding, as expressed in some system of social arrangements.

These three currents of thought have touched and influenced one another in countless ways, and produced a substantial crop of hybrids; still, the distinction among them is real. It's in this sense that "green" utopias such as Ernest Callenbach's *Ecotopia* deserve the name, despite their intensely pastoral imagery; their forests and meadows are maintained by political and institutional arrangements which are inconceivable in the primal innocence of Arcadia. It's in this sense, too—admittedly not the one he had in mind—that Karl Marx's criticism of competing systems as "utopian socialism" hits the mark; the visions of Owen, Saint-Simon, Fourier, and the like all required some amount of human effort for their fulfillment, while that of Marx relied wholly on impersonal social forces, the nineteenth-century rationalist approximation of God. Marxism is thus millenarian, not utopian, and the communist paradise of its prophetic tradition shares the defining characteristics of all millennial realms: in theory, inevitability; in practice, indefinite postponement.

These same confusions have played themselves out in the contacts between Hermeticism and utopian thought as well. There's a substantial amount of Hermetic "utopianism" that is, properly speaking, nothing of the kind. When a figure such as Giordano Bruno is described as a utopian thinker despite the fact that he wrote nothing even vaguely utopian—his closest approach to it, the mythic cosmological reform of *The Expulsion of the Triumphant Beast*, limits itself to a general denunciation of the religious arrangements of his time and a desire that men would be more virtuous—it's obvious that the terms being used have been diluted nearly to the point of meaninglessness.[3] Similarly, there's a large amount of Hermetic "utopian" thought that is pure millenarianism, depending on a *deus ex machina* rather than any more concrete (or more likely) proposals for the reform of human society.

These considerations are partly worth noting as a help to clarity, but they have a more practical use as well. It's of no great importance here if vague optimism or a wish for social change is redefined as "utopian thought," although it does tend to confuse communication. Nor is the overlap between Utopia and Arcadia a significant problem; the Arcadian tradition is all but extinct as an active force in Western thought at present, for the simple and melancholy reason that untouched natural environments no longer exist on our planet.

Millenarianism, though, is another matter. Millenarian traditions remain alive and powerful today—in traditional religious forms, in folk legendry of the UFO type, and in a range of half-veiled forms from the survivalist myth of nuclear apocalypse to the Omega Points and evolutionary leaps posited by many currently popular thinkers. This is potentially a serious matter, because—it's hard to say this gently—millenarian thinking has quite probably produced more misery and failure than any other single phenomenon in the history of human thought. The appalling end of the Solar Temple movement is only one of the most recent examples.[4] Relying on supernatural intervention as a fix for earthly problems is one of history's classic recipes for disaster, but it's a seductive idea, and one which can take more than the ordinary amount of clear-headedness to avoid.

Conflicts Between Hermetic and Utopian Thought

The confusions of language, though, don't make up all the potholes on the road to Adocentyn. A second set come from the awkward point that the basic presuppositions of Hermetic philosophy offer little in the way of support to overtly utopian projects.

Central to Hermeticism, as to most traditions of Western esoteric spirituality, is a keen recognition of the difference between what Plato called the realms of Becoming and Being—the world of social and sensory experience bound by space and time, on the one hand, and the world of absolute reality transcending space and time on the other.

Human consciousness, in the Hermetic vision, touches both these realms and has the potential to mediate between them, but the distinction remains. The geometrical metaphor is at once traditional and exact; be it ever so carefully drawn, no circle on paper can claim to be identical with *the* circle, the circle-archetype in the realm of ideals.

The same argument can be made even more forcefully in the case of Utopia. From a Hermetic perspective, the ideal of justice cannot be converted into any specific system of laws or customs, nor can it be embodied in a concrete community. The same is true of any other ideal which may be chosen. Within the context of Hermeticism, then, to speak of a perfect human society is a little like discussing a heavy, orange thought. Societies, like circles, are concrete and imperfect reflections of ideal patterns, and the Hermetic tradition gives very little encouragement to the claim that a circle can be made perfectly round if only the right kind of paper and compasses are used to draw it.

In keeping with this, the Hermetic tradition historically hasn't been an especially prolific source of utopias or of utopian thinking. To the extent—an important one—that Hermeticism has roots in Plato, it can lay a limited claim to the ideal states of the *Republic* and the *Laws*; even so, it's too often forgotten that Plato's were neither the only nor the first utopias in classical thought, and that utopian writings in the ancient world came to be associated not with Platonism but with Stoic philosophy.[5] The same pattern continues through the later history of the utopian tradition. The revival of Platonism, Hermeticism, and magical and alchemical traditions during the Renaissance gave rise to a handful of utopias—Campanella's *City of the Sun* and Andreae's *Christianopolis* are the best known of the very few examples—and to one significant burst of utopian politics during the first half of the seventeenth century.[6] By contrast, Renaissance humanism produced a far more substantial crop of utopias, among them the work of Sir Thomas More which gave its wry name—*ou topos*, "nowhere"—to the entire genre. The early years of the "mechanical philosophy," the newborn scientific materialism that overcame the Hermetic "chemical philosophy" in the struggle to define reality for the postmedieval West, were rife with utopias and utopian projects; and the zenith of the utopian tradition in the West during the eighteenth and nineteenth centuries, a period which saw thousands of utopias written and hundreds attempted in the form of actual communities, drew its inspiration not from Hermeticism or any other esoteric tradition but from the unlimited optimism of the Enlightenment's cult of reason.

A certain amount of questionable logic has crept into considerations of this last point, and it's as well to clarify matters here. The fact that people involved with esoteric spirituality were also involved with utopian schemes—as a certain number were—does not in itself redefine those schemes as esoteric, any more than the fact that (say) a number of Satanists enjoy playing volleyball would make volleyball Satanic. To point out, for example, that Transcendentalists of the stature of Bronson Alcott participated in abortive communal experiments, or that several important nineteenth-century French occultists were deeply involved in socialist politics, simply proves that these were men and women of their own time, caught up in many of the same interests and enthusiasms as their more orthodox neighbors. Claims of a closer connection between the traditions need to be backed by evidence of specific links between Hermetic thought and utopian practice—and these are few and far between.

Hermeticism and the Political Sphere

The same point can be made even more forcefully about claims that Hermeticism is itself political in nature, or defines some particular political stance. Claims of this kind have ranged from straightforward definitions of some such stance as "Hermetic politics," through a spectrum of more or less paranoid conspiracy theories, to subtle analyses of the political potential of Hermetic thought.

The first two of these can be dismissed fairly easily. It's true that some Hermeticists have been active in the political arena (although a great many more have not); it's equally true that some of their activities have been more or less secret in nature, at least at the time. The difficulty here is that the positions taken by politically inclined

Hermeticists (and Hermetically influenced politicians) fall all over the ideological spectrum, from the alchemical anarchism of Gerrard Winstanley through the socialism of Eliphas Levi, past the stolid English middle-of-the-roadism of Dion Fortune, to the reactionary absolutism of the eighteenth-century *Orden des Gold- und Rosencreuz* and the overt fascism of Julius Evola. It's hard to see how views this divergent can be turned into anything approaching a consistent position, much less the sort of monolithic conspiracy trumpeted by former Golden Dawn chief C. M. Stoddart (among many others) and parodied to death by Robert Shea and Robert Anton Wilson in their tremendous satire *Illuminatus.*

There are deeper matters caught up in the question of Hermetic politics, however, which cannot and should not be passed over so easily. In an age as dominated by mass phenomena as the present, a tradition such as Hermeticism which focuses its attention on the individual rather than the mass may, paradoxically, be more relevant to political life than many more overtly political approaches. There's a real sense in which the journey of the individual from a dependence on mass consciousness to a personal knowledge of the Transcendent is a—and perhaps *the*—supremely political act.

At the same time, this approach to Hermeticism has pitfalls of its own. These can be seen most clearly, perhaps, in Ioan Couliano's brilliant if problematic *Eros and Magic in the Renaissance*, which attempts to read the entire system of Renaissance Hermetic magic as a deliberate technology of psychopolitical manipulation. This essay is not the place for a full examination of the achievements and failures of this remarkable work, but a few points need to be made.

The core assumption of Couliano's argument is that the language of Renaissance magic can be converted precisely into the language of modern psychology—that, for example, *eros* can be understood as libido in the Freudian sense, the pneuma as the subconscious, and so forth. This equation allows magic to be seen in terms which make sense to the modern mind—as psychological manipulation grounded in a canny grasp of the motivating force of human desires—and forms the basis for his unsettling suggestion that modern methods of advertising and public relations are unknowingly following in the footsteps of the Renaissance magi.

The problem is that this equation can be defended only by doing a good deal of violence to the actual context of these ideas in Renaissance thought, and by excluding those factors—above all the transcendent and transpersonal powers central to Hermetic theory—which have no place in the modern vision of the universe. Couliano's central definition of the relationship between eros and magic, for example, claims that "all erotic phenomena are simultaneously magic phenomena in which the individual plays the role either of manipulator or of the manipulated or of the instrument of manipulation."[7] This corresponds closely to some modern attitudes on the subject. On the other hand, an identity between love and manipulation is worlds away from the Hermetically-inspired Renaissance conception of eros, which is well-documented from Ficino onwards, and plays a central role in such works as Giordano Bruno's *The Heroic Frenzies*. That conception identified love as one of Plato's four divinely caused states of madness, all understood as participations by the whole self in a realm of transcendent power—not as manipulations carried out through a passive medium by the uprooted and isolated ego.[8]

Couliano's interpretation—like most other modernizing interpretations of Hermetic thought—imposes the typical modern understanding of means and ends on a tradition which understood that distinction in a very different light. As the Hermeticists of the Renaissance saw it, the state of erotic desire, of participation in the divine power of eros, was itself an end, not simply a means to the end of sexual activity. In magic, similarly, the participation of the magus in transcendent power was the real work, the *ergon*, of magical practice; the ostensible goal of that practice was a *parergon* or side effect, however valuable in its own right.

In politics, finally and crucially, the same point holds true. It may be that the study and practice of Hermeticism leads to certain political effects; still, these are not the point of the exercise. The aspect of life we may as well call the "spiritual" is precisely that which deals with ultimate ends. To treat it as a means to some other end is to banish it, and dress up that other end in spirituality's cast-off clothing. The results are far too familiar: on the one hand, all the overt and covert pathologies of power; on the other, the sanctimonious justification of the abuses of an oppressive order, or its inverse, the religious irreligiousness of "socially aware" denominations or their more avant-garde equivalents, in which religious language has become nothing more than a slightly dowdy way of talking about political ideology.

Building Nowhere Somewhere

Questions of means and ends are also involved in the last set of obstacles in the way of Hermetically based utopian projects. Utopias have many possible uses, ranging from simple entertainment and wish-fulfillment through satire and social criticism to deliberate attempts to design and construct a new society. This last purpose, however, has dominated the utopian imagination in modern times, and it's hard to argue against it at first glance; if you have a workable plan for a better society, or think you do, why not try to put it into effect?

This approach has ancient roots. The first utopian theorist of whom any trace survives, Hippodamus of Miletus, was involved in the founding of an actual community, the Panhellenic colony of Thurii. Plato's own utopian schemes, in their turn, formed the foundation of Plotinus's celebrated attempt to create a philosophers' city called Platonopolis.[9] The list of similar projects proposed or attempted since then, seeking the perfect society down nearly every imaginable road, is enough to stagger the mind.

If sheer energy were enough to win the struggle, this vast outpouring of effort and imagination might be expected to have brought Utopia into being long ago. It has not, and with one significant exception, the long history of utopian communities is a history of almost unrelieved failure.

The one exception is monasticism. Religious communities of this very specific sort exist in most of the major world religions, and have flourished in a wide array of social and environmental contexts. Even the pressures of the consumer economy have had only a limited

success against the monastic way of life. There are several potent
sources of strength in the monastic utopia: membership is voluntary,
and depends on assent to a given set of beliefs, values and rules of life;
intensive devotional or meditative practices done as a group build deep
bonds within the monastic community; rules of poverty and celibacy,
all but universal in successful monastic systems, cut away exactly those
issues—money, sex, and family—which drive most interpersonal
conflicts.

The essence of the monastic utopia, then, is a radical simplification
of life. On its own terms, it works brilliantly; so long as it can recruit
new members to replace those that die, a monastery can exist and
function indefinitely. On the other hand, the monastic system excludes so much of value in ordinary human life that, for most people,
it can hardly be called utopian. However successful it may be, it's of
limited value as a guide to broader approaches.

Outside of monasticism, the record of utopian experiments is bleak.
The average lifespan of those which actually get past the drawing
board is about three years. The specific factors in each individual
breakdown vary with situations, and with scale—small communes
have different breaking points than national regimes—but the pattern
of failure is consistent enough that it's worth looking for a deeper
cause.

There are any number of approaches to this question, but one drawn
from issues of Hermetic philosophy raised earlier may not be out of
place. The entire utopian project can be seen as an attempt to bridge
the gap between the ideal and the concrete, and the results of the
attempt may well count as a kind of experimental evidence in favor of
Plato's division between the realms. The more a utopian system relies
on ideal factors to handle practical difficulties, the more certain it is to
break down at precisely these points.

Charles Fourier's system of utopian socialism is a case in point.
Fourier's complicated theories postulated a state of Harmony as the
natural endpoint of human social evolution, in which "passional
attraction" would end all social woes and make possible a life focused
around dining ("gastrosophy") and orgiastic sex, interspersed with

modest periods of work at frequently changing tasks. In the nineteenth century these theories were immensely popular, and dozens of Fourierist "phalansteries"—collective settlements intended as the nuclei of the new order—were established in Europe and America. All of them went under after fairly brief lives. The idealized force of passional attraction proved to be too weak to motivate the constant hard work necessary to found and run a new community, and nothing else was available to do the job.[10]

Fourier and his followers, in particular, never quite seemed to grasp the difference between a little puttering in the garden and the more than full-time job of subsistence farming. The same problem appears elsewhere; it's one of the constants of utopian history that utopians tend to massively underestimate the amount of effort and skill needed to maintain what modern people consider a comfortable standard of living. As a result, utopian plans routinely have people consuming far more in the way of goods and services than they produce. On paper, this produces a highly attractive ludic and festal quality to utopian life; put into practice, it forces utopian experiments either to accept extreme poverty, to find some way to parasitize on the larger society, or to go under as soon as the money runs out.

Another example of ideal factors as a point of utopian breakdown can be found in far too many of the alternative religious movements of the last fifty years. Here the ideal is, as often as not, akin to Plato's vision of the philosopher king: the personal spiritual qualities of the movement's leader are seen as justification for his or her absolute control of the community's decision-making process. The results are as predictable as they are unpleasant.

These kinds of difficulties can be addressed, of course; a community can develop practical ways to meet collective economic needs, or to keep rein on the behavior of its leadership. The problem is that the more this is done—the more the ideal is replaced with the pragmatic— the more the utopian community begins to resemble the unreformed world outside its borders. The history of the few successful utopian communities, like that of successful revolutions, is a history of compromise which starts with ideals and ends with a restoration of the status quo; the transition which turned the Oneida Community into a suburban development mirrors the one which replaced the tsars with commissars.[11] It's worth keeping in mind that the existing order of any society has evolved as it has for good reason; it represents whatever collective compromise people make between the desire for freedom and the fear of responsibility, and it will tend to reestablish itself with a fair degree of exactness after the turbulence of disaster or idealism has passed. It might even be said that, in this sense, we get exactly the society we deserve.

Breakdown along the fault lines of the ideal, and absorption into the larger society through pragmatism, form the Scylla and Charybdis of the utopian voyage. The rhetoric of failed utopias is a chronicle of excuses for either, or sometimes both at once. The attempt to bring the ideal society to physical birth will no doubt continue, but the results of the attempt to date may suggest that the real value of Utopia may well lie elsewhere.

Three Roads to Adocentyn

The various obstacles we've examined may seem to add up to a dismissal of the entire utopian project, at least from a Hermetic standpoint. They do not—but they do, certainly, call into question the assumption that a Hermetic approach to that project can be made successfully in a naive manner. The failure of utopian experiments is not the only sign that a confusion of the worlds of Being and Becoming is, to say the least, problematic; the disastrous history of millenarianism and the difficulties which follow on a political interpretation of Hermeticism can be traced to the same root.

To do away with this confusion and make use of the utopian imagination from within a traditional Hermetic perspective involves a significant change of focus, and it requires that Utopia remain exactly where the word implies—nowhere. It may seem quixotic to try to imagine an ideal society in the knowledge that it can neither exist nor fully express its own ideals, but this paradox is the paradox of human consciousness, the reconciler of irreconcilable worlds. Nor is this strange exercise useless, for it leads in directions which have a good deal to offer. Three of those directions will be examined here. One of them will be familiar to many readers, the other two less so: one because it has largely been hidden away in the specialist literature, the other because its connections to the Hermetic tradition—and to the utopian imagination—have gone all but unnoticed in modern times.

The Utopia of Contemplation

Plato, who gave so much to the Western esoteric traditions, apparently devised the first and most important of these directions of utopian thought. A passage from the end of Book IX of the *Republic* puts it best:

> I understand, [Glaucon] said. You mean the city whose establishment we have described, the city whose home is in the ideal, for I think that it can be found nowhere on Earth.
>
> Well, I said, perhaps there is a pattern of it laid up in heaven for him who wishes to contemplate it and in so beholding to constitute himself its citizen. But it makes no difference whether it exists now or ever will come into being. The politics of this city only will be his and of none other.[12]

The hierarchical society of the *Republic* with its rigid class structure of philosopher kings, warrior auxiliaries, and underlings, has often been taken as Plato's own prescription for an actual state. It may have been that; the society of the *Laws*, which is unquestionably designed for practical ends, shares many of the same authoritarian features that modern readers find objectionable in the *Republic*. It was also, however, an attempt to represent the ideal of social justice, as Plato saw it, through the medium of the human imagination. That is its crucial role, and as a "pattern laid up in heaven," it is intended to serve not as a blueprint for practical social change but as a focus for thought and meditation, and as a model for the inner ordering of the self.

So far, so good; but to go on as Plato does, and suggest that the contemplator of this imaginary city becomes its citizen, involved in its politics and subject to its laws, is to touch on something potentially explosive. Citizenship in Plato's time was anything but an abstraction. It's worth thinking about what it might mean to be a citizen, not of a Greek *polis*, nor of some modern nation-state, nor yet (in the facile modern phrase) of the world—but *of the Ideal*. What are the rights of such a citizenship? What are the responsibilities?

Plato's own understanding of the city of absolute justice may or may not be appropriate to Hermeticists today, who have seen many of its features parodied in the totalitarian states of our own era. The process of critical thinking and examination of ideals which is central to the dialogue has not lost its relevance, though, nor has the metaphor which tests justice in the self by projecting it onto the larger screen of a society. It may well be that process and metaphor can be best combined in the present time by the creation of new utopian images as reflections—again, as always, imperfect—of Plato's "pattern laid up in heaven."

The Utopia of the Craftsman

A second direction for Hermetic utopianism first took shape, like so much else Hermetic, in the hothouse environment of the Italian Renaissance, and like so much else it drew its inspiration from the recovery of an ancient manuscript. The manuscript was a copy of the *Ten Books on Architecture* of Marcus Vitruvius Pollio, and the movement that took its starting point from this find was one of the most intriguing facets of the Hermetic movement of that age.

Vitruvius, a practicing builder and engineer with a pedestrian command of Latin, was an unlikely source for a Hermetic revival; one more easily imagines him wearing the Roman equivalent of a John Deere cap than an adept's starry headgear. He drew extensively on older traditions, though, and gave a good deal of space to systems of architectural proportion which derived the bases of form and measurement from the human body. The humanists of the Renaissance took this in a sense far deeper than Vitruvius apparently meant it; they linked it with medieval number symbolism, surviving scraps of Pythagorean lore, and the traditional analogy that related human and cosmic forms as macrocosm and microcosm. They came to see architecture, engineering, all forms of craft as a deliberate reflection of ideal proportions and geometries in material form.[13]

The impact of this vision on the arts and architecture of the Renaissance is only now beginning to be traced by scholars, as former fringe subjects such as Hermeticism make their way further into the academic mainstream. Some of its effects went in unlikely directions—for example, the application of Vitruvian ideas to personal combat led to the birth of rapier fencing and ultimately to a school of swordsmanship which can only be described as a Hermetic martial art.[14] It's in architecture, though, that this movement came within reach of Utopia. Several important architectural treatises exist which describe the siting, plan, and buildings of an ideal city based on Vitruvian geometries. The most fascinating of them, Filarete's *Treatise on Architecture*, expands this into a full-blown narrative of the founding of the imaginary city of Sforzinda, from the location of the site to the construction and decoration of the buildings within it.[15]

It's important to realize that these treatises were not simply a reflection of the practices of their time, as, for example, Vitruvius's work seems to have been. They were conscious attempts to reorient architecture toward the ideal while still keeping a firm grasp on practicalities. The cities and buildings they describe are not intended to be built; they were intended to suggest what could be built, to explore the possibilities of the builder's art, and in a way to tackle one facet of the utopian project on its own. The actual buildings designed by these same architects handled the further step of grounding some of these possibilities in practice.

Such explorations aren't limited to the field of architecture, of course; they can be used in the context of any craft. The appalling ugliness of so much modern building suggests that architecture might well be a good place to start, and the work of architects and designers such as Buckminster Fuller and Paolo Soleri show that the concept of the ideal city is still alive in current thought. The architectural visions of a modern Hermeticism could draw on new materials, and on philosophical and geometric perspectives drawn from a much wider range of sources than the Vitruvian revival of the Renaissance had to hand. It's intriguing to think about what a Hermetically inspired ideal city of the present might look like, and how that image and the ideals undergirding it might best be communicated.

The Utopia of Secrecy

The third direction we'll be examining, like the second, has its roots in the Renaissance, although its origins were English rather than Italian. It reached its full development centuries after the Vitruvian revival had faded out with the suppression of Hermetic thought at the end of the Renaissance. To speak of it at all is to enter onto a territory awash in ironies, some historical, some innate to the phenomenon itself.

The historical ironies are worth tracing first. Imagine—as an exercise in alternative history, perhaps—that the Hermetic tradition had given rise to an extensive, semi-secret movement just at the point in history when Hermeticism itself was being forced underground; that this movement had proliferated, taken on new forms, developed extensive systems of theory and practice; that it had grown to a size unmatched by any other manifestation of Hermeticism in history, and become a major channel for the diffusion of Hermetic ideas into mainstream Western culture.

This isn't actually alternative history, of course. That movement— the fraternal lodge movement of the eighteenth and nineteenth centuries—existed, and still exists, if on a scale much smaller than it once did. The connections between Freemasonry, which is one part of the movement, and the Hermetic tradition have been explored by a few scholars in recent years, but the wider context of Hermetic influence on lodge organizations remains a nearly untouched field.[16]

The lodge system combines a method of group organization rooted in medieval guild structures with a system of ritual and symbolic expression derived from Renaissance Hermeticism. The murky process of interaction by which these two diverse factors came together in seventeenth-century Britain isn't relevant to the present discussion, but the resulting hybrid is. On the organizational side, the lodge system is a pragmatic structure of governance, evolved over centuries in a wholly practical context to meet the requirements of collective activity. On the symbolic side, the lodge system is a structure of iconic communications, in which emblems expressing a set of ideal concepts—ethical, in the case of Freemasonry, Odd Fellowship, and similar fraternal lodges; mystical or magical, in the case of occultist lodges such as the Hermetic Order of the Golden Dawn—are combined with ritual to shape the perceptions and actions of lodge members in specific ways.[17] In terms of the Platonic division, the organizational side is oriented to the world of Becoming, the symbolic side to that of Being.

Pervading both, and shaping the essential character of the whole system, is the defining factor of secrecy. It's fair to say that without secrecy the entire lodge system would lose much of its point. The secrets involved are rarely of any importance in themselves: a set of gestures, words and images; the ordinary business of the lodge; confidences received from lodge members; in occultist lodges, a set of teachings and practices which are more often than not taken from publicly available sources. The act of making these secret and of keeping them secret is what is crucial.[18]

The use of secrecy creates a liminal space, a "space between the worlds," which corresponds exactly to the liminal space of human consciousness. Like the private world of thoughts, it observes, but it is not observed; it mediates between two worlds—in this case the world of ordinary social life and the world of symbolized ideals. This liminal quality is reinforced in both spatial and temporal terms: spatially by the use of a specific and highly formalized meeting space, temporally by the lodge's ritual opening and closing and by the simple fact that a lodge only exists and functions during its meeting times. The lodge cannot absorb or be absorbed by the surrounding social context without ceasing to be a lodge. It exists in opposition to the rest of the world, an opposition veiled in secrecy.

The dominant role of secrecy in the lodge system creates a whole dance of nested ironies if, as here, there's an attempt made to talk about the nature of the system. It's precisely the act of not-saying that defines the thing discussed. Still, the liminal role of secrecy is also at the heart of the lodge system's role as the subtlest of all the Hermetic tradition's contributions to the utopian project. In most fraternal lodges and many occultist ones, the specific ideals which are central to the lodge symbolism define—sometimes very explicitly—a utopia, and this definition is the basis for standards of behavior within the lodge. The lodge thus models itself on the utopian vision, and in its turn the lodge itself becomes a model for life in the world outside it, mediating in the liminal space of secrecy between the utopian vision and the world of everyday life. The lodge itself is not a utopia, then, but it exists in a constant relationship with the utopian imagination. Like monasticism, it forms an interface between the ideal and the real by a radical simplification, but it does this without demanding a surrender of human meaning to the ideal.

The utopian role of the lodge system is, perhaps, clearest in cases where lodges have intervened in the larger social context, from the small-scale charitable work common to surviving lodges in the present to startling episodes like the Grange's war against railroad monopolies in late nineteenth-century America. It can be seen in its inverse form, as a kind of dystopia of secrecy, in the case of the Ku Klux Klan, itself a lodge organization of the classic type built up around its own repellent "ideals." These outward expressions of the system, though, don't exhaust the possibilities of the utopia of secrecy. The Invisible College of seventeenth-century England, itself a body deeply involved with the origins of the lodge system,[19] and the magical lodges which have been so significant a part of the Hermetic movement in recent centuries, may suggest others. How these potentials might be put to use in the current Hermetic revival, though, is a matter for individuals and groups to search out on their own.

Ultimately, in its focus on the hidden and the unspoken, the lodge system's utopia of secrecy expresses an insight with deep echoes in Hermetic thought and important lessons for the Hermetic utopian project. What is unseen and intangible is not necessarily powerless; the city of Adocentyn is closest, perhaps, when it is nowhere at all.

Notes

1. Quoted in Yates, *Giordano Bruno and the Hermetic Tradition*, 54.

2. Polak, "Utopias and Cultural Renewal."

3. Bruno as utopian appears in the otherwise excellent Manuel and Manuel, *Utopian Thought in the Western World*, 222–42.

4. See the collection of Solar Temple papers in Kinney, "The Solar Temple Dossier."

5. See Ferguson, *Utopias of the Classical World*.

6. Manuel and Manuel, *Utopian Thought in the Western World*, 261–366, surveys the movement.

7. Couliano, *Eros and Magic in the Renaissance*, 103.

8. The Platonic source of the four kinds of madness is *Phaedrus* 244–50. This interpretation of eros can be found throughout the literature of the Renaissance; its specifically magical implications can be traced from Ficino's writings through Agrippa's *Three Books of Occult Philosophy*, and provides the proper context—*pace* Couliano's interpretation—for the erotic imagery of Bruno's *De vinculis in genere*. See Ficino, *Three Books on Life*; Agrippa, *Three Books of Occult Philosophy*, especially 616–28; Yates, *Giordano Bruno*, 275–90; as well as Bruno, *The Heroic Frenzies*. Compare also Plotinus 4.4.40, with its insistence that the magician must act from within the universe as a participant.

9. Recounted in Porphyry's *Life of Plotinus*. See Plotinus, *Enneads*, p. 9. For Hippodamus, see Ferguson, *Utopias of the Classical World*, 48–50.

10. The standard English-language collection of Fourier's writings is Fourier, *The Utopian Vision of Charles Fourier: Selected Texts of Work, Love, and Passionate Attraction*. For the attempts at putting his system into practice, see Kesten, *Utopian Episodes*.

11. There is an extensive literature on the Oneida Community. For an overview of its history, see Lockwood, "The Experimental Utopia in America."

12. Plato, *Republic* IX, 592 (tr. R. Hackforth).

13. There are several studies of the Vitruvian tradition in Renaissance Hermeticism, but the best starting place is Vitruvius himself; see Vitruvius, *Ten Books on Architecture*. Yates, *Theatre of the World*, and Hersey, *Pythagorean Palaces*, are solid overviews.

14. This development of the tradition is the subject of Greer, "Geometries of the Sword."

15. Filarete, *Treatise on Architecture*. See also Alberti, *On the Art of Building*

in Ten Books.

16. The non-Masonic developments of the lodge tradition remain all but unnoticed by scholars. Carnes, *Secret Ritual and Manhood in Victorian America*, and Clawson, *Constructing Brotherhood*, are among the few significant studies; each is burdened with an interpretive apparatus (respectively, psychological and Marxist) that obscures more than it illuminates. Clawson does deal usefully with the role of Hermeticism in the origins of the tradition.

17. See Greer, "The Hall of Thmaa," for a more extensive analysis of lodge technique in the context of the Hermetic Order of the Golden Dawn.

18. My understanding of the role of secrecy in this context draws on an essay by Earl King, Jr. See King (1995).

19. See Yates, *Giordano Bruno.*

Bibliography

Henry Cornelius Agrippa. *Three Books of Occult Philosophy*. Translated by James Freake; edited by Donald Tyson. St. Paul: Llewellyn, 1993.

Leon Battista Alberti. *On the Art of Building in Ten Books*. Translated by Joseph Rykwert, Neal Leach, and Robert Tavernor. Cambridge: MIT Press, 1988.

Johann Valentin Andreae. *Christianopolis: An Ideal State of the Seventeenth Century*. Translated by Felix Held. New York: Oxford University Press, 1916.

Giordano Bruno. *The Expulsion of the Triumphant Beast*. Translated by Arthur Imerti. New Brunswick: Rutgers University Press, 1964.

———. *The Heroic Frenzies*. Translated by Paul Memmo, Jr. Chapel Hill: University of North Carolina Press, 1964.

Tommaso Campanella. *The City of the Sun: A Poetic Dialogue*. Translated by Daniel Danno. Berkeley: University of California Press, 1981.

Mark C. Carnes. *Secret Ritual and Manhood in Victorian America*. New Haven: Yale University Press, 1989.

Mary Ann Clawson. *Constructing Brotherhood: Class, Race, and Fraternalism*. Princeton: Princeton University Press, 1989.

Ioan P. Couliano. *Eros and Magic in the Renaissance*. Translated by Margaret Cook. Chicago: University of Chicago Press, 1987.

John Ferguson. *Utopias of the Classical World*. Ithaca: Cornell University Press, 1975.

Marsilio Ficino. *Three Books on Life*. Translated by Carol Kaske and John Clark. Binghamton: Renaissance Society of America, 1989.

Filarete (Antonio di Piero Averlino). *Treatise on Architecture*. Translated by John Spencer. New Haven: Yale University Press, 1965.

Charles Fourier. *The Utopian Vision of Charles Fourier: Selected Texts on Work, Love, and Passionate Attraction*. Translated and edited by Jonathan Beecher and Richard Bienvenu. Boston: Beacon, 1971.

John Michael Greer. "Geometries of the Sword." *Gnosis* 40 (1996), 50–55.

———. "The Hall of Thmaa: Sources of Golden Dawn Lodge Technique." *Golden Dawn Journal* 33 (1995), 121–44.

G. L. Hersey. *Pythagorean Palaces: Magic and Architecture in the Italian Renaissance*. Ithaca: Cornell University Press, 1976.

Seymour R. Kesten. *Utopian Episodes*. Syracuse: Syracuse University Press, 1993.

Earl King, Jr. "On Having and Keeping Secrets." *Caduceus* 1.3 (1995), 18–24.

Jay Kinney, et al. "The Solar Temple Dossier: Documents and Background on the Tragedy." *Gnosis* 34 (1995), 87–96.

Maren Lockwood, "The Experimental Utopia in America." In Manuel, *Utopias and Utopian Thought*, 183–200.

Frank E. Manuel, editor. *Utopias and Utopian Thought*. Boston: Houghton Mifflin, 1965.

———, and Fritzie P. Manuel. *Utopian Thought in the Western World*. Cambridge: Harvard University Press, 1979.

Plotinus. *The Enneads*. Translated by Stephen MacKenna. Burdett: Larson, 1992.

Frederik L. Polak. "Utopia and Cultural Renewal." In Manuel, *Utopias and Utopian Thought*, 281–95.

M. Vitruvius Pollio. *Ten Books on Architecture*. Translated by Morris Hicky Morgan. New York: Dover, 1960.

Frances Yates. *Giordano Bruno and the Hermetic Tradition*. Chicago: University of Chicago Press, 1964.

———. *Theatre of the World*. Chicago: University of Chicago Press, 1969.

Book Reviews

Synchronicity, Science, and Soul-Making: Understanding Jungian Synchronicity through Physics, Buddhism, and Philosophy by Victor Mansfield. Chicago and La Salle: Open Court, 1995. Paper, 260 pp., $17.95.

Reviewed by Joscelyn Godwin

IT IS A BOLD ASTROPHYSICIST, even when protected by the academic cocoon, who ventures into print with a book like this one, which his colleagues may greet with incomprehension and scorn. Little do they know that they, too, are being carried along by the inexorable power of a paradigm-shift as profound as the Copernican/Galilean Revolution. Mansfield's teacher Paul Brunton wrote of this in 1943: "[Science] is steadily moving in a particular direction which will compel it—and this prediction will be fulfilled during our own century—in the end to see, through its own facts and its own reasoning, that the world-stuff is of the same tissue as that out of which our own ideas are made." (*The Wisdom of the Overself*, p. 25) Mansfield does not quote this prediction, but his book reads like a commentary on it.

It is also courageous to pay public homage to one's spiritual teachers, if one is fortunate enough to have any. The teachers acknowledged here are Anthony Damiani, founder of Wisdom's Goldenrod Philosophic Center on Seneca Lake, New York; Paul Brunton; and the Dalai Lama XIV (both of whom visited the Center during Damiani's lifetime). To an insider, the book is a celebration of the work that has gone on there for almost thirty years. Damiani's philosophical synthesis made large use of Brunton's works, and also of Advaita Vedanta, Neoplatonism, astrology, Middle Way Buddhism, and the psychology of C. G. Jung. Mansfield focuses on the last two of these and adds to them the vital component of modern physics, "building a three-part harmony with a psychological soprano, a scientific baritone, and a philosophic bass" (p. 7). The stroke of inspiration that makes this book more than a treatise is to interpolate eleven "synchronistic interludes": stories of remarkable experiences that have happened to eleven unnamed friends, most of them connected to Wisdom's Goldenrod. Mansfield's own students, friends, and teachers are so much in evidence that people beyond upstate New York might find the atmosphere cliquey. But the themes are as universal as they could possibly be.

Mansfield has refined Jung's 1952 definition of synchronicity in the light of subsequent developments in psychology and physics. He excludes merely paranormal events, and insists on an external component (simultaneous dreams won't do), and on "some genuine guidance from the unconscious." Synchronistic experiences, thus defined, are envoys from the archetype of meaning that Jung called the Self. In the most typical ones, a significant event in the outside world reflects or confirms something previously dreamed or wished for. My favorite story tells of the women who walked by Seneca Lake chanting the lake's old Indian name, as a friendly gesture to its spirits, and found there a natural pebble with eyes, nose, and open mouth (shown on the cover of the book). When blown, it gave out musical notes. Soon after, the narrator came across a Native American "Story of the Singing Stone." All of this correlated with her meditations to give a constellation of meaning to her life.

If synchronicities, because of their epochal importance in people's lives, cannot be dismissed as mere coincidences, they raise serious questions for a physicist, for in the common view of mind and matter there is no mechanism to explain them. Mansfield treats these questions in the middle chapters of the book, which are an idiot's guide (with not a single formula!) to quantum physics and its enigmas. If, as Laplace informed Napoleon, classical physics had no need for the hypothesis of God, then modern physics has no place (or time) for a universe of independently existing objects. Brunton's prediction is being fulfilled, as the role of mind impinges on a substructure once deemed firm: the hypothesis of matter. "The quantum vision removes the independently existing dancers and populates the world with possibilities, tendencies, or propensities for particular dances. Here the melodies (waves) and the dancers (particles) are fully united until we call one of them forth or bring one of them into existence by our measurement . . . Many of the details of the symphony are not written until we listen in a particular way" (p. 106).

Such ideas on the nature of things are new only to Western exoteric philosophy. For example, "The philosophic heart of Northern Buddhism, the principle of emptiness, denies that anything, whether subjective or objective, exists independently, separately, or inherently" (p. 128). After a masterful exposition of this philosophy, Mansfield writes: "My hope is that an appreciation of emptiness, the idea that we codependently arise with the world, will help us appreciate not only the possibility of synchronicity but its naturalness. It may also help deepen our appreciation of the view of nature emerging from modern physics that must be the starting point for any unification with mind" (p. 160).

It was tactless of the publisher to ask Fritjof Capra for a word of praise for *Synchronicity*, then to print it on the back cover along with three others that say how much better Mansfield's work is than Capra's *Tao of Physics*. But it is true that Mansfield raises the modern physics-Eastern philosophy parallel to a higher emotional and experiential pitch. The life-changing stories are one part of this. Another is the presence of Carl Jung, whose life was dedicated to understanding and healing a soul that, for Buddhism, has no independent existence. Mansfield does not duck the paradox: he honors both the quest for the silent mind, and the Jungian path of soul-making. For example, if, against Jung's advice, one practices Eastern-style meditation, "there are inevitably periods when attempting to go deeper is like flushing skunks out of their dens. Then these unearthed affective contents cause great psychological agitation and make meditation extremely difficult. They can also lead to all sorts of excesses and imbalances so commonly found in spiritual communities that emphasize meditation . . . however, here depth psychology can truly come to the rescue. It can give us insight, bring order to the chaos, and generally disarm the contents by helping us integrate them into consciousness" (p. 217). The two paths are reconcilable because they concern different levels of (un)reality.

The final message of the book concerns the intimate link of the emptiness doctrine with the Buddhist ideal of universal compassion. Could a parallel link arise out of the revolution in philosophy necessitated by the new physics? This may seem visionary, says Mansfield. "Nevertheless, it would be magnificent if we could realize, as in nonlocal quantum mechanics, that the interconnections between people, races, and countries are more fundamental, more real than the independent existence of our little egos, nationalities, or nations" (p. 226).

This book is a considerable achievement. Few people possess the multiple gifts and experiences necessary for writing it. Jung's distinguished colleague Marie-Louise von Franz said recently: "The work which has now to be done is to work out the concept of synchronicity. I don't know the people who will continue it. They must exist, but I don't know where they are" (p. 22). Soon afterwards, despite her ill health, she read Mansfield's entire manuscript and offered encouragement.

The book is illustrated with many photographs, mostly by the author, and with drawings. Some of these are delightful, such as the gnome-like "Wolfgang Pauli and Niels Bohr spinning a top" and the pig in pointed boots. Professor Mansfield teaches some of this material to undergraduates, and humor is part of his strategy for charming them, and the reader. The pig illustrates one of several flagrantly self-deprecating stories. But I find his work ill-served by the fancy design features of the book. The typeface is so lightly leaded and tightly packed that reading it is a strain. Here and there are gray boxes containing "sound bites" in magazine fashion, perhaps intended for hasty reviewers but invariably ill-chosen. If this book gains the reputation it deserves, it will be on the strength of Mansfield's ideas, and a future edition would do better to present them as an unadorned and legible text.

Cosmos and Anthropos: A Philosophical Interpretation of the Anthropic Cosmological Principle by Errol E. Harris. Atlantic Highlands: Humanities Press, 1991. Cloth, 194 pp., $45.00. *The Self-Aware Universe: How Consciousness Creates the Material World* by Amit Goswami, Richard Reed, and Maggie Goswami. Los Angeles: Jeremy P. Tarcher, 1995. Paper, 336 pp., $14.95.

Reviewed by Roger S. Jones

TWO MAJOR INTERPRETATIONS of twentieth-century science are in direct conflict with each other. To some philosophers and scientists, the implications of quantum theory, cosmology, complexity, evolution, and genetics seem to reinforce the Cartesian-Galilean view of a natural world which has inert matter at its foundation and which is governed by basic laws that ultimately reduce all phenomena to the activity of passive elemental entities. To others, twentieth-century science suggests the complete transcendence of materialism and reductionism and an ironic return to earlier ideas of holism and idealism. While the former interpretation implies a universe generated and advanced by accidental and chaotic processes, and thus devoid of any value or purpose, the latter view hints at a holistic guiding principle expressing a grand cosmic design, which thus imbues the universe with meaning and suggests a central role for life and consciousness.

The two books under review—*Cosmos and Anthropos* by Errol E. Harris and *The Self-Aware Universe* by Amit Goswami—fall definitely into the second camp, and argue persuasively that one can truly rationalize and understand twentieth-century science only on the basis of an assumed cosmic consciousness and intelligence. Harris, in fact, goes all the way, and argues that science proves the existence of God. But by the end of Harris's powerful, carefully documented, and frankly teleological argument that a holistic, self-reflexive, and self-perfecting principle must underlie and govern all of nature and experience, the use of the word "God" to describe this cosmic condition is little more than a matter of semantics.

Cosmos and Anthropos opens with a thoughtful review of alternative versions of the anthropic principle, which try to interpret the all but impossible delicate balance and coincidence of so many physical and chemical parameters that were essential to the emergence of life and consciousness in the universe. Were it not for just the right charge of the electron, strength of gravity, etc., then atoms or stars or galaxies would not have formed or been stable, or else the universe would not have lasted long enough for nature and evolution to have taken their course. Was it all simply the result of ridiculously unlikely odds, or was it part of a "plan," or is the question tautological and meaningless? Harris's book attempts to give a rational and compelling answer to these questions.

Early on, Harris squarely faces the issue of teleology in nature—a seemingly purposeful plan or intention that guides the cosmos. The idea was originally promoted by Aristotle, and later rejected by the natural philosophers of the Enlightenment at the birth of modern science. Harris attacks the strongest criticism against teleology. It need not imply a reverse of causality, in which the end point of a process controls its development. Teleology does imply a plan, but not necessarily one with its final state worked out in advance. A painter does not paint a picture in order to place a predetermined final brush stroke on the canvas, but rather to create and complete a whole image, whose character is evaluated and modified during its creation according to aesthetic criteria, but whose final result is not known in advance. Harris proposes teleology in nature as a principle that guides the evolution of the cosmos towards completion, perfection, and wholeness, but which does not constitute final causation.

In his middle chapters, Harris challenges the traditional arguments in physics, chemistry, biology, evolution, and psychology, which claim that the complexity and variety of the world is the result of abstract reductionist laws. According to these laws, the properties of water are an inevitable consequence of the laws of atomic bonding. Consciousness is simply an emergent and efficient property of complex organic systems. And so forth. But Harris argues that there is an interconnectedness and a holistic pattern in the universe that cannot possibly be explained on the basis of chance occurrence. The uncommon and unique life-nurturing properties of water may be based on atomic laws, but why should such laws exist in the first place? Some natural selection mechanisms might explain the survival of certain species, but then why do so-called elemental life forms persist for millions of years? And natural selection and survival can never explain the actual emergence of life from inanimate matter, the odds for which are infinitesimal even in a vast universe of 15 billion years' duration. Nor can evolution account for consciousness, which is entirely unnecessary for survival or successful adaptation to the environment. Chance variation and natural selection are certainly supported by the evidence, but "they are not sufficient to account for the results, which are not additive accumulations of characteristics but intimately and integrally organized systems of structure and function." Only a "more organismic account of evolution . . . and . . . nothing less will do justice to the observed facts."

Harris widens his discussion to include sentience, perception, cognition, consciousness, self-reflection, and insight. At every level, he argues, not chance but some overarching principle of organization and completion is operating to bring into being the systematic unity and wholeness inherent in the universe from the start. And this completion is not possible until the universe becomes aware of and reflects upon its own nature and process. "No whole can be complete unless brought to consciousness." This is the true meaning of the anthropic principle, according to Harris. Life, consciousness, and self-reflection are not the causes, but the inevitable consequences of an organized, holistic, and self-perfecting universe. And ironically, this is what the evidence of twentieth-century science is screaming at us, though it is largely unheard through the deafness of materialism, reductionism, and dualism.

But human knowledge and empirical science do not represent the end point of cosmic perfection, which must be some unified all-knowing condition that is tantamount to our usual concept of God. Thus God is not a cover for our ignorance, but rather "the logical consequence of the very nature of our knowledge and of the structure of the universe as discovered by empirical science."

The Self-Aware Universe by Amit Goswami is a fitting complement to *Cosmos and Anthropos*, because it argues that a far more coherent and logical explanation of the weirdness of quantum theory is provided by a philosophy of "monistic idealism," than by the conventional one of dualistic materialism. And such a monistic principle can be best understood as a kind of pervasive consciousness at the foundation of all of time and space, which thus forms a universal ground of cosmic mind.

Goswami begins by briefly surveying physics and demonstrating that modern quantum theory not only supplants the older classical physics, but even expels its materialistic assumptions. The concept of "potentiality" that is central to quantum descriptions of the micro world and the principle of nonlocality inherent in quantum systems are stark and explicit contradictions to the very notions of primal matter and causal laws. The various paradoxes of quantum theory, such as Schrödinger's cat, can never be resolved without bringing mind and consciousness into the picture and giving them a fundamental role in the natural world.

The act of observation is represented in quantum theory by the so-called collapse of the wave function—an apparently acausal process in which all the myriad possible states of an electron are instantaneously "collapsed" into the one we actually observe. Thus the *choice* by an observer of the specific form of an experimental observation of an electron is the immediate cause for the physical "manifestation" of the electron. And choice, argues Goswami, is the characteristic *par excellence* of consciousness. Thus consciousness and mind are essential to the physical being of an electron, and by implication, of everything else in the universe. And so the process by which we become self-aware and construct our ego is very same process by which the universe becomes manifest.

At this point, Goswami presents the most radical and novel ideas in the book. Self awareness, which is central both to observation and ego formation, is fundamentally nonlocal or noncausal. It involves a creative discontinuity, which is tantamount to the famous "quantum leap." Imagination and creativity are thus at the heart of "physical reality," both as "objective" cosmic consciousness and as an illusory personal ego. For self awareness always entails self reference and therefore the illusory identification of a separate "I" in a process Goswami calls a *tangled hierarchy*. It is in trying to untangle the confusion of the knower from the field of knowing that a "self" arises as the apparent agent of untangling. So the formation of an ego with its subject-object dichotomy is a concomitant though illusory aspect of cosmic manifestation and self awareness.

Awareness and consciousness are not the same according to Goswami (based on psychological experiments). Awareness is the universal and nonlocal unconscious state in which quantum potentialities exist. In making manifest a particular potentiality, consciousness creates "reality" and produces the illusion of ego in the process. Thus consciousness is at the basis of all of nature and provides a logical and compelling rationale for modern quantum theory.

And so Goswami ends by relating these ideas to traditional religious philosophies and practices—primarily but not exclusively of the East—and also to questions of ethics and world community. Both he and Harris make a strong case for the ultimate integration of science and religion, which are now revealed to be very far from opposing one another, as many people and institutions have supposed over the years. It now seems that a deep and thoughtful reinterpretation of twentieth-century science, such as we find in these two excellent books, is forcing us more and more to see humanity as an essential participant in a meaningful cosmic pageant.

When Corporations Rule the World by David C. Korten. San Francisco: Berrett-Koehler, 1995. Cloth, 374 pp., $29.95.

Reviewed by James Robertson

IT IS ODD, when you think of it, that we should be so dependent on business sponsorship for music, opera, the arts, sports like football, cricket, and athletics, and other cultural, educational, social, and community activities. Some time ago I went to a church service in Bristol, and was surprised to find it was sponsored by British Nuclear Fuels. How soon will the annual Christmas broadcast of Nine Lessons and Carols from King's College, Cambridge, come to us courtesy of Multinational Moneygrubbers, Inc.? It is a strange kind of society we have created.

And that, of course, is just the froth on the surface of a very big pond. The really serious questions are about how the cancerous growth of "business civilization" continues to turn many millions, even billions, of people all over the world into victims of poverty and deprivation. How has it come about that they—and we—do not have sufficient means to support desirable and necessary activities for ourselves? Why and how has so much of our power been drained away to big business and finance? What are we to do about it? And how does this connect with spiritual transformation and the sense of an emerging new consciousness? If those questions interest you, then this is a "must read" book for you, as it is for Archbishop Desmond Tutu.

Its first five parts—Cowboys in a Spaceship, Contest for Sovereignty, Corporate Colonialism, A Rogue Financial System, and No Place for People—contain a searing critique of the corporate world order that exists today. The final part, on Reclaiming Our Power, contains four chapters discussing The Ecological Revolution, Good Living, An Awakened Civil Society, and Agenda for Change.

The book's impact is all the greater because it is so fully documented, and because the author has never been, and is not now, antibusiness. He believes that an efficient system of industry and commerce is essential to human well-being. When he was an MBA student, he believed that global corporations might offer an answer to the problems of poverty and human conflict. But he has now concluded that "the systemic forces nurturing the growth and dominance of global corporations are at the heart of the current human dilemma." To avoid collective catastrophe we must radically transform the underlying system of business.

Korten recognizes the magnitude of this task. Millions of thoughtful, intelligent people, who are properly suspicious of big government, who believe in honest hard work, who have deep religious values and are committed to family and community, are deceived by the false information and the distorted intellectual and moral logic repeated constantly in the corporate-controlled media. "Those who work within our major corporate, academic, political, governmental, and other institutions find the culture and reward systems so strongly aligned with the corporate libertarian ideology that they dare not speak out in opposition for fear of jeopardizing their jobs and their careers. We must break through the veil of illusion and misrepresentation that is holding us in a self-destructive cultural trance and get on with the work of recreating our economic systems in service to people and the living earth."

We all need to understand, as fully as Korten now does after more than thirty years as a dedicated development worker, that a principal feature of the Western development enterprise has been about separating people from their traditional means of livelihood. By breaking down the bonds of security provided by family and community, conventional economic progress makes people dependent on the jobs and products that modern corporations produce. This process began with the enclosure, or privatization, of common lands in England in the seventeenth and eighteenth centuries where it provided a launching pad for the Industrial Revolution. The colonial era extended it to non-industrial lands. After World War II, the new corporate colonialism took over. Western development assistance and development investment, supported by the World Bank and other such bodies, continued to deepen economic and social dependency. In the battle for the souls of the colonized, economic conversion replaced religious conversion. Economic growth became imbued with a mystical significance, with the consequence of ever greater dependence on the money economy and thus on institutions of money that could be controlled by the few.

This underlying theme is not new. Over the past twenty years, increasing numbers of us have been pointing out that conventional economic "progress" is a process of dependency creation, that we need a new economic paradigm—including a new direction of economic progress, new economic theories and policies, and new business values and goals—and that this new economic paradigm must focus on enabling and empowering people to take control over their own lives. Awareness of this has been spreading, and understanding of what to do about it has been growing.

But this book's great strength, and the main reason why it will help to accelerate the spread of awareness and understanding, is that it conveys more powerfully and convincingly than any other I know the crass unacceptability of the "business civilization" that dominates the world today, and of "the cloud world in which the architects of the global economy live . . . isolated from the daily reality of those they rule." The cumulative impact of the detailed evidence to be found in its pages is overwhelming. The top 20 percent of the world's people enjoy incomes 150 times as high as the lowest 20 percent. Within the USA alone, the income received by the top 1 percent is greater than the total income of all the bottom 40 percent. The $20 million paid in 1992 to basketball star Michael Jordan for promoting Nike shoes was more than the entire annual payroll of the Indonesian factories that made the shoes, where thousands of girls and young women workers were paid as little as 15¢ an hour. Highly paid directors and senior company officers are protected from personal liability for their actions. Illegal corporate acts, that would bring stiff prison sentences (or perhaps even death sentences) for individuals, lead—at most—to fines on the company which are insignificant in relation to its assets. And so it goes on. There is a treasure trove of information and insight here about the "organized irresponsibility" that characterizes the corporate sector.

In his epilogue, "Choice for Life," Korten refers to the compelling meaning he finds in the profound transformation to which the Ecological Revolution is calling us—"to experience ourselves as spiritually alive and politically active participants in the unfolding exploration of the potentials of a living universe," and he defines the need to transform today's global business system as part of the challenge to "rediscover neglected political dimensions of our societies and spiritual dimensions of our being."

In so doing, he offers a challenge—as it seems to me—to all of us who participate in "new paradigm" activities and networks. Like many other people—especially professional people—in modern society, we find it hard to integrate our interests and experience with one another's, and all too easily gravitate into separate spheres labeled Science or Philosophy or Health or Religion or Ecology or Economics; Inner-Directed or Outer-Directed; Personal or Political; Intellectual or Activist; and so on. Among its many virtues, this book challenges us to see the need to transform the business system, not just as part of a wider post-modern transformation of the institutions and power structures of the world in which we live, but also as integral to the development of our own personal values and consciousness.

Sex, Ecology, and Spirituality: The Spirit of Evolution by Ken Wilber. Boston: Shambhala, 1995. Cloth, 830 pp., $40.00.

Reviewed by James O'Meara

AFTER SEVERAL YEARS of mostly involuntary silence due to his wife's death from cancer (chronicled in his work *Grace and Grit*), Ken Wilber is back, writing big books again, and being interviewed everywhere. He's even published a book that is an interview, but more of that later. *Sex, Ecology, and Spirituality* is 831 pages, 293 of them "Notes"—many of them short articles in scope—representing Books One and Two of a projected three-volume series.

Another publisher faced with such a behemoth might have balked, but Shambhala, choosing to take it as a marketing opportunity, produced instead another book, *A Short History of Everything*, in which Wilber presents a "friendly and accessible" version. He also perfects the fine art of "log rolling"—writing blurbs for friends who will write blurbs for you—by employing as interviewer one Tony Schwartz, author of *What Really Matters* (Bantam, 1992), which not only features Ken Wilber, but boasts an enthusiastic blurb from . . . Ken Wilber. Schwartz now returns the favor, and even provides a blurb for the back of his own book! I will be treating the two books as one for this review.

Part One begins by locating the root of our current ecological and spiritual crisis in the "fractured worldview" produced by the divergence of the "two arrows of time": the increasing complexity of evolution and the decreasing energy of thermodynamics. Only recent advances in the "sciences of complexity" have enabled us to envision "hidden aspects of the material realm" that can "propel themselves into states of higher order . . . complexity, and . . . organization." To do this requires a rehabilitation of the currently unfashionable idea of hierarchy. Wilber does this by introducing Arthur Koestler's term "holon," "that which, being a whole in one context, is simultaneously a part in another." A "natural" hierarchy, or "holarchy," is simply the way holons link together in orders of increasing wholeness or integration. When higher-level holons dominate, rather than integrate, the result is a "pathological holarchy," which is what the anti-hierarchists are really opposing.

Natural holarchies, however, are the central tools of the sciences of complexity. Thus we could heal our fractured worldview if we could figure out what all these holarchies have in common. Wilber goes on to explicate "some twenty tenets" that do this. Wilber's discussion of these tenets (Holons compose the Kosmos, up and down; holons have four fundamental capacities; holons have emergent properties and emerge hierarchically, etc.) is perhaps the most valuable part of the book. It provides a framework that makes sense out of many controversies and confusions in the "new age" or "new science" areas. For example, if humans are only part of the "great web of life," how can we place greater value on our consciousness or society than on the more numerous and better-adapted cockroach? Because greater holistic depth entails lesser physical span, though you'll have to read chapter three to see why, and how this reconciles ecological awareness with deference to human cognitive evolution.

Wilber parts company with systems theorists, however, by noting that holons have not only exteriors but interiors, which "holistic thinkers" tend to either ignore, deny, or attempt to deal with by reductionism. Wilber insists that besides the individual, exterior holon—an atom, if you will—we need to deal with social or group holons, and the interiors of both. Thus only a "Four Quadrant Model" will do all the jobs that need to be done, with a special method of enquiry (empirical, hermeneutical, contemplative, etc.) adequate to each.

On this basis Wilber begins examining his main topic: human evolution, with special reference to the relations of humanity to nature, and the genders to each other. Wilber apparently endorses the view that "ontogeny recapitulates phylogeny": he directly correlates personal evolution with social or cultural evolution, as societies tend to foster development to their normal level. Wilber argues, for example, that the roots of patriarchy lay less in male malevolence than in biology, means of production (plow versus stick) and above all, worldviews that did not privilege equality or female values. Thus, liberation has been largely a function of the comparatively recent emergence and consolidation of the developmental stage of rationality.

As the leading transpersonal theorist, Wilber finds evidence, in sources ranging from Aurobindo to Zukav, that there are still higher levels of development. He refutes the charge that these levels are intrinsically unavailable to scientific evaluation—being no more subjective than the data of any other science, and susceptible to their own appropriate tools of discovery and interpersonal verification—and delineates five such levels: vision-logic (mind/body integration and the intuition of complex conceptual networks), psychic, subtle, causal, and nondual. Each is correlated with a characteristic style of mysticism (nature, God, the Formless, the Nondual), experience (somatic force such as the Kundalini, interior visions and sounds, pure consciousness, and the Nondual *sahaj samadhi*), and discussed through the writing of an exemplar (Emerson, St. Theresa, Meister Eckhart, and Ramana Maharshi).

Part Two turns from evolution to discuss the perennial problem of integrating this "path of ascent" with its necessary coordinate, "the path of descent."

The West started well, since Wilber suggests that a careful reading will show Plato to be far from the stereotypical world-negating "ascender," but the dissociation of "the way up and the way down" has continually plagued us. For nondualists like Plato, Plotinus, or Aurobindo, the watchword was "Flee the many, find the One, embrace the many as the One"; the former is Wisdom, the latter Compassion. *Agape* for the lower must balance *eros* for the One. When this integration fails, *eros* becomes *phobos*, leading to repression and alienation; *agape* may become *thanatos*, leading to regression and denial of higher possibilities. Western history has been an alternation between those who would flee the world, and those who would seek salvation in it, "French kissing the shadows."

Modernity continues these two trends. While myth has been superseded by rationality and empiricism (the "good news"), ascent, conflated with myth, has been suppressed; vertical ascent becomes an infinite horizontal "flatland." The residual problem of the nature of human subjectivity and its relation to the world has led to two false "solutions," the Ecological camp or "Eco," which seeks communion with Nature and emphasizes feeling and Art, and the Ego camp, which emphasizes autonomous Reason and Philosophy (think Kant). The Ego's problem is that the emphasis on empirical science leads to reductionism, which ironically actually alienates and represses other real goods, including both transpersonal experiences and the body itself.

The Eco, on the other hand, has the problem of reinserting man into nature, without losing the advance of reason. But since it confuses differentiation with dissociation, it overvalues emotion, conflates God with Nature, and is obsessed with a Search for the Golden Age, which

Wilber dubs the "Regress Express."

With these two positions epitomized by Fichte and Spinoza, Schelling becomes the hero of this narrative. He realized that Idealism had *dissociated* Mind and Nature rather than *differentiating* them, forgetting their common transcendental Ground. Rather than regression, Schelling called for progression beyond reason, to see mind and nature as different movements of one Spirit, manifesting in successive stages of evolutionary unfolding: Objective Spirit (Nature), Subjective Spirit (Mind). Alas, Idealism ultimately failed, not by logic but by lack of a contemplative practice by which peak experience could become voluntary and stable.

Wilber ends by noting two encouraging trends: the inability of Darwinism to account for macroevolution has poked some holes in the main roadblock to acknowledging the emergent factor in the cosmos, while the physicists now admit that they cannot explain how nature's laws have operated from the first second. The drive to self-transcendence is beginning to move ever more people into transpersonal stages. Wilber offers his quadrant analysis to help them to validate and understand these experiences and not repeat the errors of modernity.

What's wrong with this picture? Plenty, according to the many critics that, for the first time, emerged almost when the book appeared. One focus of criticism has been Wilber's treatment of his sources. The first shot was fired on the Alexandria discussion group on the Internet, where D. H. Frew posted a blistering criticism of Wilber's account of Plotinus that accused him of many errors of fact, deliberate use of outdated translations, and outright fabrication of passages. Wilber's response was unconvincing and seemed to make use of bluster and arrogance for argument. A second E-mail made an equally devastating case against his treatment of Emerson.

My take on this, which may not please either side, is that these criticisms are ultimately beside the point. Figures like Emerson or even Plotinus function in Wilber's book as *exemplars*, not grounds of argument. Their writings are used to illustrate certain timeless positions that Wilber thinks consciousness may take up, rather like Hegel's *Phenomenology*. Ironically, Wilber himself seems to want to defend his work as ironclad scholarship, producing the unintentional comedy of three bulky volumes in the best Victorian tradition, and haughty defenses of the indefensible use of equally nineteenth-century scholarship. But if, as he hints, he is operating at the leading-edge level of vision-logic, then other factors, such as the felt sense of acquiring new perspectives that solve old nagging problems, should count for as much as or more than reasoning. In fact, the post-modern reader is not interested in "systems" and "truth" anyway, but in pragmatic suggestions for acquiring new perspectives and states of consciousness.

In any event, I found that the only way I could deal with this hulking work was to take it as the very opposite of a systematic treatise. It was much more fun to use it as a sort of medieval encyclopedia, filled with randomly arranged bits of wisdom, often in unexpected places. The post-modern reader finds the idea of the DJ more useful than that of the Grand Theorist anyway. What's needed is someone to take up found elements into a new and spirited *bricolage*. As Brian Eno says, we have become "dilettante perfume blenders, poking inquisitive fingers through a great library of ingredients and seeing which combinations make some sense for us—gathering experience—the possibility of making better guesses—without demanding certainty." Even Guénon opposed any "systematized representation," and demanded that his reader "keep in mind the part played by the inexpressible, which cannot be enclosed in any form, and which is the only essential thing."

Wilber is actually at his best not when arguing but when he is explicating such tools as his twenty tenets, which the reader can use to order his own experience and create her own synthesis. For the rest, perhaps he has written a parody of the systematic mind, to free us from the chains of rationality and promote the development of vision-logic in his reader. He needs to wear his learning a little more lightly, to let it go and take it up again as needed, instead of using the cornball jokes and arch phrasing he seems to think will "lighten up" his work.

This does not mean I have no complaints to lodge here. Wilber still has not dealt with the vital "future primitive" school of thought, which challenges the "progressive" model of cultural evolution with a vigorous "Back to the paleolithic!" Wilber has never seriously engaged this literature, contenting himself with dogmatic pronouncements about brutish cavemen, and basing himself entirely on an old book by Lenski, whom I have frankly never heard of. He's added Marshall Sahlin's seminal *Stone Age Economics* to his bibliography, but I can find no actual discussion of it. Just "noting" an opponent in passing, without actually dealing with the challenge? And how much more of this is going on in those 300-plus pages of notes? Moreover, he seems politically naive, swallowing the whole neo-liberal line on the threat of the teaming Third World, the "PC threat" (a handful of postmodern feminist semioticians threaten the totally honest and balanced multinational-controlled media), and the glistening New World Order. For the balance Wilber fails to provide, I might suggest Benjamin Barber's *Jihad vs. McWorld* (Ballantine, 1995), and Jerry Mander and Edward Goldsmith, *The Case Against the Global Economy* (Sierra Club, 1996).

But as Furtwangler said of Bruckner, "It is a piece of philistinism to believe that the absence of faults produces greatness." At the end of Book Two, Wilber muses on the increasing occurrence of transpersonal breakthroughs throughout the world. "But all *depth* must be *interpreted*. And how we interpret depth is crucially important for the birth of that depth itself." Faults and all, Wilber has succeeded in giving us an essential guide for that assisted birth.

About the Contributors

David Appelbaum is professor of philosophy at the State University of New York at New Paltz. His recent books include *Everyday Spirits*, *The Stop*, and *Disruption*, all from the State University of New York Press. He is the coauthor, with Jacob Needleman, of *Real Philosophy* (Penguin Arkana), has published several volumes of poetry, and is editor of *Parabola*.

Hakim Bey is an transdisciplinary writer of social commentary, political analysis, and visionary manifestoes. His publications include *T.A.Z.: The Temporary Autonomous Zone, Ontological Anarchy, Poetic Terrorism* (Autonomedia), *Immediatism* (A.K. Press), and *Millenium* (Autonomedia, forthcoming). His writing has been described as "Fascinating" (William S. Burroughs), "Exquisite" (Allen Ginsberg), and "A splendid hoax" (*Moorish Science Monitor*). Ironically, his article on "The Information War" was picked up on the World Wide Web and forwarded to us by E-mail.

Jay Bregman teaches in the history department at the University of Maine, Orono, and has also taught at UCLA, Berkeley, and Howard University. His scholarly specialties are Hellenic Neoplatonism and the religions of late antiquity and Neoplatonism in North American thought, art, and literature. He is also an alto saxophone player and a student of the music of Charles "Bird" Parker.

Andrew Burniston has been studying modern esotericism and depth psychology for twenty years and has published in most of the journals in these fields. His most recent work, a review article on the new Eranos *I Ching*, appears in *Harvest*.

Christopher Castle, visual artist and composer, is co-artistic director of ANIMA MUNDI Dance Company. He lives in Marshall, California.

Stuart Cowan, a mathematician, is the coauthor, with Sim Van der Ryn, of *Ecological Design* (Island Press, 1996).

Kathleen Damiani is a Ph.D. candidate in philosophy, working on a dissertation, "The Circuit of Sophia and the Gnosis of Relationship." Her master's thesis was an exploration of Sophia in myth, religion, and depth psychology. She lives in Ithaca, New York, where she teaches philosophy and critical thinking.

John David Ebert is a contributing editor to *The Collected Works of Joseph Campbell*, now in preparation by The Joseph Campbell Foundation. His work has appeared in *Mythosphere* and *Mythos Journal*, and he is presently working on a collection of interviews.

Albert Einstein (1879–1955) is best known for his General Theory of Relativity, which is considered one of the greatest insights of twentieth-century science. But in addition to his work in physics and mathematics, Einstein was was a philosophical humanist who wrote on a wide variety of contemporary issues, including religion and the philosophy of science. "Science and Religion" and "The Cosmic Religious Feeling" are taken from *Ideas and Opinions*, a collection of his essays and speeches.

Christos Evangeliou is professor of philosophy at Towson State University and holds degrees in classics (University of Athens, Greece) and philosophy (Emory University). He is the author of two books and more than thirty scholarly papers, associate editor of *Skepsis*, co-editor of the *Journal of Neoplatonic Studies*, and the American representative of the International Center of Philosophy and Interdisciplinary Research, based in Athens, Greece.

David Fideler is a philosopher, writer, and educator. He is the founder of Phanes Press which, over the last decade, has published forty books on the philosophical and spiritual traditions of the Western world. A doctoral candidate in philosophy and cosmological studies, he is writing a book on the World Soul and humanity's relationship to the living universe.

Gordon Onslow Ford is a painter living in Inverness, California. His books include *Insights*, *Creation*, and *Painting in the Instant*.

Suzi Gablik is an art critic and artist who has taught at the University of the South, Virginia Commonwealth University, the University of California at Santa Barbara, and Virginia Tech. Her books include *Has Modernism Failed?*, *Magritte*, *Progress in Art*, and *The Reenchantment of Art*. Her conversation with Thomas Moore is excerpted from her most recent work, *Conversations Before the End of Time: Dialogues on Art, Life, and Spiritual Renewal* (Thames & Hudson).

Joscelyn Godwin is professor of music at Colgate University and the author of many books. His most recent titles are *Harmony of the Spheres: A Sourcebook of the Pythagorean Tradition in Music* (Inner Traditions), *The Theosophical Enlightenment* (State University of New York Press), *Music and the Occult: French Musical Philosophies, 1750–1950* (University of Rochester Press), and a revised edition of *Harmonies of Heaven and Earth* (Inner Traditions).

John Michael Greer is co-editor of *Caduceus: The Hermetic Quarterly* (c/o Cinnabar, PO Box 95674, Seattle, WA 98145). He is the author of *Paths of Wisdom: The Magical Cabala in the Western Tradition*.

Werner Heisenberg (1901–1976), awarded the Nobel Prize in Physics in 1932, helped lay the foundations of modern physics and is best known for his formulation of the Uncertainty Principle, which is central to quantum mechanics. His philosophical writings are collected in *Physics and Beyond* and *Across the Frontiers*.

Lee Irwin teaches comparative religions in the Philosophy and Religious Studies Department at the College of Charleston, South Carolina. He is the author of *The Dream Seekers: Native American Visionary Traditions of the Great Plains* (University of Oklahoma Press) and *Visionary Worlds: The Making and Unmaking of Reality* (State University of New York Press). His earlier articles include "The Orphic Mystery: Harmony and Mediation" (*Alexandria* 1) and "The Divine Sophia: Isis, Achamoth, and Ialdabaoth" (*Alexandria* 3).

Roger S. Jones is a Morse Alumni Distinguished Teaching Professor of Physics and Astronomy at the University of Minnesota, where he has been teaching and studying for twenty-nine years. He lectures and offers courses on physics, its philosophical implications, and its cultural influences. He has also written two books—*Physics as Metaphor* and *Physics for the Rest of Us*—that present physics from a conceptual, critical, and humanistic point of view.

Joseph Milne is visiting tutor for philosophy in art courses and the master's program in mysticism and religious experience at the University of Kent at Canterbury, where he is also researching a Ph.D. in Vedantic and Christian anthropology. He is a research associate of the International Institute of India Studies and a fellow of the Temenos Academy, where he has given many lectures on philosophical theology, mysticism, and seminar courses on Shakespeare. He is particularly interested in bringing together ancient and modern thought in philosophy and the arts, Eastern and Western.

Bruce Nelson is a poet, teacher, and longtime student of contemplative traditions, East and West. He has produced several journals including *Demeter's Bakery* and *Mythos*. He is administrative coordinator for the Invisible College, a contemplative and philosophical school based in Kansas City, and can be reached at *eleusis@sound.net*.

James J. O'Meara studied philosophy at the University of Windsor and has also studied at the University of Colorado, the Naropa

Institute, and Rensselaer Polytechnic Institute. He is corporate librarian at a law firm in New York City, and is a freelance writer and book reviewer.

Plutarch of Chaerona (*c.* 45–*c.* 125 C.E.) was a Pythagorean and Platonic philosopher, antiquarian, statesman, essayist, and priest of Apollo at Delphi during the last thirty years of his life.

James Robertson worked for the Cabinet Office and Treasury of the British government, where he worked on decolonization and development. Later, he directed interbank research for the British banks. Since 1973 he has been an independent writer, speaker, and consultant. His books include *The Sane Alternative: A Choice of Futures; Future Work: Jobs, Self-employment, and Leisure;* and *Future Wealth: A New Economics for the Twenty-first Century* (all available from Bootstrap Press, New York). He has recently been a trustee of the New Economics Foundation (London) and a visiting fellow at the Green College Centre for Environmental Policy and Understanding (Oxford).

Robert Romanyshyn, Ph.D., is the son of a gypsy whose vagabond soul has been wandering the desert of our techno-consumer culture in search of its spiritual heritage. His teaching and writing over the past quarter century have focused on the eclipse of soul in modern Western culture, with its consequent deanimation of the world by a mind which has taken leave of its senses. His is the author of *Psychological Life: From Science to Metaphor* and *Technology as Symptom and Dream*, as well as numerous articles. He teaches at the Pacifica Graduate Institute.

Betty Roszak is a poet and writer who has lectured and written on ecofeminism. With Theodore Roszak she edited *Masculine/Feminine: Readings in Sexual Mythology and the Liberation of Women*. Her audiotexts *Starbirth* and *The Crest of the East Pacific Rise*, poetic evocations of recent scientific discoveries, have been presented to numerous audiences, including the American Association for the Advancement of

Science and the Geophysical Union of America.

Theodore Roszak is professor of history and director of the Ecopsychology Institute at California State University, Hayward. His most recent books are the novel *The Memoirs of Elizabeth Frankenstein* (Random House, 1995/Bantam, 1996) and, as co-editor with Mary Gomes and Allen Kanner, *Ecopsychology: Restoring the Earth, Healing the Mind* (Sierra Club Books, 1995).

Stephen Rowe is professor and chair of the Department of Philosophy at Grand Valley State University, near Grand Rapids, Michigan. He is the author of *Rediscovering the West: An Inquiry into Nothingness and Relatedness* and *Leaving and Returning: On America's Contribution to a World Ethic*. He is the editor of *The Vision of William James, Living Beyond Crisis: Essays on Discovery and Being in the World*, and *Claiming a Liberal Education*.

Thomas Willard, author of "Drinking with the Muses," teaches English at the University of Arizona, a dry campus in the desert town of Tucson. A book reviewer for *Cauda Pavonis: Studies in Hermeticism*, he has recently edited the alchemical works of Jean D'Espagnet (forthcoming from Garland Publishing). He recommends the unretsinated wine of translation, and first offered the translated sayings about the Muses to his students in classical rhetoric.

List of Subscribers

THE FOLLOWING INDIVIDUALS have made *Alexandria* 4 a reality by joining THE ALEXANDRIA SOCIETY, the sole purpose of which is to support our publications program. We thank these individuals for their generosity and support, which has made this forum possible.

Patron ($250)
J. H. Bruening
Robert P. Korth
Phil Lesh
Doss McDavid

Benefactor ($100)
Anonymous (1)
Paula R. Bainbridge
Armand Courtois, Sr.
Bob Culley
Robert Firth
Federico González
Robert Hofer
Joseph & Stephanie Hoggert
David Patrick Hurley
Constance Papson Johnston
Sidney Lanier
Ruth McMahon
Jeffrey G. Mead
Lorna D. Mohr
Ann Ovodow
John G. Pladel
James B. Robinson
Alexander Sprinkle
Billy E. Taylor
John T. Walker
Roger Harman Weeks
Tom Whiteside

Sustainer ($75)
José Anes
Francis P. Broussard
Edward C. Deveney
Harry Doumas
Kenneth G. Field
John Fogarty
Jeffrey I. Friedman, D.C.
Ignacio L. Götz
Alvin Holm
Richard M. Kline
Dr. James L. McNamara
M. Joy Mills
Katherine Neville
Walter Parrish
Brenda Spencer
Loyd S. Swenson

Supporter ($50)
Anonymous (1)
Pasquale Accardo
Marc Adamchek
Richard A. Adams
Shinya Asahara
Dr. J. Keith Atkinson
Jack M. Balls
Eleanor J. Barnes
Steve Bass
Taylor Baxter

Mark A. Belisle
H. Avoise Blackway
Tony Boscarello
Dr. G. J. Bosman
Jay Bregman
Cornelius Bull
Hall C. Burbage
Joseph Caezza
John Carey
Walter R. Christie, M.D.
Christi Clogson
George Contos
Mark Crann
William Crouch
Mary Cupp
Carl Daggett
Robert & Elsbeth Diehl
Frank Donnola
William Downey
Peter Dussik
Eco-philosophy Center
Claude Epstein
Alma Espinosa
Frances M. Evans
Antoine Faivre
Llewellyn G. Farr
Richard Faust
Prof. J. Fichefet
Graham S. Fletcher
Karen Gardner, Ph.D.
Shelley Glickstein
Joscelyn Godwin
Geoffrey Gough
Julie Grabel
Andrew Green
Arthur Gregory
Mickey Bright Griffin
Zev & Heidi Guber
Dr. Hans T. Hakl
Robert S. Hand

Meredith Hardin
Peter D. Harrison
S. C. Hedger
Michael C. Hergoth
George Hersh
Stephen Hershey
Richard M. Higgins
Stephen G. Hughes
Marta Illueca
George Ionnides
Albert Jacobbe
Marie Louise Kagan
Alice S. Kavanagh
Scot Kelly
Mark Kindt
Brace Knapp, M.D.
Maurice Krasnow, Ph.D.
Janice Kyd
Nelson E. Lamborn
Dr. Melvin Land
Enrique R. Larde
J. W. Lawrence
Gerald F. Leska
Will Lewis
Bruce MacLennan
Perry D. Manack
Thomas Mansheim
Domenick Masiello
Kevin A. McCarthy
Clifford McCready
Rosa McGehee
Conti Meehan
Brian Mertz & Sharon Wheeler
Ralph Metheny
Gordon Mickelson
Brett Mitchell
Frederick Morgan
Alexander Moshos
John M. Murray
Frank G. Neves

Jane Olinger
Scott A. Olsen
Stephen Overy
Charles E. Pasley
Anne Phillips
Barry Popik
Karen K. Prince
Lawrence Principe
Alan Riche
Rev. Eric W. Robinson
Philip J. Romei
Katsuhiko Sakaguchi
Mark Sanders
Gregg W. Saunders
J. Scott Sawyer
JoAnne Schmitz
Benjamin Sells
Mark Siegeltuck
Jeffrey J. Snyder
J. Mona Sosna
Lou Soteriou
David B. Spurgeon
David Stobbs
Hanne Stranger
Göran Svarvell
Toby Symington
D. W. Taylor
Gretchen Thometz
Mary M. Tius
Erol Torun
Joanne Tsoutsouris
Knut Vaksdal
Robert Valentine
Christine Van Camp Zecca
Lill Van Eps
R. Dennis Walton
Anthony Watson
Julian Watson
Sharon Wheeler
Andrew White
Ruth G. Wiskind

Beatrice S. Wittel

Member ($35)
Anonymous (1)
David L. Ackerman
Sherry Ackerman
Afentakis Akindinos
Robert B. Albertson
Jerrold E. Allen
Cliff Amos
John Anderson
Keith E. Anderson
Norman Anderson
Robert Armon
H. Scott Armstrong
Jo Ashenden
Ann Ashworth
Pieter Asselbergs
Jacqueiline Aubuchon
Kurt Aurley
Jeanette Avila
William R. Bacher
Carol Baer
Wm. Joel Bailey
Keith E. Baird
Norman Bashor
Sarah Batchelor
Janet Bayliss
Bill Becker
Thomas Beckett
Chester L. Behnke
Sue Belden
Don E. Benson
Liza Berdnik
John F. Berglund
Bill Bernardo
Antonio Betancor
Paolo Bianconi
Rudolf A. Binnewies
Marco Bischof
Elizabeth J. Bissell

Gordon Blackford
Charlotte Blackman
Phyllis Blakemore
R. E. Bliss
Liliane Boardman
Mary Boike
Josep M. Gracia Bonamusa
Joseph Bonsuwsa
Estella Bourque
Colleen O'Brien Bowden
Rex Boyer
Anthony Bradford
Carolyn B. Brafford
Michael Brande
Neal Brandoff
Charlene Breedlove
Vija Bremanis
Thomas Merton Brightman
Dean Brown
Richard Brown
Richard Brzustowicz, Jr.
Betty Budack
William Buford
Dusty Bunker
Joseph Burke
Carter Burnell
Timothy Butler
Rose Mary Byrne
Miguel Francisco Cadete
Patricia Lynne Callon
James Earle Canfield
Janice Canning
Lucia Capodilupo
Antonia Cardona
Toni Carey
Mary Kathleen Carroll
Michael D. Castelli
Richard Chamberlain
Judson Chambers
Craig Chase
Beverly Ciokajlo

Leroy Clark
Robert Clark
Chas S. Clifton
Pennie S. Clymer
Dorothy Cochran
David Coe
Christopher Michael Collins
John Robert Colombo
Robert Cornett
H. Martin Coulter
Kirk Crady
William Cranston
Michael Crisp
Monica Cryant
Bette F. Culbertson
John Daley
Richard Dance
Elizabeth Dancoes
Gregory Danyluk
William Davis
Frederick A. De Armas
Jonathan DeCamp
Ronald Decker
Nancy Denton
Jon Dependal
Dr. Raymond J. Dezzani
Michael Díaz
Katia Anne Dich
Carl Dietrich
Mark Distefano
Bine Donakowski
Kendall J. Dood
Frank E. Dougher
Elizabeth Downs
Lewis Dreisbach
Martin Edgar
Brian David Ellison
Ms. Lee Ellsworth
Philip Emmite
George Eraclides
Jacques H. Etienne

Richard Evans
Nancy B. Fairhurst
John P. Falchi
Andrew Faust
Carol C. Faust
Robert Ferguson
Scott Ferguson
Fetzer Institute
Thomas Folan
Howie Cohen & Zicky Forbes
Brett Forray
Dr. Scottie Foss
Alastair Fowler
Norman Frank
D. Moreau Franklin
Marco Frascari
Nelson French
Nancy Freyer
Nancy Friend
Diane Gaboriault
Michele Gagnon
Virginia Gaines
David Gallagher
David A. & Marie J. Garcia
Prof. Dr. Helmut Gebelein
Urs Geissbueller
William D. Geoghegan
Demetra George
Jodee M. Giacobbe
Darren Gibbs
Derek Gilman
Sarah Gilmer
David F. Godwin
João Varela Gomes
Kerry Gordon
Kathleen Henry Gorman
Thomas Gottsleben
Christopher P. H. Grabarkiewctz
Gary Gran
Dr. Sydney R. Grant
Dianna Gray

Aaron Richard O. Green
Green Lion Bookstore
Josephine Grieve
Joseph Groell
Walter E. Gross
Adele & Steve Gruen
Arthur C. Guidotti
Joseph Guilino
Elisabeth Haarstad
Elliot Haas
Greg Hackney
David F. Haight
David Hall
Denton E. Hall
Betsy Halpern
Dennis Hamilton
Leo Hansberry
Joseph Harakal
Ken Harbour
Jack Hardie
Ben Lee Harris
Carol Harrison
Richard Harrison
Steve Hart
Lois Hartzell
Penelope Harvison
John R. Haule
Alice M. Hazer
Russell Heiman
Fritz Heinegg, M.D.
Ben Heinie
Claudia Helade
Pamela Hemmingway
David Henderson
Thomas Henderson
Helen Henry
John W. Henry
Audrey Herrin
Elaine Herring
Patricia Herron
Delbert Highlands

Keith Hill
James Hindes
Richard Hiolman
Harold Hodges
Dean Hoekstra
Ray Hogenson
Karl F. Hollenbach
Karl Hollerbach
Sue Hookins
Charles Horton
Don L. Hoskins
Alice O. Howell-Andersen
Roland & Corrine Hume
Paul Hurley
LaVerne Isenburg
Prof. C. J. Isham
Dr. Andreas Iversen
B. J. Jacks
Paul F. Jarrell
Morten Jellestad
Jens Jensen
Kelly Jill
Aldona Johnson
Anthony L. Johnson
Martin Johnson
Michael Johnson
Rudolf Johnson
Roger S. Jones
Perry Jorgensen
Dr. Roger W. Jung
Robert Kaladish, M.D.
Sylvia Kalb
Patricia Kaminsky
Reah Janise & Hadan Kauffman
Neil H. Kaufler
Lawrence E. Keith
Susan Kelemen
Bonnie & Joe Kelly
Ken Kempf
Tan Choon Kiat
Andrea Kielpinski Sadler

Michael Kiggans
Dan Kiley
Michael Kimbell
John C. Kimsey
R. Russell Kinter
S. Kirchhoff
Laura Louise Klohn
Jon Knebel
Hannah Kodicek
Bob Kogel
Chris Kolmel
Vernon E. Kooy, Ph.D.
Kathleen Korpi
John J. Kottra, M.D.
Laurel Kovacs
Randy Lee Kremer
Clem Labine
Chris Labridis
M. Lakshmanan
Kent Lambert
Mary Kay Landon
Charles Larry
Michael Leake
Kristina Leeb-Lundburg
Douglas Leedy
Vita Leicht
Kris Leroine
Flora R. Levin
Monica R. Lewis
David Dean Lim
Dr. Robert Lima
Annabel Lindy
J. Litwin
Gaye Lobban
Timothy Lobdell
Kathleen Long
Marvin Longton
Torfinn Lorvik
Mayra S. Luria
James MacLellan
John Mahoney

Farzad Mahootian
James Mai
James J. Malpas
Scott E. Mann
Rose Marie
Jim & Mary Marsden
Nigel Marsh
Joseph Marshall
Lee R. Martin
Keith Martz
Mrs. Olive Mason
David E. Mathieson
Eva Matis
Joyce Mauler
Leigh J. McCloskey
Howard W. McCoy
E. J. McInnis
Rev. Malcolm McLeod
Thomas McMillian
David W. Meany
Verdnika Meekison
Toni Meenach
Donald Melchoir
Alison Melville
Richard Merrihartt
Sharon R. Michaels
Djoko Milono
Guido Mina
David Mitchell
Kathryn Mitchell
Steve Mitchell
Tony Mitton
George J. Mobille
Dr. John L. Moffat
James & Janet Moffett
Blair A. & Ida Moffett
Lee Moffitt
Judith Mogilka
Barbara G. Moore
Regina Morella
John Morey

Cynndara Morgan
Gary Moring
Holly Morrison
Robert Moss
Margaret Moum
Jim Moyers
Edward G. Mulligan
Oscar Munoz
Curt Musgrave
Richard Myers
Raymond R. Mytko
Thomas Nary
Lucy Nauta
Jeremy Naydler
Deanna J. Neider
Bruce Nelson
Richard Nelson
Stephen Neuville
Raymond G. Newak
Peter Nicholakakos
Vanya Nick
David Nikias
W. Nookadu
Dan Noreen
Derrick Norman
Jan Noyen
Katherine O'Brien
Vivienne O'Brien
Judy Olsen
Gordon M. Onslow Ford
David Oppenheimer
Martha Orick
Kevin Oster
Scott Osterhage
Paul Paccione
Jon Parks
Jerry Pavia
Mario Pazzaglini
John Peck
David A. Peckerman
Peter B. Pellier

Timo Penttila, Ph.D.
Marilyn A. PeQuignot
David Perkins
Patti Perleberg-Owen
K. R. Perlow
Devorah Peterson
John Pettingill
Richard Pickrell
Daniel J. Pierce
Allen Pluth
Robert D. Poirier
Dr. Daniel Polland
David Porter
Frances W. Porter
Randall N. Pratt
Nicholas Psillas
Lynn Quirolo
Miriam Ramirez
Michael Randall
Scott Rasmussen
Richard Rauch
W. Campion Read
Rebecca Reath
Chris & Paul Rechpen
F. Marion Redd
Charles Reid
Christine Rhone
David Richards
Rosemary Robbecta
Marlin Roehl
Steve Ronan
Joseph F. Rorke, M.D.
Diane Rosen
Iglesias Rossi
Jere Roth
Elisabeth Zinck Rothenberger
Mossman Roueché, Jr.
Stephen Roulac
Ernest Rubenstein
Carl W. Ruppert

Emily Rushin
Val Savenko
Michael Scahill
Bernhard Scharbius
Barbara Schermer
Michelle Majerus Schmidt
Walter S. Schmidt
E. May Schneidt
Leslie Schnierer
Gloria Y. Schwartz
Brian Scott-McCarthy
Paul Sechia
Lisa Seitz
Shirley Self
Jane Seligson
Robin Van Löben Sels
Ivry Semple
Elizabeth Sewell
Stephen J. Shartran
Gregory Shaw
Kenneth Shaw
Rev. Milton R. Shaw, Ph.D.
Jay Sherry
Madeleine R. Shields
Susan Sholley
Agnes Simandi
Joseph Simmons
Andrew Sistrand
Nikolas D. Skalkotos
Joseph A. Slicker
Eugene Smith
Gary MacDonald Smith
Johnny Smith
Patrick J. Smith
Richard Smith
Ruth Smith
Francis Spataro
Willard Stackhouse
Richard J. Stanewick
Jesse Stanowski

Robert Stein
Nancy Stetson
Kirby Stewart
Monica Stillman
Carol Stoddard
Norman Strand
Jon T. Strehlow
Valerie Stromberg
Michael Strong
Tracy Strong
Gerd Stumpf
William F. Sturner
Ray Styles
Joseph H. Sulkowski
Terrence M. Sullivan
Edith Sullwold
Linda Sussman
Sondra Ford Swift
Brian Swimme
Allison Talarico
Frank Tarala
Beverly Taylor
Beverly L. Taylor
Ruth Thaler
Linda Thayer
Rev. A. H. Thelander
Gilles Therien
Monte Thompson
Charles Tilden
Doris Tillman
Roger S. Tobie
Ptolemy Tompkins
Rev. Shawn Tracy
Henry P. Trantham
Brian K. Tuller
Christiane A. Usher
Cis Van Heertum

Sharon Mariel Van Sluijs
Donald Vento
Paal E. Vevle
Jean-Pierre Vila
Ed Volker
Jaromir Vonka
Rod Wallbank
Richard Ware
Rosemary Warner
Joy & Harvey Warren
Garnet Lee Webb
Jeffrey Weidman
Edward Weinburger
Joseph Weitner
B. Robert Welton
Ken White
Dana Wilde
Thomas Willard
Charla J. Williams
Dr. Jay G. Williams
William Williams
Edgar Winger
Kieron Winn
Michael Winn
Christina F. Winter
Clifford P. Wolfsehr
Nancy C. Wood, Ph.D.
Jeff Woodart
Catherine Woods
Thomas D. Worrel
Russell Wright
Richard Yaw
Stuart Ross Yerian
Cathleen Conley Young
Steven Young
Philip A. Zemke

ALEXANDRIA

ALEXANDRIA 1 • "Revisioning the Sacred for Our Time" by Kathleen Raine • "The Orphic Mystery: Harmony and Mediation" by Lee Irwin • "Hymns of Orpheus: Mutations" by R. C. Hogart • "Michael Maier's Alchemical Quadrature of the Circle" by John Michell • "The Eternal Feminine: Vladimir Solov'ev's Visions of Sophia" by Kristi A. Groberg • "Embodying the Stars: Iamblichus and the Transformation of Platonic Paideia" by Gregory Shaw • "Galaxies and Photons" by Dana Wilde • "Esotericism Today: The Example of Henry Corbin" by Christopher Bamford • "The Waters of Vision and the Gods of Skill" by John Carey • "The Path Toward the Grail: The Hermetic Sources and Structure of Wolfram von Eschenbach's *Parzival*" by David Fideler • "The Creation of a Universal System: Saint-Yves d'Alveydre and his Archeometer" by Joscelyn Godwin • "Aspects of Ancient Greek Music" by Flora R. Levin • "A Plotinian Solution to a Vedantic Problem" by Michael Hornum • "Gnosticism, Ancient and Modern" by Arthur Versluis • "Hekate's Iynx: An Ancient Theurgical Tool" by Stephen Ronan • Reviews and more • Paperback, 384 pages, $25.00

ALEXANDRIA 2 • "The Museum at Alexandria" by Edward Parsons • "A Note on the Muses" by Adam McLean • "Bibliotheca Alexandrina: The Revival of the First Universal Library—A Report from UNESCO" • "Alexandria: Past, Present, and Future" by Eric Mueller • "Hypatia of Alexandria: Mathematician, Astronomer, and Philosopher" by Nancy Nietupski • "The Life of Hypatia" from *The Suda* • "The Life of Hypatia" by Socrates Scholasticus • "The Life of Hypatia" by John, Bishop of Nikiu • "Psychedelic Effects and the Eleusinian Mysteries" by Shawn Eyer • "The Science and Art of Animating Statues" by David Fideler • "The Alchemical Harp of Mechtild of Hackeborn" by Therese Schroeder-Sheker • "The Fish Bride" by Jane Thigpen • "An Introduction to the Monochord" by Siemen Terpstra • "A Note on Ptolemy's Polychord" by David Fideler •

"Mysticism and Spiritual Harmonics in Eighteenth-Century England" by Arthur Versluis • "Mentalism and the Cosmological Fallacy" by Joscelyn Godwin • "Printing, Memory, and the Loss of the Celestial" by Arthur Versluis • Gerhard Dorn's "Monarchy of the Ternary in Union Versus the Monomachia of the Dyad in Confusion" • "Imago Magia, Virgin Mother of Eternity: Imagination and Phantasy in the Philosophy of Jacob Boehme" by Hugh Urban • "The Castle of Heroes: W. B. Yeats's Celtic Mystical Order" by Peter Cawley • "The Availability of the One: An Interpretive Essay" by Michael Hornum • "The Magic of Romance: The Cultivation of Eros from Sappho to the Troubadours" by Christopher Bamford • "Seating Arrangements in Plato's *Symposium*" by Robin Waterfield • "All Religions are One" by William Blake • "The Dolphin in Greek Legend and Myth" by Melitta Rabinovitch • "Sacred Geography of the Ancient Greeks" by Christine Rhone • "The Cosmological Rorschach" by David Fideler • "Reports from Hyperborea" by John Henry • Reviews and more • Paperback, 440 pages, $25.00

ALEXANDRIA 3 • "Harmony Made Visible" by Michael S. Schneider • "The Alchemy of Art" by Arthur Versluis • "Ecopsychology in Theory and Practice" • "The Divine Sophia: Isis, Achamoth, and Ialdabaoth" by Lee Irwin • "Ruminations on All and Everything" by Peter Russell • "The Strange Case of the Secret Gospel According to Mark: How Morton Smith's Discovery of a Lost Letter of Clement of Alexandria Scandalized Biblical Scholarship" by Shawn Eyer • "Knowledge, Reason, and Ethics: A Neoplatonic Perspective" by Michael Hornum • "Delphi's Enduring Message: On the Need for Oracular Communications in Psychological Life" by Dianne Skafte • Anatolius "On the Decad" • Two Letters of Marsilio Ficino • "Cosmologies" by Dana Wilde • "The Invisible College" by Anthony Rooley • "Reviving the Academies of the Muses" by David Fideler • "Plato, Athena, and Saint Katherine: The Education of the Philosopher" by Christine Rhone • "The School of Wisdom" by Jane Leade • "Education in the New World Order," a trialogue by Ralph Abraham, Terence McKenna, and Rupert Sheldrake • "The Teaching Mission of Socrates" and "A Note on Myth, the Mysteries, and Teaching in Plato's *Republic*" by Ignacio L. Götz • "Reflections on the Tarocchi of Mantegna" by Oliver T. Perrin • "Speaking in Hieroglyphics" by Peter Lamborn Wilson • "Three Exemplars of the Esoteric Tradition in the Renaissance" by Karen-Claire Voss • Ships with Wings • "Apuleius in the Underworld" by John Carey • "Astronomy, Contemplation, and the Objects of Celestial Desire" by David Fideler • Reviews and more • Paper, 494 pages, $25.00

To order, enclose cost plus $3.50 shipping for the first item, 50¢ each additional. Make your check payable to Phanes Press.

Phanes Press • PO Box 6114 • Grand Rapids, Michigan 49516 • USA

POESIA·XXVII

Philosophy &
the Imagination

FOLLOWING our successful 1996 session on "The World Soul and the Soul of the World: Philosophy, Cosmos, and Culture," *Alexandria* is planning to organize a panel of papers on "Philosophy and the Imagination" at the sixteenth annual conference on Ancient and Medieval Philosophy and Social Thought, which will be held at the State University of New York, Binghamton, late October 1997. Proposals for papers should be sent to David Fideler, care of the *Alexandria* journal, as soon as possible.

If you would like to receive details on the conference, join the Society for Ancient Greek Philosophy and you will receive full information at it becomes available. Send a check for $7.50 to: Dr. Anthony Preus, Department of Philosophy, SUNY Binghamton, Binghamton, New York 13902.